OUTRAGEOUS
GOOD FORTUNE

Michael Burke

# OUTRAGEOUS GOOD FORTUNE

Little, Brown and Company
Boston–Toronto

FIRST EDITION

*Library of Congress Cataloging Publication Data*

BURKE, MICHAEL, 1918–
    OUTRAGEOUS GOOD FORTUNE.

    1. BURKE, MICHAEL, 1918–    . 2. SPORTS PROMOTERS —
UNITED STATES — BIOGRAPHY. 3. SPORTS — ORGANIZATION AND
        ADMINISTRATION — UNITED STATES.   I. TITLE.
GV742.42.B87A36   1984      796'.092'4 [B]      84-14422
ISBN 0-316-11679-3

                        MV

*Designed by Patricia Girvin Dunbar*

*Published simultaneously in Canada
by Little, Brown & Company (Canada) Limited*

PRINTED IN THE UNITED STATES OF AMERICA

For all my children with all my love . . . and for my sister, Janet, who cheered me on from our earliest childhood.

I have found life
enjoyable, enchanting,
active and sometimes
a terrifying experience.
And I enjoyed it
completely.

Sean O'Casey

# Acknowledgments

HAVING MOVED through most of my life accompanied by large numbers of people, I at first found writing a book a lonely business — that is, until friends and acquaintances from the earliest to the latest years joined me from memory and filled the room with their company another savored time. To all of them for all of the remembered occasions, I am grateful.

Grateful also am I to two young Irishwomen: Ann Youell and Niamh Nolan. Ann typed, retyped, and typed again early drafts of the manuscript, patient with my trials and errors; and as time ran short, Niamh pitched in, swiftly and skillfully, and even learned to decipher my handwriting.

I am indebted to Sterling Lord, literary agent and Knickerbocker basketball fanatic, who read the first crude outline, grinned encouragingly, and said, "I can sell this." And I am equally indebted to Bill Phillips, Senior Editor at Little, Brown and Company, who must have blanched when he saw my dog's breakfast of a first draft. Nevertheless, he deftly swept aside three great chunks about Africa, Russia, and China, setting me on a less meandering course. And at a later stage his letters to Ireland described how I could achieve order from my disorder. Glea Humez, copyeditor of this book and daughter of my English master at Kingswood School, saved me from a blizzard of grammatical and spelling errors and did so without loss of patience or humor.

Most particularly I owe a special acknowledgment to my friend Willie Morris for letting me play on his softball team and for the many long nights together in Bridgehampton pubs where he first planted the notion that I write a book, then cajoled, and insisted until I promised to do it one day.

Not least here is my mother, who kept me away from the stables and other diversions with her letters from America wanting to know when I would be done with it. She wrote, "I'm nearing ninety-five. This is no time for a waiting game."

MICHAEL BURKE
Northbrook

Aughrim
County Galway
Ireland
1984

Ireland 1981

# I

IT WAS eleven o'clock Irish time, that is to say anytime between eleven and noon, on the Saturday following Christmas 1981, at Broderick's Pub in Kilconnell, the rendezvous point for the East Galway Hunt. Horses gathered unhurriedly in the roadway, some ridden in along narrow black-topped country roads that twisted and turned between leafless gnarled hedgerows, some hauled in by horsebox, unloaded and saddled in the main street that passes Broderick's front door. Waiting for the Huntsman and the pack, most riders sat easily astride patient, unnervous horses; others dismounted and fetched glasses of brandy or port to brace themselves against the chill, variable day or to add a fillip of courage to leap the walls and fences that a fox would slither past at unbroken speed. The Treasurer, polished boots already splattered by the street puddles left by the early morning rain, passed sociably among us collecting capping fees — three pounds for members, ten pounds for visitors. Young John North called from the doorway of the pub, "Brandy or port?"

"Neither, thanks." I needed both hands on the reins to gentle CB. It was his first hunt and he was charged with excitement, too jittery to stand still, quick eyes darting here and there, missing nothing of the new scene. I was thankful that he let himself be cajoled into staying within the village limits. He was a jumper I had brought with me from America, a swift companion with whom I had shared hundreds of solitary hours on the riding trails in Westchester County, trotting across fields, leaping fences, and pounding flat out along the sea at Wainscott on Long Island. A big three-quarter-bred horse, handsome and alert, he would have been furious had I left him behind and I the lonelier without him. The more accustomed Galway horses were tolerant of a morning drink, but none of their good manners rubbed off on CB. Up and down the main street he danced, spooked off his reflection in shop windows, suspicious of alleys. Briefly he escaped out along a gravel path towards the ruins of a thirteenth-century Franciscan abbey in a field a few hundred feet from the pub. I explained to him that Cromwell had sent the friars packing in the seventeenth century, and he wheeled and walked smartly back to Broderick's as the Master and the hounds arrived in yapping confusion.

Thirty or more horsemen and horsewomen, wearing traditional riding hats, black coats, and black boots, and children home from boarding school for the holidays, mounted on their Connemara ponies, milled in the narrow street. Hunt-wise horses, sensing the start, strained to be away, and at the sound of the Master's horn, we set off along the road out of the village, following the red coats of the Master and the Whipper-In. Iron hooves clattered on the hard road surface, past the blacksmith's two-hundred-year-old forge, and sloshed across a soggy field to the first covert where a fox might be raised. Responding to his arrogant thoroughbred blood, CB shouldered his way to the front, where he assumed he belonged. I hadn't a clue whether he would last a minute or an hour in this rough West of Ireland country, but he went like a champion born to the sport, clearing every wall, sliding into and climbing out of every drain, bashing through imperceptible openings in high hedgerows with me lying flat against his neck to avoid decapitation. At one point, an hour out, the scent of the fox was lost and we pulled up for a check. A handsome lady in a black bowler and a black riding jacket with a yellow collar, the East Galway Hunt colors, halted her big gray hunter beside me, admiring CB. "That's a fine Galway horse you have there," she said.

"Thank you. He's very keen." I was loath to tell her that CB had been in Ireland less than a month. The hounds picked up a new scent and we bolted off again. Galloping across a bog, I struggled with mud-slippery reins to avoid the unforgivable gaffe of taking the lead away from the Master. Neck and neck, splashing through pools of knee-deep water, the Master shouted at me testily, "A man can kill himself that way!"

"Trying not to!" I called back. "I'm too young to die!" He threw back his head and laughed wildly because the white hair of age flared out from under my hat and because he was a wild black-maned young man named Michael Dempsey, Jr., known to bash up a half-dozen horses every hunting season as he rode with abandon. At the next hard road surface CB limped, favoring his right foreleg, and I jumped down, fearful that in my own exhilaration I had ridden too recklessly. But he had merely lost a shoe in the bog and his foot was tender. I loosened the girth, ran the stirrup irons up under the saddle, slipped the reins over his head, ran my arm through them, thrust my cold wet hands into my pockets, and set off walking home, CB's nose nuzzling my back. A passing car stopped to ask if we needed help.

"No, thanks. He's just thrown a shoe. Anyhow, he's had enough for his first day. But could you tell me if I'm walking in the right direction for Kilconnell?" The hunt had chased an uncatchable fox over such a ragged course that I was completely disoriented. Within minutes the couple in the car was back again, this time drawing a horsebox. We loaded CB and they drove us home, saving a six-mile walk. I was so struck by their kindness, which they dismissed with a casual wave of the hand, that I forgot to ask their names or where they lived.

Limping slightly, CB followed me through the gateway of the ten-foot-high gray stone wall that enclosed the stable yard. Five box stalls lined one side; the tack room and feed room faced the horseboxes across a gravel square. CB, happy to be back in his box, lowered his head for me to slip off his bridle and, as I undid the girth and lifted the saddle and pad from his back, he turned his head, sniffing my pocket for a carrot. "Not yet; wait till I hang up your tack."

In the tack room I placed the saddle on its wood rack, spread the saddle pad upside down to dry out, hung the bridle on its wall peg, and picked a handful of carrots from a box sitting on the cold potbellied stove, which on colder days was fired to take the chill off the stone-walled room. CB's head stretched alertly over the half door of his box, anxious for my reappearance. I handed him one carrot and, spreading his blanket over him and fastening it across his chest, let him maneuver the others from my pocket, something he enjoyed doing on his own. I bolted the lower half of the box door, and his reproachful eye followed me out of the yard. CB disliked being alone, and the other horses were not yet back from the hunt.

Parked beside the stable yard wall, a DeLorean car lent me

by a friend looked like something from outer space, especially when its gull-winged doors were opened. The DeLorean was a tight fit on the narrow, winding back roads of Galway, and its cockpitlike interior was more suited to the Indianapolis speedway than to dodging sheep and cows being herded from field to barn. But it was a joy to drive, even from the stable over the rough dirt road that runs through the fields of Northbrook farm to a nineteenth-century cottage a mile away, a stone cottage surrounded by a white fence that protects the lawn and garden against animals grazing in the adjoining fields and keeps out stray cattle that sometimes wander along the one-lane road that winds through the hedgerows and passes the house.

Martin, who looks after me, had logs blazing in the sitting room and library fireplaces, and tea was on the hob. I gravitated to the library at the back of the cottage, a cozier room and quicker to unchill the bones. Through a large picture window, I looked across rolling pastures that gently slant away to a distant stream. A herd of grazing bullocks and a mare in foal drifted in and out of view and birds darted back and forth against an ever changing sky. A quarter of a mile off to the right Northbrook House, a once splendid Georgian mansion, stands solitary and silent overlooking its demesne from behind a picket of ancient trees. Long abandoned by its last profligate squire, its roof is caved and the ivy blanketing its walls has crept inside through vacant windows and grows along its fallen beams.

This is where I live now, in Aughrim, County Galway, the cord with Madison Square Garden cut, my share of Yankees ownership sold, and the City of New York kissed a loving farewell. Disbelieving friends predicted surely I would soon be back. I had lived happily in the midst of the city's marvelous tumult, at the center of its action, elated by it, enthralled by it, galvanized by it from the first day to the last. Because of the high visibility of the Yankees and the Garden, I suppose, I had become part of the city's furniture. Then, suddenly, I had done all I needed to do at the Garden and no other occupation attracted me. To carry on would have been to repeat myself; to take on some other job would have been an anticlimax. I needed no institution to shelter me, no spar to cling to.

In truth I no longer wanted to be beholden to anyone, how-ever generous the conditions. The sense of independence that forever urged me to positions of least supervision pressed for-ward more urgently. From early on I had taken risks, taken a chance on an unknown outcome — a youthful leap from a pa-rochial Irish background to a Wasp prep school, a parachutage into German-occupied France, the Circus. And each survival nourished me, each self-experience enhanced me. Surely by now whatever support I needed was built in. So I chose to go to the nearest faraway place to start another life vastly different in quality, texture, and rhythm, to fill my life with new en-deavors and new people, to risk yet another new adventure for all the excitement and promise that is always in it. I had no qualms about making friends of strangers or accommodating to a life-style in Ireland, one that I had sampled in thin slices over several years. I had moved from place to place all my life, searching out the natural course for me, like water seeking its own level. At some point along the way the idea that I would one day come and live in Ireland appeared and took root. The day came in December 1981.

Idling here, sitting by a fire, reading, listening to the stillness of nightfall, my mind wandering, I imagined I could hear the long-silent clash of arms in the Battle of Aughrim fought in the surrounding fields in 1691, and I wondered what man there had the same name, the same look, the same carry-on as I. Reflecting on him — what sort of man was he; what part of him am I? did he die or did he flee with the Wild Geese to soldier in France or in Spain? — I reflected on my own times and thought to set down where I had been and what I had seen, thought to inquire how much substance, how much sawdust lay beneath the skin of events.

Of myself I thought I would find a person from the crowded middle cut of America who, given medium mental and physical equipment and an occasional burst of outrageous good for-tune, wandered out into a mostly happy life, an improvised life, making a living at things he most wanted to do, and, when instinct signaled it was time to go, moved on, the promise of the new always outdistancing the fear. Perhaps on examination it would seem an inconsistent and a sometimes lonely route as well. Somewhere along the way I knew I had discovered that a man is his own fallback position, that, when he has ventured into some daunting place and all his money is in the game, it is futile to look over his shoulder. There is no one there. The wall of a church on a side street in the French city of Tours bears a message daubed in red paint: *Homme, tu es seul.* Man, you are alone. Nothing dismaying about that, nothing to chivvy at. It is simply good to gain a natural truth early on and to deal with it as part of the adventure.

I discovered, too, the simple truth that without a woman's friendship to companion me, I was incomplete.

Given that no one ever remembers the way it was, this was to be how it seemed to me.

# France

IN PARIS at six o'clock on a November evening, 1944, the Ritz Bar was filled with uniformed men, mostly rear-echelon officers from the indoor look of them, and chic French women slimmed by wartime rations and bicycling. The cocktail chatter had segued from French-German to French-English as the city changed hands in the summer of 1944. My eye easily picked out Hemingway, large in the small Art Deco room, his torso bulky in a war correspondent's tunic, leaning forward, forearms flanking a martini on the table before him, talking intently with two Royal Air Force pilots seated opposite him. Startled when he caught sight of me standing in the doorway, he stopped in midsentence, shoved back his chair, cut a cannonball path through the closely spaced tables and gripped one of my shoulders in each of his powerful hands.

"Christ, kid, they told me you were dead!" he shouted as though I were some distance away, digging strong fisherman's fingers into my flesh to be sure it was real. He pulled me to his table, introduced me to his RAF friends, asked Georges, the *chasseur,* to bring champagne, and explained his surprise to the pilots. "They told me the kid was dead."

He wanted to know everything. "You know everything, Papa," I said, only half in jest. He was pleased when I told him I had reread *For Whom the Bell Tolls,* while I waited for the weather and the moon period to come right for parachuting into France.

"What about dinner tonight?" Hemingway asked, and I accepted happily. I enjoyed him and his companionship very much. He was a spring freshet of a companion, a generous and caring friend. We had first met in Ireland less than a year earlier, fellow passengers on an airplane. The flying boats that crossed the Atlantic landed in the Shannon River at Foynes, where passengers were ferried ashore in an open boat, fed a rich Irish breakfast of fresh eggs and bacon and mounds of toasted soda bread, before being bused to a land plane, which lifted them to Croydon Airdrome in war-rationed London. Hemingway had floated an invitation to anyone within earshot to join him in a gin and tonic, had walked past the diningroom and turned into the bar. Henry Ringling North and I, in mufti passing through neutral Ireland, had been the only volunteers. We introduced ourselves, drank breakfast, and began a lifelong friendship with Papa.

Now in the Ritz Bar Hemingway asked, "When did you get to Paris?"

"Last night."

"Where are you staying?"

"Don't know yet. Last night I stayed with René, Arnold Ostertag's old chauffeur. Did you ever know Ostertag? He was the jeweler at 16 Place Vendôme. Married my wife's sister." Hemingway shook his head. "Anyhow, René and his girl have a small apartment in the 13th; near the Port d'Italie. They fed me and let me sleep on their couch. But I don't want to disturb them. The OSS hotel is full. Of administrators, I suppose. And the Navy won't have me." It was one of the war's silly ironies. Earlier in the day, in the Rue de Berri, I had run into Brooks Peters, a Marine captain I had known in London. He was on his way to lunch at the Royal Monceau and invited me along. The elegant hotel had been requisitioned by the United States Navy as officers' quarters. True to naval tradition, the high-ceilinged, finely appointed diningroom was dressed with crisp linen, polished silver, crystal, and an abundance of food served by neat Filipinos in starched white jackets. I was dressed in a blue beret, a khaki parachutist's jacket, and dark blue trousers of rough provincial cloth, scratchy but warm, gathered in at the tops of paratroop boots. I had grown a black beard. Peters and I had been seated for only a moment or two when he suddenly stood up, in response to a beckoning gesture from an officer at another table. "Be back in a minute." He was. "Let's go," he said sharply.

"Go? We just got here." A Filipino mess boy passed carrying two thick juicy steaks to a nearby table.

"Come on!" It was more command than invitation. I followed

him out across the marble lobby into the Avenue Hoche. "That was Captain Cope who called me to his table. He wanted to know what the hell that was I had with me. I told him you were an American naval officer and he said to get you out of here immediately. Also to tell you you cannot mess or be billeted in the Monceau 'til you're in proper uniform. And you're to report to his office at 1430 today."

"Welcome home."

"Yes. Well, let's see if we can find a place that will let you in for lunch."

I had had a bath, and Freda, René's girlfriend, had cleaned my clothes so I wasn't dirty or smelly. But dress that was unremarkable in the Vosges was not acceptable to the Paris Navy.

At two-thirty I was in Captain Cope's outer office in a building off the Champs Elysées, where I waited an hour before being summoned. Cope sat behind a plain wood desk, his big body more than filling a barrel-backed desk chair that squeaked as it moved back and forward under his weight. His face was square and disciplined, his thick black hair in military trim, his complexion pale. He had the look of a man who needed more room, a man who would be more at home on the bridge of a cruiser. I guessed his age to be about forty. Certainly a professional, not a civilian in uniform.

"Lieutenant Burke, sir. I was told to report to you." I saluted uncertainly, not sure if it was proper protocol to salute indoors, without a hat and in dubious uniform.

He was angry. "Lieutenant, you know the uniform of the day is undress blues!"

"No, sir, I just got here."

"What the hell has that got to do with it? You look like a goddam tramp!"

"Sorry, sir. This is all I have. My uniform is in England."

"In England! Don't you read orders, Lieutenant? Every officer in this command was directed to have proper uniform with him." His Naval Academy sense of order was affronted. Understandably, professionals suffered a low flash point when they sensed a reserve officer playing loose with the code. None of the ribbons on his uniform were for combat. Hard luck for a career officer to be anchored to a desk in Paris while warships were fighting all over the globe. I would be irritated too if it were me, I thought, and felt vaguely sorry for him.

"I couldn't bring my uniform with me, sir. I came to France by parachute."

"What's that?"

"I parachuted into the department of the Haute-Saône in eastern France. I've been with the French underground there."

"Oh, I see." His anger fell away. "I didn't know we had Navy parachutists," he growled.

"One or two. A radio man with the maquis in the Doubs, I think, and a couple of Marines I know jumped into the south of France."

Once he had accepted my legitimacy he was intrigued and throttled back to a conversational tone. "But," he concluded, slipping back to a formal but unhostile attitude, "you understand you can't mess or be billeted at the Monceau until you're in proper uniform."

"Yes, sir. Thank you, sir." We shook hands and I wandered out into the truly beautiful city pockmarked here and there by bullets and shell fragments where Paris resistance groups and the departing Germans had clashed a few weeks before. The autumn dusk softened the city to her best light. Paris was exactly as I imagined it would be, almost as though I had been there before. I wandered across the Pont Alexandre and along the Left Bank quays of the Seine to the Pont Neuf, crossed back again, weaving through Les Halles, along behind the Hôtel Meurice and out into the Place Vendôme. The Place was empty; the fighting war might have been on another planet. I stopped to look at the measured meter fixed into the stone wall of the Ministry of Justice beside the Ritz, permanently faithful to its official length, war and occupation notwithstanding, then passed through the hotel's haughty entrance, down the long narrow corridor lined with glass cases displaying expensive gifts, and finally to the bar on the Rue Cambon side. Hemingway was the first recognizable person I saw.

At dinner Hemingway wanted an accounting of what I had been up to for the last five months. It seemed a longer time since I had last seen him, on a Sunday in early June 1944. He had given a breakfast party in his suite high up in the Dorchester Hotel in London. It was the weekend Hitler first launched his "victory weapon," the V-1 buzz bomb, against England. Someone had brought bourbon whiskey and pancake flour from New York, and Hemingway invited friends for an American breakfast. Henry Ringling North and I were there; so was Martha Gellhorn, Papa's wife, who had arrived from their home in Cuba, accredited as a war correspondent. Hemingway thought women should stay home from wars, wives especially should stay home from wars; at least *his* wife should stay home. He tried to discourage her with graphic possibilities: "What if you're with a tank column and they call a ten-minute halt and a tanker has to take a shit? What's he going to do if you're hanging around?" His arguments rang hollow. Martha's liaison with Papa had been formed during the dangerous living of the Spanish Civil War.

We drank bourbon and had a clear view of the buzz bombs flying up the Thames through the clean spring sky, could hear their engines, sounding like distant backfire of motorcycles, cut abruptly to silence, as the bombs nosed and dove to earth. Where they struck, stone and steel, timber and tile blasted high into the air, hung for an instant of slow motion at the top of their arc, then plunged to earth in mad disarray. At our distance, the sound of the explosions reached us seconds later across the chimney pots of London, past the damaged dome of St. Paul's Cathedral and the watchful face of Big Ben. When the pancakes were ready Hemingway encouraged us all to get out our Ignorers and ignore the bombs. We did, more or less. That is, we ate and drank and kept one ear cocked to be sure the buzz bombs kept their distance. They moved closer. Then one broke the loose pattern. The putt-putt sound of its engine grew louder and louder. It came on and on at a determined, unhurried, throbbing, exasperating pace. Everyone rushed to windows. This one seemed bent on joining us for breakfast. Its nose, loaded with explosive, loomed larger and blacker.

"Sweet Jesus!" cried Hemingway. "We'll have to get out our Bulldozer Ignorers for this one." At that, the engine cut out and the bomb winged over. It dove at a steep angle and plunged through the roof of the Guards Chapel across Green Park from the Dorchester. The eleven o'clock service was at midpoint. Worshippers filled the church. The blast killed most of them and defoliated trees along Birdcage Walk, we learned later. We raced across the park to help, but the police and firemen, four years' experience in their kit, needed no amateur assistance.

North and I were naval officers — he a lieutenant, I a lieutenant junior grade — seconded to duty with General "Wild Bill" Donovan's Office of Strategic Services, the OSS. In the early days of World War II Donovan, as a private citizen, ranged through Europe, the Balkans, and North Africa and related his observations to President Roosevelt. My "secret legs," the President called him, and several months before Pearl Harbor, Roosevelt appointed Donovan to establish America's first intelligence service, starting from scratch. Very simply, the two clandestine operational branches of OSS were Secret Intelligence (SI) and Special Operations (SO). Both were charged with operating secret agents behind the enemy lines. The SI mission was to gather information about the enemy; the SO mission was to harass him in unconventional warfare. North and I had operated in Italy in 1943 as SO officers and our orders to England in 1944 read: "As combat experienced OSS people North and Burke will be usefully involved in the liberation of France." At the time we were among the relatively few OSS officers who had been in combat.

For some unknown reason, when we reported to the OSS headquarters at 70 Grosvenor Street in London, we were assigned to a French Agent training school, in a charming, comfortably renovated thirteenth-century house in Sussex called Drungewick Manor. The military had requisitioned it from its owner, the theatrical producer Gilbert Miller. The officer instructors lived agreeably in the house; the French agents in training, *aspirants,* lived almost as well in a line of permanent tents in the garden of the carefully tended demesne. Henry and I fell into neither category neatly but managed to live indoors. I taught the French softball, but no game ever got past the first inning; the arguments about whether a runner was safe or out at *la première base* were interminable. We kept fit on the obstacle course, improved our language facility — all instruction and social conversation was in French — and at night we drank convivially at the Crown Inn in Chiddingfold, which people had been doing since the year 1292, and occasionally we managed a weekend in London to visit Hemingway and search out other divertissements. D-Day came and went while we sat seemingly forgotten in Drungewick Manor. Abruptly, Henry was dispatched to join an SI contingent assigned to go into France attached to General Omar Bradley's First Army. Left behind stewing in frustration, I wrote an official request to Colonel John Haskell, the chief of SI in London, asking to be detached from the training school. I thought I might be stuck there indefinitely unless I took some direct action.

Shortly I was ordered to London by an angry Haskell. I had never met him and, before receiving my request, he had certainly never heard of me. Haskell and his brother Joe, who commanded the OSS Special Operations Branch in London, were professional soldiers, West Pointers, as their father had been. If they were dismayed by some of the OSS people they found in London it would have been understandable. More than a few of personal wealth lived in suites at Claridge's or the Dorchester, were conscientious about their jobs in the Grosvenor Street headquarters but equally keen on their bridge games and London club life. Perhaps Haskell jumped to the conclusion that I was one of those. He got right to the point.

"The fighting is in France, Lieutenant," he snapped contemptuously. The training unit, he said, was slated to move to France at some point. "You can't lie around London for the rest of the war!"

I curbed my own anger, realizing that my request had hit him from the blind side. Politely, I told him that he had the wrong end of the stick, that he had misunderstood, that I didn't want to stay in England at all, nor in a training unit anywhere. I wanted to parachute into France, now. "I've been stymied. That's why I appealed directly to you, Colonel."

I knew that the Special Operations Branch had dropped American OSS personnel into France but that John Haskell's Secret Intelligence Branch had dispatched only French nationals. I was volunteering to be the first American SI agent to be dropped behind German lines in France. The mood changed abruptly. Haskell became as solicitous as he had been contemptuous. He called in a Major O'Brien, head of his French desk, and told him to get me into France. O'Brien took me around to General Koenig's headquarters in Montague Mansions; Koenig commanded De Gaulle's Forces Françaises de l'Intérieur, the FFI. At FFI headquarters we met a Colonel Vernon, a Colonel Manuel, and the infamous "Colonel Passy," André de Wavrin in real life, in an austere, strictly functional office, impersonal as their manner. Manuel conducted the screening interview, cool and detached. I was a body, not a name or a person; a body that might or might not be useful, a body that might come equipped with a W/T set, a piece of equipment always in short supply.

"*Vous êtes d'Action ou Renseignements?*" Action or Intelligence.

"*D'Action, mon colonel,*" I replied quickly before O'Brien could say different. Through my own grapevine I had learned that, at this point, two weeks after the Allied landings in Normandy, De Gaulle did not want American or British Intelligence agents joining the French underground. He wanted only paramilitary people capable of harassing the German Army rear with *coup de main* raids, train derailments, and so on. "*D'Action,*" I repeated to secure the point.

I boarded the 1445 train for Manchester and the Royal Air Force Parachute School at Ringway. The group I joined was housed at an ungainly red brick manor set in a square mile of rolling meadows and ancient trees, screened from the world by four miles of high red brick wall. Some nineteenth-century industrial baron, bricks perhaps, had confused size with taste or had chosen an architect of limited talent. But the vast house easily swallowed our class of sixteen students and left ample space for privacy when we were not together for instruction or at meals in a drafty diningroom, where we were served by smart-stepping British soldiers. Their hobnail boots scarred a path to the kitchen into the polished oak floors. With rare exception the trainees were strangers to one another, identified only by Christian names, probably false. For obvious security reasons anonymity was respected. No one ever attempted to get a fix on another student. From our group I remember only two Belgian girls. They were perhaps twenty-five, quite pretty, very feminine, and looked wholly incongruous in jump suits and parachute harnesses. If in primary school either had been your sixth-grade teacher, you would have brought her an apple every day.

On the second day at Ringway, after some ground training, we were shepherded into a bus and driven to a place alongside a dropping field to watch other trainees jump. Old Whitley aircraft flew overhead every few minutes at the agent-dropping altitude of six hundred feet, wings flapping to stay aloft, it seemed, as they slowed to less than one hundred miles an hour and dropped a stick of eight parachutists. In quick succession bodies, dark against the summer sky, appeared from the belly of the plane, plummeted for four or five seconds, then suddenly jerked like puppets as the parachute canopy ribboned out above them and then blossomed, filling with blessed air.

"You see. Nothing to it. A piece of cake," the instructor reassured us in a thick Scots burr. "Here's another. One . . . two . . . three . . . four . . . five . . . six . . . seven . . . eight.   Floating like petals on a pond." He was rhapsodic as a Rolls Royce salesman. We watched silently. "And another. One . . . two . . . three . . . four . . . Bugger! Caught a streamer!" One parachute failed to open. The canopy remained strung out above the jumper like a tail on a diving kite. The body sacked into the earth and lay dead. The instructor's tone changed from soothing to brusque. "All right. Back in the bus, everybody. Back in the bus. Step along now."

The obsolete Whitley twin-engine bombers looked like survivors from another era. Parachute training was their only possible use and, calculated or not, they provided some psychological value to the trainee; he was eager to jump before the plane fell apart in midair. The hole in the plane's belly through which one jumped looked like a straight-sided water barrel. One at a time we were to swing our legs into the hole, feet together, rump edged forward on the rim, one hand beside each thigh, palms down against the deck, head up and, at the jump master's command, push off, snapping the body straight, standing at attention in space, head up, dropping straight as a candle, holding an attention posture as we dropped, waiting for the static line attached to the plane to snake the silk canopy out of the canopy's pack strapped to each back and for the rush of air to fill it out. On the first jump the wait for the canopy to open was endless, the temptation to look down at the uprushing ground almost irresistible. And looking down, given the heaviness of the head, sends the body tumbling end-over-end, risking all sorts of unpleasant complications. I tried to dismiss the fresh vision of the streamer and the body sacking into the ground and rooted like hell for the law of averages. The jerk of the harness, the blissful billowing of the chute, the ecstasy of survival were so seductive that my mind had to be kicked into remembering that this delicious state is not forever, that in forty seconds I would hit the ground. Six jumps — one from a balloon, three with a forty-pound leg bag — earned your wings. Each time the Belgian girls were less tentative, never less feminine. Their courage made your heart sing and say an unused prayer that they would not soon die. It had not occurred to me that bravery could be endearing and that one could so long retain undiminished affection for two persons briefly seen and hardly known.

Exhilarated by parachute training and the anticipation of a mission to France, I treated myself to a first-class compartment on the train back to London, where I discovered once again that the Secret Service was no less fouled up than the Army. The mission I had been assigned to left without me, and the French were furious that I hadn't turned up; I had missed them by a couple of hours.

After several days of frustrating delays and false starts on a mission of my own, Colonel Haskell asked if I would join a team to be parachuted to a maquis band in the Haute-Saône in the northeast corner of France. *Maquis* is a Corsican word meaning wild underbrush; during World War II it was applied to the underground resistance forces in France. The Maquis de Confracourt was concealed in the mountains in front of the Belfort Gap, the gap through which the *Wehrmacht* would eventually retreat into Germany. The chief of the maquis was pleading for help. We were to take in as much guerrilla war material as twenty-two containers, carried in two B-24 bombers, could hold. As part of the Forces Françaises de l'Intérieur we would harass the German Army retreat and develop an intelligence network from a secret base in the Forêt de Confracourt in the Vosges Mountains of Alsace.

"I would, sir."

"Good!" He offered his hand.

We were driven to Harrington Airdrome. The Americans would fly us in. Through three empty gray days of summer rain we stayed in a Joe house near Harrington, a house where departing agents were isolated waiting for the weather to be

clear and the moon to be bright. It was a stone house, chill and
damp. For warmth I spent much of the time in bed rereading
*For Whom the Bell Tolls* and reading Vercors' *Silence de la Mer,*
originally printed and distributed clandestinely by the underground press in Paris. I found a village barber whom I asked
to cut my hair one inch long all over. It struck me as frivolous
to be going off to fight a guerrilla war carrying a comb and
brush.

Two bombers would lift us in. One of the planes carried
Lieutenant Colonel Waller Booth and me from OSS, Lieutenant Walter Kuzmak, detached from the 101st Airborne Division and attached to us at the last moment because he spoke
Ukrainian, and two French Regular Army officers whose noms
de guerre were Cornut and Chamard. In a sensible world
Waller Booth should not have been included; his rank was too
high and his years too advanced for that kind of mission. At
forty-plus his contemporaries and friends were rightly content
with their desk jobs in London. But Booth was ambitious to
prove some theories about irregular warfare, and his courage
matched his ambition. Cornut had not seen his wife and child
since he left Paris on a military assignment in 1938. Chamard
had fought with the ferocious *goumiers* in Morocco and with the
Free French in North Africa; he fantasized endlessly about
returning to Paris and specifically to 122 Rue de Provence, one
of the city's elegant brothels. Savoring the prospect he would
promise, *"Dites, Michel, nous passerons un mois là-bas."* We'll
spend a month there. The second plane took Captain Steve
Vinciguerra, a former Cornell football player, and Sergeant
Birdsall, an American radio operator also from OSS, together
with three young Frenchmen who had made their separate
ways to England to join De Gaulle.

In a war world you must depersonalize destruction and
death, push them outside the range of normal sensitivity. But
the kindness and simple courtesy of the people preparing us to
get off was deeply touching. I'm sure they were equally kind to
all bodies they dispatched. Deftly and carefully, as though it
mattered a great deal to them, they helped each of us into a
striptease, the jump suit worn over regular clothing for the
drop. An American lieutenant insisted on relacing my boots for
me, and the British sergeant who handed me my parachute

across a long bare table in the packing shed patted it and said cheerfully, "Oh, this is a lovely one, sir. Packed it myself." I thanked him and, exchanging smiles of private appreciation, we shook hands. Agents jumped with one chute, British style, with no reserve chest pack.

Our two planes were to join a flight of American B-24 bombers en route to some target in Germany, then, once through the curtain of antiaircraft fire over the coast of France, peel off and head for our target area in the Vosges Mountains. Our B-24 — an aircraft American crews called the Flying Coffin; the British more graciously called it the Liberator — shuddered and labored into the air, its heavy load of containers stored awkwardly in the bomb bay, and, once airborne, sighed resignedly and with a great mechanical bellow winged off to join its twin-tailed friends in flight. At the altitude we flew it was terribly cold in the dark fuselage aft of the bomb bay. I took a swallow of cognac from a flask one of the escort officers had given me at the airfield, rested my back against the side of the plane, and pulled my thighs up against my body for warmth. My adrenaline flowed and I was consciously happy, not the kind of happiness one remembers later, but the best kind of happiness, knowing it at the time. I thought of the Wild Geese who fled Ireland for France with Patrick Sarsfield after the defeats at the Boyne and at Aughrim and the Treaty of Limerick in 1692; perhaps I was a straggling, latter-day bird of that flight. I felt kindly towards the lottery of life.

The plane began its descent towards the drop zone and the sergeant dispatcher in his sheepskin-lined leather flying suit told us to hook up our chutes to the static line and get ready for the run in. God, I thought, I'll be glad to get out of this cold. Too heavily drugged with excitement to think of fear, I pulled my .380 Colt automatic out of a pocket in the striptease, put a round in the chamber, set the safety, and buttoned the gun back in its pocket. A blast of air rocketed into the plane as the bomb bays opened and the containers were released on the first run over the drop zone. Then, as the plane circled for a second pass, the sergeant pulled back the cover of the joe-hole. Above it a red warning light came on. I smiled across the open hole at Cornut and Chamard. We exchanged thumbs-up signs and shouted the customary *"Merde,"* for good luck. The ground was a blur racing past the bottom of the open hole. Then a green light flashed and in quick succession we dropped down into the night.

The moon lit the terrain clearly. I was over an open field but pulled the risers, collapsing one side of the canopy to make certain I would drift away from the bordering trees. My leg bag, hanging below me on a cord and containing my carbine, ammunition, and other gear, oscillated but not dangerously, and I landed softly in a stubble field. My body felt coiled and tight, but my brain directed it clearly and deftly to do the things it had been trained to do. Instantly I banged the release disc on my chest, shed the harness, quickly unfastened my leg bag, and rolled the green and khaki parachute silk into a crude ball. The pilot, foolishly, circled yet again and buzzed the drop zone, shattering the night, wagging his wings in a good-luck gesture, and roared off, further alerting all but the dead for miles around that something unusual was happening in the vicinity of Confracourt. Unknowingly, we had dropped into an area crawling with German troops.

Three silhouetted figures appeared from behind a low rise, first their heads, then their upper bodies. They did not wear German coal-scuttle helmets and were not headed directly for me but walked at an angle and did not see me stretched out on my stomach, elbows planted in the earth, watching them along the barrel of my carbine. They were speaking French. They must be part of the reception team, I thought, and called out, "*Alors, mes amis.*" To my own ear it sounded a pathetic salute. The three men, startled, dropped down and I heard the harsh metallic clack of a Sten gun being readied to fire. "*Je viens d'arriver. De l'avion,*" I shouted, rising to one knee. It sounded equally foolish in the still French night, but for an instant the recognition signal had blanked out of my mind. Then mercifully it flicked back. "*Le renard a couru!*" I stood up, my left hand raised above my head in greeting, my carbine hanging loose in my right hand at the thigh, and they trotted towards me. Their submachine guns, I saw with relief, were now slung behind their shoulders.

"*Bienvenu!*" the one in the lead called out. He was huge as a Notre Dame fullback. "*Bienvenu,*" he repeated and pumped my hand in his countryman's stone-hard hands. And I shook hands with the others. *"Je suis très content d'être ici, dans votre pays,"* I said. I was not only glad to be there; I was happy to be with them. They had been expecting a supply drop only, not bodies. Neither did they know the recognition sign and wondered why the hell I was shouting about a running fox, thinking perhaps I had landed on my head. Bursting with bonhomie, chattering excitedly, they helped me gather my gear and took me off like a scavenger-hunt prize to meet Commandant Darc, commander of the Maquis de Confracourt, and M. Mortier, the mayor, who doubled as Chef de Parachutage. The two stood concealed in the shadows among the trees at the edge of the meadow, a few hundred yards from where I had landed. Booth and Cornut had already been brought in. A few moments later Chamard came limping along painfully; in landing, he had torn ligaments in his knee but was no less elated than the rest of us to be on the ground and connected with our new comrades. I found him a stout stick that would do as a cane. *"Pas de cent-vingt-deux pour toi,"* I teased him. No 122 for you, meaning the bordello in the Rue de Provence.

He grinned lasciviously. *"Je m'en fous. Je ne suis pas tombé sur le membre, mon vieux."* He didn't give a damn about the ankle; his private parts were undamaged. Under Darc's instructions, roughly dressed and tough-bodied men came and went in the pale moonlight and shadows. Darc, even in the dimness, was noticeably different. From a man in his mid-thirties I felt his quiet authority, made out the soldierly bearing of his short straight figure and the intelligence of his evenly proportioned face. I heard the low voice of a man accustomed to being listened to, heard the cultured tones of an educated man. Mail fist, velvet glove. No games, no melodrama, only serious purpose. Only business handled professionally and with care. In a matter of moments I sensed that my life was well placed in his hands. What a piece of good luck for us to have fallen under his command.

Members of the reception committee gathered up the containers and loaded them on horse-drawn wagons, creaking loudly enough to wake up a surly Paris concierge as they lurched across rough ground. I went to help search for two containers that had fallen in the woods and to make certain that all eleven were on the wagons. They would have to be deep in the forest before daybreak. Young *maquisards* were collecting chutes and harnesses, careful to leave no trace of a para-chutage, careful not to tear the silk canopies, which their women would make into underclothes. There was no sign of the other plane which should have arrived before us. Men with flashlights stood by a hundred yards apart in a large rectangle ready to flick them on and mark the drop zone at the first sound of engines. At three o'clock we abandoned hope. The plane never made it to the target. Neither did our one set of radio crystals carried by Sergeant Birdsall. Without them we would have no radio contact. London would be listening for our call sign, and we would be mute.

Darc gave three maquis scouts a five-minute start, then we quietly followed their path through waist-high yellow wheat into a shallow bowl of fields that held the provincial village of Confracourt, silent as a sleeping cat. Centuries-old stone build-ings huddled around the steepled church and along short nar-row streets spoking off the village square. There was nothing contemporary about Confracourt, time-locked in an earlier century.

Two of Darc's lieutenants, Simon and Claude, led Booth and me through the gate of a small garden to the front door of a two-story house and knocked softly. A heavyset man of sixty-odd years, eyes puffy with sleep, thick gray hair matted, opened the door pulling his suspenders over a long-sleeved flannel undershirt. He would have been sleeping in long johns and, at Simon's knock, rolled from bed, thrust his legs into his trousers, and hurried downstairs in bare feet. Simon gave him a swift, half-whispered explanation about us and left. Booth and I were made welcome in the main room, the kitchen. Our host's wife, petite and spare in contrast to her large round husband, appeared. I don't think I ever knew their names, though sheltering us in their small house, a few paces from the village square, they risked death or a concentration camp. The woman hesitated, studying us uncertainly, our height towering above her and filling the low-ceilinged room, then rushed for-ward, tears streaming down her cheeks, grasped our hands and kissed them fervently in a dam-burst of emotional relief after four German-occupied years. "To think," she sobbed. "To think that General Eisenhower has sent two officers to free our village." We embraced her gently, careful not to disturb her illusion, and, curtains drawn securely, sat around a bare wooden table celebrating with champagne and cheese, apples and nearly undrinkable *café nationale,* made from acorns. It was nearly six o'clock in the morning before they let us go upstairs to bed in their spotless second bedroom. Its windows, at the back of the house, presented an easy drop into the garden and quick access to the open fields and forest beyond. A tall porcelain water pitcher and matching washbowl standing on a marble-topped bureau reminded me of my grandmother's bedroom.

Booth and I placed our outer clothes and boots carefully at hand in case we had to wake up running and climbed into the clean rough sheets. I was asleep before I closed my eyes. Nervous exhaustion, I think. And I woke with a start to find it was nine o'clock on a warm sunny morning. Darc had already sent a man around to inquire about us, but our hostess wouldn't hear of our going anywhere before she had given us breakfast of coffee, fresh baguette, and apricot jam.

The region where we had dropped was stiff with German troops, though there were none in Confracourt itself, and Darc thought it would be good for the villagers' morale if they actually saw us. We walked through the streets, two strangers escorted by two well-known *maquisards.* People had heard our plane and saw that we were flesh and blood, not rumor. We met Darc in the Café Hubacher — his Confracourt headquarters was a back room, bare except for a table and three or four odd chairs — and he described the makeup of his maquis and the whereabouts of the German troops. They were indeed everywhere in the Haute-Saône. Vesoul, the capital, twenty miles away, was an important army garrison and a Gestapo regional headquarters. Route Nationale 70, running northeast from Dijon, and Route 19 from Paris to Basel were essential German withdrawal routes to the Belfort Gap, the military gateway from Germany to France. And back. These and their supporting roads, within *coup de main* range of the Forêt de Confracourt, were our targets.

Animal instinct, training, nervous tension or all three told me we should move into the forest that day. The term *le lendemain* kept running through my head; all agent training emphasized spending but one night, the night of your parachutage, in the initial safe house. *Le lendemain,* the next day, you were supposed to move on. Darc and Booth would go together. I picked up my gear, kissed our hostess on both cheeks, and left Confracourt for the forest with Claude and Simon. Thereafter, I would spend almost every waking and sleeping hour with them — until Simon was killed.

Simon and Claude were, without question, the most valiant men I have ever known. Both in their late twenties, they were two of Darc's principal and most effective lieutenants; both were natives of the region, and spoke fluent German. They had been inseparably active in the Resistance from the very beginning. It was immensely fortunate for me that they took me in; Damon and Pythias needed no third partner. Simon's aristocratic bloodlines — his mother was a *comtesse* — were apparent in his handsome features, fine lithe figure, and graceful carriage. His cultured speech, soft tone, and gracious manners masked a fierce, almost foolhardy bravery. "*Ça ne risque rien,*" there's no risk, was his invariable opinion, offered with a shrug of his shoulders and a nonchalant smile when the risk, in everyone else's opinion, ran especially high. He had all the requisites of a great matador.

Claude's family grew fruit trees. His solid body, flaxen hair, and a blond beard that sprouted in a half-circle from chin to ears, framing a ruddy peasant face and keen blue eyes, gave him the look of a rural Henry VIII. He wore jackboots taken from a German soldier who would no longer need them, twill riding breeches, and an old Foreign Legion officer's tunic. That's all — no undershirt, no drawers, no socks. In cold weather he put on a ragged sweater under his tunic, and when he went out on a hit-and-run raid he wore a World War I French infantryman's helmet, the type with a ridge running fore and aft across the crown.

At first glance the two could not have appeared more different; in truth they could not have been more alike. Simon was the natural leader. This is not to say that Claude had to be led. Both hated the Nazis with an unspoken passion so deep you would have to be inside their heads to understand it. They never cursed or ranted; theirs was an underlying toughness. Their only outward display of feeling was the contemptuous tone in their reference to the Germans as *les Boches* or *les Schloks*. And the fierceness with which they fought.

A one-lane dirt track led out from one side of Confracourt across a mile or so of fields, rising at a shallow slope for half the distance and falling away gently to the far edge of the fields where it tunneled into the thick, tended forest of tall trees. I did not see them and jumped nervously when four young *maquisards* hidden in the underbrush rose to greet Simon and Claude. Armed with rifles and Sten guns, they bracketed the road, as others did every hundred yards or so in the diffused light of the forest as we climbed higher and deeper towards the headquarters, an impossible gauntlet for an unwelcome stranger. Headquarters was a one-roomed forester's hut in the small space cleared of underbrush and screened from the sky by a canopy of thick summer foliage. We unpacked the containers: Sten guns, Thompson submachine guns, .45 Colt automatics, ammunition, plastic explosives, primer cord, detonating caps, grenades, fog signals for derailing trains, warm clothing, shoes, and a half-million francs. Weapons and ammunition were turned over to Darc for his distribution, then we climbed a few hundred yards deeper into the forest to inspect what Darc called his Force de Surprise.

Darc's maquis was unique. In a clearing, aligned in as perfect a military order as the uneven forest floor would allow, a battalion of Ukrainians in German army uniform, 769 officers and men, stood at attention. Their uniforms, their arms, their equipment down to the polished harness brass of their horses would have been given high marks by the most demanding martinet. They were a proud military unit, complete with field kitchen, a hospital wagon, medical officer, and a battalion mascot: a twelve-year-old orphan boy they had picked up in Russia fighting in the Soviet Army, kept with them as prisoners of war in Germany, and brought with them when they were dispatched to France to fight as a punitive force against the maquis. From Darc we heard their extraordinary story.

A Resistance leader named Brun had sent word to Darc from Dampiers, a village twenty kilometers southwest of Confracourt, that an enemy battalion had arrived and was bivouacked in the Forêt Dampierre. Their mission, Brun reported, was to locate and destroy a band of terrorists operating in the vicinity of Combeaufontaine. A German Major Schulkopf was in command, supported by a cadre of SS officers and noncommissioned officers. Otherwise the battalion was composed of Russians. Later Brun identified them correctly as Ukrainians and said their own commander, a Major Hloba, had told him how much he and his comrades despised the Nazi fanatics. Simon and Claude obtained Darc's permission to attempt a Ukrainian defection and bicycled off to Dampierre. Brun hid the two young Frenchmen in his house while he obtained identity cards from his friend, the prefect of Gray. The cards bore the stamp of the German *Kommandatur* stating that Simon and Claude were employees of the prefecture. Simon was Franz Dutweiler; Claude was Dieter Stampel. Brun then arranged a secret meeting for Simon and Claude with Major Hloba behind the Brasserie de l'Est in Dampierre. Hloba, graduate of the Kharkov Military Academy and son of a Czarist colonel, agreed to throw his lot with the Maquis de Confracourt. It was the first of eight meetings between them to plan the revolt. The following night Simon and Claude, posing as Dutweiler and Stampel, boldly called on Major Schulkopf, claimed, as Alsatians, sympathy for Germany, decried their fellow Frenchmen for failing to comprehend the advantages of collaboration. They even called Schulkopf's attention to a "bad situation" in the vicinity of Confracourt where, they said, a gang of terrorists operated. They hoped that Schulkopf could get rid of them. The Nazi major asked if Dutweiler and Stampel could find out more about the Confracourt gang. They said they would try, but it would take some days.

Meanwhile the two Frenchmen and the Ukrainian major developed their defection plan. One morning at 9:45 a covered German military wagon driven by one of Hloba's Ukrainian soldiers stopped in front of Brun's house. Simon and Claude climbed aboard with their rucksacks, submachine guns, and two hundred rounds of ammunition. Hloba met them two hundred yards from the battalion headquarters tent. A Ukrainian platoon formed a semicircle behind it, a Ukrainian sentry stood beside the tent entrance. Hloba held up two fingers — two minutes to go — and the sentry hastened away from the tent entrance to join his platoon. At that moment Schulkopf pushed aside the tent flap and stepped out, pleasantly surprised to see Dutweiler and Stampel. As he hailed them, Hloba shot him twice — once between the eyes, once in the chest. Instantly the area was shredded by wild furious gunfire. In the space of an hour thirty SS officers and eighty-seven noncommissioned officers, the entire German cadre, were dead. The Ukrainians had twelve killed and twenty-one seriously wounded. Doctors and nurses in Brun's clandestine organization would look after the wounded. The dead, German and Ukrainian alike, were buried and signs of the battle were obliterated. Simon, Claude, 769 Ukrainians, and 150 horses drawing the battalion's full array of arms and equipment decamped on the twenty-kilometer journey to the Forest of Confracourt. It was one of the most audacious feats in the bizarre history of underground warfare.

Our first night in the forest Darc, Simon, Claude, Booth, Cornut, Chamard, and I slept on the floor of the forester's hut. Kuzmak had stayed with the Ukrainians. Black sheets of summer rain drove down through the thick foliage and muffled thunder rolled through the hills. One by one dark, wet forms crept in from the storm and lay down beside us. By morning seventeen sleeping bodies lay in a line head to toe, wall to wall. The air was ripe with unwashed bodies and damp wool: "the pleasant, comforting stench of comrades." Gently I moved a sleeping limb from across my Adam's apple, picked up my boots, and slipped out to look at my first morning in the Forêt de Confracourt. Through the trees the sky was admirably clear and a climbing sun dappled the wet vegetable life that grows out of the rich French earth. Birds chirped gaily in the still, wakening day. The whole clean-washed world seemed refreshed and deceptively at peace.

It was to be the day that a German regiment occupied Confracourt. The commanding colonel moved into the house where Waller Booth and I had stayed, and slept in the bed we had slept in two nights before. My heart went cold and I racked my memory of the room for any trace left behind which might compromise the old man and his wife. Now, living cheek by jowl with a force that could destroy us, we must operate with extreme care. Their presence beside us made yesterday seem almost danger-free.

The awareness of unbroken danger and the precariousness

of our position were constants, but they were not debilitating. On the contrary, all senses stretched to the limit of keenness; slackness invited disaster. If this tension were a sound it would be the single shrill note of a piper playing at a distance, audible if you stopped to listen.

Breakfast in the forest was a swallow of local *eau de vie*. In one liquid flash it woke you up, cleaned your teeth, dispatched the morning chill, burned away your appetite, and energized you for the day. Maquis life fell quickly into a pattern. Agents of Muchotte, Darc's Intelligence officer, came in with information and were sent out with new assignments. Instructions in weaponry were given to new recruits, many very young. One impressionable boy said to me, "*Alors, Michel, après la guerre nous irons à Chicago.*" After the war we'll go to Chicago. And he mimed blasting a target with his Thompson submachine gun, miming his then and future trade. Ambuscades were laid to harass the enemy. Prisoners were taken, confined to a roped-off area near the headquarters, and set to work under a grizzled German Regular Army sergeant, digging latrines and building a log lean-to where some of us could sleep on straw to separate us from the damp ground, sheltered from the rain. We left the forester's hut to Darc. The German prisoners made no attempt to escape. They counted themselves lucky not to have their throats slit by the maquis, as they had been warned to expect. Willingly they swung into any task and clung uncertainly to a prisoner of war status, silently patient with the shortages of food, silently praying that the advancing Allied armies would soon make them legitimate prisoners of war.

In time, the Maquis de Confracourt became too prickly a burr under the German saddle and was marked for extinction. From the village reports came that the number of German troops in Confracourt was mounting. A courier from Luxeuil bicycled fifty kilometers through most of one night with information that the Nazis were about to send an additional force in our direction. Columns of gray uniformed troops in their coal-scuttle helmets moved along the roads around the wood; a human noose surrounded us. A general, we heard, had taken command in Confracourt.

Darc, Booth, and I made a reconnaissance. Slipping out from a finger of wood that pointed towards one side of the village, we made our way to the top of a low hill, careful to stay out of the line of sight of a German lookout in the church steeple, and lay concealed in a clump of bushes. We watched a company of Mark IV tanks, a battery of six 88-millimeter cannon, and a stream of motor and horse-drawn vehicles arrive and take up positions on either side of Confracourt. It appeared to Darc that they planned to squeeze us in a nutcracker movement, and his military eye assessed them as a ragtag lot, not a crack outfit.

By the time we returned to the forester's hut Muchotte had collated his intelligence reports. He estimated that German strength against us had mounted to four thousand or five thousand, outnumbering us more than five to one. And there was worse news: Bazeau had been captured! The incomparably clever Bazeau. Time and again he had eluded the Gestapo. Now he had been captured by a simple army patrol. He was the only person outside the forest who knew our strength and disposition, knew anything truly useful to the Germans. He was the same handsome young mountain of a man who had first met me with welcoming shouts and an iron handshake. Usually he worked as a team with his comely wife. This time he was alone and Mme. Bazeau was home with their two-year-old daughter, Josette. The American Colt .32 he carried in a shoulder holster under his thick flannel shirt would be his death warrant. The question was would he talk. His comrades said never. Our first report told of his being taken from the *Mairie* in handcuffs and driven off in a black Gestapo Citroën. Two and a half hours later he was brought back. Beaten, scarcely able to walk, half-carried up the *Mairie*'s steps by two men, he shook his head signaling to whatever friend might see that he had not talked. Nor had *la Geste,* the Gestapo, yet finished with him, we could assume.

The Germans opened the day, September 13, 1944, with a barrage of artillery and mortar fire, pounding the front edge of the forest. Then, three pairs of tanks, separated by a couple of hundred yards, advanced across the fields, leading infantry. Their gray uniforms made clear targets against the yellow wheat under a cloudless Indian summer sky and brilliant sun. Rifle and machine-gun fire from the maquis positions, hidden every few meters along the periphery of the forest, forced the tankers to close down their covers, and after four hours of fighting the Nazis halted their probe and withdrew. It had cost them a hundred casualties to learn that the Maquis de Confracourt possessed and could use automatic weapons. The Ukrainian medic and his orderlies, I heard, worked expertly on the wounded. The French would deal with their own dead. The first attack repeated itself the following dawn, except in greater strength. Having probed, the Germans now planned to smash with a heavier bombardment, with more tanks and more infantry. But Darc upped his ante, adding machine guns and mortars manned by the Ukrainians. By noon the Germans again withdrew — their casualties heavy, ours light — and lobbed mortar shells into the forest at random through the balance of the day and through the night. Darkness added its own tensions to daylight combat; day left no time for listening to your heart beating against its ribcage.

A third attack came on the third dawn with a variation. After the heavy bombardment with 88s and mortars, the German launched himself first in two prongs against our flanks, expecting that Darc would weaken his middle to support the ends of our line. Darc anticipated him; as soon as the artillery barrage ceased, he quickly added a hundred Ukrainians, held in reserve at their bivouac, to strengthen our right and left, leaving our middle strong. And for the first time in the battle he opened up with the 57-millimeter antitank guns. The Ukrainians had brought seven with them. Once again the surprised Germans were stopped, but this time only at the tree line. We anticipated they would infiltrate the forest after nightfall. Now they could overrun us at will. We had little ammunition left to fight off another sustained attack. Individual *maquisards* could, in classical guerrilla fashion, disappear, moving like shifting hares. Perhaps some of us would escape and some of us would be captured or killed, but how does an entire battalion of Ukrainians vanish? Darc, a man of strength equal to the hour, decided we should hold on and resist as best we could.

Capture meant death, of course. Chances of survival for more than a handful appeared dreadful at best. The Maquis de Confracourt was about to be wiped out, it seemed. Flimsy as a spiderweb, we would be blown away unnoticed, too irrelevant even for a footnote in military history, of significance only to those of us who were there, worthy of no more than a postwar monument in a remote, unvisited provincial village square. London, unbeknownst to us, had already counted us dead. A British SOE team operating in the department of Doubs, just to our south, had radioed a message to OSS that we had dropped into a concentration of German troops and were doomed. Our own radio signal, monitored in London, had not come on the air confirming our safe arrival. Prolonged silence from agents in the field had but one grim connotation. *Maquisards* and Ukrainians alike were cool and resigned. No one funked. Whatever their private thoughts, outwardly they were controlled and committed. Perhaps each expected his underground existence might one day lead to a place from which there was no exit, and each man dealt with it in his own way. *Merde alors* would probably speak the resignation of the French; and American comment on the bad luck of it would be no loftier; we would neither be the first nor last to die at this young man's business of war. There was an acceptance of things.

I was surprised how quickly I accepted the reality of dying, how quietly the notion settled in. My own mood was neither morose nor baleful but one of nostalgic sadness for the years I would never know. Odd fragments passed through my mind — like taking my daughter Patricia to dinner at "21" on her eighteenth birthday — a teenage copy of her mother — and imagining how fulfilling a father-daughter relationship must be. Until then, death, even close at hand, had been neither uncommon nor remarkable but common to the day's occupation. It was something that happened to someone else, mostly to people you didn't know. I thought of God, though I had long since abandoned praying for something for myself. That seemed too egocentric. One is in the world to deal with whatever there is to be dealt with. Calling for God's instant intervention would be unseemly. My mother, I recalled, once told a priest friend that she was going to pray that I pass my Latin examination. Don't bother God, he said; tell Michael to go home and study his Latin. I couldn't remember who said: God, give me the strength to ask you for nothing. But the prospect of an early encounter with God permitted a wish, if not a prayer: that I die quickly rather than be massively wounded or taken prisoner. I did not want to survive to be a burdensome invalid, and I doubted that I would behave well under Gestapo torture, if that were to be my lot. But survival remained the first choice. Against the odds, the incandescent will to live would not be shut down.

The advancing American Army could not be far away and an air strike against the German regiment might cool them off. I proposed to Darc that I try to slither through the German circle, make contact with the advancing Americans, and send in a bombing run. I would need a guide who knew the night forest well. This was no gesture of self-sacrifice on my part. Any action, no matter how slim the chance of success, seemed to me preferable to doing nothing. Darc, sensible and collected, wasn't sanguine about my chances of getting through and was determined we should hold on through the night and see what happened.

The listening night hours took more than their allotted time. All action, no matter how swiftly paced, seemed infinitely clear and slowly measured. My senses were so alert that it was like being awake twice over. Though the Germans gained the tree line, they did not come into the wood. Instead, mortar shells lobbed sporadically into the trees exploded on the soft forest floor or burst in tree branches, spewing shrapnel out and down. At times I wished I had a steel helmet instead of a beret, but we were so well dispersed through the forest that our casualties from intermittent shelling were nil.

Night's dark tensions lessened with the sunrise. In the new day we saw that the enemy had withdrawn to lines just in front of the village. Soon an old man, one of the villagers, appeared on the wagon track scurrying towards us, willing swiftness into his aged legs, stiff with World War I shrapnel scars. He carried a message from the German commander: forty-six hostages — old men and young boys — had been taken from the village and locked up in the *Mairie*. One more shot fired from the forest and they would be executed. We decided to play a bold hand. Almost without exception German troops dreaded being captured by "the terrorists." It would be doubly so of terrorists they had been unable to subdue in three days of fighting. We speculated that they might surrender on the guarantee that they would be accorded treatment of prisoners of war under the Geneva Convention. They would not, we assumed, take the word of a French *maquisard,* if indeed he would be given a chance to speak before they killed him. That left the non-French: Booth, Kuzmak, and me. Instinctively, without a beat lost to reflection or even to thought, I said I would do it. And Kuzmak volunteered to come with me. Booth wrote an ultimatum to the German commander and signed it "Lieutenant Colonel, United States Army." I put it in the breast pocket of my jacket and we fixed a white cloth to a stick. It was a windless day and the flag hung limp. Our friends, concealed in the brush on the perimeter of the wood, covered us with machine guns, though it seemed to me of little value. We set out on the naked two kilometers to the village not knowing if each step would be the last, cut down in midstride by a slash of gunfire, not knowing if the Germans would let us walk through their lines and turn us over to the Gestapo, not knowing if they would believe we were, however unconventional we looked, American officers and accept our proposition. Whatever, the dice had been tossed.

The sun was high and hot. If it had been a peacetime Sunday, families would be picnicking along the riverbank. I wondered fleetingly what day of the week it was. We walked side by side, one in each wheel track. I don't recall who carried the flag, but I think it was Kuzmak. The Germans, I noticed, had removed their dead from the wheat fields. I forced myself to walk erect, not to cringe at the gnawing thought of being zapped by a sudden fusilade, but my body tightened with attention, irresistibly gathering itself in.

Kuzmak and I may have talked to one another, but if we did, I don't remember what we said. I doubt that I asked myself: why am I doing this? The answer begged the question. I was doing it for myself, because of my expectation of myself. There was no external reason, nothing so empty as bravado, so noble as self-sacrifice, so unnecessary as a public test. Had someone else volunteered, had I hung back, and had that other person died or succeeded, either way, I, by my own private measure, would have hated my guts forever for having finessed the risk. I don't know why that is; it simply is. There are some spheres in which reason does not penetrate at all. A brave act, if that's what it might appear to be, is less difficult to bring off if there is no alternative, even if one doesn't know why there is no alternative. For me, it may be a gene left over from some other distant contest of arms where an ancient of my tribe did what he had to do. But there was little room for abstractions during our walk in the sun. The tactic of the moment concentrated our attention. If my mind strayed at all it was to an Everyman hope that, if they opened fire, I would not be hit in the crotch. Or, if I was, to be hit everywhere else too and die quickly.

From the brow of the rise five or six hundred yards distant, the village was still and poised and curious. I expected to see soldiers; instead it was quiet, motionless. No one was about, no soldiers, no civilians. We looked for guns poking over walls or out of windows and there were none. The eye registered and the mind recorded every detail at once with the clarity of camera, the speed of a shutter. Then at the far side of the village, our line of vision angling across the square and along a narrow street, we saw a body of German troops climbing into vehicles and moving off in a column in the direction of Combeaufontaine. They appeared not to have seen us. Or if they did, they had no intention of delaying their departure. Partially screened from their view, we leaned against a wall and watched the last German elements abandon Confracourt. Then we walked a few more paces into the empty square and sat on the church steps. Slowly, one and two at a time, the villagers began to appear. One with a bicycle we sent back to the forest to tell Darc that the maquis could now occupy Confracourt. Kuzmak and I chatted quietly. Our guts unknotted, tautness seeped from our tendons, limbs and nerves loosened, and we laughed softly at ourselves at the anticlimax. A young woman, shapely and sensual in a loose summer dress, hurried towards us, her sabots clomping on the cobbled square. She sat barelegged on the step above us and filled three glasses from the bottle of *pineau* she carried and we drank to one another. A sudden surge of lust consumed me, and I swallowed the mucus that welled in my throat.

Darc and the others arrived quickly. Excited townspeople filtered into the village square. The freed hostages bore the look of men delivered by some godly stroke, pledging privately never to sin again. People sang, shouted, milled, laughed, wept, hugged, shook hands, and drank. Presently, sung in a loud clear baritone, the "Marseillaise" soared high and strong above the sounds of celebration. Another voice joined in, and another, until the whole moving square froze in a rough provincial tableau, faces from any century, figures standing straight and proud singing the most stirring national anthem of all, singing with the exaltation of new freedom, with passion, with self-respect won by selfless risks taken for one another. And they sang for France. At the outer edge of the square, self-effacing and apart, Simon sat astride his splendid black stallion and, glancing up, I saw a *maquisard* lookout Darc had ordered to the church steeple. His presence reminded me that there was still more war to be done, though no more war for the village of Confracourt. And I saw Mme. Bazeau standing in front of the Café Hubacher, erect, weeping softly, face assaulted by an awful sadness. A seven-year-old girl dressed in a pale blue school smock was in my arms. I sang along with her, and, deeply moved, wept too.

The following day we learned that the Germans were also pulling out of Combeaufontaine, five kilometers away. Simon, Claude, and the Ukrainians moved to liberate the town and Kuzmak and I were with them. Booth and the others remained with Darc. In maquis hands, Combeaufontaine and Confracourt became a spider's parlor to the German fly. Small units and retreating stragglers rode or marched unsuspectingly into our trap, and surrendered, some after a brief firefight, some with no resistance at all, until our roped-off area in the forest held more than two hundred prisoners. French women captured with their German beaux had their heads shaved by the maquis and were turned loose in bald shame.

Bazeau's body had been dumped in a ditch by the side of the road between Confracourt and Combeaufontaine. His fingernails were gone. His back was in ribbons where hooks had been inserted and yanked out. His body had been beaten savagely and, in the end, the back of his head had been blown away by a shotgun blast. He had not talked. The following day a Gestapo lieutenant and three sergeants, riding in a black Citroën, drove into our net. The trunk of their car concealed their vicious trade tools — instruments for pulling out a man's nails, hooks for tearing his flesh, shotgun shells, a shotgun. In the forest the maquis held a tribunal. We Americans were told to stay away. "Bazeau is none of your affair." Bazeau, indestructable and bursting with life, had liked us calling him *Bienvenu*. I could feel his hard enveloping hand gripping mine the night of the drop, could hear his big warm voice calling *"Bienvenu!"*

The Gestapo lieutenant, tall and slender, had a finely boned, aesthetic face. His Gestapo *Ausweis* recorded his age as thirty. His name was Creselius. Creselius had been an architect in civilian life and his rucksack held two volumes of *The Cathedrals of France,* their margins filled with sensitive and appreciative notes. He could have been the German officer in Vercors' *Silence de la Mer.* Calm, aloof, self-possessed, he gave no sign of fear. He lighted and smoked his cigarette with a steady hand, apparently resigned to execution. He bore himself as a thoughtful, intelligent man who had found perspective for his death, perhaps a perspective embodied in the ancient cathedrals of France and the simple truth that, as the Irish say, it is a small thing that does not outlast a man — a tree, a stone, a hero's medal. The three noncommissioned officers captured with him laid their neatly folded tunics in a line on the grass as they dug their graves. For a tortured Bazeau, the maquis price was Creselius plus three, a bullet into the base of each man's skull.

At dusk in Combeaufontaine, Simon, Claude, and I stood in a doorway of a shop when the first American soldiers, riding in a Jeep, rounded the corner and moved cautiously along the principal street. As they drew abreast, I put my two small fingers in my mouth and made the kind of shrill whistle you can hear any day in any ball park and yelled, "Hey, Sarge, how's army life?" The Jeep slammed to a halt. "It's OK," I added. "No Germans here." The were dubious as we approached the Jeep. My obvious American accent was probably reassuring but out of joint with the place and the look of me and my two French friends. The two soldiers were with the 117th Cavalry Reconnaissance Squadron reconnoitering on the point ahead of the American 36th Infantry Division. They agreed to take us back to their troop command post. Their captain, pleased to know we held Confracourt and Combeaufontaine and glad to have any other intelligence we could give him about what lay immediately ahead, had us lifted in one of his Jeeps the twenty kilometers back to the squadron command post, a schoolhouse in Port-sur-Saône. A short, chunky major with a red Irish face and a surly disposition sat at a teacher's scarred desk. Situation maps stood on easels off to one side. He looked skeptical. We were not prepossessing. Our clothes, an assortment that could not have been given away at a flea market, had lived as roughly as we had lived. Claude's Henry VIII beard was no more reassuring than my black *barbe*. My carbine was slung over my shoulder; Claude's submachine gun rode across his back as a natural part of him; and Simon carried on its sling a German Schmeizer machine pistol, a burp gun, taken somewhere along the line from a captured or killed enemy. I saluted and said, "Lieutenant Burke, U.S. Navy. My friends are Captain Doillon and Lieutenant Voughnon of the Forces Françaises de l'Intérieur."

"No shit!" He wasn't buying any of it; no one was going to make a fool of him. His name was McGarry, I think. I gave a swift sketch of who we were and he went to wake up his colonel. Rubbing his eyes and yawning, Colonel Hodge appeared. I repeated our story and at once he was wide awake, intrigued, amused, and hospitable.

"U.S. Navy! Christ, how'd you get here? We heard there were some crazy American bastards out in front of us somewhere raising hell with the krauts. But Navy! Jesus!" His outfit, the Essex Troop from Newark, New Jersey, was one of America's historic National Guard units; the original troop had fought with Washington at Valley Forge. Hodge said a New Yorker and his friends were welcome. We talked about Manhattan restaurants and the Far Hills Hunt while he sent someone to fetch Booth, Chamard, and Cornut from Confracourt. Kuzmak would stay with the Ukrainians, whose ambition now was to join the French Foreign Legion en masse and fight with De Gaulle's Free French. Not having them attacked by oncoming American and French armies was our tricky first priority.

Hodge, a New York broker in civilian life, was an attractive man and a tough soldier, lively and imaginative. He attached us to his squadron as Irregulars to do scouting and patrolling out in front of his troops, since we were familiar with the country, had contacts, and were experienced at moving about in German territory. For us it was a natural extension of our maquis operations and we were joined by ten volunteers from the Maquis de Confracourt. Hodge assigned us Jeeps, provided clothing and food, and the following night we moved up from Port-sur-Saône to Saint-Loup as members of the squadron. Simon and Claude rode proudly in the column driving our new Jeep. I rode on top of one of the 117th's light tanks just for the hell of it; I had never been on a tank before. It was exhilarating and I was happy there, secure and safe among the American troopers and their marvelous fighting equipment, in contrast to our precarious situation in the Forêt de Confracourt. This perspective made me smile, amused by the notion that not everyone would agree to that definition of safety and security. Nor would I at another time, but so it seemed to me then. We elected not to let the OSS people in London or Paris know where we were. Waller Booth was eager to prove how effective our tactical intelligence techniques could be in this new situation and I was a willing partner.

Word of the Ukrainians in German uniform, their 150 horses and their equipment made its way through the appropriate military echelons and they were ordered to Vesoul. Lieutenant Kuzmak stayed with them as an interpreter–liaison officer and to make certain that their courageous story was properly told, their treatment accordingly correct.

In Saint-Loup Simon and Claude searched out the Chef de Résistance of that region, a Captain La Plante, and, through him we met Lieutenant Raymond Lupin of the Francs-Tireurs et Partisans, the Communist resistance movement often at swords' points, literally and figuratively, with the Gaullists. Raymond and his ten FTP comrades from the Midi had moved north from maquis to maquis, refusing to be overrun by the advancing Americans, determined to continue the underground war in their own way. Now they wanted to join us with the 117th Cavalry, bringing with them their own weapons, all German, and their own transport, also taken from the Germans. They were young and bloodthirsty and increased the strength of Hodge's Irregulars by eleven. None knew the words of the "Internationale."

Simon and Claude and I made a side trip to Vesoul. Though Darc had undoubtedly informed his own FFI superiors of their new assignment, the two wanted to report personally to the regional FFI commander. We found him in what had been the office of the Gestapo Chief of Northeastern France. On a wall behind his head were three leftover photographs — one of Himmler, one of Hitler, and, between the two, Claude. Under Claude's photograph was a legend: *Le plus Grand Terroriste de tout l'Haute-Saône,* and a reward of one million francs offered on his head. Claude smiled shyly, half-embarrassed, half-pleased. Once on a mission our maquis party had rounded a bend in a forest road and had run head-on into a band of twenty or thirty Germans. Both sides froze, except Claude. In one motion he whipped out a grenade from his belt, threw it into the Germans' midst and swung his tommygun around, spewing fire. Everyone dove for cover. A short firefight followed, then the Germans broke off and bolted away from the road into the woods, leaving a sergeant lying on the road horribly wounded. The grenade had apparently caught him waist-high. His guts were hanging out in the dirt and he screamed in agony to be killed. "*Töten Sie mich. Töten Sie mich.*" Claude put a gun to the man's temple and fired. The sergeant's head snapped to one side and he lay still. *Le plus Grand Terroriste de tout l'Haute-Saône* knelt on one knee beside the body, carefully folded the dead man's arms across his chest, bowed his head, crossed himself, said a prayer.

Our work as Hodge's Irregulars — out in front of the squadron, crossing and recrossing front lines, singly, in pairs, in small groups, routing out small pockets of resistance — gave the squadron and the infantry divisions of the Sixth Army Corps, for whom the 117th was doing reconnaissance, useful tactical intelligence. It saved them lives and cost us casualties, particularly when the Americans' swift summer advance came to a halt in the Vosges, east of Epinal. German resistance stiffened and Patton, his long supply line taxed, ran short of gas. The squadron command post settled in Sercour. Claude, Simon, and I pushed ahead another four or five kilometers and set ourselves up in Rambervillers. So did one of Hodge's troops. Troop B dug into foxholes like infantry and held a section of the front line.

In front of us — that is, to the east — lay the Forêt de Rambervillers: the near side held by the Americans; the far, the eastern, side by the Germans. A fluctuating no-man's-land of patrols and snipers lay between. At one point the Americans had advanced as far east as Anglemont but were pushed back.

Now they sought to retake it, and a tank commander from the 45th Division wanted to know from Colonel Hodge if his tanks could move out of Rambervillers along a road running southeast to Bru, then along a road running northeast through the Forêt de Rambervillers, using the forest as cover to get his tanks close to Anglemont. In short, he wanted to dogleg through Bru into an attacking position, unseen. The key question was Bru itself: was it defended or had it been abandoned by the Germans? Hodge asked his Irregulars to find out. It was a typical request.

Simon, Raymond, and I drove straight east through the American side of the forest, planning to conceal our Jeep in the underbrush and make our way on foot along foresters' trails, approaching Bru from the cover of the forest. But at the point we planned to slip into the woods, a hot firefight snarled and spat between a small freebooting band of British Red Berets, Major Baker-Carr and his SAS paras, plus a couple of French armored cars on one side and the Germans on the other. I lay against a bank next to Baker-Carr to find out whatever we could, assessing our chances of making our way to Bru by that route. "Not bloody likely," Baker-Carr said. We stayed perhaps a half-hour while both sides raked one another with machine gun, mortar, and 37-millimeter fire, and decided we had better try another route. (Baker-Carr was killed a few days later in a similar firefight.)

We returned to Rambervillers and headed out again, this time along the road directly to Bru, passing through the American front, a line of GIs from the 157th Infantry Regiment dug into foxholes about one hundred yards outside Rambervillers. Their expressions as we drove past were not difficult to read: those guys must be out of their goddam minds. I drove slowly along the high poplar-lined macadam road, its surface several feet above the level of the open fields on either side. From Rambervillers the road rose slightly for about a kilometer to a low crown midway between the two villages, then declined at a slightly steeper grade another kilometer straight into Bru. At the crown I stopped the Jeep. We sat for a few moments observing the town. Nothing moved. There was no sign of life. We drove forward another three hundred yards and dismounted. I left the engine running. My French friends took one shoulder of the road, I the other, and we walked forward another two hundred yards, using the poplar trees as a partial screen and watching closely for any movement in Bru as we went. I called across to Simon and Raymond to stay put until I brought the Jeep closer to us, drove it abreast of where they waited lounging against a tree, turned it around, headed it towards Rambervillers, again leaving the motor idling, and returned to my side of the road. We moved forward more cautiously now from tree to tree, about fifty feet at a time. Again we stopped and observed for perhaps three or four minutes. Simon's opinion was that there were no Germans about, that we could walk right in. *"Comme toi-même à Confracourt, Michel,"* he called. Like you at Confracourt. Raymond was not so sure. Raymond was a butcher by trade, an ox-strong young man with tousled black hair, a two-day growth of blue-black beard, deep-set darting eyes, a quick smile. He read the situation and looked especially wary. Incongruously, to our left a solitary farmer and two draft horses plowed a field, plodding stolidly back and forth in unhurried rhythm, occupied by nothing more than the next furrow.

*"Allons,"* Simon called impatiently. Let's go. *"Ça ne risque rien."* His characteristic comment when the risk ran high. Swinging his burp gun from behind his shoulder to the crook of his arm, he moved off towards the village. We had taken no more than half a dozen steps when the whole side of Bru erupted. Rifles cracked, machine guns stuttered, 37-millimeter guns barked at us, ripping the air and tearing up the ground around us. The Germans had observed our entire approach, of course.

Reflex action dropped us into the ditches that ran along each side of the road and, bent double, half running, half crawling, we scrambled along in their protective cover to the idling Jeep perched on the high-standing road, naked and exposed. Bullets zinged past it. Shells exploded on either side. Very quickly the guns would have the precise range. We shouted a plan to one another across the roadway: when I gave a signal we would spring from the ditches and into the Jeep, me behind the wheel; they wherever they landed. I flew at the Jeep, threw my legs under the steering wheel, rammed my foot onto the clutch pedal and jerked the stick into first gear. Simultaneously Raymond, then Simon, leapt forward from the opposite side. Raymond had one foot on the floor of the Jeep and one on the ground when machine gun bullets slammed into his crotch, knocking him backward into Simon. Simon pushed from behind and I grabbed his flailing arms and pulled. His body fell sideways into the seat like a sack of grain. Simon dove in, half on top, half beside him, and I pushed the accelerator to the floor, crouching over the wheel to reduce my target size. The fire followed us. The Jeep's engine screamed. And Raymond moaned, too stunned yet to feel the real pain. We roared past the GIs in their foxholes and raced to an emergency field station in a schoolhouse. Raymond lay on the bare floor of the dingy schoolroom waiting for the medics to attend him. A *maquisard* pressed a half-filled bottle of *eau de vie* into his hand and, slipping an arm beneath his shoulders, raised him gently. Wild-eyed with pain now, Raymond threw back his head and emptied the bottle into his throat in huge racking gulps. Shortly, two corpsmen lifted him into an adjoining room for emergency treatment. We were told he would be taken back to a field hospital for surgery.

That night at supper in the squadron officers' mess in an annex to the Sercour town hall, fierce stomach cramps suddenly bent me double. A giant hand grabbed my insides and clenched them in an iron fist, pulling my body down against my thighs, holding me there. For moments I couldn't move. Then I forced myself to maneuver away from the table and, still bent, my torso parallel to the ground, shuffle out into the night air. Slowly the hand loosened its grip and, inch by inch, like an ancient drawbridge, I was able to raise myself up and stand straight, though soreness persisted for an hour or more. It was, of course, a delayed nervous reaction to the day's events. I was thankful my body hadn't malfunctioned earlier in the day when I needed it.

The law of averages was gaining on us. At age seventeen *le petit* Roitel looked like a child. The youngest member of the Maquis de Confracourt, he had been a wily courier for Mouchotte's intelligence network, *un bon type*, everyone said. And he had volunteered, along with nine other *maquisards*, to join us with the 117th Cavalry. A couple of days after Raymond was shot little Roitel passed through the German lines and returned with information he had been asked to get: the exact position and strength of a roadblock that had pinned down a patrol from Troop A. The roadblock was wiped out by the 45th Division's artillery. Through some tragic fluke, Roitel was sent out on a second line-crossing mission that same day, something no one would have done wittingly. He never got close. As he approached a German position, machine gun fire cut him nearly in half.

Within a day or so Simon, too, was gone. He had been sent on a carelessly requested line-crossing mission, worth no man's risk. Lieutenant Christian Gauss, an American who squirmed loose of a desk job in Paris to join the 117th Cavalry, chose to go with him. I don't remember where I was that day. But that night Gauss related how it had happened. Resting somewhere along the way, Simon lay on his back on the bank of a ditch, hands clasped behind his handsome blond head, watching the vapor trails of high flying aircraft against a cloudless sky and talking of his brother, a Royal Air Force fighter pilot. Rested, they moved on and Simon picked from the ground an abandoned German rifle. He tested its weight and balance and lifted it to his shoulder to look through its sight. At that instant one bullet from an unseen sniper's rifle crashed through his chest and killed him instantly. Simon's body rolled down a steep slope into the underbrush and Gauss flung himself down after it, out of sight. That night in a black rain Gauss led us out to recover the body, but we failed. The Germans had booby-trapped it, and we would have to wait for a more auspicious time. Claude, *le plus grand terroriste*, wept inconsolably for two days. And soon we learned that Simon's brother, Jean, had been shot down and killed. Perhaps some weird twist of fate had dispatched them on the same day. "The valiant never taste of death but once."

Each morning and evening, faithful as the Angelus, the Germans shelled Rambervillers. *Nebelwerferen*, a kind of rapid-firing rotary mortar, hurled round after round of screaming Mimis into the village. Their screams, the most nerve-racking of all incoming shellfire, kept terrified townspeople hidden in their stonewalled cellars, and one morning's barrage slammed into the courtyard outside the house where Claude and I slept. It killed twenty-seven men of the 117th's Troop B, standing in a mess line waiting to be fed breakfast.

Simon gone, Claude and I were the only customers in the small Rambervillers restaurant where we three had often been given dinner. It was there that I received a message that my friend Henry North had driven out from Paris in an Army command car and was waiting for me at the squadron's headquarters in Sercour. Searching for me, Henry had worked his way forward to the Seventh Army headquarters, on to the 45th Division headquarters and on up to the 117th's Cavalry position, which on the map looked like a short finger thrust into the German Army's belly. Rambervillers was the nail on the end of the finger. I drove the Jeep back to meet him and we passed the night in an air-cooled room of a Sercour farmhouse: a shell had sliced off a corner of the building, letting in the chill October night and yellow harvest moonlight through the gaping hole. When he returned to Paris Henry proposed to someone that my number might be running thin and recommended that I not stay until I too was killed. The Marcel mission, as we were identified on the OSS records, was recalled to Paris. At the same time Claude was ordered to duty by the Free French, promoted to captain in the Foreign Legion, and placed in command of the Ukrainian battalion. We did not know then, of course, that our Ukrainian comrades, who had fought so gallantly, would be forcibly repatriated. An agreement among the Allies at Yalta had condemned them to return to the Soviet Union to be executed en masse by their own countrymen.

Our part of the war in France would be lost in the space on the head of a bullet. But if a person were to dig deep into the records of bravery and heroism, he would find that the teenage Roitel was awarded the United States Medal of Freedom, that Bazeau was awarded the United States Medal of Freedom with Gold Palm, and that Simon and Claude were awarded the Legion of Merit and a Certificate signed by President Roosevelt — three of the four posthumously. I never learned whether Raymond lived or died. Lieutenant Colonel Waller Booth remained a career soldier and it was he, I believe, who shepherded these citations through the bureaucracy and saw to it that their families received an acknowledgment of the price paid and the unpayable debt owed.

Everyone was saying that the war would end before Christmas, 1944. Colonel Hodge assigned one of his troopers and a Jeep to lift me across France to Paris and my eventual rendez-

vous with Hemingway at the Ritz Bar. Driving in a cold gray
November rain up to Nancy and then west along Route Nationale 4 through Saint-Dizier, Sézanne, and Rozay-en-Brie, I was
grateful for the raw metallic whine of the Jeep's motor, grateful
for the rhythmic roar of the Red Ball Express trucks barreling
east with gas for Patton's tanks, grateful for the slashing rain
and slick roads that concentrated the driver's attention, leaving
me withdrawn silently inside myself, alone with thoughts of
silenced friends, for six hours and two hundred miles, as subdued coming out as I had been exhilarated flying in. As the
fighting distanced itself behind us, the body's tightness lessen-
ing and the tension of the mind slowly subsiding, I wondered
vaguely if anything that lay ahead could cause me fear or
whether I had used up my allotment. Certainly I had been
forever shaped by this war embedded in me, and yet there was
an unreality about that slice of time, and I wondered too if I
had experienced it at all.

# Beginnings

## 2

BEING FEARFUL of the dark and admiring of ladies' legs are my earliest childhood recollections. That was in Connecticut. Just before the turn of the century my grandparents had emigrated from Ireland to villages on opposite banks of the Connecticut River, thirty miles upstream from Long Island Sound. Michael Fleming, my mother's father, bought a farm in Suffield; Patrick Burke owned a saloon in Enfield, where I was born. Irishry in our family ran centuries-deep in myth and mist, pride and prejudice. Blood-is-thicker-than-water was heard a thousand times to settle an argument on which side of an issue you should come down. Deviation from the Church of St. Patrick was a calamity. Time obscured the plain fact that not all generations of Burkes and Flemings were godly or even good. Both families were among the band of six hundred Normans who invaded Ireland in May 1169, one hundred mounted knights and five hundred archers, "a mixture of aristocrat and bandit, tough, acquisitive and a law unto themselves," as Emily Hahn described them in her book, *A Fractured Emerald: Ireland.* Once ashore, they abandoned their fealty to the English King Henry and struck out to establish private kingdoms for their own account, at first ruthlessly, then by being adaptable. Being adaptable meant nipping into bed with native Irish girls. William de Burgo (Burke) married the daughter of Donal Mor O'Brien; magnanimously he agreed not to seize his new father-in-law's estates until the old man died. And he brought up his own children more Gael than Gaul. By 1227 the Red Earl, Richard de Burgo, controlled all of Connacht and Ulster and managed to govern that unruly area, according to Emily Hahn, "because he was popular with the people, had O'Brien blood and talked Gaelic." The Irish considered him one of themselves.

The Flemings established themselves at Slane on the banks of the Boyne in 1175 and lived in Slane Castle until 1641, when the estates of Christopher Fleming, the 22nd Lord Baron of Slane, were confiscated by the English king and Christopher was sent packing with whatever he could carry. The king made a neat profit selling Slane Castle to the Scots Connynghams, who had the foresight to be Protestant and to fight beside the king, not against him. The Connynghams live in Slane to the present day. To hell or Connacht was the choice given the mere Irish by Cromwell, and by the end of the nineteenth century it occurred to all my grandparents that there was a third alternative. With the desperate courage of most émigrés they opted for the New World over the West of Ireland, for Suffield and Enfield in place of Galway and Tipperary. In America they became friends. Many a night Michael Fleming was the last man to leave Patrick Burke's saloon and then only because his horse, who had been standing at the curb all night, lost patience, crossed the sidewalk and peered through the window searching him out. The sober Pat helped the less than sober Mike into his carriage, where he slept soundly while his horse found its familiar way through the sleeping village, clattered across the wooden bridge and up the mile-long hill to the Fleming farm. In the stableyard the horse halted, and my grandfather, awakened by the absence of motion, unhitched him and hung up his harness. Each made his own way to his bed.

As a child I shuttled back and forth across the rattling wood-planked bridge connecting the two towns, equally at home in both Burke and Fleming houses, listening to tall tales and embellished history that telescoped the past and present, creating a sense of continuum, of belonging to a long unbroken line.

Suffield and Enfield were lovely towns for childhood. White frame Colonial houses, set on broad, deep lawns among great old trees, faced one another across a hundred yards and more of green fairway divided by a two-lane road. Even now they seem little changed, secure in the quiet, unhurried confidence of age. Suffield was farming, dairy and tobacco mostly. Enfield's principal business was a red brick carpet factory alongside the river. My grandfather Burke's saloon and his big gray frame house behind it were near the factory gate, and the mill-hands were his customers. Though he dealt in whiskey, he never drank. Dressed in an aging black homburg and black chesterfield coat, he attended Mass faithfully and strode at a heavy gait to the same pew each Sunday, down front on the left. In a courtly half-turn he ushered his trailing wife into the pew before him, made a hint of a genuflection and established his aisle position. A tall, portly, pink and white man, the color of his face accentuated by his untrimmed white hair and large white moustache, he said his prayers in a loud rumble and was terrified of leprechauns. He won a local reputation for bravery by once disarming an enraged barber about to slice a customer's throat with a straight razor. But one night in his house I was awakened by sounds on the landing at the turn of the stairs just outside my bedroom. My grandmother, petite and delicate-featured, stood beside her husband, looming in his nightshirt, listening to strange noises from below. "It's an intruder," my grandfather concluded in a hoarse whisper. "Go down and deal with him, Bridget."

The first automobile of his that I remember was a Peerless, a huge seven-passenger maroon touring car with wheels as high as my head and a body shaped like a lifeboat. He sat grandly on the back seat, left the driving to his sons, and sent two of them to Yale to learn other skills. Grandmother Burke appeared frail, but she must have been made of Sheffield steel. She looked after everything, while my grandfather held court from his rocking chair in their big kitchen. Once in my pre-memory I took hold of and could not let go a steam pipe that ran up through her pantry to the floor above. She pried loose the burned hand and tended it. I think of her with love each time I look at my scarred right palm. At the end of her life she came to live in my parents' home, and I carried her tea to her bedroom every morning and sat on her bed and chatted before I left for school. Bedridden, she remained keen to know all that was going on in my young world. And before she died she gave me her wedding ring, a gold band engraved with fleurs-de-lis.

Grandfather Michael Fleming bought me a pony, Dolly O, and I rode out with him when he went to oversee the haying or to visit a pasture of dairy cows. Like most farmers, he took more care with his outbuildings than he did with his house. The stables were wonderfully well built. Draft horses were kept in wide straight stalls. At the head of each a chest-high feed trough stretched its width, and above the trough a wooden half-door gave the horses a good view of the goings-on in the hay barn and the cow barn. My pony luxuriated in a box stall to herself in one corner. I would have slept there on a pile of hay but for my worry about an occasional rat. Rats repelled me. When Dolly O grew old and cranky she tolerated only my grandfather and me in her stall. Others she bit and kicked.

Michael Fleming remained loyal to horses, but in 1914 he bought a Cadillac, and thought it perfectly proper for his young sons to drive as long as he was in the machine; to him an automobile was always a machine. On Saturday nights he drank with gusto and danced as long as the fiddler would play and on Sundays I sat at his elbow as he drove a carriage to Mass and he teased me about going to church with the ladies while he waited outside with the horses, smoking his pipe. Though he took a dim view of the Catholic Church and kept the clergy at a distance, he was strict about my being properly dressed to accompany my grandmother.

My mother was the third of four children, the only girl. She was bright, bold, good-looking, dressed smartly and, by her own admission, thought she was "the cat's whiskers." She became a legal secretary. My father graduated from the local high school and, at age sixteen, entered Holy Cross College in Worcester, Massachusetts. Four years later he went on to Yale Law School. My parents had known one another casually and were thrown together when my father found a summer job with Abe Lasker's law firm in Springfield. My mother was Mr. Lasker's secretary. On their first date my parents disagreed about everything. They were married during my father's final year at Yale, took the train to New York for a honeymoon at the McAlpine Hotel, and were asked to leave the roof-garden dance floor. My mother's ankle-length dress was designed with a risqué split up one side to the knee and their style of dancing was too sexy for the management. Ever since I can remember, they danced fluently and indefatigably and deep into life.

As I grew older, I spent long periods of time at the farm, especially in summer, turned out each morning like a colt to pasture to improvise the day. By then my Uncle James worked the farm and his children were my friends. Except at night;

then my Fleming cousins became my tormentors. Possessed by the normal cruelty of children, they invented "a man" who hid at night in the dark lane between their house and my grandfather's. An ogre with a great sack would carry me off, never to be seen again. When the three-hundred-yard flight through the dreaded blackness could no longer be put off, I flew from their high veranda on wings of terror, vaulting the steps, sped across their lawn, raced into the black sleeve of a lane, raced past the chicken yard with its restless cherry trees, past the lurching corn crib, the low crouching cowbarn and the pale, gaunt silo, zoomed around Bridget Fleming's circular flower bed, past the stables and the lurking shapes in the open carriage shed and shot arrow-straight for the back entry as fast as my skinny legs could flail the dirt drive. The devil himself could not have caught me. After such a fearful run, to sleep in my grandmother's bed was my breathless, heart-pounding prayer. Pressed close to the wall, I held myself rigid as a dry stick for fear of disturbing her and losing that safe, protective place. By morning I had earned her gentle admonition, "Sure, boy, you kicked me black and blue in the night."

Her kitchen, too, was the main everyday room where my grandfather rocked and smoked his pipe and she sang Kerry songs to him in her soft Irish voice. She tended her own kitchen garden and, as Grandfather Fleming boasted, "she could throw a stick in the ground and it would grow." Her pantry held everything from jugs of cider to jars of cookies to a cardboard box labeled "string too short to use." When she was eighty her hair was still jet black and, loosed from its bun, hung to her waist. She must have been a young woman of great beauty.

My own father, Patrick Burke, Jr., took me everywhere with him: to night court, where he sat me on a front bench, feet dangling short of the floor, while he, a young lawyer, defended some beleaguered immigrant; took me to the circus in Boston and afterwards to midnight supper at the Parker House where a sensible old waiter protested that I should not have coffee at midnight and my father insisted I should. "If the lad wants coffee, bring him coffee." Often too I caddied for him when, dressed in plus-fours, he first took up golf on Enfield's cow pasture course. The greens were protected from wandering cows by barbed wire fences and were entered through turn-

stiles. A bit older, I played along with him using one club, a
wood-shaft mashie-niblick. He showed me how to swing and
taught me always to play the ball where it lay. To improve your
lie, he said, was to cheat yourself. (Golf, Dave Anderson once
wrote in his *New York Times* column, has a history of conscience.) During Prohibition I drove with him in a barely-
remembered Chandler touring car on night trips over the
Connecticut hills to Waterbury, where some distant relative sold
him five-gallon tins of alcohol, which he ferried back to Hartford for himself and his friends to make bathtub gin. Whatever
the weather, we fastened on the car's rain curtains, slipping
them on their metal supports and buttoning them to the canvas
roof, to obstruct the outside view of our contraband. Like my
grandfather Fleming, he too drank and danced and sang joy-
ously. Each of them, as Sean O'Casey said of James Joyce, was
"a man born with a dance on one side of him and a song on the
other; two gay guardian angels for any man to have." Michael
Fleming, a man of solid earth; Pat Burke, Jr., a man of graceful
intellect. They were heroic figures, graced with chivalrous instincts, residual of the knights from whom they were anciently
descended. A sense of noblesse oblige remained in their mar-
row centuries after their lines had been dispossessed of all title.
They were intrinsic gentlemen. So, too, was my grandfather
Patrick Burke, though he was a more remote figure, not physically remote, but less approachable by children.

I did not achieve a close friendship with my mother until she
was in her seventies. By any measure she was a good mother —
raised us, fed us well, clothed us with care, nursed us through
childhood diseases, kept a comfortable and spotless house. She
and my father seemed happy together, enjoyed one another,
shared good times, good friends, a good life. She was proud of
him. She was proud of us: of my sister Janet, a brilliant scholar
and a lady of saintly disposition; of my brother, a blithe spirit;
of me. Yet she was afflicted by a strain of petty Irish bigotry.
Persons other than Irish Catholics often caught the rude edge
of her tongue and even within that ethnic circle she was
brusquely selective. But she was equally guilty of Irish inconsis-
tency. Over the years some of her close friends, as they say,
were all kinds of other people. Perhaps I was made vaguely
uncertain of her because she never spoke to her own father. As

a child, I was puzzled by this awkward, unexplained silence between them, and it made a deep impression. She would make caustic asides about him when he had drunk too much and I would side silently with him. I would guess this rift, which was never spoken about, caused my grandmother considerable sadness. My father chided my mother good-humoredly for her lack of charity. Yet some time before my brother and I went to war, she joined the Red Cross and set off every morning, looking very smart indeed in her blue-gray uniform and képi-like hat, to roll bandages and perform all the other hospital services those wartime ladies performed with great dedication and industry. I had in effect left home at age sixteen, and the image of her I carried with me until my middle years was limited to the perspective of childhood memories.

The first landmark event of my life occurred when I was about seven or eight years old. We had moved to and lived briefly in Springfield, Massachusetts. Crossing a vacant lot on my way home from my first day at the Catholic school, I was jumped by three public school boys, beaten up, and went home crying. For some reason my father was there, heard my tearful story, gave me a quiet talk about bullies and told me to lay into them if they attacked again. They did, the next day. I flailed out, bashing, kicking, biting, invaded by some new courage. I felt I was winning even when they had me in a headlock or otherwise painfully twisted and pummeled because I was bleeding, now on one boy's sweater, now on another's trousers. My bleeding nose was a staunch ally and I was encouraged that it bled so profusely. Eventually they quit, bloodied with my blood, left me alone holding the high ground, bloodied with my own blood. Never have I felt more triumphant. I was pleased for my father. It was a major victory. There were other grade school fights along the way, of course, but none were memorable. Most of my boy-energy was spent on games, any game. I discovered I could do them better than most and that gave me a certain standing in my boyhood community and a certain beginning sense of myself. This made the transition to new schools and the accommodation to new schoolmates less difficult when my family moved down the Connecticut River and my father joined the legal staff of one of the insurance companies headquartered in Hartford.

Somewhere in the growing-up years I saw my first major-league baseball game. We were staying on Governors Island, the United States Army post in New York Harbor, guests of an Army colonel friend of my parents in one of the handsome antebellum houses the Army had built for its senior officers, high-ceilinged and cool even in the July heat. My father and Colonel McDonald and I took the free ferry across Buttermilk Channel to the Battery and, for a five-cent fare, I think, rode the Lexington Avenue subway to 161st Street. Dank air blasted through the car's open windows, a relief from the hundred-degree temperature on the streets above. But I was too excited to notice the heat, and the roaring rattle of the train hurtling itself towards Yankee Stadium only heightened my anticipation. We had seats in the lower grandstand a few rows back from the third-base dugout, and I hadn't opened my first bag of peanuts before Babe Ruth came to bat, looking just as he did in newspaper photographs, and hit a long high home run into the right field stands. I never dreamed that a baseball could be struck so high and so far. We stood and clapped and watched Mr. Ruth's mincing trot around the bases, and I became a Yankee fan forever. When I was a little older Frank Crosetti was the great Yankee shortstop and my baseball idol. Taking infield with my pals — all summer long when we weren't actually playing a game, we were endlessly at infield practice — I must have fielded a million ground balls pretending to be Crosetti. "The way to look, Cro," my friends would yell when I made an especially good stop. I never actually saw Crosetti play except in my mind's eye, but I was sure my form was as faithful as my admiration.

In high school I became better at basketball than baseball. As a sophomore making the hour-long bus trip from West Hartford to Bristol, I was just another member of the squad who might spell a first-team player for two or three minutes. Or I might not play at all. But one of the regulars twisted an ankle in a freak pregame accident and I joined the starting team. Bristol High was virtually unbeatable in those days, primarily because of two marvelous athletes named Gurske and Palau. Later both became three-sport stars at Fordham University; Gurske was the fullback and Palau the quarterback on Fordham's nationally ranked football teams of that era. Even in high school in 1932 Gurske was a young bull. I was a broomstick matched against him. But I stuck closer to him than his shirt. My contribution to our offense was nearly nonexistent but, as it turned out, so was Gurske's. Throughout the game I held him scoreless, an unspeakable annoyance to a high-scoring player. On the bus ride home I was no longer just another bench-warmer, and in the corner drugstore at West Hartford Center where some of us went for milkshakes, the conversations up and down the soda fountain told variations of the story of young Burke holding the great Gurske scoreless. Listening to this sweet praise of peers, responding modestly to adult curiosity, drinking my chocolate malted, I experienced the warm seductive glow of the spotlight and wanted the evening never to end.

As the only nonsenior on the first team, I was tapped for the captaincy the following year. That is, until it was discovered that on nights when I should have been home studying I was playing for a semiprofessional team under an assumed name and was fired from the high school squad. Suddenly, then, at age sixteen I was open to other options.

## 3

KINGSWOOD SCHOOL for Boys was beyond the financial reach of those of us who went to the public schools. Realistically, we coveted no more than one of their handsome maroon and black football jerseys, if we could swipe one. Then one day my friend Jack Carey and I learned through the teenage grapevine that Kingswood's athletic director was ambitious to flesh out his sports teams with public school athletes who would run and pass and kick and generally throw their bodies about with greater abandon than the paying students. Scholarships were available.

On a day in June, together with a couple of dozen other athletes from central Connecticut high schools, Carey and I appeared at the school's summer-vacant grounds at the end of a drowsy tree-lined residential street in West Hartford. A gravel drive passed through an open iron gate between high red brick gateposts, each surmounted by a huge stone Wyvern, and divided itself into a long narrow oval that curved, at the far end, in front of the wide stone steps of a red brick ivy-covered chapel. Inside the gate, immediately to the right, was the school's administration building, a sedate three-story red brick Colonial building with casement windows, which also housed the common room and library. The Green, where only the faculty and members of the senior class were allowed to walk, was a half-moon of lush lawn bordered on the flat side by the drive and on the curving side by a row of four identical white, slate-roofed buildings that looked like Elizabethan cottages. These were evenly spaced in a semicircle between the administration building and the chapel. Each building held two classrooms on the ground floor, and on the floor above masters' apartments looked onto the Green through dormer windows. Carefully tended playing fields spread out to the left of the drive: football, baseball, tennis, running track. Thick, even grass, green as dollars, contrasted strikingly to the worn, grass-barren public high school athletic fields we were accustomed to. In all, the designers had successfully simulated the look of an English boys' school. It lacked only a century or two of aging.

In a splendid new gymnasium beyond the semicircle of class-room cottages we aspirants dressed in shorts and sneakers and, on still another series of sports fields, near a brook, ran and threw and caught and vied to show off our best physical form. The following day we were tested academically. All but two candidates were eliminated, Carey among them. It became a wrenching time for me, and I considered forgoing Kingswood. Carey and I were all but joined at the hip. Together we played every stick and ball game known to man. Our summer world was contained by the four lines of a baseball diamond; in autumn football and zones were the limit of our horizons. Aspiring to become college footballers, we were up at dawn to run and build our legs and our stamina. We neither drank nor smoked but shared secrets of our first adventures with adventurous girls, as innocence receded. Black-Irish, handsome, and personable, Carey carried on at the high school, captained the football team, as he did later at Trinity College, died too young of an Irish disposition to drink more than the mind and body can abide. I opted for the opening world of Kingswood. Our lives diverged and the texture of our relationship changed. We remained friends who grew apart. For me Kingswood was life's major turning point, the opening of a new and wider experience.

My acceptance at Kingswood had the opposite effect on a public school friend named Vivian. That is to say, she moved closer. Physically precocious, Vivian could easily have been cast in a French film as the convent girl who seduces the village baker for the sheer naughtiness of it. After Kingswood, she declared, I would play football at Dartmouth College and we would be married in my freshman year. At that point being a college freshman appeared terribly sophisticated, and safely distant. Vivian had converted a young lad's fantasies to warm flesh. Once having tasted, I would have outswum a salmon up the cascades to taste again. And again. So I was loath to cavil at a distant marriage prospect. Forever was a year and a day. At the time, pregnancies, like a misplaced epidemic of mumps, broke out among my public high school classmates. Girls named Peggy and Ruby and Sue were hastily married to boys named Warren and Joe and Ed. But Vivian's family moved to a distant city before teenage heedlessness trapped us in premature parenthood, marriage, and God knows what kind of afterlife.

My parents were pleased by Kingswood, though apprehensive, pleased by my initiative and apprehensive about my hurling myself into an unfamiliar circumstance, to live among young people differently, more genteelly raised than I. In his wisdom my father kept his doubts to himself, his own Irish Catholic doubts about the potential hostility of a Wasp school. In those years before the Second World War employment ads warning "Irish need not apply" had long since disappeared from Eastern newspapers, but neither the memory nor the mindset that inspired them was altogether dead. As for myself, I had no recollection of the anti-Irish prejudice that surged during the Al Smith presidential campaign of 1928, for instance. In 1933, among my father's generation if not mine, it remained a current though muted issue. But the Jesuits, who had given my father fluency in Greek and Latin and secured his religion, also imparted a sophisticated view of life, one that accommodated a wider-ranging world, the handling of a long spoon if one must sup with the devil. My father was an intelligent and enlightened man, unfettered by antique prejudice. When my mother learned that Kingswood's religion was Anglican-based — the school derived from the original Kingswood School in Bath, England — and that the students attended chapel each morning, not Mass, she envisioned my soul sliding from grace and lost.

In the mid 1930s Irish-Catholic was as deep as Kingswood dipped into the minorities, but I never sensed that I was treated differently from anyone else. If I was different, it was because I was a scholarship boy and I was a better athlete than most others. Also, though I had stood second academically in my public school class, I was a lagging student here. The scholastic level at Kingswood was markedly ahead of me.

Despite family foreboding, the only hostility I encountered

was an overheard conversation between two of Hartford's scions standing at adjacent urinals, while I sat closeted in a toilet. They deplored the practice of bringing in "tramp athletes" to fill football team positions that rightfully belonged to "legitimate" students. They had a point, but if theirs was a general attitude, it waned quickly; if religion was an issue, I was unaware of it. As a good athlete, helping the school teams to win and having a capacity for easy friendship, I found acceptance more swiftly than had I been a withdrawn, prickly scholar. The doors simply opened.

First Red Shepard, a member of the football squad, invited me to his family's spacious country home for a weekend. His father was rich in tobacco land along the Connecticut River and his clothes had the cut of a good New York tailor. On the Friday night, Mr. Shepard, as gruff as Mrs. Shepard was kindly, declared any man six feet tall, my height, was too clumsy to get out of his own way, and he snorted when I abstained from the meat course to avoid what I then thought to be sin. I was unsettled by his manicured appearance contrasted with the granite-quarry look of my grandfather and my sun-blackened, lath-thin Uncle James. They were my image of tobacco farmers. The following day Mr. Shepard discovered I knew about tobacco from beginning to end: that seeds topped from the previous year's plants were bedded in boxes of soil-like substance scraped from the core of decaying apple trees and preserved during the winter in the coal-stove warmth of the kitchen; that in early spring the seeds were planted in long low glass-covered beds, slanted to catch the best sun.

In the fall at harvest time I had worked in the tobacco fields, at first handing the cut plants to a man who pulled six stalks onto a lath, spearing these through the base to hang topside down. Then I was promoted to carrying the lathed plants from the spearer's caisson to a waiting tobacco rack, and in time worked my way up to the dream job of like-minded twelve-year-olds: driving one of the long, narrow, horse-drawn tobacco racks between the field and the sheds where the tobacco was hung to dry. A boy who drove a rack also got to ride his horse to the field each morning and back to the stable at the end of the day. Mr. Shepard was much less gruff with me after our talk about Havana broad-leaf tobacco.

At the end of my first football season at Kingswood, the team elected me their captain. To celebrate, Philip Judd, a classmate, gave a dinner party at his family's baronial estate. The front lawn was a full-sized golf course and the garage held eleven cars, eight of them Rolls Royces. A long narrow building alongside the kitchen gardens contained the bowling lanes. Philip's grandfather was a famous nineteenth-century financier known as "Bet-a-Million" Gates. He must have won most of his bets, I thought. The girl I brought was quite pretty but not cut from the same fine cloth as the others, and I hoped it wouldn't be awkward for her. My concern was misplaced. At the end of dinner, served by maids in crisp uniforms, champagne was opened and my captaincy toasted. It was a totally new experience. I didn't know whether to sit or stand, drink or not drink. I felt like a great bloody clod and sat fumbling in confusion and ignorance, flushed with embarrassment, saved only by the casualness with which my new friends sailed past what for me was a painful social milestone.

I had so much to learn. Sports had given me a certain cachet, an opening to a different social world. The manners I had been taught as a child and those I had learned by example were good manners, though not as polished and nicely rounded as those of my new friends. Apart from the confusion I experienced at being toasted, I was not a social embarrassment to them or to myself. They seemed to like, to seek out my company, and I enjoyed them and their mode of living. They lived naturally with the trappings of the well-to-do and, at their invitation, I was adaptable enough to join them and enjoy it. While I looked and listened and learned, it never occurred to me to pretend I was anything but what I was. This may have been some misguided adolescent conceit. More likely it was traceable to the wonderfully secure environment in which I grew up. I did not for a moment feel a sense of inadequacy, only a lack of precocious social polish.

Two fellows in the sixth form (the twelfth grade), one year ahead of me, became my special chums. Geer was a stocky, feisty football quarterback and baseball shortstop, son of a stockbroker; Moray was a big, square, rather ungainly end, a serious student and a generous friend. Moray's father, an insurance company president, lived in New York, leaving his son loosely looked after by an aging housekeeper in a rambling eighteenth-century farmhouse several miles outside Hartford. Loosely looked after, because on occasion we were able to take girls there, the kind of girls who protested as one fumbled to undress them in the dark, then helped unfasten a troublesome button and get along with it. On Saturday nights we drank beer and went to all-night diners for hamburgers. Sundays we re-hashed the previous night's foolishness: did this or that happen before or after the fight? Almost always there was a fight. Geer, who looked like a pugnacious Mickey Rooney, compulsively challenged people bigger than he. Often Moray and I con-sidered letting him fight it out on his own, but invariably we joined in. We fought anonymous people without anger, to no purpose. Even then it seemed stupid to me. One foray in a saloon put me in jail. Actually I had been in the men's room when the shoving match started at the bar and returned just in time to be thrown out into the street by the police. Cockily I told Geer it wouldn't be necessary for him to give up his car keys as the cops had demanded, a piece of advice the police took instant exception to. With the speed of a jai-alai ball I was bounced into a squad car, caromed off the booking sergeant's desk, and slammed into a cell. The iron door clanged and locked behind me, leaving me in solitary darkness listening to the wracked bodies of derelicts and petty criminals snoring, sleep-mumbling, moaning, being sick in nearby cells.

My friends, being friends, came to rescue me. I heard Mo-ray's strong voice echo through the stark metal and concrete building: "Do you have a prisoner named Burke here?" Lights in the cellblock went on again, footsteps clapped up the cement stairs. I stuck my arm through the bars signaling my location, but Moray and Geer, each in the punishing grip of a cop, were marched past me and shoved into a cell of their own farther down the line. Other prisoners, twice awakened now, cursed and yelled angrily for quiet and, when the lights went out, settled restlessly into their fitful night. In the morning Judge Schwolsky lined us up before his bench, gave us a tongue-lashing and turned us loose. I had not liked being locked up. The clank of absolute nonfreedom, the iron door slamming closed behind me clangs in the memory each time I read of a man going to prison — for a month, a year, for ten — and my freedom-loving body chills along its spine and shudders at the thought.

Thus my first year at Kingswood was filled with games, socializing with friends, living well enough on the twenty dollars my father sent me each month, skipping classes on a whim, guilty of silly deportment, making sporadic incursions into the school's academic program. To be a star athlete and a companionable friend was all that was expected of me, I wanted to think. It wasn't, of course. My year-end examinations were a disaster, and a summons to the headmaster's office was inevitable.

In his muted, wood-paneled study I was motioned to a straight-backed chair facing his disordered desk. George R. H. Nicholson — he was called "the Duke" beyond his earshot — stood stiffly at one side before an unlit fireplace, a black academic gown over his civilian clothes. For a long moment of wintry silence he studied me from an angle and, when he had frozen my attention, came sharply to the point. He spoke in a slipped Oxonian accent. "Burke. You are a bad element!"

I had torn up my ticket to a new world. Listening with half an ear and a plummeting heart, I scarcely heard the reasons for his conclusion — I knew them well enough — and braced myself, cringed perhaps, against an onrushing sense of loss, against the sinking sensation of dismissal, floundering in the bog of my own mindlessness, a soggy place I had half-hoped to slither past. My face burned at the reality of failure, having set out so pridefully, burned at the prospect of returning to the high school I had cut away from so expectantly. An irreplaceable opportunity had been tossed away heedlessly as a gum wrapper. For the first time I was face to face with my own foolishness and it scared me.

Burke, you are a bad element. I had no response to Mr. Nicholson's summary of my performance. Embarrassed and genuinely contrite, I screwed up enough courage to raise my head and look at him.

"I'm sorry, sir."

Outside the open window the gardener and his lawnmower went the length of the Green and back before the Duke spoke again. His tone sounded less stern.

"Well, Burke. We are going to give you another chance."

Somewhere I found the wit to ask, "Why, sir?"

He made a gesture of exasperation, as much with himself as with me. "Because, Burke, there must be some good in you somewhere. We have yet to find it."

I was tempted to say that he could have used a little help from me, but didn't; it would have sounded flippant. I thought to promise to do better, but didn't; it would have sounded hollow and too late. Perhaps he read the one thought that was running round my head: if I am too stupid to grasp this reprieve for myself, then fairness and common sense demand my best shot for a man who would give me a second chance. Still standing before the fireplace, his hands clasped behind him under his black academic gown, he seemed less aloof, less steely, more flesh and blood. Along the sides of his straight, ascetic nose and on the skin stretched tight across his cheekbones, a network of thin red road-map lines hinted that a gin and vermouth at sundown eased days vexed by unshaped minds and by adolescent behavior. Some days must have called for more Booths Bombay than others. I thanked him very much.

Finding some good somewhere, giving some form to a lank of boy was delegated to W. O. Williams, "Wow" of course, who would be my master in the sixth form, and to Joe Gargan, newly returned to Kingswood and to his former post as athletic director. The two men were vastly different and fast friends. Williams, transplanted to America from England, epitomized the traditional English schoolmaster, a real-life Mr. Chips. Gargan was a soft-spoken, tough fibered Irish-American with a degree in Physical Education from Springfield College in Massachusetts and a fine record as a scholastic coach. Both were men of rare quality; they cared as much about the development of a boy's character as his mind or body. Wow was addressed as Sir; Joe as Joe.

Wow was all of a piece: a spare frame little higher than five feet, keen face, small clean features, darting movements swift as his mind. At sixty, I would guess, he was quick as a waterbug. No one would ever dream that he was an avid cowboy fan. In the secrecy of his rooms he would strap a gun belt around his boy-sized body and practice quick-drawing a six-shooter. Incongruously, too, he drove a 1928 Packard Phaeton at thundering speeds, peering gleefully over the steering wheel through steel-rimmed glasses, leaving the blurred impression as he flew past of a powerful machine running away with a small boy. Making no concessions to summer, he dressed year-round in thick three-piece suits and wore high shoes that might have been made by Edward VII's bootmaker. He was the perfect schoolteacher. He could help anyone learn anything, coax the most reluctant brain out of its sloth and exercise it into a working part.

The direness of my case pricked Wow's special interest, I believe, plus the fact that he had once seen me play a basketball game against Westminster School. On that day, because of an injury to our regular center, I had been drafted to jump against a player seven or eight inches taller than I. A center jump followed each basket in those days and all afternoon I launched myself into the air and never once touched the ball. My persistence, despite its futility, impressed Wow, though I told him, without being either disingenuous or coy, that it seemed to me a perfectly ordinary thing to do, to keep trying. Perhaps he sensed he could induce me to try learning and that I might keep trying. He invited me to his apartment above the sixth form classrooms to talk about my solid geometry and trigonometry, subjects that were eluding me. Wow speculated, discreetly and obliquely, about my inability to learn from my math teacher and suggested I come to his rooms each afternoon at four for private tutoring. It became an adventure. From mathematics we branched out into all manner of subjects and his alchemy soon changed the chore of doing lessons into the joy of discovery, of learning. In lighter moments he taught me how to draw a perfect freehand circle, how to make a proper cup of tea and confided that his own schoolboy sport in England had been Hare and Hound. He was, he admitted with shy pride, the only Hare the Hounds never caught during his scholastic career. Clearly he was as proud of his undefeated record as, say, Joe DiMaggio of his 56-game hitting streak and might have equated the two had Joe DiMaggio ever come to his notice.

Often in the late afternoon and early evening I sat in the sixth form classroom doing my studies. It was, I told myself, a more conducive atmosphere than Mrs. Parsons' boardinghouse on Farmington Avenue where I lived with a mixed bag of middle-aged secretaries and energetic young salesmen. More truthfully, I always hoped for a glimpse of Marion Hepburn, the famous Katharine's younger sister. Marion came from home to tutor with Wow and passed the sixth form classroom door arriving and departing. I took care to leave it open and sit at the front desk in the row nearest the entrance. Several times we smiled and said a passing hello. Then one evening her light feminine step sounded on the worn wooden stairs from Wow's apartment and stopped at the pay telephone in the vestibule. She must have misdialed a couple of times and gotten a wrong number; she was seized by a fit of giggling. After a moment of timidity, I offered to help, dialed her number, and passed her the receiver. I think she said into the phone that the chauffeur should come and fetch her and was told that he was on his way. But we did chat and she was disproportionately grateful for my having got her number and I felt disproportionately gallant for having done so. She was very gay, very pretty, and less angular than her actress sister. With a delightful sense of occasion, as the fall moved into winter, Wow overlapped the end of my tutoring with the beginning of Marion's and called it Afternoon Tea. Marion brought cakes baked for us by the Hepburn cook and in Wow's cosy, cluttered schoolmaster's quarters the early New England darkness was less dreary by far. In the spring Marion invited me to her family's home for Sunday dinner. Dr. Hepburn was away and Mrs. Hepburn graciously put a gauche schoolboy at ease. In the library after dinner she took my hand and read my palm, embarrassingly raw and ungainly in her delicate cared-for hands. The scar at the base of my index and middle fingers stood out pale and jagged against the redness of the rest. No foretelling included Marion. I had a crush on her, of course. But she was destined for a Kingswood classmate, an exceptionally nice fellow with impeccable credentials, social and financial.

Joe Gargan inherited me as captain of his 1934 team and a football schedule that included a game, the fourth of the season, with a big public high school which had a reputation of supplying colleges with outstanding football players, a school whose pool of athletic talent far outstripped Kingswood's. We won a moral victory by playing them to a tie. I scored our touchdown and kicked the extra point. Wow was so thrilled he recommended a school holiday be declared, but the Duke turned a cold eye on it. That night I celebrated at the local movie with some pals. In the lobby afterwards I entertained them — and anyone else who cared to watch — by holding my nose and blowing an egg-sized swelling under my right eye, depressing it with my fingers and blowing it up again. An easily amused knot of people gathered for a few moments until, by chance, a cousin of my mother's passed by. He was Richard Buckley, a brilliant young brain surgeon who kept half an eye on me since my family had moved to Philadelphia. He elbowed through the little group of onlookers and took hold of my arm. "Stop that foolishness and come with me!"

In his office Dr. Buckley examined me and discovered a fractured sinus bone. I couldn't remember any particularly sharp blow in the face, but one of my teammates told me later that I had got up a bit groggy from one tackle and on the next play thrown a forward pass out over the sidelines, rather than down the field where the receivers were. I had no recollection of that either. For the balance of the season I watched from the bench, forbidden to play. But Joe Gargan let me put on a football suit for the final game and let me go onto the field for the very last play so that I would be with my friends to finish Kingswood's first undefeated football season in many years. We were so excited that, when the referee handed me the game ball, we galloped off the field shouting and thumping one another, rudely forgetting the sporting custom that now seems quaint: huddling at the game's end, win or lose, to give a cheer for the opposing team. I was disappointed not to have played enough during the season to be considered for the All-State prep school team, happy that my teammate, Bob Filon, did make it and thrilled that the team itself had done so well. But the moment of truest elation at Kingswood was getting the trigonometry problem to come out right on the final examination in June. Wow would hear of it; a quick smile would flicker across his eyes, and he would be terribly pleased.

Dressed in our white flannels and blue jackets, we had our class photograph taken beside the ivy-covered wall of the sixth form cottage, and in the chapel, after the speeches, twenty-two boys — boys named Jones and Grant, Oldershaw and Judd, Barrett and Filon, Beach and Gill — filed past the headmaster accepting their diplomas. My parents drove up from their new home in Philadelphia for the graduation exercise. I smiled to myself wondering whether my mother had crossed herself as she entered the chapel and had missed the holy water font at the entrance, as I first had.

Afterwards, socializing with the other families in the spring sunshine on the Green, I was especially glad my parents had come. My mother was a particularly attractive raven-haired lady in her early forties, her oval face lifted to another level of beauty by a perfect nose, like the lady in Renoir's *Portrait de Modèle*. My father, tall and straight, his long intelligent face supporting a strong Roman nose, had the fair look of an ancient Irish prince, and the soft flow of his language from its Greek-Latin-Irish source marked his quality. He said he noticed that Mr. Nicholson, as he handed out the diplomas, had held his handshake with me a few seconds longer than the others, and he interpreted that to mean that the Duke was well pleased with my having won the Carvalho Prize, an award given annually to the member of the football team making the greatest improvement in his studies. I did not have the heart to tell him that it was I who had clung to the headmaster, signaling with my hand, my arm, and my heart, I hoped, how grateful I was for the second chance. It did not seem necessary to blight the day with a confession of how narrowly I had escaped dismissal and, but for the Duke's grace, a different life entirely. Looking back, I realized that, though no course in Civility was taught at Kingswood, civil behavior was fundamental to school life; even the dullest of us learned this lesson and carried it away as part of our education.

Still, the thoughts of youth are not long and I would go to college to play football, to pursue an adolescent dream, to be part of the pageantry and tempo of autumn Saturdays in a time when college football was king, to perform in a magnetic stadium before festival crowds making a dancing time of it, high on a fix of promise and expectation: pretty girls, flags in the autumn breeze, yellow 'mums, bright sun in a cool blue sky, green turf lined in white for swift young athletes in vivid jerseys. The whole romantic fantasy. Some youngsters were hooked on fishing, chemistry, automobile engines, the piano. I was possessed by football. When I was a child the walls of my bedroom were covered with thumbtacked newspaper clippings of the Purdue Boilermakers' backfield and other distant, unknown figures I had read of and fantasized about.

An invitation came, among others, from the University of Pennsylvania football coach to visit their campus. As I stood on Franklin Field's deep summer turf, my mind's fancy filled the steep-banked, double-decked stadium's 78,000 empty seats with cheering fans, rimmed the high brick walls with pennants flaunting their colors in the breeze, raced me from the sidelines to a red-and-blue-jerseyed huddle on some opponent's twenty-yard line. This was how I chose my college. Later, our group of schoolboy football prospects was fed lunch at the training house, was shown through the campus, saw the dormitories, even had the library pointed out.

As had thousands before us throughout two hundred years, we arrived on the Penn campus in September, slightly bewildered strangers trying to remember which was College Hall and where Political Science lectures would be held on Tuesday. We bought and wore the demeaning freshman skullcaps, beanies, submissively kissed the toe of Ben Franklin's statue, and looked around for kindred spirits. Almost at once I met Ned Fielden in the tuck shop in the Freshman Quad. He was a boy from a rival New England prep school. Two years earlier on a bitter November day (the only time my father ever saw me play football at Kingswood) Ned, instead of tackling me as I caught a forward pass, hit me hard in the face with a clenched fist. The blow must have hurt his hand. I came to on the trainer's table. The doctor was poised with a needle to sew my mouth together with a dozen stitches and my father stood behind him cursing the unknown Providence player who had slugged me. That winter our schools played a basketball match. Ned and I were put out of the game for fighting, continued our battle privately in the common shower room as the game went on without us in the gymnasium. In the spring he caught for the Providence baseball team. When I came to bat he asked casually through his catcher's mask where I was going to college.

"Penn," I replied.

"Me too. See you there."

It may seem odd that two boys who had battered one another

in various games would become instant friends at college. But boys, physical boys, get caught up in games, in competition, in contesting skills unleash their energies on one another, without anger, without personal animus, and in fact with considerable respect for the other fellow's skills and courage. I felt that way about Ned Fielden and he me. Besides he was a wonderfully personable young man — an All-American boy, the college newspaper described him — from a background comparable to mine. His father was a doctor in Fall River, Massachusetts, a man of quality, much like my own father. We shared similar tastes and interests and liked different girls. He was as close to me as my brother and when he was killed during the war a part of me died with him.

We traded in our assigned single rooms for a double and roomed together for four years. My father grew very fond of Ned, and we never told him it was he who had knocked my mouth permanently lopsided. We both took for granted that we would do well academically. Our concern was making the freshman football team. Beginning prospects looked dim. More than a hundred players turned out for freshman football, forty of them prep and high school captains from athletically prominent schools. In the first selections I was buried on the sixth or seventh team, issued old, ill-fitting equipment, and sat on the bench unused throughout the first game. Self-worth and dreams of glory sagged. The following week a freshman B Squad was taken to play in Maryland. Withdrawn and morose, I went along, sat alone in the back of the bus atop the equipment and watched the game dejectedly from the substitutes' bench, bent by an inward bruise, as though watching a young friend die, distraught that he should be gone so soon, disheartened by the empty place that would be left. I had lived with football as long as I could remember, slept with it, waked up with it, once rejected my father's offer to buy me a basketball. "It doesn't bounce so crazily," he said. I held out for a football; no matter how crazily it bounced it was my game. It never dawned on me that I would not be a college football player. It was the distant beckoning fire in the darkness, and that was as far into the future as I could see. Now, within the space of a few days that vision was vanishing. I had no other ambition.

Someone hollered my name and I was sent into the game to replace an injured player. The ball was punted to me. Anger and frustration exploded, I suppose. Some demon inside me slashed and cut and sprinted sixty yards for a touchdown. When the second half began I was in the starting lineup, fielded another punt, ran seventy yards for another touchdown. My mind recorded no detail of the runs, only the desperate, half-crazed will that nothing should stop me. Reflexes had operated my body. After the game a coach threw his arm around my shoulder and said something about hiding my light under a bushel. No useful response occurred. The black was still too thick on me, and I remembered my Uncle Roxy once asking me whether I would play college football.

"If I get a break," I said.

He peered at me for a moment, searching perhaps to see what I was made of. "Mick," he said, "in this world you make your own breaks." And walked away.

In the morning there was a telephone call from my father. He had read in a Sunday paper about Penn's discovering "a dazzling new running back." Sensitive to my having had a rough time, he was hesitant, hating to ask the question yet having to ask it. Burke was not an uncommon name in Irish-heavy Philadelphia. "Is it you they wrote about?" His tone was gentle in case it was not, praying silently for my sake that it was. We had not discussed my torment but, knowing me, he knew. And he knew as well that it was my wont, when hurt, to take refuge within myself, to crawl into my own hole like a wounded animal and to come out when I was healed.

"You too?" I snapped. "You gave up on me too?" No sound but a wounded silence came from the other end. I could have cut out my tongue; I hated myself for that sudden bleat of self-pity. I despised whining.

"I'm sorry, Dad. I didn't mean that. Yes, that was me. Everything's OK now."

The following Monday I was issued new equipment and played in the first-string backfield for the balance of the season. At the end of it we heard that the freshman coaches had assessed us and advised the varsity staff that they were sending up five boys who could play football. Ned and I were two of them. Whew! Another plateau.

Life at sea, I expected, would toughen my body for next year's football, and I took a summer job as a seaman on the Furness Bermuda line's *Queen of Bermuda,* which sailed each Saturday noon on weekly cruises from Pier 54 in New York. It was a poor choice; my slim body grew slimmer. The gang I was assigned to was the lowest form of life on the ship. We lived in a glory hole on E Deck deep in the ship's airless bowels, were routed out at five in the morning to set up the dining saloons for breakfast, and ended our day scrubbing decks after the last passenger had left his dining table at night. In between we polished brass and other surfaces and were occasionally drafted to wait on tables in the second-class dining saloon. Our own meals were taken standing at a shelf along a bulkhead in the galley, eating whatever a meat chef, a fish chef, a vegetable chef chose to give us, or not give us, at his whim. And on the first voyage the rolling round-bottomed ship made me vomit a lot until an old sailor pulled me away from the water cooler with gruff advice. "Lay off the piss."

My sophomore year was a football purgatory. I had taken one step forward then two back. Not that I balked at practicing with the scrubs through the week, nor did I begrudge watching Penn's famous Destiny Backfield play well enough to be invited to the Rose Bowl. (The university refused the invitation.) I could bide my time. Very difficult to cope with was the fact that Ned, my friend and roommate, was a first-string varsity and that I was so poorly regarded. I was humiliated, not by his success, but by my own apparent inadequacy. It was a private pain I had to live with and pretend to the outside world that it didn't exist. For some reason it never occurred to me to quit. Perhaps I could not abide defeat or accept that I might not be good enough. So I was driven. A dervish bashed and slashed at the other scrubs and my abandon fascinated one of the minor coaches, Nig Berry — a great Penn and professional running back in years past. He made me a personal project, coaching me to exaggerate my natural high-knee, loose-hipped running motion. Time and again, after the others had left the practice field, and until my legs literally gave way, he made me race down a sideline stripe and cut at right angles, striving not to lose speed. His personal attention revived my spirit and my expectations. The crucible paid out. The next season I vaulted over all the in-betweens into the first-string backfield to stay. I loved every minute of it for the next two years, especially Saturday afternoons.

I was an emotional player. Friday nights were restless and Saturday mornings I woke tense, quiet, and withdrawn. From the jock-house on Spruce Street where many athletes lived, I ambled slowly and alone through the campus towards the stadium, consciously absorbing the quality of the day, the dignity of the ivy-covered buildings unruffled by the excitement rising around them, the cheeriness of students' good-luck calls, the lovely wine-red brick of the Engineering School beside a leafy walk, the early traffic moving impatiently along Thirty-third Street towards the parking lots, the vendors hawking programs, the furtive body language that gave away the ticket scalpers, the pennants decorating the stadium's rim, signaling the wind direction. Savoring it all, I reminded myself that an adolescent dream had become reality and that I should fix it in memory. Soon you'll be grown up, I told myself, and it will be pleasant to remember how happy you were, how lucky.

Lunch in the training house was at 11:30. I could eat little. A few bites of lamb chop, a taste of baked potato, a few sips of tea was all my nervous system could deal with. Some boys tended to horseplay, others to banter; I retreated into silence. Lethargy, quiet as fog, invaded my body and hung there heavily. Hard thighs turned the consistency of the custard I couldn't eat for lunch. The hundred-yard walk from the training house at the west end of Franklin Field to the players' locker room under the south stands was a trek. A plaque on the wall just outside its door bore a legend: A team that won't be beaten can't be beaten. It stirred no one. No one ever looked at it; half the players didn't know it was there. It was remote, bronzed cant belonging to someone else, having nothing to do with our nervy, contemporary moment. For some unremembered reason — perhaps rooming together on road trips drew us close — James Patrick Connell, our fullback, and I always made the trek together. Connell, another black-Irish football friend, was more mature than the rest of us. Hard as anthracite, he had arrived at college a freshman from the Pennsylvania coal fields with a good-looking dark-haired wife and two babies. Invariably as we scuffed past the rehearsing band, we asked one another why hadn't we taken up the tuba instead of football.

At the moment tooting and marching was infinitely more appealing than banging heads with Michigan or Navy or whomever we were to play that day. None of which we meant, obviously. But there was comfort in sharing the misery of pregame queasiness, the nausea of excitement. Penn State upset our pregame ritual when they broke Connell's leg, as they said they would; Connell had clotheslined one of their quick runners the season before and put him out of action.

Pregame sickness began to diminish in the crowded locker room clatter — metal lockers, cleats on cement — overtaken by the precise routines of having ankles taped by the trainer, fitting shoulder pads into place, lacing high cleated shoes. And all tension was shot away by the opening gun catapulting us into the game. Especially I loved those last suspended moments, both teams spread out on the white-striped grass, theirs lined up across midfield to kick off, ours dispersed to receive, me isolated at the goal line, dancing lightly to stay limber, like a tennis player about to receive a first service, shaking my hands, loose and limp on hanging arms, to keep them supple, loving the fact that I was there, naked and alone, that 78,000 keyed-up people edged forward in their seats to see what I could do. Christ, how lucky, I thought, appreciating the moment. Come on, kick the goddam ball before I explode with happiness and tension. The kicker moved forward and the crowded stands vanished. Once the ball was in the air, nothing else existed, not even the other players, until the ball was gathered in. The spectators might have been stone, so total was the concentration for the next couple of hours of running and passing, tackling and blocking. The era of the two-platoon system lay somewhere in the future. A man played both offense and defense in that time and no one broke out the *Guinness Book of Records* when you played a full sixty minutes.

Once against Yale I took the opening kickoff at the goal line, ran straight, veered right several strides, cut back, crossing the right leg over the left at full speed, hit a Yale helmet with a driving knee, drove through it without feeling, spun on a few yards into a gathering of Yale shirts. The man whose head had been hit by my knee lay still, unconscious. The Penn team stood in a loose huddle a few yards away while the doctors and the stretcher-bearers looked after him.

"Who hit him?" Connell asked.

"Who the fuck do you think?" I snarled at him.

"OK, OK," he said, laughing. "Don't get mad at me. I'm on your side."

The player taken to the hospital with a concussion was Stewart Hemingway. I visited him every day till he was released, fully recovered. So did Frank Reagan, Rix Yard, and others. Everyone liked him. Later Cornell came to Franklin Field for our traditional Thanksgiving Day game. I threw a forward pass and a Sherman tank hit me from the blind side. "Jesus, was there only one of you?" I asked a Cornell player who was lying on me.

"I'm Stewart Hemingway's brother," he said simply. I laughed. More power to you. I loved the give-and-take of it. The evening up, the balancing of life. It was a wonderful career-ending game. Cornell was the top team in the nation that year. They had defeated Ohio State the week before, and we had lost by a touchdown to Michigan before a crowd of 101,000 in Ann Arbor. Cornell and Penn played to a tie, satisfying to us. I intercepted two passes in the final quarter, satisfying to me. Twice Brad Holland, Cornell's All-American end, and I leaped for the ball together; both times I came down with it.

There was more to college than football. Often on Sunday nights we went to joints on Race Street, then Philadelphia's Harlem, to hear superb black musicians and hope some lovely black girl would invite us home. They never did. Benny Goodman's sextet played at our Junior Prom. Bulky tackles and rangy ends shook the floor of the training house dancing the Big Apple; laughter and the animal health of youth bent the walls. In our rooms we listened to Bunny Berrigan's "I Can't Get Started with You," and sometimes we were invited to the grand houses along the Main Line by some generous magnate who got his kicks from college football. In New York for the price of a one-dollar drink you could stand at the bar of the Onyx Club on Fifty-second Street and listen to Maxine Sullivan sing "Loch Lomond" and, again on Sunday nights, along with college kids from Columbia and Princeton and other places, pile into the German-American A.C. on Seventeenth Street under the Third Avenue El to drink draft beer and sing "Who Put the Overalls in Mrs. Murphy's Chowder."

We also attended classes. It was not difficult to earn reasonable grades, though by national measure Penn held to stiff academic standards. Some very talented football prospects disappeared after their freshman or sophomore years and turned up playing for other well-known colleges with more flexible requirements. After discharging the obligatory freshman courses, I ranged all over the university. As though it were a smorgasbord, I helped myself to some of this and some of that: philosophy, English, music, sociology, economics, French, logic, political science, Oriental studies, psychology, and so on with no sense of direction. I hadn't a clue where I was going. Academic inspiration, such as it was, came in different forms. Once I knocked at the door and entered the office of the head of the Oriental Studies Department to inquire about his course.

"Are you the football player?" He was disdainful. Dumb athlete.

"Yes, sir."

"Two lectures a week. No exam until the final." He bent over his desk, the discussion ended. Well, you prejudiced old bastard, I said to myself. His patronizing so irritated me that my mind locked on showing the old goat that I could learn more than the football play book. I earned a grade higher than a future Rhodes scholar in the class, proving nothing to anyone but myself. And, like a host of undergraduates, I was bewitched by a Dr. Twitmeyer and his Abnormal Psychology course. Among my friends, two ends, a tackle from the football team, and the captain of the basketball team — we lived together in the same house on Spruce Street — also signed up for the course. But I told them they needn't attend the lectures, if they were so disposed. I would be there every time, take notes, and tutor them before the finals. I did. They were all graded B; I achieved a mediocre C. So much for the grading system. In any event, at the end of our third year Ned Fielden and I were among the twenty members of our class elected to the prestigious Sphinx Senior Honor Society.

I enjoyed a number of subjects but nothing really caught my fancy except Faith Long, a New York model. She came over from New York on weekends, sat with my parents during football games, and waited for me afterwards outside the dressing room, drawing a postgame crowd of her own. She was a lively, gregarious, extroverted girl and looked the way a New York model should look. She was a strawberry blonde, and we fell in love and wanted to live together for all time to come. During the Christmas break in my senior year we were married secretly upstairs over a garage in Greenwich, Connecticut. We couldn't wait until June; Faith feared she was pregnant. A mechanic, the justice of the peace, crawled out from under a car, washed his hands, and pronounced us man and wife, and we spent a weekend honeymoon at the Roger Smith Hotel in Stamford. She was not pregnant, and I went back to college after the holidays.

Faith and I knew our families would have a fit if they found out about the justice of the peace in Greenwich, so we finessed that. We would tell our children, but we told our parents we planned to marry in June, after my graduation. No one was surprised. It was quite a normal thing to do in those days: get a diploma and get married. My parents were fond of Faith. And for my weekends in New York Faith's mother had fixed up an apartment for me on the top floor of their house. I was not a stranger. Only her father, Frank Long, was unhappy. "You aren't dry behind the ears yet," he said. He was right; I didn't even have a job. Faith and I were simply two appetitive young animals who mistook lust and possessiveness for love. But in the end Mr. Long relented and joined the others and we were married, properly, by Father Donnelly in the university's Catholic chapel.

Football was big business at Penn in those years. Each autumn Saturday Franklin Field was sold out. On Sunday the Philadelphia Eagles of the young National Football League were overjoyed if they drew 5,000 fans to Municipal Stadium. Usually it was fewer. In our senior year Penn played before more people than any other college in the nation except the University of Southern California. Never for a moment did I feel exploited. On the contrary, an education was lying there for the taking, and altogether the juice of young life was flowing free. The college years were rich, vivid, full of friends — friends one played with and against. I don't know if I learned anything useful in Penn's classrooms, but I learned a great deal in Franklin Field: about myself, about friendship, about a time to come and a time to go.

About myself I learned that I could persevere, at least in a football context. Friendship rooted itself in a thousand things, like this one. An all-day rain formed larger and larger puddles all over Franklin Field one Saturday when the University of Michigan came from Ann Arbor to play. Despite the weather, as Penn's safety man I was having what is known in the sports trade as a good day. I ran back punts for more than a hundred yards, more yards than the entire Michigan team advanced the ball all afternoon. So good a day that Michigan's line coach, a tough old boot named Hunk Anderson, who had played at Notre Dame under Rockne, told his players, "Get that number 22 out of there." A large, raw-boned end named Smick, I think, took it on as a personal assignment. Each time I ran back a punt he came along from somewhere with a rabbit punch, a forearm or an elbow to the face. There were no face masks in that era. I told Smick I'd rather he not do that, or words to that effect. But my teammate, Rocky Shinn, an All-American tackle, grabbed a fistful of Smick's jersey and put it more directly. "If you do that to my friend again, I'll kill you!"

On my next punt return Smick struck once more. So did Shinn; a haymaker from grass level laid Smick flat on his back. Not waiting to be ruled out of the game, Shinn pulled off his distinctive red helmet — the rest of us wore red and blue — flung it in a defiant arc toward the players' bench, and trotted straight to the locker room. To the referee, to 78,000 fans, and to the national radio audience this was clearly an infraction of the rules, a case of unsportsmanlike conduct. To me it was an act of pure friendship. I voted for Shinn to be captain in our final year, as did everyone else.

Seasons end. Chapters close. Football had been tremendous fun, important even, if only to those of us who had the years together. No one could ever take them away — they were our years, but they were over. Last year's halfback is just another fellow sitting in the stands. I had seen enough oldtimers drifting irrelevantly around the periphery of the team, trying to hold the fading afterglow, to have made up my mind never to be one of them, never to allow college football, much as I loved it, to be the high point of my life. It was time to go, taking my vivid memories and fast friendships with me. I didn't make a laundry list of these insights at the time. They simply became a part of me and only in retrospect can I sort them out.

Professional football tempted me briefly, but early on I noticed that the fellow standing next to me in the huddle — he had been in the league seven years — seemed punchy in dummy scrimmage, even before the head-banging started. The basic pay scale was $125 if you played in a game; $100 if you did not. Only Davy O'Brien, who quarterbacked Texas Christian and won the Heisman trophy, had a lucrative contract, $10,000 a season. Burt Bell owned and coached the team then, before he became the National Football League's first commissioner. Bell's fatherly advice and my own common sense prevailed, and I switched to a career in marine insurance. The North America Company at 90 John Street in lower Manhattan said they would have me as a trainee, at thirty-five dollars a week. For more than a year I traveled the New York waterfront from the North River to Red Hook, learning how cargoes should be stowed, that bilge and cantline stowage was more graphically bilge and cuntline to Anglo-Saxon mariners, that furs left the piers in astonishing numbers wrapped under longshoremen's pea jackets, that a case of Scotch whisky could be dropped skillfully on its corner and if you blinked at the splintering sound you would see nothing left but kindling and straw, that a cargo hook in the hand of a longshoreman can be intimidating, and that my trenchcoat was inadequate protection against the winter winds off the harbor but more practical than a chesterfield, which was the only other coat I owned, still have, and still wear.

On a fateful day, December 7, 1941, Franklin D. Roosevelt's Day of Infamy, a doctor confirmed that Faith would have a child. Walking home from his office we heard the news of the Japanese bombing of Pearl Harbor. She was apprehensive, but the reality of war was remote. The so-called Phony War in France, even the fateful Battle of Britain and the London Blitz were distant events that didn't really touch us. We listened to Ed Murrow's news broadcasts from London, heard what he said, didn't really comprehend it as something that would affect us. President Roosevelt said in a radio broadcast that he wanted to assure and reassure us that there would be no blackout of peace in America. Our attention was centered on one another and on establishing a foothold for ourselves. We speculated that a married man with a child would not be called up in a draft. Faith's anxiety diminished, but there remained an under-lying unease. War was now a fact of American life, confused and topsy-turvy at first. National Guard units were called up, draft boards created. Most people were unsure how to react. "Draft dodger" became a contemporary term. At first I thought my role as husband and father was an honorable reason to stand apart, to carry on as a civilian. But as weeks passed and the war dominated all of life, I knew I must go. This was my generation's war. Simplistically, subjectively, I could not abide the thought of other people — my own friends perhaps — fighting to defend my wife and my child while I sat safely at home shielded by a technicality. The world divided itself into black and white. My country was at war, and, though it may seem quaint in today's more sophisticated climate, I thought I should fight for my country. The nation crackled with action and, willy-nilly, if you had any spirit at all you were caught up in it. Life is action and passion, Oliver Wendell Holmes, Jr., said; it is required of man that he share the passion and action of his time — at the peril of being judged not to have lived. Perhaps Justice Holmes wasn't thinking of war, but I was drawn ineluctably to the action of my time.

Faith, like wives from the beginning of the world, could not comprehend why I had to go, why of my own free will I would leave a wife and an infant in order to risk death. An irreconcil-able conflict as old as man and war. The argument that if you were willing to create life you must be willing to defend it was too abstract. And perhaps it was a rationalization for what I wanted to do. So much of a man is not definitive.

# The OSS

# 4

SO YOUNG was the world then that heroes were still the good guys. It was the nature of things and we didn't know what an antihero was. In a vague distant sort of way "Wild Bill" Donovan was a hero of mine. I discovered him in a 1930s film called *The Fighting Sixty-ninth,* the story of New York's famous Irish regiment in World War I and of its heroic leader, Colonel Donovan. He had won the nation's highest combat decoration, the Medal of Honor, and had marched at the head of his regiment up Fifth Avenue when New York welcomed the doughboys back from France in 1918. As an impressionable movie-going youngster I was struck by how much more handsome Donovan looked in photographs than George Brent, the actor who portrayed him. I identified strongly with Donovan the man and not at all with Brent the actor. And it occurred to me that an actor's life must be an unenviable one, always pretending to be someone else, always a shadow of real-life substance.

Donovan disappeared into the background of my memory and I was unaware that he had returned brilliantly to law and that as a private citizen in the years before America entered the Second World War he had undertaken missions to Britain and the Continent at President Roosevelt's behest. And I took only glancing notice when, in mid-1941, Roosevelt appointed him to the bland-sounding post of Coordinator of Information.

Then in the spring of 1942 football opened another door. By chance I met on the street a wealthy Philadelphian living in Washington and doing some sort of war work. I had known him casually as a Penn football buff, and he invited me to his Georgetown home for dinner. Donovan, I was thrilled to discover, was among the guests. He was a stunning-looking man of great magnetism. A fallow boyhood image of the soldier-hero leapt into real life and I was awed, impressed, and taken anew. There was nothing wild about him but his leftover name. He was courtly and soft-spoken, at once alert and at ease. A well-cut blue suit concealed an expanding middle; closely cut gray hair and a healthy Irish complexion emphasized clear Mediterranean-blue eyes that looked at you with genuine interest. His attractiveness to ladies, as one heard it talked about, was apparent; women in the room gravitated to him.

Surprisingly, he said he remembered seeing me play football at Penn — he had been a quarterback at Columbia University — and asked what I was doing in Washington. I told him I had come to join the Army, the Navy, the Marines, whichever service would have me in its officers' training program. Donovan sketched briefly what the Coordinator of Information was about. The President had commissioned him to establish America's first Intelligence Service. In those beginning days Donovan recruited wherever he happened to be — a cocktail party, a boardroom, a college campus; young and old, brains and brawn. I would guess he classified me as young and brawn.

"Why don't you come and join us?" It was a stroke of blind luck. I didn't think once, let alone twice, but jumped at the invitation. Security checks in those formative months were mostly finessed. I was first assigned to a man named Freeman Lincoln, who was in charge of the courier service. It sounded romantic but in truth I was a glorified mailboy. At the munificent salary of one thousand dollars a year I flew back and forth to New York on commercial planes, lugging a sealed bag and carrying secret documents from one office to another, until I was sent off to a series of agent training schools in Maryland and Virginia. While the COI adjusted its charter and changed its name to the Office of Strategic Services, the OSS, I was learning the usual gamut of agent tradecraft.

Actually, the original Coordinator of Information split and became two separate organizations: the Office of War Information and the Office of Strategic Services. At the outset the OSS was responsible directly to the President of the United States, then later was moved under the command of the Joint Chiefs of Staff. The new agency took all manner of flak from the established services — the Army, Navy, and State Departments — each one protective of its own turf and almost paranoid about possible incursions by an upstart OSS, but the bureaucratic infighting occurred at a level far above my station. Initially the thrust of the OSS mission was research and analysis, and brilliant academics and area specialists were recruited to prepare briefs for President Roosevelt. Very quickly clandestine services were added. The two main branches were Secret Intelligence and Special Operations. The first was designed to conduct espionage against the enemy, the latter to carry out unconventional warfare against him. I had joined the clandestine service to fight the Secret War — innocent, ignorant and eager; that is to say, I was starting even with almost every other American. In the beginning the British taught us all we knew; it was they who supervised setting up the OSS training schools, modeled on their own, drawing on their clandestine operational experience during the first years of the war. The British SIS (Secret Intelligence Service) was the model for the OSS SI Branch; British SOE (Special Operations Executive) was the counterpart of our SO Branch. When in 1940 Prime Minister Winston Churchill formed SOE as a paramilitary force, he instructed its chief: "Now go out and set Europe ablaze." When I joined OSS in April 1942 there were fewer than four hundred people in the clandestine branches, including secretaries, hardly enough to set Albania ablaze.

Assigned to one of the training schools for, say, a four-week course, you simply dropped out of sight. Like others, I had to tell my wife that I would be away for a month, could not tell her where I was going or why; in an emergency there was a phone number she could call. It was an anxious development for Faith, and sensibly she agreed to spend the time until my return with her parents in New York.

At Area E School sixteen students were set down together in a big rambling house on a secluded Maryland estate. All of us were in our twenties or early thirties, all a bit uncertain, masking edginess with silence, guarded because we had been individually admonished that our identity must be kept secret from every other student throughout the course. It was part of the clandestine training. Two men I already knew, though we didn't acknowledge one another. Four of us shared a room. Every night one man knelt beside his army cot and prayed; later he parachuted into Yugoslavia to fight alongside General

Mihailovich, fighting against other OSS people who had been sent in to join Tito's partisans, and after the war he became a distinguished New York judge. Classroom instructors taught us codes and ciphers, how to use a one-time pad to encode messages, morse code, how to operate a W/T (wireless telegraphy) set, how to shadow a man or elude one trailing you, how to pick a lock, to use a mini-camera. We were drilled in the cellular structure of an underground network, the correct use of couriers, cutouts, and letter drops. All the usual tradecraft. Outdoors we were trained to strip, reassemble, and fire a .45 automatic pistol, a Thompson submachine gun, a Sten gun. The Sten was a submachine gun that looked as though it was made from plumbing pulled out from under the kitchen sink and felt, when you fired it, as if it would fly apart in your hands at any moment. An uncomplex, inexpensive weapon, it was designed to be supplied to guerrillas in quantity. When we had mastered the guns, we moved on to simulated house-to-house fighting — day and night — blasting away at targets that popped up like ghosts in a fun house. We learned how to put together detonating caps, primer cord, and plastic explosive to blow up a bridge or a rail line; we learned close combat and knife fighting and wondered how much, if any, of this stuff we would ever use. I knew I would never be worth a damn as a W/T operator; my speed with the sending key was woefully inadequate. I was better with the guns and explosives and close combat than some of the other students and less clever at coding and decoding. On the threshold of an entirely new experience, with us not knowing what it would be like, where it would lead, how it would come out in the end, the training for a clandestine life smacked of melodrama, of unreality. I felt like a character out of a low-budget film or a novel. I was self-conscious and of two minds about taking it seriously. What if I ended up sitting at a desk? But mixed into the same line of thought was the hard fact that the war was real, that the bullets I fired tore huge holes in the straw-men targets, and that if I didn't learn my lesson well I might one fine day be dead. The unknown made me generally apprehensive of what lay ahead and specifically serious about the work at hand, however bizarre some of it, like lock picking, might seem at the moment. At maritime school on the lower Potomac River we were taught the techniques of sea infiltration, a certain amount of celestial navigation, and how to handle a foldboat — a collapsible frame-and-canvas boat designed for two men to paddle to an enemy shore from a submarine or a PT boat. All the water exercises took place at night, and each two-man team was required to assemble its boat in the dark and break it down again, once ashore after a simulated infiltration. Luckily I drew as a partner a man who had spent his life sailing in the South Sea islands. But the cleverest of the trainees was a group of eight delightful Indonesian boys. They disliked the Navy-type food and were desperate for fresh fish. One night after everyone was asleep they paddled into the river and caught several big fish, broke into the galley, baked them whole and concocted a sauce from whatever they found on the shelves. I know this only because one of the boys laid a hand on my shoulder and woke me gently. "Maak. Maak." It was as close as they could come to "Mike." "Come," he whispered. They were in seventh heaven and insisted I share their feast. I tried. But at two o'clock in the morning an entire fish, uncleaned and unboned, covered with a repulsive mixture of catsup, mustard, peanut butter, and chili sauce, had limited appeal. I'm still haunted by the wonder of whatever happened to them. Did they live or die, those lively flashing-eyed, laughing brown boys? And my foldboat partner? Not knowing was a condition of the compartmentalized structure of the clandestine business. In the secret world you encountered fleetingly and liked very much many anonymous people, then each went his way and you rarely ever knew how they fared.

The naval commission for which I had applied was slow in coming and Commander Bill Vanderbilt, the OSS liaison with the Navy Department, inquired about it. Word came back that an Ensign Bond of Naval Personnel, who had screened me, concluded that I did not qualify as "an officer and a gentleman" and turned down my commission. One of the questions on the application form asked if the applicant had ever been arrested. Perhaps naively, I had admitted to an arrest and a night in jail in Hartford while I was at Kingswood School. Bond asked me to elaborate and I described the teenage foolishness light-heartedly, as though telling a funny story on myself, something to be laughed at. But Bond took a sterner view; his sense of caste was offended by my reference to the police as "cops." Commander Vanderbilt vouched that, by OSS standards at least, the incident and my colloquial language describing it should not disqualify me. Most but not all OSS people were in the armed services; being in uniform facilitated movement in the war zones.

On the same day in July 1942 Patricia, my first child, was born in Alexandria, Virginia, and I was commissioned an ensign in the United States Navy, seconded to duty with the OSS. Like a number of young transients, Faith and I found a temporary apartment and permanent friends in Alexandria, a few miles down the Potomac from Washington: Lieutenant Wallace MacGregor was a Navy supply officer; Major Elroy McCaw was an Air Corps communications genius; Gurney Wilkes was an attractive, raven-haired girl whose Regular Army husband was missing in the Pacific — a typical wartime Washington combination of friends. Far from harm's way, we traveled back and forth to the Pentagon, to the Navy Department, or to the OSS by bus like peacetime commuters, and sometimes at the end of a day to give our uniforms a wistful taste of water, MacGregor and I sailed home on the Washington to Richmond riverboat, which stopped at Alexandria.

The war suspended real life. We handed responsibility for ourselves over to our military superiors to tell us what to do and when to do it, though the OSS, by its newness and nature, invited individual initiative. For me its great attraction was an absence of regimentation, the loose structure, the flexibility to try almost anything that appeared potentially disruptive to the enemy. Free spirits were incited rather than checked. The OSS unit to which I belonged, Special Projects, was dreamed up by a resourceful, wily naval lieutenant of Lebanese extraction named Johnny Shaheen. John had slipped into OSS on the strength of his Arabic, which when tested was found untrue. But Donovan winked at this linguistic shortfall — "I know all about Shaheen's Arabic" — and read Johnny's artifice and determination as useful. He was right. Shaheen was one of a kind: a slight, wiry body, a sallow Middle East complexion, and an almost hunted look were superficial cover for a tireless internal engine. He was undefeatable. His plans might be shot down in flames a hundred times, but each time he rose out of the ashes, his resolve undiminished. During his parachute training he became airsick and vomited every time the plane left the ground, but he had the guts to stick out the five jumps and qualify for his wings. In the winter of 1942 Special Projects consisted of one room in Q Building in the OSS compound at the Potomac River and Constitution Avenue, three naval officers — Shaheen, Navy Lieutenant Percy Wood, a mature, perceptive former Chicago *Tribune* writer with an oblique, low-key sense of humor, and me — plus Helen Platt, a secretary. Sensibly, Wood ran the office and left Shaheen and me to forage for mischief. Our first target was a ship loading precious ore in a West African port, destined for Germany. It eluded our hijack plan by sailing earlier than scheduled. Tennis shoes we had requisitioned to scale her sides were thrown into a corner, and we looked around for other things to do. Like kidnapping Hermann Göring. Shaheen and I flew to New York to meet Captain Eddie Rickenbacker, the famous World War I flying ace, then president of Eastern Airlines, and asked him to tell us all he could about Göring, an antagonist in the first air war; the captain was generous with his time and knowledge. Our plan was to lure Göring aboard the seagoing yacht of his friend Axel Wenner-Gren, a Swedish industrialist, and make off with him. Its flaw was Wenner-Gren's total lack of enthusiasm. Strangely, no one thought these ideas were nutty, least of all Donovan.

Finally we connected.

Paolino Gerli was a wealthy, highly respected Italian-American silk merchant who lived in New York. He alerted Bill Donovan to Marcello Girosi, an Italian married into a prominent New York family. One of Girosi's brothers was Admiral Massimo Girosi, a member of the Italian Navy's Supreme Command; another brother, Cesare, was an Italian Navy commander; their father had been an admiral. By family and naval tradition the Girosis were royalists, loyal to King Umberto, thus thought to be antipathetic to Mussolini. There was a chance, it was calculated, that the Italian fleet, given the right opening, might abandon Mussolini and Hitler. The gambit, then, was to contact Admiral Girosi, using his brother Marcello to establish our bona fides, and to present the Italians with an opening. Donovan gave the assignment to Special Projects, and we named it the MacGregor Mission, after my friend and neighbor in Alexandria. Shaheen went ahead to North Africa to prepare the way; I would follow with Girosi.

There was a hitch. After Girosi had been formally recruited, the OSS Security people suspected that he might be an Italian agent, and I was called to the Chief of Security's office. Weston Howland was a tall, craggy, Lincolnesque man with more jowls and less hair than the President he resembled. A permanent look of foreboding suggested that the good man carried his responsibilities very heavily.

"You have got to watch Girosi night and day," he said, implying the worst, though the degree of suspicion was too thin to scrub the project.

"I can't. It isn't possible. When do I sleep?" Howland and his aides agreed that a third person could be added and produced a list of Italian speakers in various stages of OSS training. Running down the page, my eye stopped abruptly and focused on a familiar name: Joe Savoldi.

"Is that Jumping Joe Savoldi? The old Notre Dame football player?"

"Yes. Turned professional wrestler. Born in Italy. Came to this country at age twelve."

"I'll take him."

"You know him?"

"No. But I read the sports pages." Savoldi was brought in from a training site. He was built like a gorilla and moved as lightly as a leopard. His wrestler's face had been mashed against the ring canvas a thousand times. He was enthusiastic; I thought he would be perfect. He would terrify Girosi and maybe the entire Italian fleet.

A few weeks earlier over coffee and cognac in Gerli's Manhattan drawingroom, a clandestine mission to Italy probably had a disarmingly theatrical cast to it. But reality sobered Girosi precipitously; his swarthy Neapolitan complexion paled as we created a new persona for his trim body: Marco Ricci, Lieutenant, United States Naval Reserve, complete with uniform, Navy identity cards, serial number and travel orders, all synthetic. His receding hair and coarse skin made him look somewhat overage in his rank and his nerves were too jumpy to make him a convincing military figure.

In Washington Girosi and Savoldi were kept apart. Savoldi

knew the profile of his assignment but he did not yet know Girosi's identity. Jumping Joe would travel as a civilian on military orders "to entertain the troops with wrestling exhibitions," and he was not to appear to have any connection with Girosi and me until we arrived in North Africa, even though we would be flying in the same military aircraft. Girosi and I would travel together simply as naval officers being posted to duty in the Mediterranean; he was to know nothing of Savoldi until we arrived in Algiers. The afternoon before our departure I met Savoldi in Q Building, gave him his travel documents, instructed him to report to the Military Air Transport Service at the National Airport at eight o'clock the following morning. I remembered the apocryphal stories about Joe when he played fullback for Knute Rockne: his memory for plays was said to be so frail that they were diagrammed on the leg of his football pants. So I carefully repeated his instructions not to acknowledge me until we arrived in North Africa, four days hence. I did tell him that the naval officer traveling with me was to be his assignment, but he need not concern himself until we reached Africa. I did not want Girosi to become windy about Joe too soon. Meanwhile, Joe should conduct himself discreetly; the transatlantic leg would be a high-priority flight, full of generals and other senior officers.

That evening, July 8, I dined with Girosi at the Wardman Park Hotel, where he was staying. He picked at his food and complained of feeling unwell. I tried to screw up his courage, said I would fetch him at seven in the morning and drove to Alexandria to spend my last night with Faith. In bed she held on fiercely, gripped by uncertain fear. She knew only that I was going to North Africa and that I would be back in a few months. I never doubted I would return, although my certainty did not convince her nor dislodge her intuitive sense that I was taking some unspoken risk that need not be taken, which was true.

In the morning when I picked him up at the hotel Girosi looked as though he hadn't slept. His olive skin was sallow and his expression pained. This bastard may chicken out, I thought, as the taxi carried us to the Military Air Transport Service hangar at the National Airport. *Discreet* secret agent Savoldi was already there, boisterously signing autographs for about a hundred GIs. En route to Newfoundland, Girosi whimpered about the cold, demanded a blanket, moaned about feeling progressively worse, and finally said he must lie down. The pilot agreed to let him come forward and stretch out on blankets spread out in the companionway just aft of the flight deck. Later he came back and spoke to me. "I'm going to put this joker off in Newfoundland when we stop to refuel. I can't have the sonofabitch die on me over the Atlantic."

"He's not going to die, for Christ's sake. He just moans a lot." The pilot agreed to carry Girosi across to Scotland, the next leg of our flight, only if an Air Corps doctor at the Newfoundland base certified that he wouldn't die in midair. While the plane refueled, a Jeep raced us to a perceptive young doctor, who recognized a loss of nerve when he saw one, and we sped back with a reassuring note for the pilot. From Prestwick, in the cover of night, a stripped-down Royal Air Force bomber flew us along the German-held coast of France, around Spain, and into Marrakesh in the Atlas Mountains of Morocco. As junior officers Girosi and I spent the night in a tent while Savoldi, singled out as a VIP civilian, was put up grandly with general officers at the famous Mamounian Hotel, probably in Winston Churchill's suite.

Next day, four days after we had left Washington, Shaheen met us at the Maison Blanche Airport in Algiers and we were driven to an OSS safe house where we could lie up until we could determine what to do next. Girosi had written a longhand letter to his brother the admiral proposing a secret rendezvous in Italy. To confirm its authenticity, the letter included a reference to a childhood nurse the Girosi brothers had shared, identifying her by their pet name for her, a name unlikely to be known by anyone else. The first step was delivery. The local OSS station gave us one of their agents, a young Italian courier called Tommy. We planned that he would be parachuted into Italy during the light of the moon that ended July 24, but neither the British nor the American Air Force would spare us a plane. General Donovan signaled from Washington that we should try to get in by way of Sicily. Sicily had been invaded by the British and Americans on July 10, and on the day the Americans captured Palermo, July 22, Shaheen and I flew there and asked Commander Stanley Barnes, commander of Torpedo Boat Squadron 15, if one of his boats would lift us up the boot into Italy. Barnes was game, but there was a problem. The Mediterranean was operationally divided: the British Navy patroled waters north of 38°40', the American fleet south of it. Barnes had to obtain permission from the United States Naval Commander to sail north of the demarcation line. We wanted to run as far up the Italian coast as the PT-boat range could take us, giving our courier with the Girosi letter the shortest overland distance to travel to his target. We aimed for the Gulf of Gaeta, two hundred miles deep in German-held territory, about halfway between Naples and Rome, a point the British and American armies did not reach until December 1943.

Palermo was a shambles; baking in the July sun, it stank of bodies rotting in the rubble. In a villa on the outskirts of the city we found Henry Ringling North, whose uncles had founded Ringling Bros. Circus, functioning as the finance officer of a small Sicilian-American OSS unit attached to the U.S. Seventh Army. He and I had met and become friends at the OSS headquarters in Washington. Since I had last seen him there, dysentery had shrunk thirty pounds from his normal weight and his six-foot frame looked dangerously thin. He was not enchanted with his assignment, and we asked him to join our mission.

Days passed and Admiral Hewitt, the Commander-in-Chief of the Mediterranean fleet, continued to withhold his permission. As fed up as we, Commander Barnes, a Naval Academy man with an imagination that outdistanced the book, gambled on taking us up to the Gulf of Gaeta. We would have to be wary of two hostiles: the Germans and the British. North of 38°40' with no way to identify ourselves convincingly as friendly, we could expect the British to blow us out of the water. Well, nothing is without risk, and time was running against us. Mussolini had been deposed on July 26, King Umberto took over the government, and the German Army took over Italy.

The date was August 10. General Lucien K. Truscott's gallant Third Division was still ten tough, bloody fighting days away from Messina. At sundown two torpedo boats, PT-208 and PT-209, shoved off from Palermo, each carrying on deck, between the after torpedo tubes, extra drums of fuel. Without this deck load we wouldn't get back. Aboard the 209 boat, in addition to the ten-man crew, were Shaheen, North, the Italian courier, and me. It was a glorious summer dusk. Slowly the calm Tyrrhenian Sea darkened to a cobalt blue. North and I sat on the charthouse just forward of the bridge, our backs resting on the windscreen that shielded the helmsman and Lieutenant Ed duBose, the commander of our little flotilla: two 78-foot boats each armed with four torpedoes, a machine gun forward, two 50-caliber machine guns on either side of the bridge, and two 20-mm Oerlikon guns in tandem on the after-deck. Twin Packard engines gave the boats a cruising speed of 25 knots, 40 knots flat out. An Associated Press correspondent who had been given a lift by the squadron across from North Africa to the Sicilian invasion wrote that torpedo-boat sailors should be given both flight pay and submarine pay — half the time the PT-boats were in the air and half the time under the water. It certainly seemed so in rough weather, and at times the Mediterranean could become very wrought up indeed. But on the evening of August 10 it was rolling softly in a silken breeze. Twin propellers drove the boat's stern down into the water, lifted its bow high, skimming it across the gentle sea, leaving a long white wake in the darkening water. Henry and I watched the night settle and millions of stars canopy the world — distant, silent, overwhelmingly beautiful.

"Wake me up when we get there," Henry said. He went below and lay down in duBose's bunk to keep his chronic sea-sickness in check.

The moon was up and nearly full, flooding the sea with its pale light, when General Quarters sounded. Everyone leapt to his battle station; the skipper cut the engines, made a 90° turn and idled away from our wake, which lay on the black sea like a white arrow pointing in our direction. Three German JU-88 bombers, returning from a raid on Palermo, closed on us five hundred feet above the sea. I felt completely exposed and use-less. DuBose held command, the helmsman held the wheel, the other crew members gripped the machine guns and the Oerli-kons. I stood beside the bridge with my hands on my hips for want of somewhere else to put them and was suddenly seized by cold terror. My teeth chattered together, my knees knocked against one another, my whole body, out of control, rattled like a skeleton hung out in a gale. My mind could not will my body to stop shaking. I locked my jaw shut and still could not stop my teeth banging together. Fear had attacked my body separately from my mind, and my mind's eye, looking on with shame, saw its body behaving like a comedian in an old-fashioned ghost film. From early on, probably soon after completing my OSS training, I had dismissed being killed from my mind. This was not a conclusion reached by analysis, but rather a condition that emerges almost unnoticed from some inner defense mechanism to buffer the minds of men at war. I don't suppose anyone thinks *his* number will come up, not until the very last moment.

In a few seconds the planes had flown past and were consumed in the darkness beyond the moon and the silence of the night. The boats resumed their course, and I climbed back to my seat on the charthouse and wondered where this fit of terror had come from. Was it a drop in nerve? All courage had leaked away like water when a plug is taken from a sink. Or was it a seizure that everyone must suffer once to immunize his system? I devoutly hoped the latter and was grateful for the quiet returned to my body. Fear, that baleful companion, had released its cold hand, gone as suddenly as it had come. The stars were in their heavens as they can be only when seen from the night sea. They will be there tomorrow night whether I am here or not; they will be here a hundred years from now when all of us are gone. They sent down a silent message of perspective to the speck of aloneness that was one man sailing north along the Italian coast to an unknown place, to an unknown outcome.

The moon was down off Terracina and we began our run in towards the landing point at half-speed. I went below and raised Henry. He and I were to row the courier ashore in a rubber boat, then row it back to the waiting PT-boat. DuBose already held the Navy Cross for extraordinary heroism; he would take us as close as depth permitted. On the afterdeck, between the torpedo tubes, where the jettisoned extra fuel drums had been carried, we prepared the boat, the agent, and ourselves and stood by. Tommy couldn't be still. Even in the dark I could sense the tightness of his thin restless body. He was twenty-two and looked like a street urchin grown up. He kept reminding us of our promise that he would meet Loretta Young, the film actress, when the war was over. The crew too was tense. No one had asked them if they wanted to go on a two-boat mission two hundred miles deep into enemy territory. No one had to tell them that the landing point, by a stroke of hard luck, might have been ill chosen, that it was a crap-shoot whether the coast there would be free of German troops or full of them. We would not know if we were in the lion's mouth until it closed and swallowed us. The words *bocca di leone* kept jumping in and out of my mind, unattached to anything.

Then, at one moment, we sighted a string of twenty or thirty lights strung out at equal distances. At first we thought it might be a German truck convoy moving slowly along the coast road, but the lights did not move along as a convoy would. The boat's engines idled now and we moved forward very slowly until it was clear that the lights were on the water, not on the land. As we drew closer the lights were seen to be flares very close to the surface, perhaps only a foot or two above it. Fishermen. Obviously there with German permission. Probably under German watch. Our boats lay dead in the water now. We lowered the rubber boat over the side and discussed what to do. Our radar picked up a German E-boat sliding out of its base at the north end of the gulf, but it moved out to sea without spotting us or hearing us. Every now and then a swell would lift the stern of one of the boats clear of the water and the exhaust, unmuffled by the sea, would roar out into the silent blackness. The fishermen would assume it to be a German patrol boat. We counted on any Germans who might hear us thinking the same, never dreaming that an enemy boat would be this far behind their lines. At length we decided we could not put our courier ashore here, this night, without discovery. We would try another place, another night. The rubber boat was hauled aboard and the two torpedo boats came about and idled towards the open sea, revved up to half-speed, and, at a safe distance, throttled up to twenty-five knots and headed home. Only when the enemy coast began to fall away was I aware of the intensity of my alertness. It was as though all my senses had raised themselves to the second power and now, going home, slowly lowered to normal. DuBose had navigated four hundred and fifty miles through British and enemy waters without being detected.

On the twelfth of August we went out again, this time to a less ambitious distance though to a potentially more dangerous infiltration point. Calabria, at the lower end of the Italian boot, was now thick with the main body of German forces, withdrawn intact from Sicily across the Straits of Messina while a relatively small force fought a fierce delaying action against the Americans. As a service to the British, we took along one of their agents to be infiltrated along with our lad, Tommy. Ashore, they would go their separate ways. Once again at dusk we sailed from Palermo Harbor, Henry and I again sitting on the charthouse, backs to the windscreen, marveling at the suffused beauty of the sea and sky like holiday cruisers, until he went below. I doubt Henry actually slept but lying prone kept his seasickness from erupting.

We moved in cautiously on the Calabrian coast above the town of Belvedere. Two hundred yards offshore we put the rubber boat over the side. I leapt down, helped the agents aboard, and Johnny Shaheen pulled me back onto the PT-boat. The two paddled off alone, a line fastened to the stern of their little craft, and were quickly lost from sight in the darkness of the sea and the denser blackness of the mountain rising out of it. Tangible threatening silence fell between them and us; blackness impenetrable as death concealed the enemy shore and set the imagination twisting and turning. Were we playing a huge game of Russian roulette? What dark disaster awaited the next tick of the clock? Each minute arrived, established itself, then gave way to the next at deliberate pace. Night-schooled eyes and ears strained towards the shore. No one spoke. Then in quick succession came three flashes from Tommy's infrared light, the signal that they were ashore and had shoved the rubber boat clear of the beach. Wordlessly we hauled in the line hand-over-hand until the empty boat was alongside and then lifted aboard, freeing the agents of time wasted burying it and the risk of its discovery. The torpedo boats crept back to sea and then picked up speed to be back in Palermo by dawn.

Running west along the northern coast of Sicily, we watched artillery fire stab at the night and heard the muffled cannon fire. The Panzers bedeviled the American infantry and General Truscott's Third Division blasted the Germans from their strong defensive positions near Brolo on the narrow coastal plain and in the treacherous ridges that ended against mountains passable only for a few men and for mules. Poor goddam brave dogface soldiers. *"Le courage de la nuit"* was Napoleon's tribute to this kind of men, and they were Sassoon's "unheroic dead who fed the guns." In peacetime their route was a spectacular scenic drive. Now it gave the Germans every alternative for defense.

Sailing into Palermo, I woke Henry. Home again. No more scenic boat rides until August 27, when we had a rendezvous to pick Tommy off the beach at Terracina, again risking that area to save the agent a long overland journey south, down the boot.

At midnight on the twenty-seventh we were at the rendezvous point lying two hundred yards off shore, waiting for Tommy's light signaling us to come and fetch him in the rubber dinghy. This time we saw no fishing boats; perhaps it was one of the nights forbidden to the Italian fishermen. Several pairs of eyes searched along the shoreline, back and forth, straining to penetrate the darkness for any sign in case Tommy had lost his infrared lamp. Other eyes fixed themselves on the watery green radar screen, watching for the image of E-boats coming out of their base at the northern tip of the gulf. The E-boat was a formidable version of the American PT-boat, bigger and with greater firepower, a middleweight against a lightweight boxer. An hour passed, then two, with no sign of Tommy. In the immense silence there was no sound except the occasional night-splitting roar as one of the boats' exhausts rolled clear of the water, loud enough to wake Caesar's ghost or shore batteries that could smash us to smithereens. We idled slowly along the shoreline in case Tommy had miscalculated the rendezvous point. Still nothing. By 2:30 A.M., dejected and overtaken by time, we left. Some distance had to be put between ourselves and the hostile coast before daylight.

Frustrated by the lost contact with Tommy and expecting that the invasion of Italy was now only days away, we decided to go ashore with the British forces and somehow, in the confusion of battle, make our way through the lines to Admiral Girosi. A Lieutenant Fuller, Royal Navy, gave us a hitch to the invasion. At 2 A.M. on September 9, his British torpedo boat cast off from Palermo Harbor and at 6:30 A.M., eight miles off the Salerno beaches, a lifting morning mist unveiled the tremendous fleet. The first wave of assault troops had landed at three o'clock that morning. One of the motor launches escorting a convoy of landing ships agreed to take us to the beachhead and we leapt from one raking deck to the other.

Amber Beach was a huggermugger of confusion and wreckage. At one spot a British officer directed his men coolly, indifferent to the roaring sounds and grim sights of battle beyond his immediate responsibility; a hand grenade's throw away, other men would suddenly be dead, scythed down by the shrapnel of German mortar bombs and 88-millimeter shells. Life and death moved invisibly among the invaders, always but a few paces apart, operating at random. In war everything goes awry and at Salerno everything went wrong in spades.

At a British command post we were told that they had been met by the Sixteenth Panzer Division, not by the expected Italians, and were fighting desperately to hold a sliver of a beachhead. As we pushed north along the coast towards the town of Salerno, the warships to our left pumped high explosives over our heads and into German strong points; to our right, in the tobacco fields and meadows and orchards, the British engaged the Panzers in a wild disjointed series of firefights. We passed through Salerno, devastated and deserted, and two or three kilometers up a winding hill road to Vietri. Sounds of cannon mortars, machine guns, and small-arms fire ricocheted off medieval walls and cobbled surface of the village square; a British commando unit fiercely battled elements of the Hermann Göring Panzer Division. Raking machine gun and mortar fire closed off our road towards Naples and our only alternative was to leapfrog up the coast by sea. But for two days we were trapped in Salerno while the German artillery dug into the surrounding hills, controlled the harbor, and toyed with our destruction. At length a British motor launch dared to pluck us off this end of the harbor cove and streak back to sea, pursued by the whispering, sliding, screeching whine of approaching eighty-eight shells and sprayed by their explosions, and brought us home to Squadron 15 in Maiori Bay. Next day Commander Barnes moved his boats to Capri; and we learned that the Italian fleet had sailed into Malta and other Allied ports and surrendered. Thus, our mission to contact Admiral Girosi was overtaken.

Off Salerno the Allied fleet had been stunned by the devastating accuracy of a German weapon used: radio-controlled bombs. A single Luftwaffe aircraft flying above the range of antiaircraft fire had put a bomb down the stack of the British cruiser *Uganda,* knocking her out of action. Guided missiles became an instant Intelligence priority and, on the spot, General Donovan assigned our MacGregor project to that target.

On Capri Marcello Girosi discovered old Neapolitan friends, and through them we were led to Admiral Eugenio Minisini, an inventor of naval ordnance and a world authority on naval and air torpedoes. He had commanded the Italian Navy's torpedo station at Baia in the Bay of Naples and, together with Professor Carlo Calosi, had perfected an electromagnetic device for detonating torpedoes as they passed beneath the hull of a ship. Called a Sic Pistol, it was a device all the navies of the world had been working on, including the American Navy, but none had perfected it except the Italians. With the Allied invasion imminent and to prevent his devices being carried away by the Germans, Minisini had had all the "pistols" loaded onto a barge, towed into the Bay of Naples, and sunk. Professor Calosi and his key technicians scattered into hiding in Naples. Minisini and his wife were spirited off and hidden in Capri. Through Girosi, Minisini offered his services to the Americans. He was fearful of being kidnapped or executed by Gestapo agents for what the Nazis regarded an act of sabotage. It was imperative to keep him safe and to get quick permission to bring him and his wife to the United States. As an interim step we decided to slip him out of Capri. It would be only a matter of time before the Gestapo picked up his trail.

At 4:30 in the predawn darkness Girosi and I fetched Admiral and Mrs. Minisini from a secluded villa in an old Lancia touring car and drove through sleeping Capri down the twisting road to the Marina Grande dock and boarded PT-214. Our old friend Lieutenant duBose was the skipper. We were under way before six. It was a lovely day on the water. Mrs. Minisini, short, round, and chirpy, sat in a canvas director's chair behind the bridge between the two forward torpedo tubes, and Girosi wrapped a Navy blanket around her knees. The admiral, bare-headed, his short white hair whipped about by the wind, his ruddy intelligent face aglow, struck a sturdy sailor's stance on the bridge beside the helmsman, yet looked more scientist than seadog. Both were relieved to be safely away from Capri, to be en route to America, but underlying their excitement and anticipation, one sensed a deep sadness. They were, after all, Italian. They were of a certain age, their country was, in a sense, twice defeated, twice humiliated, and now was fought over by two foreign armies. Destruction would go on and on.

By noon we were in Palermo. At the OSS station a cable ordering him to Algiers awaited Shaheen, and he flew on at once. Early next morning we were again at sea, headed for Bizerte in Tunisia. The sea was angry and the boat pitched and tossed through a nine-hour voyage. I had cabled OSS people to have a car meet us there and drive us to Tunis, but no one showed up. The PT squadron fed us in their mess, showed us a movie, and freshened the two officers' bunks on the boat for the Minisinis. Marcello and I slept above them on deck, in rain, cursing the bloody OSS staff people. In the morning duBose borrowed a Navy station wagon and drove us to Tunis. The OSS contact had us led on foot to a house deep in the Casbah, where the Minisinis would remain hidden until permission came to fly them to Algiers and to America. Tunis was rife with Gestapo stay-behind agents. In deepening dusk the labyrinth of unlit, unpaved streets, hardly more than passageways between windowless white walls and closed wooden doors, must have been a daunting prospect for Signora Minisini. Girosi held her arm and spoke softly to her as we followed our Arab guide past silent burnooses concealing dark men, and veiled women who brushed against us with an unaccustomed touch. We stopped before a faded blue wooden door set flush in a white wall. Across its threshold we crowded into a small dark flag-stoned entry. An inner door opened onto a tiled patio, abundant with plants and flowers, the centerpiece of a luxurious house furnished characteristically with mahogany and teak, leather and brass, a secret Eden hidden from the squalor of the Casbah. During their occupation of North Africa the Gestapo had used this house as a clandestine radio base. Its owner was a rich Tunisian. The single entrance through the wooden door in the front wall provided good physical security, as did its location, remote from European traffic. I worried that the Gestapo might be interested in how their secret radio base was being used and wondered if a shadowy burnoose brushing past us in the fading light might have reported our unusual party entering it. But I speculated in silence and spoke enthusiastically to the two older people about so safe and comfortable a haven.

Shaheen had hit a snag. Arriving in Algiers in response to the cable he had received in Palermo, he learned that without specific orders from their high command the Air Corps would not fly the admiral and his lady. The Minisinis were classified as enemy aliens and regulations proscribed them from U.S. aircraft. We were stymied, and it was agreed that I should fly to Washington and seek General Donovan's help. I took off from Fort Lyauty in Morocco in a luxurious Sikorsky flying boat. Its route was by way of the Shannon River in Ireland and Goose Bay in Newfoundland and finally to the Marine Terminal at La Guardia Airport in New York. The few passengers slept in Pullman car–like berths on clean sheets and soft mattresses. I was awakened at the end of the first leg by the Shannon's waters splashing against the porthole as the plane skimmed across the river's surface and, slowing, settled into being a boat. A belt, I found, had been lashed across my body while I slept. I unfastened it, pulled on my shorts and trousers, and drew back the curtains. All the bunks had been folded into place and the other passengers sat fully dressed in their daytime seats. I learned from the captain that during the night we had flown through the worst storm he had experienced in seventeen years of flying, so fierce that the tail surfaces of the plane had been bent. I had slept through it all, seduced by the sheets and the mattress and conditioned by torpedo boats bouncing around the Tyrrhenian Sea.

In Washington I went directly to General Donovan's office, taking two at a time the broad stone steps of the two-story red brick administration building in the middle of the OSS complex. I was dressed in my khaki summer uniform and carried all my personal belongings in a musette bag hanging from my shoulder. A secretary demanded testily to know if I had an appointment. I had not, of course, but I told her I had just arrived from North Africa. A hard little number, she was un-impressed by the distance and, with an indifferent gesture, said I'd have to wait outside. Later we became friends and laughed about it, but at the time I took a seat obediently in the corridor, my feelings bruised and my straight-from-the-front self-impor-tance deflated.

A half hour later Colonel Otto Doering, the head of General Donovan's secretariat, came hustling by and saw me.

"My God, Mike! I thought you were in Italy."

"I was. I just came in to see the general. We've got a prob-lem."

"Does he know you're here?"

"I don't know."

"Just a moment." He disappeared, was indeed back in a mo-ment, and showed me into the general's office. Donovan could not have been more welcoming had he been my father and was eager to hear our story.

"Get a night's rest and meet me here at eight o'clock in the morning. You and I will go and see the Secretary of the Navy. And Mike," he called after me as I was leaving, "wear your blue uniform." He sounded like my grandfather telling me how to dress for church.

Freeman, General Donovan's chauffeur, set us down at the front door of the Navy Department on Constitution Avenue. Like a dory towed by a battleship I followed the general across the sidewalk, past the Shore Patrol guarding the door, past the commanders, the captains, and the admirals — my ensign's sol-itary gold stripe more conspicuously out of place at each ad-vancing level — and sailed into Secretary Knox's office. The two men greeted one another as warm friends and the general introduced me almost offhandedly.

"Frank, you know Mike. You've seen him play football against the Navy."

"Oh yes." Mr. Knox was unconvincing simply because he didn't know me from the Navy goat and there was no reason why he should, Donovan's generosity notwithstanding.

"Mike is one of my young men. He's just come back from the fighting in Italy to see me and I thought you'd want to hear his story first-hand."

The Secretary turned his chair slightly to face me and listened politely. I swallowed a lump of nervousness and launched into a summary that quickly came together in my head. When I finished Mr. Knox leaned forward, his forearms resting on his huge desk, and asked quietly, "What would you like me to do, Ensign?"

"Well, sir. It would be great if you would signal Admiral Hewitt to have the Minisinis and Shaheen and Girosi flown to Washington, sir."

He wrote out a longhand cable addressed to Hewitt, Commander of the U.S. Naval Forces in North African waters, and read it aloud to Donovan and me.

"Is that all right?"

"Yes, sir."

"Anything else?"

"Well, sir. There's Lieutenant Henry North. It would be very helpful, sir, if Admiral Hewitt would put a ship at Lieutenant North's disposal. He's salvaging Admiral Minisini's devices from the bottom of Naples Bay, and he'll have to transport them and Professor Calosi and his technicians to North Africa. So they can be flown here."

The Secretary wrote out another cable to Hewitt and handed both messages to a yeoman. I suspected Hewitt would not be thrilled by the one about giving Henry a ship.

"Where do you think Minisini would be most useful?" he asked.

"Perhaps at the Torpedo Station in Newport, sir."

"I suppose one of our ordnance admirals should meet him when he arrives," Knox said, more to Donovan than to me, and told the yeoman to ring an admiral whose name I can't recall.

"Admiral," he said into the phone, "Frank Knox. I've got Bill Donovan here and Ensign Burke. I'll be sending the ensign over to your office. He'll give you your instructions for the next few days."

I went to the ordnance admiral's office and very respectfully — taking directions from some snotty ensign, for Christ's sake! — explained the situation to him. I said I'd alert him to Admiral Minisini's arrival as soon as I learned it. Later in the day the ordnance admiral telephoned me and, speaking hesitantly, as if it were some illicit subject, said, "You know, Ensign, for some time . . . well, my wife . . . we'd made some plans for this weekend. And I was wondering . . ."

"Yes, sir, go right ahead, Admiral. Minisini won't be arriving until Monday or Tuesday. Have a nice weekend, sir." I was thankful he was in Ordnance, not some hard-assed old battle-wagon sailor.

"Thank you, Ensign." He sounded so relieved I wondered what manner of terrifying woman his wife might be. That evening I flew to New York and had dinner with Faith and my parents at a Spanish restaurant in Greenwich Village my father liked. Washing up in the men's room, I told him about my morning with Donovan and Knox.

"I think this has been the greatest day of my life, Dad." And I meant it. It seemed nothing so grand had ever happened to me before, having an audience of two important men who were gracious and generous with a youngster and, in the circumstance, equated him with themselves. It was characteristic of Donovan to have done it that way. At the time I did not know how politically important our venture was to him and to the OSS. Apparently the bureaucratic jockeying to unseat Donovan was fierce, and he badly needed a win. Our having seized a target of opportunity produced one of the very first concrete results that OSS could cite to demonstrate its usefulness.

The Minisinis and Calosi were settled in Newport, Rhode Island, to work with officers at the Naval Torpedo Station. Girosi returned to civilian life. The MacGregor project ended and we looked around for other things to do. Johnny Shaheen resumed control of Special Projects and spoke of blowing up Tokyo Harbor with unmanned midget submarines. One day General Donovan invited Shaheen, North, and me to his office and in his soft-voiced, gentle-mannered way he summed up: we had done our mission well; we had been decorated; we'd had our respite in America. Now it was time to go out and rejoin our generation. He said we could choose where we wanted to go and, as he did so, moved to a wall map of China, pointing out the five great rivers. "Like fingers on a hand," he said. Or we could go back to Europe for the invasion of France. Outside, going down the steps of the administration building, Henry shuddered at the thought of China. "I'm for France," he announced.

"Me too."

"Not I," Shaheen declared. "I'm staying here."

"But the general said to move out."

"I'm going nowhere." And he didn't. He was to do creative work from Washington and was miffed that Henry and I would leave him. It was essential for John to be near the power source. Equally it was imperative for me to be, as the general had said, with my generation, near the action.

Faith was no more reconciled to my going back to war than she had been to our first farewell. An ambivalence had infiltrated our relationship. I sensed the disapproval of her family, particularly as I was contrasted with her sister's young husband, who remained safely at accounting and at home. Faith's father, a short-tempered man, worked at his bank on weekdays and tended his garden on weekends. Mr. Long had promised his own mother he would not marry before he was thirty and had lived up to this bargain. Thereafter he narrowed his attention to feeding and clothing four children through the Depression and managing his branch bank. His bafflement at my leaving a wife and child to go again to war was understandable. So too was the manner in which her entire family encouraged Faith's sense of abandonment. Faith's own interest in the world at large was unfocused, almost flippantly indifferent. Her attention was limited to her immediate surroundings. Romping carefree through three years of young marriage, absorbed with one another, we were in harmony. War intruded and changed the tune for me. Then, too, Faith was a spirited and physical girl. She was not the sort to be stored on a shelf like a jarred preserve waiting for some other season to be tasted. Given the harsh fact of war, we reacted differently, our differing values came into play. As I had cast my die, so she would do whatever she herself felt compelled to do. I understood this, understood it, and accepted it with an odd mixture of regret and release. Had I connived to stay at home, say at a desk in Washington, I would have shriveled into something far less than I expected myself to be. I had no bone to pick with the farmer and the factory hand, the cobbler and the accountant, who worked at what had to be done at home. But I was not they, and I would have betrayed all my instincts, devalued myself, had I subscribed to values other than my own, had I been persuaded out of combat. For me it was a Hobson's choice. Patricia, my first child, would one day come to understand this. But in contemporary time I had to know how fair stood the wind for France. And went to find out.

# At Liberty

# 5

IN PARIS, after the Maquis de Confracourt and the 117th Reconnaissance Squadron, I went to live in Henry North's garret
apartment in the Hôtel Princesse in the Rue Pressbourg, off
the Etoile and waited for the OSS to tell me what to do next. A
month passed before they remembered me. Meanwhile, each
morning Henry and I breakfasted on peanut butter — he had
scrounged a gallon tin from an Army mess sergeant — and
toast and coffee brought to us by a sprightly *femme de chambre*
of forty-odd whose joi de vivre and self-image would be forever
a ripe twenty. Most days we lunched or dined with Papa Hemingway and Mary Welsh. Mary had supplanted Martha Gellhorn as Papa's woman and would become his fourth and final
wife. I'm not sure that she was thrilled by Henry's and my being
around so much. But Papa was a boon companion — generous,
considerate, witty, humorous, and knowledgeable of an astonishing range of subjects, though fools he refused to suffer.
Persons subjected to his darker moods would give him different marks from me. At that point he had plenty of time for
companionship. The Army had loosely confined him while they
investigated the charge that he had violated the Geneva Convention, which forbids war correspondents to bear arms. Papa
had collected his own armed maquis force, joined the attack on
Paris, and liberated the Ritz Hotel. He was restricted to the city
limits while some Army body debated whether to return his
war correspondent's credentials. As he whiled away the time,
his flights of improvisation went free-soaring. One afternoon
at the Ritz Bar he invented the Valhalla Club, improvising the
rules. Charter members would be himself, North, and me. He
dubbed us Hemingstein's Junior Bearded Commandos in the
same nonsense way that he referred to himself as Ernie Hem-
orrhoid, the poor man's Ernie Pyle. Pyle was a war correspon-

dent who affected a homespun persona and journalistic style. The first and most sacred rule was that no member would ever be dunned for his bar bill. Only good guys would be taken in. Chickie, a sage old dog of Papa's, would "bring the word," indicating whether a candidate for membership was acceptable. If not, an elephant from North's family circus would wrap the reject in her trunk and drop him into a chute that ejected into the street below. If a member should become too boastful of his war exploits, he would be led to a wall map and pressed for details. Where precisely were you? Where were they? How many of them? How many of you? On this, like most days, the barroom banter had no higher purpose than to help pass the afternoon out of the rain.

At length, the OSS realized I was missing and, naturally, found me through North, but when I asked for a brief Christmas home leave before being reassigned, they agreed. Home was quite different from my leave in 1943 when I had come back from Italy. Now Faith and our daughter Patricia lived on Park Avenue with her older sister, Verna. In 1943 Faith had met me at the door of her father's house wearing a sweater and skirt and loafers. This time she wore a sleek Balenciaga dinner dress which no junior grade lieutenant's wife could have afforded. The beautiful Verna was rich. Verna had decided early on to marry a wealthy old man and live a rich widow, marrying Ostertag, the famous Parisian jeweler, more than twice her age, who was dead within a year. Verna had always taken a dim view of Faith's marrying me — he's a pencil pusher, she said. The look of the Park Avenue apartment and the life-style of the sisters made it plain that Faith had moved out of my orbit. The following morning Patricia, then two-and-a-half, stood by the sink and watched intently as I shaved.

"Jean doesn't shave like that," she said.

"Oh, he doesn't?"

"No. He shaves different." Jean Poivrel, I learned, was an affluent French glove merchant who found New York more agreeable than France at war. I could not help marveling at the irony: I in the French Resistance movement in place of him; he in my bed in place of me. The gods seemed to demand a price for everything and I had paid for it. That was my first thought. Or, on second thought, had he? I moved into a university club before noon, visited my parents, saw my brother off to join his Navy fighter squadron in the Pacific, and felt deeply sad throughout. On Christmas Day I telephoned Faith to ask if I could drop off a present for Patricia and kiss her a Happy Christmas. I was scheduled to fly back to London Christmas night.

The whole Long family had gathered in Verna's apartment: the mother and father, Faith's younger brother, Jack, her sister Betty with her accountant husband. And Jean Poivrel! I looked twice to make sure I wasn't hallucinating. But it was he, sitting cozily in the family circle. I was speechless, first with surprise, then with fury, fury at their collective insensitivity, the absence of simple decency. Christ! Couldn't they have invited Poivrel to join them five minutes later or hidden him in the bathroom? Anything. Or was this a punitive act, rubbing my nose in a mess of my own making? Whatever, I had to fight back tears of rage and left quickly, chafing to be out of it, to be away. Patricia came to the door with me and I kissed her good-bye. She was a beautiful child I hardly knew.

In February, at the start of an ordinary day, a cable from my father was waiting for me at the door of 70 Grosvenor Street, the OSS London headquarters. "Ensign Robert Burke reported crashed in Pacific by Navy Department. Body recovered. Will be shipped home. Sorry. Patrick Burke." I turned back into the street and walked without destination, my mind too dazed and sore for thought. By noon I was in Wapping Wall near the East India docks and turned into the Prospect of Whitby, ordered a whiskey, and stood on the sagging porch of the oldest pub on the river, absently watching the Thames traffic, remembering and recalling, until the publican called "Time, gentlemen," announcing the midday closing.

You would have had to be a contrary person not to have liked my brother Robert. He was a good-looking, outgoing boy who came at life eagerly, tongue in cheek, without malice. Once during the fall of his first year at the University of Pennsylvania, the freshman football coach telephoned me in New York.

"I want your brother to be my quarterback," he said, "but he keeps skipping practice. Yesterday when I asked him where he'd been he said, 'In the dorm. Sleeping.' And just laughed."

"What do you want me to do?" I asked.

"Speak to him. Tell him we're counting on him. He's got a lot of potential."

"OK." I telephoned Bob and described our conversation.

"I don't want to be a football player. Just because you played everybody expects me to. And I don't care that much about it."

"You don't have to do it just because I did, for Christ's sake."

"Well, you know how it is."

"What would you rather do?"

"Join the Mask and Wig Club. You know, singin' and dancin'."

"Well, do it. To hell with football."

"Don't you think Dad will be disappointed?"

"Of course not. You're a nice kid and I love you, but you're real dumb. Just tell him straight out. He'll understand. He's not insisting you play football."

"What about the coach?"

"I'll call him and tell him to bug off. No, I won't. I'll tell him we've talked and decided that you're going to do some other things. No discussion. Subject closed."

"OK. Thanks."

"Take care. And dance good."

He quit college at the end of his freshman year, signed on as a Navy flyer, worked in a steel mill for several months waiting to be called up, and when he was commissioned an ensign and had won his pilot's wings, he married his best girl. They were both twenty.

It was dark when I drifted into the Dorchester Hotel and stood at the end of the bar, withdrawn from the gay talk and brittle cocktail laughter but less alone because of it. A very pretty girl smiled on her way to a phone booth nearby. On the way back to her table she smiled again and called, "Cheer up." She made another phone call, "For a dinner reservation," she said when she stopped to talk and invited me to join her and her friends for a drink. I explained why I couldn't. They were the first words I had spoken all day except to barmen. In a moment she was at my side, together with an RAF pilot. "Come on, mate," he urged. "Can't make it on your own forever." Each took an arm and tugged me gently to their table. I took a drink with them — two Americans and two British flyers and four girls — and protested that I would dampen their dinner party, but they insisted I come along. The pretty telephoning girl sat me next to her and said we must dance and, when it was time to leave, told whomever she had started with, "I'm taking him home with me." On that first night, the absence of my brother from the world growing stronger, she was a solace, a compassionate lady who knew everything without explanation. I could speak with her about his good young days and she perceived a hurt too deep for tears, a grief too private to share. She was the daughter of a British general. Often I wished I might have seen her again. Or even known her name.

Some weeks later a letter arrived from my father:

My dear Mike, We laid our dear little pal to rest on the 20th. He lay in state in the den amidst a profusion of the most beautiful floral tributes, white predominating in keeping with his youth and character. Baskets and vases filled with flowers occupied all available space in the living and diningrooms and in the corridors as well. Since he loved *all* of his home we felt he would like it this way. We received literally hundreds of letters, sympathy cards, Mass cards etc. And for hours on Monday evening there was a steady procession of people who came to pay their last respects. At times the line extended down Montgomery Avenue. The church was filled on Tuesday so you can see he was well regarded and well remembered and no finer tribute could have been paid him.

He looked exceedingly well and very much at peace, and it was hard, in fact impossible, to believe that he would never again call you "the water boy" or kid me about my rocking chair golf swing. It seems such a pity that one so young and capable of doing so much good in this lousy world should be denied the privilege of making his influence felt in broader fields. We indeed were fortunate that he was one of us and were given the privilege to know and enjoy and love him and to be loved by him. God must have wanted him very badly, but not nearly as much as we.

While he was lying in state we pinned your medal on the flag and just before we said our last goodbyes it was pinned on his breast. Yours was a beautiful tribute, Mike, and a very touching one. Only you would think of it, but coming from you, it was not surprising.

I loved him very much and miss him acutely to this day.

To have lived in London in late 1944 and 1945 was to have been very lucky. It was good to be alive then; the war was going our way, V-2 bombs, bigger than the V-1s and silent in flight, still fell with devastating effect but not in overpowering numbers, and they gave a strange edge to normal things. I never encountered a person whose nerve had gone. Civility, compassion, awareness, good manners, understanding, tolerance, kindness, and the rich prize of being alive were the texture of life. Human behavior on a wide scale reached a level of quality unapproached before or since. For my friend Rob Thompson and me London was an enviable, winding down assignment. Thompson had spent the earlier part of the war running guns across the Adriatic Sea to Tito in Yugoslavia. He was a big-boned, flat-muscled man with a strong, uneven face lit by intelligence. He had the look of a man who in an earlier century could have bossed a wagon train, but in his own time he edited the *News* at Yale and became a journalist. I don't know which was greater, his capacity for bourbon whiskey or laughter. His big laugh would fill a ballroom, fill Berkeley Square. In London we were thrust together into a demanding, urgent professional assignment and a full civilized social life as well. Sleep seemed wasteful of good living time. At Les Ambassadeurs we danced until dawn closing. It was at Les A that we put our housing problem to all the ladies with whom we danced, and one said she might be able to help. Next day I spoke with her on the telephone. She had only one reservation: the "naval type" might be a bit unmanageable. Thompson was an Army captain.

"Oh, don't be concerned," I assured her, studying the stripe and a half of gold on the sleeve of my Navy jacket. "I'll vouch for the Navy. Lovely chap really." That is how we found our flat in Sloane Street. We hired the chef from Claridge's Causerie on his day off to cook for our housewarming. He arrived at eight in the morning with his girlfriend. We gave him a bottle of gin to help him through the day and a hundred eggs — some duck eggs — that Thompson, an egg freak, had scrounged the countryside to find. By evening every flat surface was covered with food and the chef was heroically drunk.

Our colleague, Freeman Lincoln, the mildest of little men,
who had been commissioned an Army major and assigned to
Research and Analysis, brought an attractive full-bosomed
young English lady. She placed herself on a footstool in front
of the fireplace until heat and gin pitched her onto the floor
like a voluptuous grain sack. Freeman, outweighed by many
pounds, wrestled her limp body into the street, bribed a general's chauffeur to drive to her home through the blackout,
and hoisted her up three flights of stairs only to find the
door keys were in her purse left in our flat. He telephoned for
help.

"Jesus, Freeman," I said. "We can't find the floor in this
crowd, much less some woman's purse."

"What'll I do?" he pleaded.

"I dunno, Freeman; you're a novelist. Do something novel.
Like take her to your place." In real life Lincoln wrote sea
stories.

"Oh my God," he moaned and hung up.

I opened the door for two girls. One I recognized as a friend
of Thompson's. At a glance the other was something special.
Attentively, I showed her to the bedroom where we were piling
coats, helped her off with hers, learned that her name was
Stella, asked if she would like to go to supper when our guests
thinned out. I dared not risk turning her loose among the
predators inside before staking out my own claim. Absent a
theatrical look, she resembled Vivien Leigh — a continental,
slightly imperfect Vivien Leigh. She was French and a war
widow. Her husband, an officer in the British Eighth Army,
had been killed in the desert. At dinner Stella told me that just
that day she had written a girlfriend of her aloneness, listing
all the things she did in bed: sewing, reading, telephoning,
writing, breakfasting; closing, she wrote, *"Je fais tous au lit excepté le bon."* I do everything in bed except the good thing. That
was the beginning of Stella. A few years older than I, she was
the essence of European woman, layered with centuries of female wisdom. She exuded the nowness of life and made me
wiser than I had been. Stella was the woman I needed to relate
to and, in the tempo of the time, I was swiftly captivated by
her.

Martha Gellhorn, estranged from Hemingway, was in and out of our Sloane Street flat. She and Rob Thompson enjoyed reading aloud to one another. For me this was an instant soporific and invariably before the reader reached the bottom of the first page, I was asleep in the chair. Another frequent visitor was our friend Moe Berg, a truly extraordinary character — son of a Newark pharmacist, Princeton Phi Beta Kappa, major league baseball player, lawyer and linguist; he spoke French, Italian, German, Japanese, and Russian. We had no clue where he went or where he came from on his OSS Scientific Intelligence missions, but in London the latchstring was always out for him at our flat. He told no one, of course, that, among other assignments, he had parachuted into Norway to determine whether a German heavy-water plant in Rjukan, damaged by saboteurs, had resumed operation. In Oslo he obtained the information he needed from a Norwegian scientist and was lifted out by small plane from a field controlled by the Norwegian resistance. Back in the thirties, as a private citizen lecturing at the University of Tokyo, Moe used the hospital room of the wife of the American consul, whom he didn't know, to gain access to the hospital roof and took panoramic film shots of the city with a 16-mm Bell and Howell movie camera. It was his film that General Doolittle used planning his famous bombing raid on Tokyo in 1942.

Moe was a prodigious walker — for distances and at speeds that would have done in Caesar's legions — and had fascinating comments about everything along the route. His civilian shoes were made by some bootmaker in Boston who had made his baseball spikes, and looked it. Except for a white shirt, black was his only color. To add a bit of dash to his wardrobe Henry North once brought Moe a tie from Charvet in Paris — black with a black design. Tall, handsome, and black-haired, Moe was enthusiastic about women, and I introduced him to Helvi, a Finnish girl I knew. He was also an ideal undercover agent, not by training alone but by nature. He would go anywhere without fear, he had a gift for language, and his alert, supple mind could adapt itself quickly and comfortably to any new subject, however esoteric. Through reading and travel he involved himself intellectually in international affairs. In Paris or Rome, London or Bucharest, he was on familiar ground and possessed an unusual capacity to live alone contentedly for long periods of time. An agent's life is sometimes, most times, a lonely one. Not everyone is suited to it but Moe was.

Social life notwithstanding, Thompson's and my professional duties were serious and taken seriously. Because of our behind-the-lines experience we were put in charge of a freshly created element of London's Secret Intelligence branch: the Operations Office. We tossed a coin to determine who would be chief, who would be deputy. It came up heads, Thompson's call. Our urgent brief was to organize and dispatch agents to Germany and Holland. The complacency that had crept into the closing months of 1944 had been shoved roughly aside by Hitler's surprise attack through the Ardennes Forest in December. For six bloody days the Germans advanced in what became known as the Battle of the Bulge. Bill Casey, head of the Secret Intelligence branch of OSS in London, was then our brilliant young boss. (In 1981 he would become the director of the Central Intelligence Agency.) Casey said to get the job done and provided us near-magical support, especially aircraft. From London we prepared and dropped forty-six agent teams, eighty-six people. At the outset a fifty-percent agent loss had been anticipated. In sum, one agent, a woman named Selma, was known to be dead, shot by frontier guards while returning into Switzerland. Ten persons were missing. Three were known to have been captured; three were known to have been alive when the Russians entered Berlin. Of the remaining four nothing was known when we wrote our final report in May 1945.

It was in May, too, over BBC Radio that the king of England, resolutely fighting past his stammer, told us the war was over. Pals gravitated to our Sloane Street flat, drank to being alive and drank to our friends who were not and, like all of London, we took to the streets. As the sure-handed football player, I was entrusted to carry a precious unopened bottle of Scotch whisky. At midnight in Trafalgar Square the bells rang, whistles blew, and I took Stella in both arms, lifting her off the ground. The forgotten bottle of Scotch whisky smashed on the stone steps of St. Martin-in-the-Fields. To this day I cringe when I pass the church. For my clumsiness and passion I was banished from my friends' lives for all time to come, or at least until they dried their tears of laughter. And we all went our separate ways. For Stella and me it was a sweet-sad, inevitable, end-of-war good-bye.

# 6

AFTER FRANCE and England and surrender, the bonds of war and interdependence were broken; comrades had died or were scattered by peace. An adventure was over and the real world took us back, restive and unready. The home public, like the home publics of all wars, could not relate to what we had been doing, so we had no one to talk with. Hemingway said it best for many who had heard a shot fired in anger: "As long as there is a war you always think you might be killed so you have nothing to worry about. But now I am not killed so I have to work. Living is much more difficult and complicated than dying." *Unprepared* and *alone* were the words written on my slate; unprepared because I knew nothing useful, alone because Faith was now living in a Fifth Avenue penthouse with her French beau and wanted to discuss divorce.

We met on a bench in Central Park. Her scheme, she confided in her gay, thoughtless way, was to marry Jean, divorce him five years hence and come away with a settlement on which she and Patricia and I could live happily ever after. She was neither dismayed nor diverted when I said it was a depraved idea, urged her to hurry along to Reno for the divorce, and said good-bye. She kissed me on the cheek, a preoccupied mother's kiss for a small boy deposited at boarding school for the first time, a scene to hurry through without tears and be gone, unencumbered. She left behind a faint scent of Shalimar.

I felt blue. Slowly I walked along a paved path, through the zoo and across Fifth Avenue to the Pierre Hotel bar because it was the nearest place. I was saddened as one is sad at any ending, no matter how long expected, how inevitable, and, in a way, how relieving. My thoughts nevertheless flipped back through the good time and how short a time it was. I suppose it was aloneness that depressed me so: no woman beside me;

and only emptiness where my brother Bob and where Ned Fielden, both dead of the courage of war, had once been. And Simon. And brutalized Bazeau. All my life had been cushioned by companionship — school chums, college football team-mates, the lads of PT Squadron 15, the *maquisards* of Confracourt, the troopers of the 117th Cavalry, OSS pals, and women companions throughout. All that dissolved into mere memory and I felt isolated and adrift. At the bar I drank a Scotch and soda and prodded my mind to move along, but it was bogged in melancholy. Next to me a cheerful couple shared a bottle of champagne, celebrating one another. The young lady smiled sympathetically. "It can't be that bad, sailor."

"It is," I said, not in self-pity but in apology for my moroseness. I paid up and moved my private depression to the street. Where now? I asked myself. I had no answer but to board a double-decked Fifth Avenue bus, climb to an empty wooden bench at the rear of the open topside, and ride to Washington Square and back again in the mild September twilight, wondering if somewhere in this great throbbing city there would ever be a niche for me. At the moment survival in civilian life was my most ambitious hope. I am alive, and it is time to grow up, was as far as my soggy thoughts would reach. I hadn't a clue where to begin, but some inner voice, impatient with my mood, told me I could not ride the Fifth Avenue bus forever.

I had always had an aversion to men's clubs. They seemed a refuge for womanless, half-complete men, places to be avoided. Yet here I was, one of the womanless creatures living at the tacky, cheerless University of Pennsylvania Club on West Fifty-eighth Street because it was convenient and inexpensive to men in uniform. I had been released from active duty but as yet had no civilian clothes. A message from the writer Corey Ford was at the front desk with the key to my room and I rang him. He said Warner Brothers had bought the film rights to *Cloak and Dagger,* the book Ford and Alistair McLean had written about the OSS. A technical advisor was needed to work with the script writers. Would I be willing to go to Hollywood for a month? Warners would pay for my transportation and put me up at the Beverly Hills Hotel and my salary would be six hundred dollars a week. That was eight times the rate of my junior grade lieutenant's salary, including parachute pay, twelve times without it. Within forty-eight hours I had bought a civilian suit, boarded the Super Chief for Los Angeles, and settled into a five-day time capsule of eating, drinking, sleeping, and reading and being solicitously looked after by a beautiful breed of black gentlemen known as Pullman car porters. I watched an unknown, changing continent move past the windows and was awed again and again by the vastness of the empty plains, the stunning beauty of the seemingly impassable canyons and mountains, and I felt myself a hothouse flower compared with the men and women who had made this route by wagon train. This land was so endless, so beautiful, so unspoiled and reached so far back into time that it could have been God's unfinished story, and I smiled at the foolish notion that I might have been killed somewhere along the line and this was the approach to heaven. But I forgave myself for such fantasies on the flimsy excuse that I was still in transition from the years just past. Then we arrived in Los Angeles.

To an Eastern person, conditioned to stone and steel, the buildings along Hollywood and Sunset boulevards appeared to be made of cardboard, the ambience as impermanent and transitory as I was. We could both be gone in the first high wind, but we would have enjoyed our visit in the sun. Warner Brothers studios in Burbank looked like a movie lot in films about Hollywood. Twenty-two huge sound stages, if I remember accurately, were making real movies; synthetic city streets and cowtown streets waited in the back lot to be populated; unit managers, like top sergeants, kept crews on the hop, and in the genial, unself-conscious green room the costumed Coopers and Grants, the Olivia de Havillands and Alexis Smiths relaxed at their mid-workaday meal. Curiosity about this new world absorbed part of my loneliness.

Fritz Lang, who had directed some of the great film classics in Germany before fleeing the Nazis, had been signed to direct *Cloak and Dagger*. Milton Sperling, the producer, had come across the continent from Brooklyn in a secondhand Ford, married one of Harry Warner's daughters, quickly made four children, and was said to be one of Budd Schulberg's prototypes for *What Makes Sammy Run?* Sperling's offices were in a charming bungalow in the middle of the Warner lot. It had been built originally as a sumptuous dressing room for the film star Marion Davies. I went there every day to attend story conferences. From the beginning I sat on the perimeter waiting to be asked a question while Sperling and Lang and first one team of writers and then another pair who replaced them argued, shouted, and despaired over a series of rejected story lines. In *Cloak and Dagger* Sperling had bought a title. The book had no beginning, middle, and end. Rather, it consisted of a series of vignettes, and a film story remained to be created.

Meanwhile, when I wasn't sitting in a corner of Sperling's office enjoying the banter and billingsgate and responding to an occasional question, I was enjoying the lush vegetable existence of Southern California. An actress I knew in New York, Bobo Sears — later she became Bobo Rockefeller and set a contemporary world record for divorce settlements — lent me a car she had left stored in Beverly Hills. So I was mobile in California's automotive society. My friend Irwin Shaw was writing a screenplay for someone. His Malibu Beach house became the Sunday gathering place for wartime pals. Marion Shaw made sandwiches and salads and everyone brought his own drinks and his own girl: Bob Capa, the war photographer, was on a lark playing a bit role in *Arch of Triumph*, mostly to be around Ingrid Bergman; Peter Viertel was collaborating on a film story with John Huston; Gene Kelly was dancing for MGM; Artie Shaw and Ava Gardner came over from next door. One Sunday, as I sat on the sand drinking wine and watching the sun lower itself into the Pacific, my mind arranged an outline from bits and pieces of my war experience in Italy, adjusted them to fit the requirement I'd seen developing in Sperling's story conferences, and, next day when the story session broke down, I suggested tentatively that I might have a story idea.

"Yeah. Sure." Sperling's voice lacked enthusiasm. But the field was barren. My sketch took but a few moments and certainly was crude. When I finished Sperling leapt out of his chair like a character in an embarrassing movie.

"You sonofabitch. You've been holding out on us!" He seemed genuinely irritated.

"Holding out?" I laughed at the absurdity of it. "Come on, Milton. I was hired to answer questions. I'm not a writer."

"You're now a writer!" He shouted at someone, "Get him a new contract!"

Two incumbent writers were dismissed and Ring Lardner,

Jr., and Albert Maltz were hired to do the screenplay. I worked congenially with them, learned something about screen writing, liked them both. Later McCarthyism sent them to prison, two of the unholy ten who took the Fifth Amendment rather than answer charges that they were Communists.

Gary Cooper was to play the lead. Opposite him Lilli Palmer, then Rex Harrison's wife, would have her first American film role. Shooting would start early in 1946. On some chore I can't recall, Sperling sent me to New York at Christmastime. I debated whether to stay on and celebrate New Year's Eve in New York — with whom? — or to go back to California and shoot an arrow in the air. I went back and chanced into an old OSS friend, Jack Reese, one of the technical advisors Twentieth Century–Fox had hired for their OSS film, *24 Rue Madeleine.* Jack and his wife were going to a New Year's Eve party given by a former Air Force pilot who had flown a famous B-17 bomber, the *Memphis Belle,* about which a film had been made. They took me along. We joined the others at a restaurant–night club on Sunset Boulevard where Hollywood ends and Beverly Hills begins. A dozen of us sat at a round table, the men all recently demobilized from war; the girls all working for film companies, on and off the screen. We had not yet become civilianized, and the champagne and kindred companions turned the chemistry of the night into a wartime, no-tomorrow party. I could hardly credit the good luck of it; I drew a seat next to a delicious-looking girl with dark eyes, soft shoulder-length hair, and a subtly sensational figure. No homing pigeon ever flew a straighter course. Unfortunately the following day I could remember only that she had graduated from UCLA, that she was a superb dancer, and that her name was Campbell. My OSS friend had the impression that she lived at the Garden of Allah Hotel on Sunset Boulevard, not far from the Beverly Hills. I rang and asked for Miss Campbell and was put through.

"Hello." It was a pleasant voice.

"Hello. Is that Miss Campbell?"

"Yes."

"How lucky for me. I thought I might never find you. This is Michael Burke. We were at the same party last night."

"How nice for you. Good party, wasn't it?"

"Terrific. But I'm glad you're not lost forever. We had such good dancing that I hoped we might try it another time."

"Dancing?"

"Yes. You were great."

"I was? I don't remember dancing."

"You don't? My God, you danced all night!"

"I don't even remember music."

"Your feet heard it."

"It's Michael, isn't it?"

"Yes."

"Whose party did you go to, Michael?"

"I don't remember the fella's name. Vince something. He flew the *Memphis Belle*. It was in a club at the end of the Strip. Not far from you."

"Sounds exciting. But I was at the Goldwyns'."

"At Goldwyn's? Oh. Then it's not Miss Campbell?"

"Mrs. Campbell. Dorothy Parker Campbell."

"Dorothy Parker?"

"Yes."

"Miss Parker, I'm sorry, really sorry to have bothered you. I was just trying to find a pretty girl named Campbell. I danced with her a lot last night."

"Well I'm sorry it wasn't me. You sound so enthusiastic."

"I am. But I'm really very embarrassed about disturbing you."

"Don't be. I want you to find the girl."

"So do I. And again please forgive this intrusion. Good-bye."

"Oh, Michael! Call me when you find her. I'll worry about it if I don't hear."

"Yes, ma'am. I will. And my apologies to Mr. Campbell as well for this gaffe."

"I'll tell him we danced all night."

It took me a couple of days. Miss Campbell lived alone in a house on Holloway Plaza Drive. We went dancing at Mocambo, dined by the open fireplace at the Bel-Air Hotel, and picnicked on empty beaches up the coast from Malibu. I gave back Bobo's car. I had fallen in love with Miss Campbell.

She was called Timmy. Her family roots were in Tennessee though her father had ventured in silver mines in Nevada, orange groves in California, and hotels in Arkansas. He died when Timmy was five years old, leaving her with only a vague recollection of a funeral and a big house in Nashville. For reasons unremembered, probably unknown to Timmy, the young restive widow and her two children moved in with a sister on a large Nebraska farm, moved on to another sister in Pasadena, California, came back to Tennessee to stay with a stern aunt, then moved once more to settle in Pasadena when Timmy was aged ten. Tenuous connections with the Campbells of Tennessee dissolved, and from this early age Timmy was connected only to her mother and her much older sister and, as she matured, grew less close to them. Out of college she had been offered an acting contract by Howard Hughes. Instead she did publicity for Warner Brothers, then fashion for Sam Goldwyn's studios.

On Saturdays we shopped for food at the Farmers' Market and lunched at the Tail of the Cock with a group of her friends who took me in. In Beverly Hills record shops we bought Helen Wiley and the Philadelphia Orchestra and rummaging through bookstores I became aware of how dreadfully undereducated I was, how little of the world's great literature I had read, especially poetry. Until Timmy, I hadn't a clue that John Donne was the source of Hemingway's title *For Whom the Bell Tolls* and that Scott Fitzgerald's *Tender Is the Night* was taken from John Keats. Timmy found and gave me a complete set of Shakespeare's plays bound individually in red hardcover pocket-size books. Often we went along the Hollywood Strip to hear Nat King Cole or to dance at the Mocambo or to listen to Slim Gaillard's jazz band do "Cement Mixer" and "Dunkin' Bagel" with its crazy "Matzo Ball O Rooney" lyrics. Timmy took me to my first ballet and I was fascinated by the physical grace of Eglefsky and Maria Tallchief.

At the studio I was alert to learn whatever I might. Fritz Lang's directing attitude was severe, except for Cooper, with whom he was gentle-spoken and considerate. But then Cooper needed only to be told what was expected of him in a given scene and he did it. With Palmer, Fritz was extremely harsh, more so, the company gossiped, after she rejected his invitation to bed. None of us knew whether he made this proposition, but certainly his treatment of her became increasingly abusive. Maybe this was his formula to incite her best performance, or a sadistic impulse toward women under his professional control. Maybe some of each. Whatever, his verbal lashings made me cringe and one day sent Lilli bolting from the set in tears. Production stopped. Rex Harrison was rushed over from Twentieth Century to comfort his wife and participate in a Sperling-Lang-Palmer meeting that resolved the problem well enough to resume production. Everyone on the set liked her and, particularly because of Fritz, made special efforts to let her know it. Coop was exceedingly gracious to Lilli. He was also fond of watching Lilli's stand-in, whose most fascinating feature was her high full firm breasts, which Coop untiringly admired with the distant pleasure of a discerning spectator.

I liked both Cooper and Palmer immensely, and I got on easily with Fritz as well. Often I went to his home for dinner and afterwards watched him sketch with meticulous care the camera angles of scenes he would shoot the following day. Fritz was not a gregarious man and appeared to have few friends. A female secretary-companion, a tall, poised, Slavic-looking woman, lived in his airy house on the side of a canyon looking down on Beverly Hills. One night when Timmy and I arrived for dinner Fritz announced we would dine out.

"Where are we going?" I asked, more to make conversation than really caring.

"To the Brown Derby."

"The Brown Derby?" I wasn't sure I had heard correctly. It surprised me that Fritz would have chosen an obvious tourist place.

"I go there once a month." We drove with the top down on his yellow Buick convertible. At the restaurant, as an attendant held the door, Fritz put his steel-rimmed glasses in the glove compartment, fingered a monocle from the breast pocket of his jacket, clenched it in his right eye, and, stepping onto the pavement, stiffened into a Prussian military posture. It would have been futile for him to have tried to pull in his stomach. The front door was held open for him, the velvet cord that restrained tourists waiting for tables was unfastened, and the maître d'hôtel deferentially bowed Fritz through. A captain led us — Fritz, Timmy, the Slavic lady, then me — through the center of the restaurant to a conspicuous table, preceded by unnecessarily loud pronouncements that Fritz Lang was arriving. Fritz ordered imperiously. We ate reasonably well, conversed as normally as Fritz's abnormally rigid posture would allow. From time to time a more daring autograph seeker would approach and be whisked away: Mr. Lang is here privately and must not be disturbed. There was no mundane nonsense about paying or signing a check. We were escorted out in the same ostentatious way, Fritz affecting a nonseeing disdain for the peasants. Once back in the car, the monocle dropped from his eye, normal glasses went back into place, and his heavy body fell gratefully into its normal slouch. It was a first-rate performance of its kind that everyone seemed to enjoy, including me.

For the amusement that was in it, Fritz said I should take a screen test, and I looked at the result with Sperling. "Jesus, you're a tall sonofabitch." That seemed to be the limit of my talent. The bit part I did with Cooper and Bob Coote was in a segment cut out of the film entirely, sparing me the embarrassment of being singled out personally for the cutting room floor. But Fritz was right; it was a fun thing to have done, once.

Sometime after the filming of *Cloak and Dagger* was completed, the United States Navy, moving with glacial speed, awarded me a medal for work done in France in 1944, and the presentation was made at a small luncheon at the Warner studios. Navy brass was there and the French consul general. The wardrobe department outfitted me in a junior grade lieutenant's uniform that Cary Grant had worn in a Warner Brothers war film. It was a bit tight through the chest and shoulders but otherwise fit well enough. Coop and Lilli came, which touched me deeply. Cooper, on a midday break, strode in wearing the boots, breeches and, beneath his contemporary sports jacket, the ruffled shirt of an officer in General Washington's army. Lilli, a German lady, lingered afterwards and we talked privately about the war period of her European life. She was moved by a reference in my Navy Citation about freeing hostages.

Not long after *Cloak and Dagger* had been edited and scored and was ready for distribution, Warners discovered that they had no burning need for me, no need at all. Any notion I might have had about staying on in their stable of writers was fanciful.

Even if I had the craft — I didn't — they were paring down and already becoming paranoid about infant television. Once again, having postponed real life until I had seen Lotus Land, I was back at square one.

Fritz Lang threw up his hands in dismay when I told him Timmy and I were to be married. "Why do you Americans always have to marry them?"

"I don't always, Fritz. I just want to marry this one." He shook his head sadly at what he regarded as a friend's folly.

It was impossible for Timmy and me not to reach out for one another, to touch, to be together. From the very outset everything between us, every facet of a man-and-woman relationship was so natural, so fulfilling that the matter of marrying or not marrying never really came up. Nothing cluttered our relationship. All instinct and desire moved us towards it and there was no question. First Timmy had to be divorced from a hasty, brief marriage to a drafted soldier, a very nice, very wealthy young man from Chicago. We drove to Reno in her pale gray LaSalle convertible and, dropping her at a ranch for the obligatory six weeks' residence, I headed across the country to Sarasota.

Mrs. North, Henry's mother, had asked me to visit them in Florida, and by the time I reached her large white house, solitary and serene among the tall palm trees on Bird Key, my stomach felt as though it was rotting away, probably from driving so hard, stopping only for quick meals at greasy-spoon joints. That sweet lady had her doctor come and examine me for something dire, but I was put right by a couple of nights' sleep and her wonderful German cooking, especially the kuchen she baked for breakfast. Her main purpose in wanting me to come to Florida was to persuade my friend Henry to do something, do anything, rather than hang about waiting for his older brother, John, to look after him. Henry had done nothing in the two years since the war's end except to divorce and remarry. John North, as executor of his uncle John Ringling's estate, was deep in a complex lawsuit with the State of Florida and maneuvering to regain control of the Circus, which he had run from 1937 until 1942. Henry, younger by six years, was simply marking time, anticipating that John would be successful and that he, Henry, would in time be put on the Circus payroll. His mother, on the other hand, was desperate to have

Henry make some show of independence, however symbolic, to demonstrate that he could make his own way, not be forever beholden to John. She thought it was essential that Henry win John's respect in that way. I proposed to Henry that together we do a magazine story on the Ringlings and the Circus, aiming ultimately to interest one of the major Hollywood studios in the film rights. We spent a couple of weeks assembling raw material, but when the time came to go to New York and put our plan to the commercial test, Henry backed away. "At age thirty-eight," he said, "I want to be the youngest retired person in America." In New York Philip Rose, the literary agent, thought the *Saturday Evening Post* would buy my circus piece, but the *Post* said it had a tacit understanding with Joe Bryan, a good friend of the Norths, that he would do all their circus stories. No other magazine saw merit in the piece.

When Timmy arrived from Reno, Bill Horrigan, an OSS comrade, now back practicing law, provided a local judge and was best man at our wedding, and Bill Grell, another OSS friend, who had become general manager of the Drake Hotel on Park Avenue, gave us a honeymoon suite at twelve dollars a day, an endearing rate even then. Absent employment or prospect, we started married life with a blind confidence that would have frightened the angels, subletting a cheerful apartment at 17 West Tenth Street in Greenwich Village, and later, for reasons of economy, moving to a sparsely populated, wooded area beyond Croton-on-Hudson, wintering in a summer house.

Characteristically, my cousin Billy-the-Horseplayer, whom I hadn't seen for years, materialized like the proverbial genie from a bottle. Billy had no visible means of support, no known address, and no disposition to make the acquaintance of the Internal Revenue Service. His grapevine informed him that I was back from Hollywood, that Timmy was pregnant, and that we lived in some distant forest. One of the first things he wanted to know was what kind of car I was driving. From my earliest recollection he had always been a car buff.

"A secondhand Ford? You can't do that," he shouted into the telephone, scolding me as though he were still responsible for delivering me to the kindergarten nuns at St. Patrick's School en route to his own eighth-grade class. "Suppose the kid starts to come in the middle of the night and you gotta drive to

St. Vincent's and this heap falls apart?" He was so distressed that the next day an almost new Cadillac appeared in the dirt lane in front of our house. An elusive young man slipped me the keys and a terse message from Billy to "keep it till the kid comes." Another car, waiting a hundred yards away where our dirt lane joined Furnace Dock Road, took him in and sped away. It seemed discreet not to ask where the Cadillac had come from. Of course we did have to make the hour-long drive into the city, to Eleventh Street and Seventh Avenue, in the middle of the night, and while Timmy had a difficult, drawn-out time with a breech birth, I sat, useless and guilty at the unshared pain, in the bar of Charles' excellent French restaurant on Sixth Avenue, drinking very slowly, without relish, and watching John, the barman, mix dozens of the martinis he was famous for.

When Doreen was born, Billy's crowd — Lieutenant Hennessy from the New York Police Department's Loft Squad, Goldie the taxi fleet owner (two cabs), O'Boyle, a barman who sometimes said he was a detective, Ott-the-Cop-with-a-Hole-in-His-Head, who would have been an Olympian if there was a running-backwards event, which is how he got the hole in his head — invaded St. Vincent's Hospital, frightening the nuns with their Runyonesque speech and unbridled behavior. They brought a radio, a football, flowers, wine, candy, whiskey, stuffed animals, and a tricycle. And back at Croton-on-Hudson in the dark of Thanksgiving Eve we heard a great commotion in the underbrush and trees and switched on the outside lights. It was Billy and his Broadway friends lost in the wilderness. For them, 161st Street was the northern limit of the inhabitable world. But they persevered. Triumphant as Lewis and Clark, they arrived carrying all the ingredients for a Thanksgiving dinner.

"Too soon after the baby for the little woman to be cooking dinner," they said. Ott-the-Cop was a surprisingly good chef, O'Boyle handled the wine with a certain professional flair, and I did the interpreting. Timmy couldn't understand the argot. She didn't know that when Billy said: If it weren't for Uncle Pat he would be up in the iron house with the frying pigeons, he meant that if it were not for my father, Billy would be on death row in Sing Sing Prison waiting to be electrocuted. Driv-

ing home from an Italian wedding, where he had apparently
refused none of the wine, Billy had struck a car making a U-
turn across his path under the Third Avenue elevated tracks.
My father had arranged for Billy's successful defense after the
fatal accident. Billy was forever grateful, and his gratitude carried over to me.

That winter in the summer house, snowed in by the famous
blizzard of 1947, I developed an idea and outlined several episodes for a radio drama about a secret agent called Solitaire.
Ted Ashley, then a talent agent and years later chairman of
Warner Brothers, liked it and took it to Pat Weaver at Young
and Rubicam, who wanted it for General Foods. The only un-
resolved point was whether the episodes should be one hour or
one half-hour in length. A slice of General Foods' network
radio budget was allocated to Solitaire and the agency assigned
a talented radio writer to ensure against my inexperience.
Then at some late hour General Foods decided to switch Solitaire's money "to Jack Benny for Jell-O." So much for my radio
writing career.

I found employment of sorts with Marcello Girosi, my old
OSS companion from our 1943 summer in Italy. Financed by
Paolino Gerli, Girosi was importing Italian films, including operas, for American distribution. He was ambitious to expand
the beachhead established by Rossellini's *Open City* and DeSica's
*Shoeshine*. I wrote subtitles for films of far lesser quality. For the
operas I wrote introductory synopses and entr'acte notes to be
recorded by Deems Taylor, the *New York Times* music critic, and
by Milton Cross, whose rich damask voice announced the Metropolitan Opera's radio broadcast each Saturday afternoon.
And I wrote a screenplay about the love affair of Caroline,
Princess of Wales, and an Italian Count Bergamo. The final
and historically accurate scene showed Caroline pounding her
fists against the locked doors of Westminster Abbey, screaming
to be admitted. Inside, her husband was being crowned King
George IV of England. Marcello, a pregnant Timmy, and I
drove to Los Angeles, conferred with Zollie Lerner, a director
at Twentieth Century–Fox, who agreed to direct the film.
When the preproduction money ran out, Timmy and I returned to New York. The subject interested no one but Girosi,
and the film, blessedly, was never made.

Mrs. Franklin D. Roosevelt offered an interlude to our scrape-along existence. Timmy and Faye Emerson had become friends in California while they were at Warner Brothers, Faye as an actress, Timmy in publicity. After Faye married Elliott Roosevelt we met his family. Apparently Mrs. Roosevelt inquired about us and, learning of our narrow circumstances, invited Timmy and Doreen and me to spend the summer of 1948 at the Roosevelt estate in Hyde Park. We were given a farm cottage, consisting of a sitting room, bedroom, kitchenette, and bath.

Faye and Elliott lived in Top Cottage, where the President and Mrs. Roosevelt had lived before his death. The former First Lady had moved down the hill to Stone Cottage, a hundred yards from us. Generously the Roosevelts included us in all their social activities and we, in turn, screwed up our social courage and invited them all to lunch with us one Sunday. Timmy prepared a very good buffet. Everyone but Mrs. Roosevelt sat on the floor to eat; she was given the comfortable chair, an old-fashioned rocker with one runner broken off at the back. Gracefully she took no notice of its precarious condition, and presided like a benevolent Queen Mother at a family gathering in Buckingham Palace. Sitting cross-legged at her feet were Jimmy, Franklin, Elliott Roosevelt, and an assortment of wives and children. The conversation was almost entirely political, and it fascinated me how eagerly her sons sought her views and how genuinely her opinions were respected.

Swimming in the pool next to Stone Cottage was allowed only at a fixed time each afternoon, so the small army of young children could be watched. Doreen, aged one-and-a-half and tied into a life jacket, bobbed about like a happy cork, and Mrs. Roosevelt always started her afternoon swim by diving off the end of the board. One day, sitting beside her on the pool's edge, feet dangling in the water, I admired her courage.

"I really hate diving," she whispered. "I do it only to set an example for the children."

The year 1948 was a disaster. The move from Hollywood to New York was a plummet down a mine shaft. That year, I earned three thousand dollars and borrowed five thousand dollars from my father to keep my wife and infant daughter from going hungry. I honed dull razor blades against the inside of a water glass to scrape out another shave or two, and in desperation I undertook to write a technical training film on alternating current, a subject I knew absolutely nothing about. Like a schoolboy boning for an exam, I crammed enough highly perishable information into my head to invent two cartoon characters who told an illustrated story. The client paid happily and said it was so good that he couldn't afford to make it. Someone stole Doreen's carriage from in front of our garden apartment at Fifty-third Street and Second Avenue and we could ill afford to replace it. Rejection slips piled up like autumn leaves, and every day now was closing down with a taste of failure. Clearly, writing for a living was an option not open to me. What could I do was the question. The distressing childhood image of a derelict World War I Medal of Honor hero, whom I remembered vaguely, faded in and out of my thoughts. I recalled people shaking their heads sadly, saying the war destroyed him, staking him to another meal, another drink. I forced my thoughts past the notion that I might end up one of those. I knew that line of thought was evasive nonsense. In contrast to countless others', my war had been a piece of cake. I was simply unprepared for peace, for anything. A reviewing of my own bidding carried me back to the headmaster of Kingswood School for Boys, and I bucked myself up with Mr. Nicholson's exasperated observation that there must be some good in me somewhere; I had yet to find it. I had two skills: football and guerrilla warfare. It was too late by far for football, so when the knock came at the door, I was prepared to become a mercenary in the underground war.

CIA

# 7

FOR THE next five years we vanished into the CIA and lived in two European countries. Even now, I have been reminded, I am proscribed from writing definitively about my covert activities or indeed identifying the places where we resided. Although I lived openly, using my own name, to the world at large I was not what I represented myself to be. And that's the rub.

This, then, is a discreet account of those years — I believe the official term is "sanitized" — giving the tone and texture of that period, if not the names and numbers of the players. Accordingly, this version remains with the rules.

The initial CIA approach came in a telephone call from Washington. The man at that end said an ex-OSS friend of mine had suggested they talk with me and asked if we could meet for lunch in New York at some "discreet, quiet place." The Algonquin Hotel on Forty-fourth Street off Sixth Avenue was suitable, I thought. Its worn gentility and semblance of Old World gentility attracted English character actors and established American literary types. In the dark paneled Oak Room I sat across from the two CIA men, wondering if they felt safer with their backs to the wall facing the other patrons, and smiled inwardly at the notion that the actors and literaries, had they known the substance of our meeting, would have rejected the scene for a play or a novel; life's imitation of art was too prosaic.

While the CIA people ordered second martinis, I gazed into the dark wood behind their heads striving to look reflective, to give the appearance of weighing their proposal that I create a revolution in a communist country. I reined in my eagerness, masking the fact that I would have agreed to unseat Stalin had they asked. Wiser, I thought, to allow them the satisfaction of persuading me over lobster salad, *escalope de veau,* two bottles of Sancerre, and a smattering of contemporary American policy. The tempo of the Cold War was mounting and a Western response was essential.

They had in mind an exploratory action, a clinical case that suited my experience. They said as a contract agent I would be paid $15,000 a year, made up of an $8,000 salary plus a $7,000 tax-free living allowance. In 1949, with the gray-market rate of exchange favoring the dollar, one could live very well on that income. I asked some obvious questions, knowing the answers better than they. Not that they were unintelligent fellows. On the contrary. But they were transparently new to the clandestine business, political analysts, theorists, innocent of the nuts-and-bolts of underground operation. I was to be the nuts-and-bolts person.

"What kind of cover did you have in mind?" I asked at one point. They foundered and looked in vain at one another for a response to a predictable question. They were not prepared for it or even quick enough to finesse it to someone in Washington, and I sensed I could do better on my own than relying on their limited resources. American peacetime intelligence was a fledgling. CIA itself was but two years old. The Covert Action element was at its very beginning. I was reassured by the fact that the responsible officer in Washington was an able, proven fellow who had operated with Tito in Yugoslavia during the war.

"I'll arrange my own cover," I volunteered.

"You mean you've agreed?"

"Yes. I'll take it on." I hoped I appeared a fire horse, content in the stable but responsive to the bell. In fact I was near my wits' end and charged with excitement at the prospect of getting back to action, into a racket where I had some professional competence. During the war British SOE people often referred to their service as The Racket. Clandestine operations, compared with being an infantry soldier, say, were a lark, a big crapshoot in which you threw the dice — parachuted into the enemy night — and gambled that you would make your number. The term gained such currency that one day a notice appeared on the SOE bulletin board: "Hereafter members will refrain from referring to this organisation as The Racket." But by any name underground activity offered a special kind of high to the risk-takers of the world. And I could feel my adrenaline flow stepping up, rising to the old lure.

Pleased with himself for a good day's work done, the carefully spoken fellow with the fine blond hair, fine blond moustache, and gold-rimmed spectacles drifted — he did nothing swiftly — into a satisfied smile and ordered himself a bonus cognac. In one so young — less than thirty-five, I would think — his lethargic softness was half annoying. Perhaps, I guessed, it was his mind that was all sinew. Then, some weeks later, another dimension revealed itself when I met his very vivacious, very sensual-looking wife, learned that they always slept late, and that he was forever arriving late at the office. I presumed that the cause of his lassitude lay in the most gallant of reasons, was annoyed no more, and quickly grew to like them both very much.

His colleague's reaction to my acceptance was to whip out a comb from his breast pocket and slide it through his impeccably combed brown hair, like a nervous tic. Throughout lunch he kept touching an expensive attaché case, highly polished as a cavalry officer's boots, that lay beside him on the banquette. In his three-piece tailor-made suit he could easily have been an intense young bank executive nervous about missing the 4:45 Paoli Local to some suburban station along Philadelphia's Main Line. You knew that all his life he would be the aide, the second man, the one who carried the briefcase.

They paid. We shook hands at the sidewalk. They would put in motion the required FBI security check. Meanwhile I would start laying on my cover. They urged all possible speed.

Timmy was thrilled at the prospect of leaving our dim railroad flat at 50 West Ninth Street in Greenwich Village. Probably I was somewhat vague about the specifics of our next life, but not untruthful. She knew it was a secret CIA assignment and about the duality of our existence, overt and covert. Perhaps she did not focus on the fact that not everyone would be friendly to our side.

She hated guns and I kept my new .380 Colt automatic and shoulder holster out of sight. The .380 fires a .38 caliber cartridge from a .32 frame. I preferred the higher caliber coupled with the smaller gun, the impact of a .38 and the compactness of a .32.

But on the night of my arrival in the first European city from which I would work I left the hotel, strolled to a nearby park, and sidled away from the dimly lit walkways into the darker shadows of the tall pine trees until I found a trash barrel, stood beside it, looking and listening to be certain no one was about, then buried the shoulder holster under the surface debris. The cumbersome holster had worried me. It was more difficult to conceal than the gun itself and not the kind of thing you tossed into the hotel wastebasket for the maid to find, give to the housekeeper, who would give it to the manager, who would give it to the police. Besides, my long stringy frame did not accommodate a shoulder holster well. They are for beefier persons in large, shapeless suits. The pocket of a trenchcoat or the barrel stuffed into the waistband of my trousers suited me better. When I met my new foreign colleagues with whom I would work, I was amused to see that they, too, favored the waistband style. They were always armed; I almost never. Normally, carrying a gun was more a security risk than a safety measure.

We met for the first time in a small spare apartment in a block of flats deep in a working-class district, each of us coming alone by different routes to avoid notice by counterespionage agents or anyone else hostile. As each man arrived he introduced himself in broken French or English or Italian.

In their own country they had been political activists — agrarians, socialists, royalists. In exile, like all refugees, they were a threadbare lot, drawn loosely together in common cause against a communist dictatorship and by a longing to go home, albeit to a near-primitive European country. The group was more a rallying point than a valid base for a political revolution. Nothing was done to discourage the expedient pretext that they were a kind of government-in-exile. It brought together disparate political philosophies and personal interests; a modest but regular allotment of U.S. dollars was the glue. As the youngest person in the room, representing a young and rich country, I commanded their attention. As an individual I would have to earn their respect. This would take longer, but, I told myself, it could be won as they discovered I was not new to covert operations, not obtuse about the political conflicts among them, and not clumsy in human relations.

I sat down at one end of the bare rectangular wooden table.

The others fell in along either side, leaving significantly empty the seat at the far end, opposite me, for the oldest member, respectful of his age, prestige and toughness. He arrived accompanied by his bodyguard-interpreter, shook hands warmly, pulled a pistol from his belt, set it on the table in front of him, and sat down in the empty chair. Our first meeting was convened.

Legend in his home country was that the old man and an adversary would disappear into a hut or tent. Sometimes they would reappear together in agreement; or on occasion a single shot would crack and echo through the mountain silence and his granite face, thick iron-gray hair, and stocky iron-strong body would emerge alone, one side of the argument settled for eternity. I liked him from the start and grew fond of him as our enterprise progressed, though apart from smiles, embraces, and other body language our communication was through the interpreter, inasmuch as he spoke no language but his own, and could write nothing but his name.

Given the black-and-white definition of the Cold War there was no shilly-shallying about morality. Who is not with me is against me. The first operational phase was equally straightforward: recruit a limited number of refugees, train them as agents, and place them clandestinely on their native soil. There they would seek out any incipient resistance elements that might exist, though the chances of finding resistance groups that had escaped annihilation were slim. We would be attempting to create an underground movement supported covertly from the outside. No one underestimated the difficulty.

All this was discussed frankly with the group and they understood the risks. Each member committed himself to find among his political followers in the refugee camps and elsewhere suitable men who would volunteer to be pathfinders, who would parachute into their country in pairs, establish initial contacts and form the first resistance cadres. If the results were positive, a larger body of men would be recruited for paramilitary training and would be infiltrated in commandolike units at some propitious time.

Plans could be simply stated. Their execution would be complex, sometimes delicate, and always sensitive to security considerations, always mindful of the plausible denial stricture imposed by the American government, however theoretical. There would be casualties; this was not a parlor game.

I flew to a nearby country to search out a former OSS colleague; I needed his help. Let me call him Ben. Ben had left an Ivy League college to drive an ambulance in France during the 1940 Phony War. As a U.S. Marine captain fighting in the South Pacific, he was wounded and decorated for gallantry, and, in 1944, as an OSS Jedburgh, parachuted into southern France to join the French Resistance. I found him in a fishing village rubbing linseed oil into the deck of a boat he had raised from the bottom of the harbor, where it had been sunk in a wartime air raid. Had I to pick one man in the world to have alongside me in a live-or-die situation, it would be Ben, blond, weathered by the sun and sea, lean and tough as rope. He agreed to join me.

I began to establish a work pattern. In order to give substance to our cover, Timmy and I sought out legitimate people we knew and began to widen our circle of friends. Often a number of us breakfasted together at a popular sidewalk café, taking orange juice, espresso, and brioche in the midmorning sun. It was an amorphous group to which passers-through added and subtracted themselves and regular members departed and arrived in the normal course of their trade. Consistency would have been abnormal and the irregularity of my own life blended conveniently into this rhythm. The acceptance of our cover was enhanced by Timmy's earlier professional work; trade talk came easily. I was mildly surprised at how uncurious people were and how very easy it was, when it suited my purpose, to direct attention away from myself simply by asking the right question of other persons and being a good listener, or at least appearing to be.

The clandestine side of life formed itself simply. I followed the basic rules of tradecraft — moving about unobtrusively, holding meetings in places and at times least likely to attract attention, changing routines before they fell into predictable patterns, remaining alert to being followed should any suspicion have been aroused. Security was holding firm, so I thought. What I did not know at this time was a simple sinister fact known only to the KGB, and to precious few of them: Kim Philby was a Soviet mole functioning in the top bracket of the British Intelligence Service.

When I first met Philby in London in March 1950 I was aware that he was legitimately privy to my assignment; what surprised me was his easy familiarity with operational matters. Frankly, too, I was pleasantly surprised and flattered that a man of his rank would invite me to dine with him privately.

We decided on Wheelers in Dover Street, ate sole and drank Meursault, and talked easily and freely about all manner of things. His considerable charm was disarming, his slight stutter sympathetic, his face almost handsome in a neglected way. He gave the appearance of wasting no more time shaving or combing his hair than he did with his clothes, which were unfashionable and unpressed. Entirely likable and very much at home in and on top of his profession, Philby's surface persona seemed to go right to his core. His social class and his education at Westminster School and Cambridge University presumed loyalty and commended him to the Establishment. It was unthinkable to suspect that those traditional credentials would conceal a Soviet agent, and the degree of self-control, of self-discipline demanded of Philby to sustain his enormous deception over so long a period of time is immeasurable.

After dinner we strolled along to pay our respects to Kim's father, St. John Philby, the famous Arabist, who was in London on one of his rare visits from Saudi Arabia. The bearded, scholarly-looking Philby Senior was dining at his club surrounded by a collection of contemporaries, chairs pushed back from the dinner table, sipping their port, an archetypal nineteenth-century scene. The two Philbys embraced, Kim respectfully, his father benignly. Personal diffidence and English good form inhibited a fuller expression of the affection one sensed they felt for one another. We stayed for no more than a quarter of an hour and St. John Philby said he expected that two young men had more stimulating things to do with the young night and we were dismissed. We went on to some late-hour club Kim knew. He was a heavy, indiscriminate drinker, but his protective mechanisms were so deeply rooted that no amount of drink betrayed him.

Soon after Timmy and Doreen had arrived from New York, we found a villa where we were able to rent the top floor and the roof, a spacious hanging garden where Doreen rode her tricycle among huge terracotta flower urns and tree boxes and from which we had a spectacular overview of the city. Our quiet street was lined, as Timmy hoped it would be, with oleander trees, and graced by other large villas set among vivid flower gardens and screened by luxuriant trees. Our villa was set back about a hundred paces from the street. Entry to the grounds was through a high iron gate, and a gravel drive led to twelve broad stone steps mounting to a wrought-iron and glass front door. Inside, a curving marble staircase climbed to our apartment, secure behind a heavy wooden door, barred and chained on the inside. In the sitting room, floor-to-ceiling french doors along one wall looked into neighboring gardens and warmed to the morning sun. At night the street and the drive were so dark that our clandestine friends could come and go unrecognized.

One night we invited some of them to dinner. At eight o'clock, an hour before they were to arrive, the lights went out. But, then, the lights in the whole city, or in parts of the city, often flickered and died in those early postwar years, only to return in a few minutes, a few hours, a few days. But in a while I noticed that ours was the only dark house in the neighborhood. A fuse box attached to an outside wall was a mare's nest of red, yellow, green, blue, and striped wires. To venture your hand was to court electrocution, so we entertained our guests by candlelight.

A terrified shriek pierced our dinner conversation, and I ran down the hall. The maid, pale even in the fluttering light, stood shaking at the bathroom door and could only point inside. An ugly black weapon rested on the washstand. One of our guests had used the toilet and forgotten to stick his gun back in his waistband.

The shutters of the tall glass doors that formed one side of the sitting room were drawn closed for security. We drank brandy, and cigar smoke mingled with that of the smoldering candles. The good food and wine and the sociable talk had eased the normal tensions of their émigré life and the political wariness among them. Their clothes, cheap and ill-fitting, looked the more forlorn against the elegant period furniture, the rich marble floor, and the high molded ceiling of the villa. Yet their manners were gracious and even courtly in an Old World way. They seemed to be allowing themselves a moment of contentment and, in this social context, perhaps perceived more clearly our human sympathy for their plight and our sense of shared equality with them as individuals. Near midnight, one by one, they kissed Timmy's hand and vanished down the gravel drive, through the high iron gate and into the moonless night.

Laced into our fluid clandestine existence was an almost normal family life. I say "almost" because throughout there was the duality of it to cope with: the natural social intercourse of ordinary things like dinner parties or Sunday by the sea alongside the clandestine occupation hidden from our normal friends. Keeping the two lives compartmentalized was in fact an interesting mental exercise for us. Between Timmy and me it created a special kind of closeness, not self-conscious, not dissected by tedious analysis or even talked about. Rather it was a secret shared, and shared easily, that created no internal tension or problem; quite the contrary. After the constant worry about next month's grocery bill in New York, our new life-style was sheer heaven. A very attractive villa, a cook, a maid, a nurse for Doreen, the beauty of the ancient city itself, a beach cabana a half-hour away, October holidays on the Mediterranean, summer visits to Austria, marvelous journeys on the Scandinavian Express through the spectacular Italian and Swiss Alps and out into the beautiful forests and lakes of Bavaria. Often Doreen accompanied us, a bright and eager young traveler, and we regretted that Patricia's mother would not permit her to join us, even though legally I was entitled to custody in the summer months. True, there was a submerged tension that ran beneath this agreeable life-style, not a frightening or worrying tension, more an extreme alertness, alert to the fact that there were people abroad in the world who were opposed to what we were doing, violent people. One morning a man's body, a fellow national of my new friends, a man whom I did not know, was fished out of the river. Who had eliminated him or why we never discovered. So there remained constant the threat of unspecific danger. It floated in the air like an unanswered question: Who? When? Where? I accepted the risk without knowing its measure. Given the persistent optimism that nothing untoward would happen to me, clandestine activity spiced more than menaced our lives. It was intellectually and psychologically stimulating.

Apart from that we lived as normally as any. We bought a small station wagon — forest green with gray corduroy upholstery, eye-catching in the sparsely trafficked capital. I did not use it for work, of course, and always felt comfortable when Timmy was seen in it in one part of the city while I was on clandestine business in another. A wonderfully insouciant decoy, Timmy amassed a staggering number of traffic tickets, leaving the car parked in the wrong places while she searched for antiques through a labyrinth of back streets where she became known affectionately as the Fighting Lady. But she did have to give up wearing a slinky black-and-white skirt made of unborn calfskin; in it her shapely legs and well-turned bottom were simply too tempting a target for the local gents.

Returning late from a visit to another country, I thought Timmy would be in bed, but instantly when I rang the bell, she called out, "Who is it?" I heard anxiety in her tone. She slid back the bar, opened the door a crack, and, obviously relieved to see me, unhooked the chain. An hour earlier, expecting me, she had opened the door and was terrified to see a policeman in uniform who wanted to come in. Fortunately, she had not unfastened the chain, so the door opening was fixed at three or four inches. But for some minutes the policeman's toe blocked her closing it while he tried to persuade her to let him make himself available to a comely young woman who, as he had apparently observed from his beat, was often alone. While we were sharing a bottle of beer and I was calming her, footsteps sounded on the stairs, followed by a gentle but audible tapping at the door. I moved softly across the marble floor, pushed back the bar, and looked out. He was back, giving her a second chance, I suppose. In a fury, I yanked open the door and before his dim wit could recover its surprise, flung him down the stairs, ran down and, while he was still off-balance, shoved him out the lower door spewing New York waterfront invective after him.

In the morning two somber, uniformed policemen arrived with a summons for my arrest: assaulting a police officer. I was to report to the local station at 4 P.M. Under the Napoleonic Code I could go to jail and stay there until I proved my innocence, or served my time. Immediately, I went to the American consulate, as an ordinary American citizen, and asked their advice. Had I done as they charged? Yes, I had. The consulate assigned a lawyer to represent me. "I'll do all the talking," he said. "You're not in a very enviable spot." After some formalities, we were ordered back the following day at noon and I slipped away for clandestine meetings and an overt social dinner at eight.

The lawyer and I were at the police station the following day. In the chief's office the climate was hostile, dark with scowls and angry undertones. Again my counsel cautioned me to be polite, even submissive, and under no circumstances to raise my voice or lose my temper; I had committed a serious offense. A door opened and the officer was brought in to identify his assailant. "That's him! That's him! He's the one!" he screamed, pointing at me and behaving as though I had raped his sister. Having served his purpose, he was taken away, leaving his superior officers in a very unfriendly mood. Amidst a comic opera of shouting and arm-waving, though not so comic for me, the lawyer remained collected, reasoned calmly, moved patiently in my defense. Despite the officer's denials of carnal purpose, what was his reason for seeking entry at midnight? Admittedly his client had pushed the officer away from his door, but his client was a law-abiding person, a foreign visitor, living peacefully among us. Without provocation he would not have taken such vigorous action. Again we were told to return the following day for a verdict.

I had picked a hell of a time to be jailed! We were on the threshold of a major covert operation. Through the afternoon and evening I hurried from one rendezvous to another, tying an operational knot here and there in case I had to spend time in the slammer. The next day, after much shouting and thrashing of arms, I was obliged to make a statement of contraction; the case was dismissed and I was allowed to leave.

I flew off to meet Ben and to dispatch our own first agent teams to their homeland.

"How are we going to move the bodies from the farm to the airfield?" I asked him.

"I bought a truck. Secondhand, maybe third-."

Our agents, waiting dispatch, were held in a safe house, an isolated farm on the outskirts of the city in which Ben lived. The plan was to leave the farm at 9:15 P.M. for the thirty-minute run to a naked brown field where our air crew of foreign nationals would be waiting in an unmarked aircraft. Into the back of the truck we loaded six parachutes and six containers of equipment — two for each two-man team — helped the agents pull on their striptease jump suits over their regular clothing, checked all the other predispatch details — documents, side arms — and boosted the men atop their gear. Ben and I climbed into the cab, Ben behind the wheel. He pushed the starter button and the engine responded with a dull metallic clunk, and dead silence.

"It worked this afternoon," he said, and fifteen nervous tinkering minutes later Ben had it going again. The moon was not yet up as we lurched off into the starlit night along a route of secondary roads. The truck labored but didn't falter. Suddenly ahead of us was a roadblock. It had not been there when the route was reconnoitered the night before. A half-dozen soldiers lolled on one side of the road; a single wooden police horse, the type used to hold back parade crowds, straddled the road. Ben took his foot off the accelerator and the truck lugged as though it were dragging an anchor. It was one of those moments when a click of the human eye registers a scene, and the brain, shortcircuiting thought, responds at the same instant, a reflex rooted in training and experience, like a halfback instinctively running for daylight. To stop and think is to be finished. Here, I saw an unintimidating barrier, a few unalert, indifferent-looking soldiers, no vehicles, probably no communication. And we were loaded with inexplicable cargo.

"Christ, Ben, we can't stop now! Gun it! Keep going!"

He pushed the accelerator to the floor, and the old machine picked up momentum, bowled through the flimsy barrier, and roared off into the night leaving the soldiers shouting and confused. Clearly they were not first-class troops, and I hoped they would conceal their negligence in silence. The men in the back chattered excitedly, but we signaled through the rear window that everything was fine.

A rising moon dimly silhouetted the plane poised silently at one end of a large arid field. Ben turned off the narrow road, shifted into low gear. As we bumped across the rough ground we could see our "air officer," an American we had recruited from a freebooting air freight service, standing by its nose.

"Make a half circle and back as close to the side of the plane as you can," I said. "It'll be easier to transfer the containers." Ben swung the machine around in a wide arc, stopped, put the gearshift in the reverse position and let out the clutch. The entire transmission fell onto the ground. We transferred the containers and chutes from there, shook hands all around, and boosted the agents into the aircraft. The plane's twin engines coughed and roared and it lifted off quickly, shaking free of the uneven ground.

The crew made their scheduled three separate drops of bodies and containers and, though they wouldn't admit it, probably swanned around the unfriendly skies just for the hell of it, for the pure high of taunting death. They were a wild and wonderful lot. On the following two nights they flew out again trying to pick up ground-to-air signals from the agents, confirming that they had landed safely and were well. There was no response from the ground, not an encouraging sign. Did the special air-to-ground voice communication equipment fail? Had they been injured? Were they hiding, reluctant to risk communicating so soon? Had they met friend or enemy? Ben and I, harking back to our own experience in France, put ourselves with them on the ground vicariously and pictured a dozen possibilities, mostly unpleasant. It was an empty exercise, of course, but we identified with them, and were apprehensive.

It was November 3, 1950. We did not then know that we had dropped these men into an alerted security net. The training of individual agents who were to follow the Pathfinders was carried on in ignorance of a high-level betrayal, and additional recruits were filtered through a screening process and prepared for paramilitary training. Everything appeared to be in order and on schedule, except for the silence of our parachuted agents. Their silence could be the silence of the dead.

Early in December Timmy, Doreen, and I left for our first official visit to Washington. We boarded the overnight wagon-lits to Paris, spent the next day shopping and, leaving Doreen in the care of a *femme de chambre* at the Hôtel Meurice, we treated ourselves to a quiet dinner at the Grand Vefour, danced not so quietly at the Eléphant Blanc, took up with a raunchy crew of instant friends in Pigalle in the hours before dawn, slept little and bore our baggage and our hangovers to the 8:30 boat train for Le Havre. The *Liberté* sailed at eleven. Aboard for the six-day crossing to New York we were delighted to find General Donovan traveling with his very attractive blonde daughter-in-law, Mary. We also ran into Steve Crain, an old Hollywood acquaintance traveling with a French version of his former wife, Lana Turner. The ship was aglow with a gay preholiday spirit. We too were aglow, but beneath the homeward-bound Christmas cheer, worry about the silent parachutists churned.

In Washington, the CIA people proposed that I move to another country to take charge of affairs there. I would cease to be a contract agent and become a full-fledged member of the Agency. I don't recall any administrative formalities; perhaps my name was simply added to the roster. The people we met socially, mostly members of the intelligence community, were warmly hospitable. One dinner party followed another and Doreen's baby-sitter at the Wardman Park Hotel read her a young child's version of *The Wizard of Oz* so many times that Doreen was able to recite it, word for word.

Ironically, the largest, jolliest, and wettest of these parties was given by the Philbys on February 24, 1951, at their home on Nebraska Avenue. Timmy and I and Ken Downs, the only people without cars and awaiting a taxi, were the last to leave. Downs, still carrying one more martini for the road, fell from the porch into a thick hedge, landed flat on his back, and held up his glass triumphantly to show that he hadn't spilled a drop. The Philbys and we cheered him extravagantly from the top step. We all hugged one another in semidrunk camaraderie, rescued Downs from the bushes, and left the Philbys awash in bonhomie. It was that kind of party, not at all the kind of party Philby had arranged for our agents returning to their homeland.

MI6 moved protectively in its traditional old-boy fashion. Philby resigned in 1951 to spend five years in the shadows, his loyalty still stoutly defended by his British colleagues, and was put on hold both by them and by his Soviet controllers. In 1956 he surfaced as a Mideast correspondent for the London *Observer* and the *Economist*, his appointments arranged by MI6 friends. Then one night in 1963, Philby failed to show up for a dinner date at a friend's home in Beirut. He simply vanished.

The British were at last closing in, and Philby's nerve began to crack under the now unbearable strain. His Russian handlers actioned the long-laid plan to spring him, and Philby decamped to Moscow.

It was virtually impossible for me to reconcile the Philby I knew and liked with the Philby I did not know and recoiled from. I could understand his having become a Communist in the despairing British political climate of the early 1930s, and I could comprehend his renouncing his country; however dubious, it was in a sense an abstract, a personal, decision. What I could not assimilate was the magnitude of his treachery, for Philby's direct action had betrayed and caused the deaths of an untold number of men who counted him an ally.

## 8

WITHIN THE CIA, as in the OSS before it, there were two principal clandestine branches. Officially they were called the Office of Special Operations (OSO) and the Office of Planning Coordination (OPC), but under these euphemistic identities their functions were Secret Intelligence and Covert Action. Communications Intelligence, intercepting the other side's communications, was a highly sensitive subdivision, as was Counter Intelligence, which defended the Agency in its operations against hostile penetration. Plainly, Secret Intelligence meant covertly gathering information about other countries, information about their strength and their intentions, espionage in its traditional sense. Covert Action, if you set aside guerrilla warfare, which goes back to Sun Tze in 500 B.C. at least, was a more contemporary facet of clandestine operations. In CIA terms it was defined as "any clandestine activity designed to influence foreign governments or persons or events in support of United States policy." Freely translated from basic bureaucratic, this meant that the CIA was to disrupt and unsettle, to harass and counter the Soviets by all special means — paramilitary, sabotage, black propaganda, political action — to turn loose among the chickens as many foxes as we possibly could get away with.

Except for General Walter Bedell Smith, a career soldier, or Allen Dulles, who succeeded him as director of the CIA, most people down the line in the new agency were young, so thirty-three, my relatively slender chronological age, was not remarkable. With the war and the earlier CIA venture I had logged more clandestine time than most and had far more operational experience than all but a few. This gave me a certain cachet, I suppose, among the people in Washington deciding who should take charge of Covert Action in one of the foreign areas. For my part I knew the business and I liked it.

Leaving the sun and sea and free-form life of our first European base for the gray discipline of our second was not a privately attractive prospect, but it was professionally compelling. I would have been reluctant to take a CIA post in Washington, if that option had been open to me. Washington would have been too distant from the action, too confining a life-style. I wanted to touch the ball, as the basketball players say. A decade or more had passed, but I was still of the same bent as the college boy standing alone and exhilarated at the goal line at the opening kickoff imploring the ball to come to him. That is not to say that there was anything collegiate in my approach to a serious Cold War assignment. It was not a time for games. More swiftly than in ordinary years, a war and a frustrating civilian experience had matured and seasoned me.

The Iron Curtain had been slammed down and the threat of new conflict was persistent. How far would either side go? No one knew. This was the giant conundrum of the day, deriving from the gravest issue of our times — the relations between East and West. Philosophies and wills were being tested — most acutely in Germany, where armies faced one another from opposite sides of the Demarcation Line and Berlin was a divided island a hundred miles deep in the Soviet zone. Germany was the hottest arena in the clandestine Cold War. For my part I was not looking for a quiet corner. On the contrary, I was eager for a new level of responsibility. It waited for us in full measure.

I inherited a large disparate body of Americans with varying skills and talents, dispersed in a dozen locations throughout the country, a myriad of ongoing activities of varying quality, and hundreds of indigenous men and women agents ranging from individual couriers to organized resistance movements. Looking back, I find it curious that I had no qualms whatsoever about taking charge of what was then the CIA's largest and most comprehensive field operation. I was sure I could deal with this assignment as well as anyone I knew. This wasn't a matter of overblown ego or empty conceit, for I knew I would have to apply myself relentlessly, learning a new clandestine topography under forced draft. But running clandestine operations had become as natural to me as law to a lawyer, balance sheets to an accountant. It was my profession. Perhaps I was imbued with a young person's sense of invulnerability. Instinctively, as though an electric switch were thrown, I was on the main current, wired to the taut, uneven vibrations of the secret war. An all-consuming business, it demanded total concentration and honed the mind to sharpest capacity. In retrospect, I realized that my brain had been half asleep until I had taken on the first CIA task, at a time when there was no textbook and you made up the game as you went along.

From the outset, in 1942, I took to this unorthodox life because it was so unstructured, offered so much independence and so many opportunities to improvise. The covert world demanded that you find more within yourself — in your head and in your stomach — than the conventional world did. And the element of danger, potential or real, the element of risk, added attraction. This may not be everyone's cup of tea, but I found it was mine.

Accepting this new CIA assignment had not been a soul-searching decision on my part. The Cold War was a hard fact, blunt as the nose of a Russian tank, black-and-white as the shooting war had been five years earlier. In East Germany scores of Soviet divisions massed along the East-West frontier, forty miles from Frankfurt, poised to sweep across Western Europe. Allied forces facing them were a fraction of the Russians' strength, capable only of briefly slowing an assault. Contemporary debate centered on how many days it would take the Soviet troops to reach the English Channel. Every CIA person was equipped with a personal evacuation plan — a route west, emergency supplies, gold sovereigns. Friends in America said I was foolhardy to place my family in such jeopardy. As I am incapable of an apocalyptic view of life I thought them too windy; circumstances often appear more ominous at a distance, distorted by sensationalist headlines, than they are up close. It was for the Soviets to gamble whether America would use the bomb against them if they were to overrun Western Europe; I gambled that the Russians would not take that gamble and I was hardly alone in this estimate. During the Russians' blockade of Berlin in 1948 and 1949 General Lucius Clay, the American military governor, thought the chance of war was only one in ten. Besides, on a purely subjective basis, I knew this was where I should be. This was the trade I knew. Intelligence is — perhaps was more then than now — as much a business of instinct as intellect and I had long lived by instinct.

Technique carries one a certain distance; logic, reason, and fact come into play, of course. But to calculate the incalculable, instinct is essential, the finger feel of a situation when there is nothing to touch. That and a certain acumen about people.

Obviously in the CIA, as in any secret service, the chemistry, the motivation, the fields of interest of individual members differed as much as their looks or their personalities. And like any large government body the CIA's staff contained a cross-cut of America, people who by some different quirk of chance could very well have found themselves in the Department of Agriculture, the Aetna Life Insurance Company, the University of Arizona, or the Cincinnati Police Department. There was no CIA type. What they may have had in common was a good mind, an ability to learn quickly, some specialized knowledge, discretion, balance, and a belief that their work was essential and that an effective intelligence service was indispensable to a modern nation.

The price of anonymity was probably offset by an air of romance and mystery that cloaked the profession, by an elixir of glamour that curled up from their secret papers, by danger vicariously shared with agents operating on hostile ground, by the possession of a secret — a host of secrets — that set them apart, placed them among an elite few. These would have been unspoken, if humanly understandable, indulgences. But in practice, they could not afford to romanticize their work; they must be as pragmatic as dentists. Above all — and perhaps the most difficult intellectual discipline to sustain — they could not allow themselves to fall in love with the game for the game's sake.

Timmy and I flew from our old to our new home, which, in 1951, was still grim with miles of buildings broken by wartime bombings. The hotel where we first stayed, across the square from the vaulted, soot-blackened railroad station, had been war-damaged but was operating fitfully and under repair at the same time. Our plain clean room had no bath, but a scrubbed and starched young maid said we should undress, don our robes, and bring soap and towels. We followed her along a drafty corridor, across a wooden scaffold spanning a gaping hole in the outer wall, down a dimly lit stairway smelling of wet cement, along another hallway to adjacent doors a few feet apart, one marked Herren, one Damen. I bade Timmy a mock *auf wiedersehen* and went through the Herren door into a small room containing a washbasin, a toilet, a hook to hang a robe, and, at the back, a closed door leading to the bath. Shaving and brushing my teeth, I sorted through my first impressions of Germany and the Germans — I had last seen them in any numbers as the enemy in France in 1944 — and concluded that my mood was one of uncertainty. I felt neither hostility nor sympathy. I was vaguely uneasy; or perhaps simply keyed up a notch or two, more nervously alert as one often is entering an unfamiliar place. I hung up my robe, slung the towel over my shoulder, and pushed through the door into the bathroom, startling Timmy, who was already bathing and relieved to see that her unexpected tubmate came in a familiar body. It was a commodious Edwardian tub. Four strong clawed feet gripped the floor, a match for any combination of weights and measures, singly or in pairs. The hotelier must have been a Gemini, possessed of surface propriety and submerged mischief. No doubt his apprenticeship had been served in Switzerland and in France and he had brought home the best of both worlds. Score one for the home side. It was an engaging beginning.

That night we found our way on foot through the unlamped streets to a restaurant alongside the Rhine. Allied bombers had used the river as a landmark — as the Luftwaffe, bombing London, had used the Thames — and released thousands of bombs on sight. Roadways were clear now, of course. Rubble was piled where buildings had once stood. Our footsteps echoed through empty, silent streets lit by a pale half moon, diffused in light fog. The message in the damp air was one of peace more than death. Walls that had not fallen, their empty windows looking out on empty space, stood like giant headstones listing silently over the dead, inviting respect for the ghosts below, citizens of another world, untroubled now by the siren's wail, the shrill downrush of bombs, or the muffled thunder of collapsing buildings. It is not possible to be indiscriminately angry at the dead. Or the survivors. Coming to Germany, we concluded that it should be to live among individuals — some good, some bad, some of no particular account. Simply that. Forgiving nothing, forgetting nothing, putting aside preconceptions and the understandable distress caused for some of our friends by our coming to live among people who had made the Holocaust.

No sign marked the entrance to the restaurant. A small cleared space in the rubble led to a long stone staircase descending to a stone cellar, deep beneath the ruins. In years past it might have been a wine cave. The music was lively, the food excellent, the wine delicious. The clientele celebrated being alive. How they had spent the years prior to 1945 was anybody's guess. But with the wine and music my own specific disquiet eased, partly I think because no one in the restaurant was in uniform. Not that uniforms represented a threat, obviously, but earlier in the day my body had tensed at the sight of railway guards and customs officials in gray-green uniforms and black jackboots. To this day my eyes register jackboots, now without anxiety but duly noticed, like seeing the number 22 from my college football jersey in some other context.

My first impressions were that Covert Action projects, all aimed at Eastern European targets, were scattered in loose profusion, and that the Secret Intelligence cadre was antipathetic to the entire concept of Covert Action. The SI attitude was understandable; intelligence operations are successful only when unseen and undiscovered. Covert Action, by its very name, calls attention to itself; only the catalyst remains secret, one hopes.

A thick winter fog that often settled on the West German plain grounded all flights to Berlin and for the first time I traveled by overnight train, sealed for its hundred mile, stop-and-go journey through the Soviet zone. Leapfrogging the Russians on an ordinary commercial flight to Berlin was little different from flying the New York–Washington shuttle, except for the tight squeeze of landing at Tempelhof Airport in the middle of Berlin, but traveling overland through Russian-controlled territory had a more ominous cast to it. The sleeping compartment was comfortable, but I slept unevenly, awakened by frequent stops and starts, by long waits in unknown stations for unknown reasons, by Russian and German voices shouting back and forth in the darkness. Dense gray fog hooded the station lights and Russian soldiers in bulky greatcoats, machine guns slung over their shoulders, hardly more than silhouettes, paced heavily up and down the chill fog-shrouded platforms, past the compartment windows, close enough to touch. Common sense said there was no danger. Yet I was tense, unable to resist speculating whether anyone inside or outside the train knew who I really was, what I was really about. Perhaps I had read too much Eric Ambler. Shoulder and stomach muscles tightened and had to be coaxed to relax, though not convincingly until morning and the train reached the Allied sector of West Berlin. I shaved and dressed, annoyed at myself for the night's needless anxiety, and disembarked into Berlin, the Broadway and Forty-second Street of the clandestine Cold War.

For me the loneliest and most testing times revolved around penetration of Soviet airspace, parachuting agents into Russia from an unarmed, unmarked, four-engine, propeller-driven plane crewed by foreign nationals. Prior to our first overflight, professional airmen gave our plane little chance of getting past the Soviet radar screen — or of getting back out if it did slip through.

The initial clandestine air penetration was meant to drop intelligence agents into the Moscow area. Also, highly sophisticated electronic equipment, designed to gather information about Soviet radar defenses, was installed in the aircraft. On the morning of the scheduled night flight I listened very carefully as briefing experts laid out the disposition of Soviet fighter aircraft, the radar warning system as they then knew it, the weather forecast — all pertinent to the route the crew proposed to fly. Ironically, a major threat to the mission's success lay at its very end: early-morning ground fog that might make it impossible for the plane to find its home field. And, of course, a crash or a landing at an innocent airport would blow the mission.

The briefing ended and the room fell silent. The time had come for me to make the go or no-go decision. The experts had painted a realistic picture, not an encouraging one. I asked one of my colleagues if he had heard anything we had not already discussed. None, he said, except the prediction of morning fog. I sat quietly for a few moments, drawn within myself, "balanced all, brought all to mind," conscious that the room was absolutely still. We were in a high-risk, high-stakes business. The overflight had been prepared sensitively and meticulously. Nothing had been left to chance but chance itself. The ramifications were clear. By some mishap or through Soviet alertness, we could lose the crew and the agents, killed or captured. If I were one of them I would not want to be captured and introduced to the cellars of Lubyanka prison alongside the KGB headquarters in Moscow's Dzerzhinsky Square. Its gruesome history was too well known. The unmarked aircraft downed in the Soviet Union would create a major international word storm. None of these were last-moment thoughts; they simply kept repeating themselves, insistently. But you can rattle the dice next to your ear just so long. Then you lay them down quietly and walk away. Or you suck up your gut, roll them out across the table, and watch for the number that comes up. It seemed to me the moment had come to toss the dice.

"OK, we'll go," I said quietly. "And thank you, gentlemen, very much," I said to the briefing officers. They filed out of the room, their diagrams and maps and weather charts under arm. It was a sober moment.

During the night I was too tense for sleep. My imagination flung up a thousand possibilities, all disastrous. The scene inside the plane was vivid, a known experience; the inside of Lubyanka could be conjured up well enough, and the very thought of it made me shudder. From the terrace of our house I watched the false dawn and then the dawn came up and peered into the fog that hovered in the park trees trying to judge how soon it would begin to drift away. The silence of the sleeping house was shattered by a ringing phone, and I jumped at it before it woke Doreen. They had landed, a voice said. No problems. Not until I became conscious of my body loosening with relief did I realize how taut I had been. Reliving the mission in my mind's eye, I didn't hear Timmy until she came into the library carrying two cups of coffee.

"Is it all right now?" she asked. She knew nothing of the overflight of course, nor would she have dreamed of inquiring. Her intelligence, her sensitivity to our business, her common sense gave her all the equipment she needed as wife to a husband who could not tell her what he did all day. Or all night.

"Yes, it's OK now." I didn't know the crew, didn't know the agents. There was no need for me to know them personally —

basic rules of tradecraft proscribed it — yet I felt an intimate involvement with them, a close human connection. "Until next time," I added and smiled at myself for jumping so far ahead so fast. The nanny had Doreen dressed for school, and we all breakfasted together like any other family in the morning.

Over the next three years the crew repeated their initial success. Each time we followed the same preparatory procedures. Each time they flew a different route. At length one overflight provoked our first known Soviet reaction. En route home the plane's radio picked up a sudden burst of Russian orders to scramble fighters into the air, but they saw none. The Russians must have been wild with frustration at the vulnerability of their radar defense and their inability to track and intercept our plane.

In April 1954 I went to Washington and had lunch with Frank Wisner, the head of Covert Action, and Allen Dulles, who had succeeded General Walter Bedell Smith as director, at Wisner's home in Georgetown. We discussed a number of matters, but one issue I was most concerned about was the overflights. I said, in essence, that listening to briefing information and deciding to send or not to send a plane, I had no idea what Washington consideration, even at presidential level, should be factored in. I suppose I was looking for some reassurance that on the day and hour that I was in an operational briefing, making what seemed a lonely decision, the people in Washington would be synchronized with us and alert us in good time to scrub the mission for reasons unknown to us on the ground. This was probably an unnecessary point to make and reflected the timeless schism between field and headquarters, the differing perspectives that plague every field officer and sometimes cause him to wonder if the Washington types understand anything at all. In reality, they would of course signal to abort a tentatively scheduled flight if there were a political or other reason to do so. If this was a problem at all, it was soon overtaken.

During their final flight over the Soviet Union and coming out across Hungary our crew sighted two planes sent up to intercept them but eluded the fighters in cloud cover. Another mission would be pressing our luck too far. The Soviets were obviously becoming more adept. At our field operating level we said that's it, no more overflights. Invaluable information on the Soviet radar defense system had been recorded by the electronic equipment rigged in our aircraft and the crew had earned their pay and our admiration. The agents dropped into the Soviet Union faced a grimmer task and tremendous odds; their odds of eluding the most formidable security system in the world would be no better than fifty percent.

Such was the texture of the time that the KGB also reached into West Germany when the Soviet Central Committee authorized lethal action to be carried out by their Bureau of Special Tasks — kidnapping, murder, and assassination. A tacit understanding between Western and Soviet intelligence organizations held that their staff people would not be kidnapped or killed. But as far as the Soviets were concerned, this unspoken covenant did not include their own countrymen who were defectors, spoiled agents, or hostile émigrés. In the early fifties the Central Committee approved four assassinations that I know of within the Federal Republic. The targets were Russian émigré leaders. These "wet affairs," as they were called in Russian trade jargon, were the responsibility of the Ninth Section of the Second Directorate of the Soviet Ministry of the Interior.

On February 17, 1953, Captain Nikolai Evgenyevich Khokhlov entered West Germany through Switzerland. His mission was named Operation Rhine and its object was the murder of Gyorgi Okolovich, the Covert Operations Director of the Natsionalni Trudovi Soyez, the National Labor Alliance, an anti-Communist organization founded in the 1920s. They called themselves Solidarists, but by whatever name, the Soviets assumed that the NTS was supported by the CIA. NTS people had been infiltrated into the Soviet Union and, among other clandestine operations, their agents had successfully smuggled millions of anti-Communist propaganda pamphlets and leaflets into the barracks of Soviet troops in East Germany and Austria. Marking the leadership for assassination was a measure of NTS success and a measure of the Soviets' near paranoia about security.

Nikolai Khokhlov had been recruited by the *Spetsburo,* Special Tasks, in 1942. During World War II he organized the murder of Wilhelm Kube, the Nazi *Gauleiter* of Byelorussia. So neatly was the operation mounted and executed that young Khokhlov was rated a rising star, kept in the *Spetsburo,* and patiently prepared for future assignments, future wet affairs. He was sent to Rumania for four years to learn to live illegally, to become to all appearances a Rumanian. Thus his dress, manner, idiom, and local familiarity would support his cover when he was sent abroad documented as a Rumanian. For his 1953 mission Khokhlov was equipped with a Rumanian passport, a complete plan of Okolovich's apartment in Frankfurt and his office in Bad Homburg, a photograph of Okolovich and his wife, and a detailed outline of their normal daily routines. He was also supplied with a murder weapon disguised as a cigarette case. It contained three dumdum bullets poisoned with potassium cyanide, was silent, activated by a battery, and accurate at twenty-five feet.

In the early evening of February 17, Khokhlov knocked on the door of the Okolovich apartment in Frankfurt. The door was opened by Madame Okolovich. She said her husband was not at home. Khokhlov thanked her politely and said he would return later. Disquieted instinctively, Madame Okolovich made a nervous phone call to her husband. The apartment was staked out by the time Khokhlov returned. Immediately he declared that he had come not with the intention of killing Okolovich but to defect and to ask the Americans for asylum.

Khokhlov was a slight, blond, scholarly appearing young man of thirty-two. He wore rimless glasses and spoke gravely. He expressed himself well, answered questions adroitly, and pleaded that his wife Yania, also thirty-two, and their two-year-old son Aleksander be brought out of Moscow as quickly as possible. It was Yania, he said, who had convinced him to defect rather than to become an assassin. He claimed he would have sealed his own death warrant had he refused the assignment. Now he begged the Americans to save Yania and the child.

The phone in Khokhlov's Moscow flat was answered by his mother. "I know nothing," she said. "I do not want to speak with you." And she hung up.

In time it became clear why Khokhlov had arrived in Germany so brilliantly briefed. One of the most highly regarded instructors at the secret NTS agent training school was Nikita Khorunsky. He was also a Soviet KGB agent. Betrayed by one of his couriers carrying information to the KGB headquarters in Karlshorst, Khorunsky was arrested, imprisoned, and eventually returned to Russia in an exchange of spies. The NTS agent training center where Khorunsky had been an excellent instructor and a productive Soviet spy was in Bad Homburg, a quaint town that looks like a charming photograph found in your grandmother's attic. Innocent and sinister people inhabited the same turf, passed through the same revolving doors, traded at the same fish market.

In that same time, an assassination attempt on NTS President Poremsky failed, but his deputy, Alexander Truchnovich, was kidnapped from West Berlin. And one of Khokhlov's fellow members of the Bureau of Special Tasks, Bogdan Stashinsky, murdered Dr. Lev Rebet and returned to kill Stefan Bandera, a Ukrainian émigré leader. Both were killed in Munich: Rebet on the steps of the office of an émigré newspaper, *Ukrainski samostnik;* Bandera at the front door of his apartment in Zeppelin Strasse. Both were killed in the same manner: a phial containing 5 cc of hydrocyanic acid fired into the victims' faces from a gas pistol. Finding no sign of injury, no trace of poisoning, pathologists concluded that both deaths were from natural causes. And so it rested until 1969 when Stashinsky, like Khokhlov before him, defected to West Germany and told his story. A West German court sentenced him to prison for eight years.

On the other side, the CIA had no assassination brief and no capability. From a purely pragmatic operational point of view, an assassination is an immensely difficult act to bring off, and it accomplishes absolutely nothing. So the subject was not only not discussed; it did not even enter our thinking. Quite simply it was something their system permitted and ours did not. Our overriding concern was to keep our own people alive.

Eisenhower had campaigned on a promise to liberate Eastern Europe, and the task of supporting Eastern European resistance movements to that end fell to the CIA's Covert Action element. But the Eisenhower promise fostered an impossible dream of resistance armies and paramilitary liberation. The Soviets watched, infiltrated, gathered all they had to know, and, during the Christmas season of 1953, they simply wiped out first the Polish resistance, then the others. World War II–type paramilitary resistance movements simply were not on for Eastern Europe. There were very realistic limits to what could be accomplished by the CIA or any other instrument of the government, and it was incumbent upon the operators to advise the policymakers which policies wouldn't work. Even if underground movements had succeeded in gaining enough strength in numbers and arms to rise up, what armies of the West would intervene to ensure their success? None. None could lift a hand on the seventeenth of June 1953 when the East Germans rose up spontaneously and the Soviets moved two hundred tanks and twenty-five thousand troops into East Berlin to crush them; none stirred three years later in Hungary when stone-throwers were mashed under Soviet tanks and bottle-throwers cut down by submachine guns. Western military intervention would have provoked the major war that every rational person in the world wanted desperately to avoid.

On the positive side, our own Political Action people performed skillfully and effectively. Classical espionage worked quietly and well; its first priority remained early warning of a Soviet attack. And in one of the great intelligence coups of the era, a tunnel dug from the Western to the Eastern sector of Berlin tapped the main Soviet telephone lines from their Army headquarters in Karlshorst to Moscow, and Soviet military conversations were monitored for months, yielding valuable information before a sinking road surface gave away the tunnel.

Social life tended to limit itself to one's own breed. Most entertaining was done in private houses, giving dinner parties for one another, welcoming a new arrival, saying good-bye to a colleague moving elsewhere in the world, hosting foreign counterparts or visitors from Washington. On such occasions one could relax the guard that instinctively dropped into place when one was among non-CIA people, and talk shop. One night the fey wife of our Political Action chief stood apart from clusters of CIA men and women drinking cocktails and chatting, and gazed pensively through a picture window of her apartment, watching the running lights of Rhine barges floating past on the strong night current of the river towards Amsterdam and the sea. Perhaps to herself, she said softly, "I wonder what people in the real world are doing tonight." It was a rhetorical question of course, posed half in jest with a half smile. But it spoke of the isolation imposed by a clandestine profession, more trying for wives who shared little of substance of their husbands' work, and thus bore the limitations without the involvement, the penalty without the reward of achievement.

This communal closeness sometimes tempted organizational incest. Inevitably some husbands and wives were attracted to others than their own. More than one distraught wife sought Timmy's counsel. She would tell me and I would talk privately with the husband, striking a position somewhere between a worldly priest and a sympathetic brother, treading gently around private lives, mindful that professional considerations did not cause me to intrude too deeply in a colleague's purely private affair. It was a different matter, of course, when a man or woman became involved outside the circle. Then security considerations could be sensitive. One case involved a man, a first-rate professional and Russian linguist, who was assigned to interrogate an attractive woman defector. He fell in love with her and confessed it to his wife. His head understood that it was an affair that could not be, but his heart was gone. And of course, so was he.

Hopefully the officer and his wife regained their balance once back in a normal environment, free of the narrow lanes through which the clandestine world twists. On the other hand two close colleagues of mine — one an administrator, one a propagandist — divorced the wives they had brought with them, married local women, and, as far as I know, lived happily ever after.

Our own personal life in Germany was exceedingly pleasant. The village where we lived clung to a medieval castle and was physically untouched by the war. Ours was a spacious neo-Tudor house set in well-landscaped grounds looking out on a meticulously tended park. Overweight ladies and liverish gentlemen drank sulfurous waters and strolled along well-groomed footpaths that wandered among old trees and around a shallow lake in which floated graceful swans. For us, it was an uncommonly agreeable place in which to live a dual life. There

Timmy entertained with gracious good taste — diplomats and correspondents, indigenous and transient friends, and a stream of CIA colleagues. We listened to opera in Berlin and Munich and attended the Salzburg Music Festival. On holidays we drove to Spain or Switzerland or France. In Spain the Duchess of Valencia invited us to her castle in the ancient walled city of Avila. Avila rises dramatically out of the Spanish plain; the eighty-six towers that reach up from its walls have scanned the surrounding country since the twelfth century. Often we visited Irwin and Marion Shaw in Klosters, where Irwin taught me to ski in his Sherman tank style, and once Doreen unwittingly gave measles to the entire village. Doreen, at three-and-a-half, had made the quickest adjustment to Germany. Her German was native-fluent by the time her sister was born at 3:30 A.M. on April 11, 1952. The *kindermädchen* called the new baby Mäuslein and she was Mouse until she grew up, went to the Sorbonne in Paris, and took her proper name, Michele. On a holiday in Spain Timmy succumbed to nausea, which she attributed to the olive oil on everything we ate. We drove back to France, and in Paris she saw a doctor who thought she had a touch of amoebic dysentery and put her on a diet of dry toast and tea. But another in Munich said, "No, good lady; you are hungry and you are pregnant." That was to be our son, Peter.

It was in 1954 and the time was closing in. I knew that I could not spend a lifetime in government service, much as the work in CIA was absorbing and, it seemed, meaningful. I enjoyed the responsibility and authority and serving abroad carried attractive perquisites — house, servants, car. But I did not fancy the inevitable return to duty tours in Washington and a lower living standard. A number of my colleagues, people whose friendship and companionship we most enjoyed, were men and women of private means. I lived on a salary. At the highest level government pay presented a modest financial ceiling, and I wanted us to be able to carry on the gracious style of living we had known. I could do that only by going out into the commercial world. From what I had done thus far with my life I knew that my head worked reasonably well and that my body generated an abundance of energy. I was confident that, within reason, I could learn anything I had to learn and make a living in a conventional way.

There were second- and third-level reasons as well, although they were not plain and easily defined. I had begun to sense myself swirling like water in a funnel, being drawn inexorably down into the spout where I would lose sight of the real world, and I became wary of abandoning my entire life to the underground province of clandestine service. Then, too, somewhere near the core of me, I noticed the beginnings of tiredness — not physical or mental tiredness but rather a surfeit of war. The hot war had made off with nearly four years of my life and the Cold War another five. Actively contesting against one hostile force or another began to pall, and I felt vaguely that I might like to switch to a trade where I would be doing something for rather than something against; the thought was no clearer than that but it supported decision to leave.

We sailed from Bremerhaven on the SS *United States,* Doreen and Mousie in hand, Peter taking shape inside his mother. The captain was concerned that our son might be born at sea. The February North Atlantic was mean. Sitting in a deckchair, my legs wrapped in a rug, reading, sipping bouillon, I was only half aware that the other deckchairs were emptying and finally that I was alone. I watched the deck slant up and down as the ship rolled heavily from side to side, fascinated by the steepness of the angle. I smiled a smug inner smile, patronizingly sorry for those who suffered seasickness, the land-bound creatures who had never experienced the pitch and roll of a torpedo boat in the Tyrrhenian Sea. I made my way to our cabin, whistling, lurching down the companionway. Timmy and the children were dressing for dinner. Somewhere between shaving and showering and toweling down, the sin of smugness struck, humiliating me with a treacherous attack of mal de mer.

"Why don't you and the children go along to dinner, dear? I'll just stretch out for a bit." The ladies kissed me sympathetically, skipped blithely off to dinner, and left the old seadog groaning in his bunk.

# The Greatest
# Show on Earth

# 9

JOHN RINGLING NORTH suggested we meet for lunch at "21." That surprised me. I had never known him to get out of bed before six in the evening, unless he hadn't gone to bed at all the night before. Short, paunchy, and impeccably groomed, he sat at the corner table in the bar, just to the left as you come in, drinking a bourbon old fashioned with strawberries and stacks of pineapple floating in it. We had a drink or two, ate lunch, and talked, drank, and talked through the afternoon, through the comings and goings of the cocktail hour, through dinner and the after-theatre crowd. By three o'clock in the morning we were alone. The chairs had been set on the tables, their legs pointing to the ceiling, and a single work-light burned over the bar. Letting us out, a sour night watchman was unmoved by John's jubilant announcement: "This is my new boss." In empty Fifty-second Street we shook hands. I had joined the Circus. To celebrate our new business relationship we walked up Fifth Avenue to Fifty-eighth Street and had breakfast at Reuben's: scrambled eggs, Canadian bacon, rye toast, and bourbon whiskey.

Johnny's proposal had been very seductive. *He* had no wife, no children; he could think of no reason why *my* children shouldn't be beneficiaries of some share of his wealth — real estate in Florida, oil wells in Oklahoma, and the Ringling Brothers Barnum & Bailey Circus. Someone he could trust implicitly was needed to look after these several interests while he, at age fifty-two, repaired to the south of France to embellish his well-established reputation as a bon vivant and epicure.

"You're our brother. And you've got to earn a living somewhere."

"Without question. I need a job." Since I had no middle name, he urged me to add the name Bailey so the names Ringling and Bailey would be perpetuated with the Circus. I don't know why he didn't suggest Barnum; perhaps Michael Bailey Burke had a better ring to it. When I protested that I hadn't a clue how to run a circus, Johnny laughed and said, "You've been training for it all your life. You just haven't known it." I had also hesitated to accept until I knew that his brother Henry didn't covet running the Circus himself. The last thing I wanted to do was to cut across a friend's bow, but Henry was still bent on being the youngest retired person in America. "You know Henry doesn't want to work." John's attitude towards his younger brother was very benign.

Timmy had misgivings. She liked the Norths very much. In Rome, Paris, Baden-Baden, we had enjoyed gay times together with them, and Henry had stayed with us on a long visit to Bad Homburg. But she was apprehensive about my being carried off for extended periods of time, running away with the Circus. I, on the other hand, believed that the Circus would be only a part-time job. In any event, I had made the decision to accept Johnny North's proposal because it seemed to me the wisest thing to do. The Circus held out the kind of life that excited me. I did not want to be an observer; I wanted to be in the game, whatever it was. Nor would I have done well in work that seemed, in my terms, prosaic or commonplace. I was not well suited to be a *rond-de-cuir*, as the French say, a leather-ass, forever seated at a desk. My high energy level needed to be physically as well as mentally engaged. Just as important, I wanted to be in a business of people rather than things. I knew little of money or merchandise. I had learned something about people and my own capacity to treat with them.

So Timmy went along uncertainly but without opposition. Perhaps, as Faith had when I had determined to go off to war, Timmy read a mind made up. Not that I was insensitive to her feelings. Rather, I accepted without question my responsibility to support my family and it followed that I must decide how best to do it. She chose Washington as a base because she had more friends there than elsewhere, and we rented a rather dramatic house in Georgetown. Doreen entered her third school in her third country; Mouse entertained her new pre-school playmates with German nursery songs; and Peter would soon be born.

I first saw the Ringling Brothers Barnum & Bailey Circus under a blue sky and brilliant February sun. It was spread over the two-hundred-acre Winter Quarters and in the full sway of rehearsal for its new season, all color and movement and unlike anything on earth. I walked the grounds picking up its electric theatricality, thrilled by its rich sweat and muscle: fragments of different languages, splashes of color, the new sounds of a snapping whip, a bear's growl, a tiger pissing straight back, splattering a wall. I decided at once I was going to like this.

My first Circus days were a jumble of visual impressions. In the sail loft Leif Osmundsen stitched the final panels into the Big Top; every year he fashioned a new one from 26,000 square yards of canvas. Trevor Bale rehearsed his Bengal tigers. Hugo Schmidt trained fifty-five elephants. Doc Henderson tended a hundred horses. Barbette, a former wire walker and female impersonator, drilled athletic girls to perform an aerial ballet on the webs, lines that hung from the rigging circling the tanbark like thick streamers. Blacksmiths hammered, and harness makers measured animals for new fittings. Max Weldy, the natty former Parisian couturier, directed an army of seamstresses who sewed tens of thousands of spangles onto two thousand costumes, executing sketches of Marcel Vertès, the French artist who had designed the show. Originally Vertès wanted raffia skirts for the elephants in a jungle number but had to be discouraged. Elephants are mad for raffia and would have eaten themselves naked. The Barstows, Richard and Edie, staged the elaborate spectaculars — one for Madison Square Garden and one for the show under canvas. Pat Valdo, who had been a clown in John Ringling's Circus, was now the distinguished, gentlemanly director of performance.

The dainty, beautiful Spanish aerialist, Pinito del Oro, practiced her heel slide on the high trapeze. The Great Alzano walked the wire as casually as most of us walk to the corner news stand. The Palacios from Mexico flew from one to the other on their flying trapezes. Alex Konyat and two elegant-looking girls — Marian was American, Nadia was French — put handsomely groomed horses through their dressage routines. Unus balanced himself on one finger atop a glass globe. José Tomás wrestled playfully with Gargantua II and Melle Toto inside cages most visitors could not approach without a tinge of fear. Tumblers tumbled, jugglers juggled and clowns were busy inventing new routines.

There was nothing new to be added to hobo clowns Emmett Kelly and Otto Griebling. They needed only to pull on their ragged clothes and paint on their sad faces to evoke sympathy and compassion. Emmett was the only clown ever to be given star billing with the Circus. Pathos was the essence of his sad-faced Weary Willie, losing endlessly at his endless game of so-litaire, his plaintive gaze sharing with his audience a common understanding that life's deck is stacked against us, or patiently sweeping a round spot of light into a diminishing circle, then flicking it out with a last triumphant flourish of his worn broom, the small satisfying victory we all seek and need.

English was the lingua franca, accented more often than not by Spanish, German, Hungarian, Italian, French, Polish, Schweizer Teutsch. Costume-fitting instructions were printed in four languages — English, German, Italian, and French. And add to the list of Circus tongues the vagrant patois of the roustabouts — the winos, derelicts, traveling men who ap-peared from nowhere, bore no name, worked a week, a month, a season, and disappeared again into the limbo of the lost.

On a railroad siding at one end of the Winter Quarters the silver Circus train, scrubbed and polished, a freshly painted Ringling red stripe running its full eighty-car length, glistened in the sun waiting to carry us all to New York for the annual spring opening at Madison Square Garden.

A trio of old Circus hands ruled from the top. Each year's show was conceived, designed, and staged by others, but once the Circus was on the road, everyone worked for them. They moved the show. McClosky, the general manager, was the boss — tough, beefy, always dressed in a baggy blue suit. He drove a Cadillac, and the wad of bills bulging in his trousers pocket like a fist was disproportionate to his modest $15,000 annual salary. Lawson, the manager, and Kirnan, the assistant man-ager, were his legmen. They had no authority and no specific function. Kirnan was also known as Forbes; I never discovered why.

At night, trying to bring the pieces into some cohesive whole, I diagrammed on a piece of foolscap what appeared to me to be the Circus's organizational structure. Lines from all the department heads led directly to McClosky: the canvas department raised and struck the tents; the property department rigged the Big Top and moved the props in and out for each act; the seat department rolled the seat wagons into place side-by-side in a huge oval; the train department loaded the show onto the eighty-car Circus train; the ticket department sold tickets from ticket wagons lined across the entrance to the midway; the sideshow, the cookhouse, the menagerie, and the publicity departments. It made no organizational sense, yet worked with unfailing precision. The Circus had no organizational chart, no functional statements, no job descriptions. Like Topsy, it just grew from the small wagon show created by the five original Ringling brothers into the huge Ringling Brothers Barnum and Bailey Circus Combined Shows Inc. It was a kind of ballet choreographed almost a century before, the choreography passed on by word of mouth, generation to generation. Variations were rare; tractors replaced horses, metal seat wagons replaced wooden bleachers — that's about all. A cadre of old pros, lifelong circus people, knew what to do, how to do it, when to do it. The train master, iron-haired, red-faced, unbending as a spike, loaded and unloaded the train under the lash of his Irish tongue. The boss canvas man, tough as harness leather, silent as stone, raised and struck the tent. His crews drove the long thick tent stakes, set out in the Big Top's oval shape, then, like a tug-of-war team, hauled the mammoth canvas aloft and secured the guy ropes. He spoke to no one but his men from the beginning of the season to its end, and at the end he vanished as wordlessly as he had arrived, gone, it was said, to spend three sybaritic months and his full season's pay with a beautiful young wife who waited for him. I would see him sitting, back resting against a bale of hay, silent, alone, and detached, and wondered if it was memory or anticipation that absorbed him. He needed no social traffic with the rest of us to fill out his life.

Lloyd Morgan, the lot superintendent, traveled with the first of the train's three sections, the section that carried the cookhouse — tent and equipment — the commissary, laundry, blacksmith, harness maker, menagerie, animal men, grooms and hostlers, some trucks and tractors, stake-driving machines, ticket wagons, and the sideshow tent. Morgan laid out the lot, decided where the Big Top would go, where the cookhouse, where the animal wagons. His beer-barrel belly and apple face promised a jolly man, but he was surprisingly somber.

The heavy end of the Circus was carried in the train's second section: the Big Top, wardrobe tent, pole wagons, ticket sellers and ushers, elephants. Last to leave and last to arrive at the next town, the third section, drawn by a third engine, brought along the performers, seat wagons, costumes. At the very end of the third section rode the *Jomar,* a private car built for John Ringling and his wife Mabel in 1910, a time when America's financial barons traveled by sea in their private yachts and by land in their private railroad cars. Johnny North had its interior modernized in the late thirties, but riding as the last car, the brass railings of its observation platform shining in the sun, the *Jomar,* and the whole passing Circus train, looked like a visitor from that earlier era. The *Jomar* was my new home.

Emily Dickinson wrote: "Friday I tasted life. It was a vast morsel. A circus passed the house." I had been handed this Circus to run, this vast morsel, given this new taste of life. I was standing in the shoes of Phineas T. Barnum and of John Ringling. I was standing in as surrogate for Johnny North, and was not quite sure what that meant. I had no clear conception of what specifically I was expected to do, but clearly I was excited, eager, elated, and too green to comprehend the Circus at a glance. As a schoolboy guest of the University of Pennsylvania I had stood in an empty Franklin Field imagining the cheering crowds, conjuring up football heroics yet to come, and knew unhesitatingly that it was the place for me. And when I wandered through the Winter Quarters on that first day the same gut feeling took hold. I was too ignorant of its complexities, too carried away by its unreality, to be hung up by doubt. Whether or not I was a fool to rush in I wouldn't know until I tried. But neither had I known that I could play top-flight college football, be a *maquisard* in France, organize an incipient revolution, or run covert operations successfully against the Soviets. So I wasted no time wringing my hands. Nor did I delude myself that it wasn't going to be tough. I accepted that fact going in, but I felt I had acquired enough savvy, enough flexibility, and enough toughness of my own to be reasonably confident I could cope.

For eight lion cubs, for twenty-two baby elephants and for me, this eighty-fifth Circus season would be our first. For Ruth, the grande dame of the elephant herd, it would be perhaps her sixtieth. No one could say precisely when she had been a First of May, as those in their initial circus season were called.

It was something of a jolt when I discovered just how difficult my job was: the Circus was one million dollars in debt, a deep hole for a business that *grossed* only six million dollars a year, and for seasons immediately past it had made substantial losses. Income from the sale of the motion picture rights to *The Greatest Show on Earth* kept the show afloat, barely. I was curious that Johnny North had not mentioned this. In contrast to the expectant air and lusty action across the palm-fringed Winter Quarters, the plain one-story frame business office was as gray and dull as a file cabinet. It was there, after I had been in Florida for a few days, that I discovered our plight. In response to my question, the chief accountant said that we had about three thousand dollars in the Circus checking account.

"What about the other accounts?"

"What other accounts?"

"Where you keep the main money?"

"There's only one account." He was slyly enjoying my bewilderment.

"Are you telling me that Ringling Brothers Barnum & Bailey has three thousand dollars to its name?"

"Yes."

"Do we have any trade bills? Do we owe anybody?"

"Everybody."

"How much?"

"I think about $250,000." On closer examination it turned out that we owed four times his estimate.

Workmen were working, performers were rehearsing, a hundred horses and fifty-five elephants were eating tons of hay, and the wild animals roared for meat. The Circus was scheduled to leave Sarasota in twenty-eight days on its traditional train journey to New York and its Madison Square Garden opening. I drove across the short causeway onto Bird Key, where Johnny North was staying with his mother in her big airy white house secluded among ten acres of palms and surrounded by water.

"What do I do now?" I asked.

"That's why I hired you, El Burkello. You're a resourceful fellow." He grinned his most engaging grin and I had to laugh. My predicament was too ironic not to be laughed at. No one had to paint me a picture. It was clear enough that the Circus was in deep financial trouble. Wordlessly, my involvement in North's Oklahoma oil and Florida real estate interests had been swept off the table. My first and only chore was to determine whether the Circus could be salvaged.

The $100,000 NBC fee for televising our Garden dress rehearsal would cover our most pressing trade bills — but the railroad would not move the Circus train unless we paid them up front, like any passenger buying a ticket. In order to get the show to New York we borrowed $40,000 from Madison Square Garden against our advance ticket sale. I moved on to the *Jomar* and prepared to travel.

On opening night in New York, a benefit for the Police Athletic League, Marilyn Monroe rode a pink elephant and I hurried to Washington to be with Timmy at Peter's birth. When I returned, the Garden had some stiff news for us. General Kilpatrick, the Garden president, and Ned Irish, who ran it for him, informed us that next season's rent would be raised to $10,000 a day for a four wall lease, up from $6,000. The Circus was to pay for everything and everybody else, plus an extra $200 a day if we asked for the air conditioning to be turned on. Their terms appeared harsh, and Irish was unyielding. The Circus had played nowhere in New York except the Garden, going back to April 1874, when Phineas T. Barnum opened his MONSTER CLASSICAL AND GEOGRAPHICAL HIPPODROME on the northeast corner of Madison Square in the converted railroad shed where the New York and Harlem Railroad had stabled its horses and collected its freight. A change of venue would be a severe break with tradition, but we had to reject Irish's demands. They seemed exorbitant. Since I was forced to think of an alternative, one solution seemed so obvious I wondered why it hadn't been tried before: pitch the Big Top in Central Park. How wonderful for city kids to see a circus under canvas! Neither the mayor nor the governor was foolhardy enough to arrange an introduction to the crusty parks commissioner, Robert Moses, but a lawyer friend did. Had I

not left his office swiftly under my own power, Moses would
have thrown me out through the window, so little enthralled
was he with the prospect of Central Park being defiled by a
circus. I remained convinced that it would have been a charming New York experience, but Mr. Moses did not suffer foolish
notions gladly. Horace Stoneham was more genial by far. He
owned the New York Giants football team then, and I asked
him if we could put the Circus in the Polo Grounds. In his
lemon-yellow Cadillac convertible we drove up through Central
Park, through Harlem to the ball park on Coogan's Bluff.

"Do you really want to play here, or is this a ploy in your
negotiations with the Garden?" His wry, squinty smile told me
he knew the answer.

"It's a ploy." Horace fell into the game enthusiastically for
the sheer fun of it. Newspapers published our photographs
standing at second base, accompanied by engineers from the
Kaiser Aluminum Company, pointing at an imagined aluminum canopy stretching from one grandstand roof to another,
covering the entire infield. It was impractical, provided brief
diversion, and did not for a moment fake Irish out of position.
We accepted his terms for 1956, outrageous as we thought
them at the time.

The Circus moved on to the Boston Garden for a week and
then went under canvas: Baltimore, Washington, and other
regular-route cities. We would not play in a building again until
we reached the Cow Palace in San Francisco in September. On
the road, under the Big Top, I learned the circus business. At
times, too, I allowed myself to slip into a solitary vagabond role,
alone and unlonely, adrift in a world apart. Rolling and rattling
across America from one city to the next, I often stood on the
*Jomar*'s observation platform and watched the Mississippi flow
along beside me in the night, gazed on the great still Western
plains, pale and endless in the moonlight, was enthralled by
sunrise stroking the Colorado canyons rose and red. It was
inescapably romantic to be sliding through the night on a circus
train loaded with six hundred circus animals and eight
hundred circus people. The Circus, someone said, was "a
bright spangled girl with a date in another town a hundred
miles away tomorrow morning." But I was traveling with her to
our date in the next town.

Living on the *Jomar* was comfortable and gracious. From its observation platform you entered an Art Deco sitting room that spanned the car's width and ran twice as deep. From there a passageway ran forward along one side leading to a suite of three bedrooms and two baths. Forward again, the dining room was as wide as the car, and at the very front end were the galley and accommodations for the French chef, Marcel. In an odd way it pleased me to be the first non-Ringling resident.

Very quickly I became accustomed to the train's erratic motion and slept soundly through the jolting about in marshaling yards, metal clanging on metal. My children were entranced by it. Peter first joined out in Chicago when he was three months old. The temperature was 102°. The Big Top was pitched in Soldiers Field. Inside the tent was a purgatory. Parents dissolved in the heat and wondered if some sacrifices made for their children were too great. I listened to the rising heat roar through the vents at the top of the tent, sounding like a blast furnace, and took my children swimming in Lake Michigan. I was learning.

Long before the show reached Chicago I had learned about the Sneeze Mob. The Sneeze was Circus argot for the men who controlled the rackets on the show: dice, whiskey, beer. Johnny North had said the rackets should be cleaned up. He didn't tell me that our general manager was the Chief Sneeze.

I had no problems with McClosky at the very outset. No doubt he saw me as a friend of the North family, a wartime buddy of Henry's, and assumed that my presence around the Circus was a sinecure of some kind, a convenient way to take care of a pal whose true role was drinking companion to Johnny North. He didn't expect to see much of me around the show. When it became clear that I had come to work, his attitude changed from indifferent to guardedly hostile. I called all the department heads together to tell them that the Circus was close to bankruptcy and that we'd all have to give it our best shot to stay in business. Dave Blanchard, a rough cob who ran the truck department, had been primed by McClosky to ridicule me as a know-nothing First of May. The meeting was short, futile, and a dumb idea. It was also our last meeting. The lines were drawn.

I got lucky early on. Toto became my driver and my friend.

He was a very tall, gangling young black with arms that hung almost to his knees, or maybe it just seemed so because his hands were so huge. He looked worried, a little frightened, his big voice low. "Yuh be careful, heah? Stay out o' the Big Top."

"Why?"

"Th' Sneeze'll git yuh." The grapevine had picked up the message.

"What are you talking about?"

"Drop a san'bag on yuh haid. Drop a pole."

"Who's going to?"

"The Sneeze." I told him I'd be all right. "Yuh be careful, heah?"

It seemed too melodramatic to take seriously, but in the mid-fifties a Southern black's fear of private law was understandable. The times were leading up to the trauma of Selma, Alabama. Actually I took care to spend more time in and around the Big Top than I might have. I wanted to make sure the Sneeze Mob knew that they couldn't intimidate me physically. Even so, not being entirely foolhardy, I kept alert, my body gathered to move quickly if a pole toppled or a sandbag fell. From Toto and others I pieced together the Sneeze Mob's private schemes.

A number of people were allowed to bilk the show as long as they paid the Sneeze for their bilking privileges. The Circus operated as it did when the five Ringling brothers were handling their own money. Now it was other people who handled the Circus's money. The advance men paid for hay, bread, fish, butter, spaghetti, everything, in cash. The truck boss decided when, where, and how many huge, expensive tires needed replacing and paid cash. Receipts were a joke. The menagerie superintendent bought the horsemeat for the wild animals; by a curious coincidence he was also the fellow who *sold* the horsemeat. The Sneeze directly controlled the dice, whiskey, and beer rackets, forbidden by show policy and the law. When the Circus train left Sarasota you couldn't find an extra bit of space to store a lady's hatbox. But in Philadelphia in May, Hamburger Jack, the head porter, had taken aboard fifteen hundred cases of beer, I learned. Beer was sold to the captive people on the Circus train at a five hundred percent profit. The dice and whiskey systems were tied into ushers and ticket

exchanges. The price of a seat at one end of the Circus tent —
in the blues — was one dollar. Once inside, if the customer
wanted a better location, he could go to an exchange booth on
the tanbark in front of the blue seats, get credit for his one
dollar ticket and buy a seat priced at two or three dollars. That
was the official procedure; that money came to the show. There
was also an unofficial procedure. Ushers working the blue areas
would induce people to move, and then they would share the
money paid with the ushers seating the unticketed movers. No
usher got one of these lucrative posts without the approval of
the Sneeze, and approval came only with the implicit understanding that the candidate shoot crap and buy his whiskey in
the prop tent. There the Sneeze relieved him of his take. Dice
games in the property tent and alongside the trains standing at
the crossings were worth assigning a professional, and Jimmy
Blue Eyes, the Miami gambler, attached one of his men to us. I
found we were transporting and feeding him as though he
were one of our own. A new phase of my relationship with
McClosky started with a simple comment.

"Get the gambler off the lot, Frank."

"What gambler?" Frank dummied up.

"This is not a discussion. I want him off the show." McClosky
did nothing, and I let the word out through the Circus grapevine, swift as Indian drums, that I wanted to see Jimmy Blue
Eyes' man. He found me standing in the midway near the entrance to the Big Top before a matinee performance.

"You're looking for me."

"Get your ass off the show," I said. He assumed the air of a
man being patient with a minor nuisance.

"Jimmy Blue Eyes wouldn't like it," he said as though that
would close the subject.

"Fuck him."

The gambler sidled close to me, like a Miami Beach Iago.
"People see us talking. They'll think you're in on the take."

"Not if they never see you again," I told him. "Let me make
it simple for you. Fuck off!" I shouted so loudly and gestured
so broadly that no one within sight or sound could mistake the
point. I never saw him again. Maybe McClosky told him it
would be better if he left, at least until the Sneeze had got rid
of me.

Michael and Bridget Fleming, my grandparents, on their twenty-fifth
wedding anniversary, Suffield, Connecticut

My mother, Mary Fleming, in black — the femme fatale of Suffield, Connecticut

Patrick and Mary Burke, my parents, after Sunday brunch, which always started with whiskey sours (*Michael Burke*)

With my father, the
young lawyer, on the
street where we lived in
Enfield, Connecticut

My father with my
brother, Robert, who
joshed him about his
"rocking chair" golf swing
and always made him
laugh

Wow (W. O. Williams) and the Duke, George R. H. Nicholson, my headmaster, at Kingswood School (*Photo courtesy of Kingswood-Oxford School*)

Myself on Franklin Field. At the University of Pennsylvania we called this the "*New York Times* pose."

Faith and I shortly after we were married

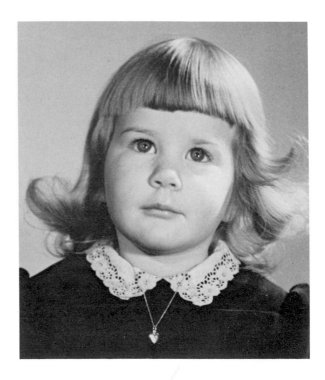

Patricia, my first child

Henry Ringling North and I in Paris, November 1944. After a champagne lunch with Hemingway I borrowed a uniform jacket from Henry, and we recorded our wartime beards for posterity.

Gary Cooper and Lilli Palmer came to a lunch at Warner Brothers and watched the U.S. Navy put a medal on a uniform supplied me by the costume department. *(U.S. Navy photo)*

With Gary Cooper and Robert Coote in a scene from the film *Cloak and Dagger.* The entire sequence — and my film career — wound up on the cutting-room floor. (© *Richard Feiner and Company, Inc.*)

Timmy Campbell on the steps of her Beverly Hills house
shortly before we were married, wearing my grandmother
Brigid Burke's wedding ring

Doreen and I on the
rooftop garden of our villa
when I was a deep cover
CIA agent. I think the
beret and jacket were left
over from my days as a
*maquisard* in France.
*(Timmy Burke)*

On a holiday in
Capri in 1950 during
a break from
clandestine life
(*Timmy Burke*)

Timmy in Greece,
1950 (*Michael Burke*)

Timmy and Doreen
in Baden-Baden,
1952, on a weekend
respite from the Cold
War (*Michael Burke*)

My CIA career is closed out with a medal from Allen Dulles, director of the Central Intelligence Agency.

1955. Ringling Brothers Barnum & Bailey Circus Winter Quarters in Sarasota, Florida. The eight-month-old lion cub was not talking to reporters that day, so I spoke for him. A few moments later he lacerated the arm of his keeper with one swipe of a paw.

Under the Big Top, Washington, D.C., 1955, with the famous clown
Emmett Kelly and Vice President Richard Nixon. Tricia Nixon is a bit
uncertain about the advantages of a front-row seat.

Doreen and Mouse became New Yorkers again in 1956 and happily.
(*Michael Burke*)

Peter, Mouse, and Doreen swimming in the sea below our villa in Saint-Jean-Cap-Ferrat, France, summer of 1958 (*Michael Burke*)

Timmy and Mousie in
front of a chalet we had in
Gstaad, Switzerland,
Christmas, 1959
(*Michael Burke*)

Doreen feeding her horse,
Kinvara, at the stable in
Fawley Green in the
Chiltern Hills, Berkshire,
England, 1960
(*Michael Burke*)

Peter on his pony, JP, behind Cheers Orchard, the Elizabethan country house we rented during our years in England (*Michael Burke*)

Timmy and I in Tanganyika (now Tanzania) during our first African
excursion, south of the Sahara, 1960

More brazen was the printing of duplicate tickets. After a time my eye grew quite good at estimating the house, and from time to time, when the final night's figure was tallied by the treasurer in the ticket wagon and was reported to me, I was surprised at how much I had overestimated. I was puzzled until the night I saw the first two rows around the tent fully occupied and, on a hunch, went to the ticket wagon and checked the racks. Our official tickets were still there, unbroken. McClosky and I had another talk beside the horse tent.

"Frank, money is running down a hundred rat holes. You know them all better than I do. If it doesn't stop, this show just ain't going to finish the season. If it weren't for the million dollars from the de Mille film, we'd be in the barn now." It was by way of final warning. Nothing changed. I phoned Johnny North in New York and said I thought we should fire the three top managers, and I would assume the general manager's job myself. It was a desperation move. Johnny agreed to come to Chicago and talk about it and to meet with the three men. McClosky arrived at the Ambassador East Hotel drunk on whiskey that was to give him the courage to face up to North. Seating himself, he missed the chair and fell onto the floor, and his friends carried him out, too incoherent to talk. Johnny was disgusted and told me to get rid of them. It was plain that John North had no stomach for handling the messy affair himself. A generation earlier John Ringling had solicitously urged one of his general managers to take a midsummer holiday, to go fishing in Montana. Then Ringling sent him a telegram: Don't come back; you're fired. Apparently dealing by indirection with disagreeable situations was a family trait.

Chicago had melted attendance. Timmy and the children flew back east to spend some time with my parents at their home on Long Island Sound in Old Saybrook, Connecticut, and the Circus moved on to play Beloit, Madison, and La Crosse on Monday, Tuesday, and Wednesday and to St. Paul on Thursday, August 4, an eventful day. I told the Sneeze to meet me in the Red Wagon at 7:30, just as our evening performance started. It was a good house — about eight thousand, I guessed, one thousand short of capacity. As usual, three wild animal acts, one in each ring, opened the show. The Red Wagon, my office on the lot, had space enough for two small desks, one for a secretary, the bandleader's wife, and one for me. When McClosky, Lawson, and Kirnan piled in, it was crowded, but our meeting was short.

"You guys are fired. Through. I want you off the lot, off the train, gone before midnight." They laughed. The show would never make it to Minneapolis, tomorrow's town, they said. By morning I'd be begging them to come back. A First of May trying to run the Ringling Show! It was the best joke they had heard in years. They exited laughing. Well, that's done, I sighed, relieved, a fever broken. What now? I didn't have to wait long for the answer. Bobby Dover, the assistant performance director, came running from the tent looking desperate.

"Nobody's striking the animal cages!" he cried. "Nobody's in the prop tent!" We raced around the outside of the Big Top to the property tent in the backyard. Bob Reynolds, the boss, and his crew had evaporated into the night. A lone member who had not fled sat morosely on a bale of hay.

"Where's everybody, Blackie?" I asked him.

"Took off. Sneeze pulled 'em out."

A clown walk-around always followed the opening wild animal acts. During it, prop men normally dismantled the animal cages and set up the next act's props. At the moment Ringling Brothers Barnum & Bailey Circus was staging the longest clown walk-around in Circus history. Hoots and hollers and catcalls rose in volume. There was no alternative but for me to walk to the center ring and pick up the Ringmaster's public address microphone. "Ladies and gentlemen, could I have your attention for a moment, please. I have an unfortunate announcement to make. Due to circumstances beyond our control we will be unable to put on our show for you tonight. Permit me to offer our sincere apologies." A wave of boos and angry shouts cascaded down from the crowd, who were riled at having been bilked by Circus mountebanks, and it was not easy to get their attention again. "You can get your money back at the ticket wagons. Or your tickets will be good for tomorrow night's performance in Minneapolis. God willing." Grumbling and grousing they shuffled out, some holding their tickets for the following night, some forming lines at the ticket wagons. And, as it always seems to do in a moment of crisis in the outdoor show business, it began to rain. Performers drifted uncertainly back to the train. Bits and pieces of information gravitated to the empty Big Top, where Morgan, Blackie, and a knot of roustabouts collected near the unstruck tiger cage in the center ring.

When the Sneeze left the Red Wagon, each member had gone directly to a department head. Bob Reynolds was told to pull out his property men and did. David Blanchfield, head of the truck department, and Whitey Versteeg, the electrical boss, refused, not for any particular loyalty to me but because of an unbreakable loyalty to their own code. The show must go on. They might have been persuaded to defect before the performance started, or after it was over, but never during. Versteeg had been told to throw the lights, leaving seven thousand terrified people stranded in the dark, three animal trainers caged in darkness with lions, tigers, and bears. He had the good judgment to foresee criminal liability and refused to do so.

The Sneeze had won the first round. What to do now? Morgan, the lot superintendent, became manager on the spot, a kind of battlefield promotion. "Blackie," I said, "you are now head of the property department." He needed hands. We sent a message to the train asking for volunteers among male performers to help strike the rigging so we could move on across the Mississippi to Minneapolis.

Until that moment I had not fully appreciated how fiercely the performers resented the Sneeze Mob, their arrogance, their exploitation of the Greatest Show on Earth. Most of them were generations deep in European circus tradition. The capstone of a circus career was to make it to the Ringling show, the Big One. For them Ringling Brothers Barnum & Bailey Circus was an institution, not to be sucked dry but to be cherished as a historic form of entertainment at its most sophisticated level. Word flew along the train that I had fired the Sneeze Mob. Men hastened back to the lot and pitched in — flyers, wire walkers, jugglers, bareback riders. All had served their apprenticeship in small shows, had the skills to do what had to be done, and plunged in with fresh enthusiasm. The division within the Circus world disappeared and the Circus melded into one family body. Performers cared genuinely about their circus tradition and had an abiding respect for each other's skills. I appointed myself to the vacant post of general manager, and they carried me through the balance of the season. We played to capacity houses in Minneapolis during the following two days and thereafter with our makeshift arrangement, did not miss a single play-date.

The Sneeze must have sulked, but they were not idle. They found their way to Jimmy Hoffa, we learned, and would learn more. In Denver the grapevine signaled that a Teamster organizer, a man named Joe Karsh, would be looking for me. He could have been sent by Central Casting. It was not difficult to identify Joe Karsh through the door as he stood with two human gorillas on the observation platform of the *Jomar* and pressed the bell. I stepped out and closed the door behind me.

"What can I do for you gentlemen?"

"You Mike Burke?"

"I am."

"Joe Karsh." He was medium height, compact, solid. His hard, flattened features looked to be familiar with street fights. His complexion was dead and lifeless as a fallen leaf. His fists were square and looked hard. "Jimmy sent me to have a talk with you." He spoke the words roughly as though it would be embarrassing, a sign of softness, to pronounce a whole word, speak an ordinary sentence.

"Which Jimmy is that?" I asked, affecting innocence.

"Hoffa." He was not sure whether I was putting him on.

"Oh?" I switched to an expression of puzzlement. "*The* Jimmy Hoffa? What could he want?"

"Why don't we step inside and talk?"

"About what?"

"Let's go in."

"Why? I don't even know what's on your mind. You may be talking to the wrong guy."

"You're the right guy, all right."

"OK. What's the message?"

"Jimmy wants us to talk about a contract."

I laughed. "A Teamster contract with the Circus? We don't have to sit down to talk about that. In fact, we don't have anything at all to talk about." Karsh was turning from edginess to anger.

"What do you mean?"

"Just what I said. There's nothing to talk about. We don't want to be organized by the Teamsters. It's that simple."

"It ain't that simple. We gotta go inside and talk."

"Not necessary, Joe. We've had our talk." He blew up. The glowering gorillas on either side of him stood like inanimate objects.

"Lissen. I aint never been t' no Ivy League college or nuttin'. So don't give me none o' dat fancy talk. 'Re ya tellin' me t' go fuck myself?"

"Joe, I couldn't have phrased it more eloquently." If I had been Karsh, I would have thought Mike Burke every class of an arrogant shit.

"You'll hear from us!" he shouted, shaking his fist. He and his companions climbed down the steps onto the railbed and I watched them disappear around the bend in the tracks.

Later that day I heard of another visitation and another disappearance. Federal agents had come looking for Hamburger Jack. They had picked up the scent of his rolling unlicensed beer racket that broke interstate commerce laws every time the train crossed into a new state. Jack rolled himself over a fence and hid out in a lumberyard. At midnight as the train's first section pulled out, he crawled from beneath a pile of lumber and scrambled aboard a moving flatcar and, for the moment, eluded the law.

We trouped through Idaho, Utah, and Washington and played down the West Coast to San Francisco for a week's run at the Cow Palace. Our engagement ended on a Sunday night. Johnny North had joined us again and was staying at the St. Francis Hotel. We had made a date to meet for dinner at Trader Vic's at eight o'clock. At five, dressed for dinner in a shirt, tie, and a blue pinstripe suit, I was at the Cow Palace. So were about two thousand Teamsters and Longshoremen, *not* dressed in their Sunday clothes, massed at the gate just outside the high wire fence behind the arena, forming a human roadblock through which our trucks, tractors, and equipment would pass on their way to the railroad crossing. We had heard from Karsh. He had recruited additional muscle from the tough San Francisco Longshoremen's Union to plague our departure. Normally our first section loaded about six o'clock, just after the company had been fed and the cookhouse tent struck. In the backyard five or six trucks were lined up inside the gate. No one knew quite what to do, what to make of it. I went from one truck to the next, giving their drivers the same instruction:

roll up the windows of your cab; lock the doors; put the machine in gear. When the gate is opened, just go. Stop for nothing. They did, and the mob parted rather than be run down. Next in line were three or four open tractors. The only thing their drivers could be told was to plow through. They hadn't gone fifty yards before the drivers were pulled off their seats. My blood up, common sense lost in rage, I ran out the gate, slashed through the mob to the lead tractor, jumped up on its axle, and grabbed the driver's arm, pulling him behind me. "Get your ass back in that seat," I shouted, and yelled back at the other drivers, "Come on, you bastards! Get up and drive!" There was a moment of disorientation, of uncertainty, in the Teamster gang. Something unexpected had happened. The drivers hopped back onto their seats. I rode a kind of awkward postillion and was called names that reached back to Billingsgate and beyond. The police arrived soon after and kept a path open for the rest of the moveout, and I met Johnny North at Trader Vic's at eight. Sipping a mai-tai, I thought what a stupid thing I had done. My body had taken over from my head. Only the element of surprise saved me from getting my skull bashed, I suppose. The enemy suddenly among them dressed in his Sunday-best suit had startled the mob, confused them momentarily, just as it startled and confused me replaying the scene in my mind's eye. In 500 B.C. Sun Tze wrote: "When the strike of a hawk breaks the body of its prey, it is because of timing." I had been an uncalculating hawk.

Karsh stuck with us for the balance of the season, throwing up a desultory, nonviolent picket line in each city. Familiarity made us almost congenial.

In Bakersfield, en route to Los Angeles, the train's electric supply failed; the *Jomar*'s deep freeze went out and several gallons of Blum's ice cream I had bought in San Francisco turned to soup in the 100° temperature. In Los Angeles Cecil B. de Mille came to see the show and visit friends he had made while filming *The Greatest Show on Earth* a few years earlier. Ruth and Walter Pidgeon, old friends of Timmy's and mine, had dinner with me on the *Jomar* before the Circus moved on to Arizona and New Mexico. Business was good in Texas, better than anywhere except Madison Square Garden, so good that we stayed a month: El Paso, Odessa, Abilene, Forth Worth,

Dallas, Wichita Falls, Amarillo, Plainview, Lubbock, San Angelo, Brownsville, Temple, San Antonio, Corpus Christi, Victoria, Houston, Galveston. We played across the Southern states, and by the time we reached Miami Joe Karsh had a visitor waiting for us in the person of Harold Gibbons, Hoffa's number-two man. Long, intense, well-spoken, Gibbons had started life as a schoolteacher, I believe. Clearly he was not a man who needed to flex his muscles. Rather, he spoke reasonably, even though neither of us changed his position, and he said Hoffa would want to see John North and me sometime later in the winter when the Teamsters would hold their annual meeting in Miami. Anytime, I agreed. I liked Gibbons. A few years later he challenged Hoffa for the union's leadership and lost. Bad luck for the rank and file, I think.

It had been the longest season in the Circus's history. We reached Winter Quarters in Sarasota on December fourth, having traveled twenty thousand miles and played to two million people in a hundred and seventy cities. An astonishing number of executives from NBC and the Benton & Bowles advertising agency in New York found their presence in Florida in December essential to the television spectacular we would stage at Winter Quarters, called *Christmas with The Greatest Show on Earth*. Those who were not swimming or golfing gathered in my office for a production meeting while outside the Circus shifted itself from the train to its winter home. Wild animals were being transferred from their road to their menagerie cages. A circus hand rushed in with an excited message that a leopard was loose, had slipped away during a transfer. The room went dead silent. Blood drained from freshly sunburned faces. The wisdom of a Florida visit came into question, and people wondered wildly whether to stand on a chair or run for a closet. The frightened animal was quickly retaken and a charming live television show was broadcast from Sarasota: the Circus family giving itself a family Christmas party. The $100,000 fee was a sorely needed credit to the Circus account. John and Henry North gave a private family party at their mother's home on Bird Key, and the next day I flew home to Washington to rejoin Timmy and the children.

The seven-day-week, twenty-four-hour-day hurly-burly of the Circus set aside for a few days uncovered in me an inward

bruise of loneliness. At eight years of age Doreen, courageous
as a young lioness and tolerant as an angel, had enrolled in the
Potomac School in Virginia. She required special tutoring in
English, and a patient teacher taught her how to make the *sh*
sound as in *shush* and other things. Mouse, a demure and definite personality at age three-and-a-half, topped the bill of her
preschool Christmas pageant with a beguiling solo rendition of
"Tannenbaum" in her natural German.

Timmy had cushioned her aloneness with the children, with
attention to an interesting house and with the sporadic awkward social life of an unaccompanied woman, worn with wondering what would become of her truncated marriage. A sense
of estrangement dropped inevitably into our lives, silent as a
towel dropped on a bathroom floor. We had not become
strangers, but the fluid closeness of earlier times flowed less
freely. My sense of guilt and her feeling of hurt imposed a self-
consciousness on a relationship that had been unencumbered.
I knew I had miscalculated, knew that I must redress the pattern of life dictated by the Circus.

"Hang on," I asked Timmy. "We know where we want to
come out in the end. I just don't know how to get there yet.
But I will." And when Christmas was done, Timmy and Doreen
came with me to Havana, where for two weeks the Circus would
put on a one-ring show at the Sports Palace. Earlier a typed
letter had come from Mary Hemingway and a postscript from
Papa, written in longhand, curved downhill from left to right:

Finca Vigia, San Francisco de Paula, Cuba

Dear Mike,

We were delighted to have your letter with word, and hope that
you and John and Henry and Dodie, if she is with you, will
come to the finca for Christmas lunch, as Johnny has done
before. Do let us know if you can get here.

It is our favorite time of year in Cuba now with the nights
cool, the bougainvillea and the poinsettas rampant, the garden
pushing up spring vegetables (they make me feel so economical,
which of course is ridiculous). We'll just have our usual informal
family fiesta before the Circus opens (the signs at the sports
palace say the 25th).

But this year I hope you and Papa will forego the footballing a La Place du Tertre. About a month ago the Cubans gave him a decoration at the same sports palace, complete with TV lights and speeches. He sweated tremendously in the heat and caught a bad cold in his kidneys and liver, and the docs. have kept him in bed and immobile for nearly three weeks. He is improving steadily, following the prescribed regime with absolute discipline and should be up and enjoying himself by Christmastime, though may not be quite so riotous as usual. Anyhow it would be splendid to see you all. I want to hear every curdling detail of the summer, and all about you. Until then — the best of everything.

Mary.

Can't wait to see you Mike. The kidney thing is finished. Both OK. The one I ruptured with the aircraft blew a gasket or something. The drs. said it was sort of pneumonia of kidneys and want me to let the scar heal good. Don't let Mary worry you. We'll be able to throw a few blocks. Along this summer I was worried maybe you had those circus characters mixed up with the Ukrainians. Never lost faith.

Be wonderful to see you. Understand John and Buddy never go anywhere together but maybe we can meet on different holy days of abnegation.

Hemingstein.

A year earlier he and Mary had suffered two successive airplane crashes in Africa, first in Murchison Falls when their plane struck an abandoned telegraph wire that stretched across the gorge, and then when an unairworthy rescue plane crashed and burned during takeoff. Papa had broken open his head, had suffered a ruptured liver, spleen, and kidney, temporary loss of vision in one eye, loss of hearing in one ear, a crushed vertebra, a sprained right arm and shoulder, a sprained left leg, paralysis of a sphincter, and first degree burns on his face, arms, and head. Characteristically, he told reporters he had never felt better. A night or two after we arrived in Havana, Johnny North, Timmy, and I were having a predinner frozen daiquiri at the Floridita Bar when a wisp of a man came alongside me and touched my arm. I didn't know who he was.

"Please excuse me. Are you Michael Burke?" He spoke softly with a liquid Spanish accent.

"Yes."

"I'm *Il Monstro*. Papa Hemingway's friend." He had been a flyweight boxer in Spain and Hemingway had become his friend during the Civil War and christened him Il Monstro. Now, still at his fighting weight, he worked in the photo department of Sears, Roebuck in Havana. "Papa is sad that you have not yet been out to the *finca*."

"Would you tell him we'll be out tomorrow afternoon? I'll have my Circus business all attended to by then." He said he would and glided away quietly, walking on cushions of air with an athlete's lithe movement. The next afternoon Timmy and I and Doreen drove the fifteen miles out to San Francisco de Paula. Dusk was gathering as we drove up to the two-story white house sitting on a hill half-hidden in a tropical growth of ancient trees, thick shrubbery, and brilliant flowers. The *finca* was not grand in appearance but rather looked at ease, enduring, and in harmony with its environment. Behind a screen door, the front door was open. The house was very still. I knocked and we listened to the vacant sound of no one home. We opened the screen door and stepped into a large foyer, dim in the deepening dusk. The noise of someone stirring came through an open door to our left and Hemingway's voice demanded gruffly, "Who's there?"

"It's me, Papa," I called, and we moved through an open door into a big, cool room full of books and pictures, first Timmy, then Doreen, and last me. Papa sat alone in a large stuffed armchair, an Indian blanket wrapped around his waist and covering his legs like a long skirt. Gripping the armrest, he pushed himself to his feet through layers of stiffness and soreness and, gaining balance, shuffled forward to greet us. He looked awful: like a bearded and battered Triton, hair disheveled, beard tangled, face gray with pain. He had aged very much in the years since I had last seen him. The bounding energy and aliveness that lit him like a midway had been browned out. Timmy had not met him before, but with good woman-instinct she crooked her arm around his neck and kissed his ragged beard. Doreen curtsied in the manner of European children, and I shook his hand. Tears filled his eyes. He was struck mute, overcome with emotion.

Papa let himself down painfully into his armchair — plywood under the seat cushion and behind the backrest kept it rigid — and we sat around him making small conversation, pretending not to notice his inability to talk, pretending not to see the tears brushed back from his eyes, accepting an occasional nod as his contribution to the conversation. Minutes passed before he was able to mumble thickly, "It's so good to have family back again." We were not family in the usual sense, of course, but the mysterious force that governs such things had caused a close and kindred friendship to happen, though the total number of days he and I shared were relatively few. From the beginning our relationship had been as natural and uncomplicated as the rising sun. His public personage never got in the way, was never present. Intense competitiveness that provoked some of his less attractive moments was never a factor with me. I was a generation younger, a nonwriter, so never a potential target for — nor did I ever witness — the black rage that had eroded his friendships with Dos Passos, Gustav Durán, Archibald Mac-Leish. He held combat soldiers in unlimited admiration, and some of the things that had happened to me as a sometime combatant attracted him, things he would have chosen for himself. And by accident of birth I had been a good athlete. Papa liked that. He once said to his first wife, Pauline: "Things that please me are simple things. Most have to do with natural reflexes and coordination." Somewhere in that soldier-athlete quarter we connected, and from Papa I received only kindness and generosity and the kind of affection that exists in an undemanding friendship.

"Mary is shopping," he told us when the emotions touched off by our arrival subsided. "Good stuff for dinner." By dinnertime he had bathed, trimmed his beard, combed his hair, donned fresh clothes. Papa always responded to an attractive young woman's presence. His spirit, if not his body, was lively as a cricket and he was in irrepressible form. Making certain that the child did not feel left out, he announced that he and Doreen were drinking champagne; the rest of us were free to join if we liked.

Thereafter each night at dinner Papa would announce plans to take the girls for a drive in the station wagon on the following day to show them the cane fields, the abandoned stone cane factories, and would propose that he and I "shoot a few bottles off the back garden wall in the morning." Neither happened. He was not up to it physically.

Timmy was smitten by him. Alone at night we talked of the

possibility that he might kill himself, as his father had done, and we wondered if a passage in *For Whom the Bell Tolls* might be turning over in his mind: "Dying is only hard when it takes a long time and hurts so much that it humiliates you." Loving life in an all-embracing, physical way and unable to raise a hand to it, much less take it in his arms, must have been a demoralizing prospect. A message in some silent cipher foretold that he would rather be dead than incapacitated, though apart from his having been moved to tears by our arrival and his impatience with the battered condition of his body, there was no sign of the personality disintegration that later overtook him. One day in a quiet dialogue, dropping his voice to a confessional whisper, he confided that he wouldn't be in this rotten shape if it were not for "Mary and her fornicating photographs." It was she, he said, who insisted that the plane make a third and lower pass over Murchison Falls to get better pictures. At that lower altitude the plane struck a cable strung across the gorge and crashed.

Time came to leave Cuba. Papa pressed us to stay longer. "Doreen must get back to school," I explained. "She's being tutored in English grammar."

"What's wrong with me? I'll teach you grammar, Doreen," Hemingway offered.

"You!" Mary scoffed and warned Doreen. "Papa doesn't know anything about grammar."

Papa snorted. "You know, grammar wasn't chiseled in stone like Moses' tablet. Some guy didn't wander out of the mountains with a rock under his arm and say: 'Here it is. Here's grammar.' You stick with me, Doreen; I'll teach you." Driving back to Havana I encouraged Doreen to fix these days with Hemingway in her memory. When she was older and read him, read what people have written and would write about him in the years to come, it would be good to remember how gentle and kind he was to her, how considerate, generous. To all of us.

Hoffa fixed a meeting in Miami in February and Johnny North and I were driven over from Sarasota in his limousine. Joe Karsh, the Teamster organizer I had first encountered when he and his two enforcers tried to board the *Jomar* in

Colorado and later when he tried to roadblock the Circus in San Francisco, had been designated as our escort. He met us at the front entrance of the Hotel Monte Carlo. En route to Hoffa's quarters, we followed Karsh into a poolside suite looking for some other Teamster official. He wasn't there but Karsh, prideful as though he were calling attention to the union's pension plan or medical benefits, pointed out the king-size bed. "Ya see. When ya get t' d' top o' dis union, ya get a bed big enough ta go ta bed wit' t'ree broads." Perhaps the occupant and the three broads were on the beach recouping their energies in the midday sun.

Harold Gibbons was in Hoffa's apartment along with two or three others. Hoffa kept us waiting half an hour, then, fresh from the exercise room and a shower, he bounced into the room like a steel ball bearing on a marble floor. He was considerably shorter than the tall Gibbons, wore a white shirt a size too small to accentuate his solid, hard-muscled torso, strong arms, and flat stomach. His hair was cut close as a Marine drill sergeant's. Short of wearing a sign, he made it certain that everyone understood he was a hard man. Introductions were clipped, all business, no niceties. No one spoke for the Teamsters but Hoffa. He shot a glance at me and said, half challenge, half sneer, "Tough guy, eh?"

I was slightly taken aback. "No. Not necessarily." I wasn't quite sure what was coming.

"I heard all about San Francisco."

"That was pretty dumb of me." The subject was closed. He wanted a Teamster contract with the Circus, wanted the Teamsters recognized as the bargaining agent for all our nonperforming personnel. Johnny parried, saying that we used Teamster standby drivers during the New York engagement at Madison Square Garden but that we couldn't afford an across-the-board contract. I said our people saw no advantage in being Teamster members or paying Teamster dues. He looked at me as though I were a cretin.

"Your people!" He was exasperated. "Who gives a goddam about your people. We're just a couple of parties making a deal. Don't give me any of that crap about 'your people.' "

We said we couldn't sign up and he said he would put us out of business. The meeting didn't take long. John and I went to

Joe's in Miami Beach and ate marvelous stone crab and drove back to Sarasota. I had moved into the penthouse apartment atop the Ringling Hotel, and Timmy and the children joined me there. Among a German family of tumblers, the youngest became Doreen's special friend, happy to find a playmate who spoke her language. Mouse announced that she didn't like riding baby elephants — "They prickle my legs" — but she was drawn irresistibly to the sideshow tent, fascinated from a safe distance by the snake charmer, but attracted closely to the midget Doll family, the nearest people to her size on the show. In the world within a world that is the Circus, the two girls wandered through the Winter Quarters, and the Circus lots on tour, among elephants and camels, schooling horses and rolling tractors, at home and unafraid, and I knew a hundred pairs of eyes watched over their safety, eyes of carpenters and painters, welders and wire walkers, and even the wine-bleary eyes of nameless roustabouts, the flotsam and jetsam of the Circus whom we fed and bedded, the derelict spirits who drifted to us and on some moon and tide of their own fancy, drifted away.

The Boston Red Sox baseball team trained in Sarasota, and each morning as he left the Ringling Hotel breakfast room, Joe Cronin, the team's manager, touched Mousie's curly blonde head for the day's luck. Neither of us then suspected that we would be close colleagues in baseball one day. The Circus season immediately ahead of us was as far into the future as we looked, the season jeopardized by Jimmy Hoffa's threat to put us out of business. John North and I went to New York ahead of the Circus train. Marcel, the *Jomar*'s chef, packed all the ingredients for our meal on the overnight train from Tampa — fresh fruit for Johnny's bourbon old fashioneds, our wine and the steaks which the dining-car chef would grill for us. We boarded before noon, ate, drank and talked in the dining car until 7:30 in the evening, went to bed in our compartments at nine o'clock, and slept until we arrived in New York the following morning. That was John's way. Harold Gibbons chose "21" as the place to meet with Johnny and me and Anna Rosenberg, President Roosevelt's former Secretary of Labor, whom we hired to mediate with the Teamsters. Nothing came of it but a pleasant lunch.

April Fools' Day and Easter Sunday were one and the same

in 1956. The Harlem Globetrotters played Madison Square Garden the weekend before the Circus came in. Their rental agreement ran out at 11:59 Sunday night; the Circus lease picked up at 12:01 on Monday. On the stroke of midnight Jimmy Hoffa's Teamsters, joined now by the American Guild of Variety Artists, threw a picket line around the Garden, the one on the west side of Eighth Avenue between Forty-ninth and Fiftieth streets, the Garden built by John Ringling and Tex Rickard in 1925. The Teamsters' standby drivers, hired by custom from Johnny O'Rourke's New York local, refused to cross the picket line. Trucks loaded with the dirt to cover the Garden floor during the Circus run lined the dark streets at a distance from the Arena. Immediately outside, Forty-ninth Street was blocked not only with Teamsters in strength but also with people from the Guild of Variety Artists. The AGVA demanded to become the bargaining agent for all Circus performers. Emmett Kelly, an AGVA member, refused to cross their picket line. I spent most of the night in Forty-ninth Street, arguing, jostling, cajoling, shouting, even pleading. To absolutely no avail. If I recall, the Teamsters' street negotiator was named Kavner. His authority was limited to withdrawing the pickets only if we suddenly caved in and agreed to Hoffa's terms.

The CBS people were very anxious. The television spectacular of our Garden dress rehearsal was scheduled to be broadcast at 7:30 Tuesday night. But they were no more anxious than I, who could see our $100,000 television fee vanishing in the turbulent night of futile street wrangling. Inside the Garden, Johnny North telephoned and woke up John McGrath — Reavis and McGrath were the Circus' New York lawyers — and McGrath woke up a judge. McGrath and I met in the judge's chambers at eight o'clock. He argued for and the judge granted us a twenty-four-hour restraining order, and both the Circus and CBS rushed equipment across the sidewalks into the building. But the dirt for the floor had disappeared in the night. Manager Lloyd Morgan and his people found — God knows where — a supply of synthetic material that came in twenty-foot squares. Ugly and uneven, it covered the cement floor well enough to put on a performance. It lasted eighty-five performances because it had to. Teamster and AGVA pickets were back on line as soon as the restraining order expired and they stayed throughout the Garden run. Circus fans didn't seem to be dissuaded; perhaps to them it was akin to picketing Santa Claus.

After the CBS telecast of our dress rehearsal, I sat alone in the empty side-arena seats watching the riggers adjust the rigging, watching two or three acts polishing their routines, watching roustabouts hauling equipment into place for tomorrow's opening. It was perhaps two o'clock in the morning, and Johnny O'Rourke strolled up casually and sat on the seat beside me. O'Rourke ran the Teamsters' New York local. A handsome, silver-haired Irishman, he was always dressed to the nines: a camel's hair topcoat, a gray homburg hat, gray chalk-striped suit, beautifully polished shoes. He had the look of a man whose barber shaved and toweled and massaged his face every day at noon, while a manicurist polished and buffed his nails. He spoke quietly in the carefully cultivated way of someone who regretted having dropped out of grade school, spoke in a manner to match his carefully selected clothes and the gentlemanly image he meant to convey.

"Long night," he said.

"Not as long as last night," I replied. And we smiled thinly at a point mutually understood. In time he came around to the purpose of his friendly visit; something just between the two of us, quietly.

"Sign a Teamster agreement now. Get rid of the picket lines. And Jimmy won't enforce it until next season."

I laughed. "Johnny, that's putting a noose around my neck and letting Hoffa decide when he's going to kick open the trap." So well affected was O'Rourke's disappointment at my lack of faith that I almost felt guilty. With a warm handshake and a last reproving look — or was it pity? — he left as smoothly as he had come. I couldn't help liking him and being taken with his whole persona, though I had no doubt that if it was necessary he would, without a qualm, arrange to have a leg broken or a skull bashed, including mine. But I had no reason to fear that.

As an experiment we tried what we called an Early Bird Matinee, an additional ten o'clock morning show on Saturday. We ran three performances that day and grossed $110,000, the highest single day's receipts in Circus history. It was our last piece of good news. An uneventful week in the Boston Garden followed our six weeks' New York run. Then we went outdoors, under canvas. To Baltimore, to Washington, where Doreen and Mousie brought their school classes and Vice President Richard Nixon came with his wife and young children.

The Teamsters drew first blood in Philadelphia. Circus trucks moving from the railroad crossing to the Circus lot were the target. As they passed under a trestle, rocks dropped like bombs through their windshields. Rocks and shards of glass slashed the faces and arms of the drivers. A friend of mine at the University of Pennsylvania introduced me to Police Commissioner Gibbons. We got extra police protection and gratefully contributed to the Police Widows and Orphans Fund. But once under canvas, playing in open lots, we were vulnerable to almost any Teamster guerrilla action. Sand was poured into vehicles' gas tanks, immobilizing them. Winch cables were frayed so that they snapped as they lifted the huge rolls of canvas onto a truck. Truck drivers were waylaid, beaten, and driven off, and our cadre of drivers shrank. Replacements, recruited hastily by our advance men in the next route stop, turned out to be Teamster infiltrators. Ostensibly these men set out to drive from the Circus lot to the railroad crossing. Instead they drove our loaded trucks to some distant place and abandoned them. Their recovery took time.

The rhythm of the Circus — the rhythm of movement that General Rommel, Hitler's Desert Fox, had studied before World War II — was broken. Departures from one city and arrivals at the next became later and later. Teamster tactics were effective. Early on, we were late starting matinees; then we missed matinees entirely as the tempo of Teamster assaults stepped up. An act of God got July off to an ominous start. It was a Sunday. We were scheduled to play only a matinee in Geneva, New York, but the local police had the parking concession and insisted that we put on an evening performance as well. The second show was just under way when a tornado spun wildly over the hills and roared through the Big Top, shredding it as a capricious gorilla would shred a lady's handkerchief. Aluminum tent poles became projectiles shot crazily through the air. Hard rain followed the wind, soaking and calming the thrashing canvas, muffling the hysterical cries of spectators and the shouts of Circus hands as they dove into the wreckage to aid the injured and guide the unharmed to safety. Miraculously there were no fatalities, although there were broken legs, broken arms, and bruises, none critical. One roustabout had been struck by a flying quarter pole, but neither he nor anyone else knew he was seriously hurt until he slumped suddenly to the ground; he had worked furiously alongside his mates for more than an hour with a broken back. The power plant functioned and props had suffered no irreparable damage. Several bullmen had been roughed trying to keep the baby elephants from stampeding; the big ones had stood firm. A frightened lioness had killed one of her new cubs. It was four in the morning before the Circus picked itself out of the wreckage and loaded into the train, minus a tent to play under. It would be four days before a reserve Big Top would reach us from Sarasota. One alternative was to go directly to Buffalo and wait, canceling Elmira, Olean, Dunkirk, Batavia, and Niagara Falls.

"To hell with that," I said to Morgan. "Cecil B. de Mille wouldn't film it that way. His movie would play those dates without a Big Top." That rather childlike image of life imitating movies worked magic. Everyone plunged enthusiastically into a fancied role in a de Mille film. Everyone prided himself on being a showman and in true fashion the show went on. In Elmira, seat wagons were rolled into their normal positions, center poles stood at their normal attitude, supporting the rigging. Lights that normally hung from the top were placed on the ground, ringing the tanbark, shining up rather than down on the performers, creating a beautiful and dramatic effect. Even the gods who had blown our tent away thought we deserved a last, fleeting smile. They gave us cloudless summer skies. That night the upward-beamed lights turned a billion stars and a midnight blue sky into a velvet Big Top, drawing the earthly Circus into its infinite space. The aerialists especially seemed to belong more to the universe than to the earth. Morale soared and the Fourth of July, a day traditionally celebrated on the Ringling show with a kind of lusty family picnic, arrived to a spirited company. Between shows the steward, John Staley, prepared an especially good dinner and, as was the July Fourth custom, the troupers staged a show for themselves, goodhumoredly lampooning one another's acts. Dick Todd, a pop singer traveling with the show for kicks, acted as singing ringmaster. Bareback rider Justino Loyal, wearing a version of Pinito del Oro's brief, sexy costume and putting on an amusing spoof of her high trapeze act, was the star of the show. The tiger trainer's daughter won the small children's footrace. The prop department won the old-fashioned stake-driving contest, though to anyone watching fifteen men, five circling each of three stakes, flailing huge sledges within the circumference of the center ring, survival alone seemed a triumph. So Circus life glowed at its intimate best. Little Frankie Saluto, a dwarf, made his way through the crowd-filled midway before the evening show. His stumpy, topheavy body rolled from side to side, his stubby legs navigated the rough ground like a small boat in a choppy sea. He came as an emissary from his fellow dwarfs and offered his small hand. "We've never had a meal like that in our whole lives. It was just wonderful. We'll never forget it." His weight shifted from foot to foot as though striving to generate more eloquence from his limited vocabulary. "Gee, we'll never forget that meal." The moment lay calm in the eye of the storm.

A few days later in Buffalo a sheriff's party visited the lot and arrested me. At 9:30 on Saturday night I was carted off to jail. A local newspaper account said, "Michael Burke of New York City was escorted from the lot by Cheektowaga plain-clothes men." A warrant had been issued by a police justice. Apparently the justice was under Hoffa's spell and acted on a trumped-up charge. By Sunday the show's "fixer" — he was said to have a law degree — had contacted the Circus' New York law firm, who in turn contacted a Buffalo lawyer, Laurence Goodyear. Mr. Goodyear detached himself from a Sunday luncheon party in the lovely gardens of his estate to spring me. He phoned his wife to tell her he was bringing the prisoner back with him to join the party. The startled lady gasped, "My God, I hope you know what you're doing!"

A week later an era ended. The Circus of the Ringlings, of Phineas T. Barnum and James Bailey was no longer viable. James Hoffa had given it the coup de grâce. The Big Top was struck for the last time in Pittsburgh, Pennsylvania, on the sixteenth of July 1956. Time and progress, with a violent assist from Hoffa, had torn a vivid strand from the fabric of America. Cash left in the till was enough to get the Circus train back to Sarasota, pay off the troupe, and put the show in the barn. To run against the Teamsters' costly harassment would have been self-defeating; to agree to Hoffa's demands was economically prohibitive. More fundamentally, it was a delusion to think that a three-ring circus playing under a big canvas tent, traveling the country in an eighty-car train was viable in 1956. It simply was not. Railroads were once allies; now the very presence of the huge Circus train was an irritant, and the cost of moving the Circus train had risen two hundred and fifty percent in a decade. Convenient open space, large enough to accommodate the Circus, was increasingly difficult to find in spreading cities. The Circus had been overtaken by television, traffic congestion, and mounting costs. For John Ringling North it was a Hobson's choice. In a statement issued by the Circus press department Johnny pronounced the end of an era: "The tented city is a thing of the past."

For the Circus people it seemed the end of the world. Inconceivably in midseason there would be no show tomorrow. In disbelief, Cigarette Bill leaned against a tiger cage, smoke curling up into a distant stare; Cross Country Eddie mechanically stowed his tools; Straight Ahead Willie stood alone near the coffee wagon silently drinking a "Pittsburgh," a black coffee, from a paper cup; and Grease, a canvas man for fifty years, spoke quietly of his unfulfilled ambition to earn twenty-five dollars a week. A bareback troupe, sweaty from their matinee performance, washed themselves from water buckets lined beneath the Big Top's guy ropes, as their forebears had for generations.

The final night performance, given on a drab parking lot at the Heidelberg Raceway on the city's outskirts, was a sellout. A newspaper lead read: "They buried the Circus here before an overflow crowd." All the 9,856 seats were filled and hundreds of other circus lovers stood in the exit gates. Children and their parents laughed and cheered in the manner of circus crowds from time immemorial. Performers labored in an air of tragedy and mustered their best smiles at the end of each act. A clown took a little boy in his lap and told him to "put away a lot of memories tonight." At the finale the entire company, performers and animals alike costumed in red and white, paraded around the tanbark in the show's closing spectacular, Peppermint Candy Party. Taking their final places, spread from one end of the Big Top to the other, they stood waving, blowing kisses, giving thanks to their final audience. The ringmaster announced the requiem. "That concludes this performance. . . ." A sob choked off the rest of his words and the band played "Auld Lang Syne" in lieu of the usual medley of circus tunes. The time was 12:02 on the morning of the seventeenth of July. A morning paper recorded: "The Big Top, furled forever, started its funeral ride today."

The three-day stop-and-go Circus cortege towards oblivion clanked and rattled, mostly in driving rain, from Pittsburgh to Sarasota, shunted again and again onto sidings to make way for cargoes with a future. The clanging of metal on metal, for which I had acquired a deaf ear, now cut through the subdued melancholy of the train in angry protest. Even the animals seemed to sense that the natural rhythm of Circus life had changed abruptly.

John North made the entire journey in his pajamas, slept not at all, drank bourbon whiskey, and foretold that the future of the Circus lay in buildings like Madison Square Garden and San Francisco's Cow Palace. To survive in the modern world the Circus must be restructured to move from building to building as new arenas appeared in cities across America. In the new beginning it would be forced initially to abandon the famous Circus train and shrink itself to a truck show, a Mud Show in Circus vernacular. The rate of construction of new arenas would dictate the rate of Circus resurgence. In the future it would reappear as an indoor show, brassy and colorful and daring as ever, but it would not be the same. Gone the Goliath of a canvas billowing in the summer wind, pennants flying from the tops of its four giant center poles, guy ropes staked to the ground holding her fast like some untamed species, restless, straining to be on her peripatetic way "to a date in another town a hundred miles away"; gone the ripe smell of earth enriching all the ripe smells and scents of the Circus; gone a measure of magic, of romance, of innocence, lost to the mechanization of contemporary life.

For me the doleful three-day journey to Sarasota, the normal schedule of summer broken, was a time for reflection. Was this the moment for redoubled effort or a clean break? At the beginning Johnny North had said: "Write your own deal." But in practice that meant attending to the ailing Circus, nothing more. Once Johnny had said to Timmy, only half jokingly, "I'll give you back your husband in five years," a remark that disheartened her and clearly fixed Johnny's price. Common sense pointed out that I must never hitch my wagon to a single star. And I would risk the disintegration of my family if for ten of each twelve months I swanned off with the Circus. Johnny North's heady promises about his legacy and my children's future material welfare had faded from discussion and evaporated. I had erred on the side of trust. In the end the decision was made easy for me.

Once we were back in Sarasota, living aboard the *Jomar* on a railway siding at the Winter Quarters and focusing on the future of the Circus, Johnny decided to rehire a man named Art Concello. Concello had been a star circus performer. Some years earlier Johnny had hired him to be general manager of Ringling Brothers Barnum & Bailey, then, after a period of years, fired him. If the black stories North had told me about Concello were merely gray, he was not a fellow I wanted to be involved with. He comes; I go. Concello came and I told Johnny I could no longer stay and why. And since I had come at his persuasive bidding, we agreed it would be equitable for me to receive a six months' salary, paid monthly, giving me time to find my way into a new life, whatever it might be.

I left for New York with the first month's check in my pocket. To this day I have not seen the second, much less the fifth or sixth. I asked George Woods if he could persuade North to make good on his commitment. Woods was chairman of the prestigious First Boston Corporation and, as a long-time friend of North's, a member of the Circus board of directors. He was a brilliant banker, a man of impressive intellect, an incisive mind. His Wall Street friends found his Circus association improbable. "I'm with you on this," Woods said and went off to Europe. I remembered vividly an unpleasant scene in the Floridita Bar in Havana eight months earlier. Woods and North and I were having dinner and the two of them got into a nasty argument. I don't remember the substance, but the date was Friday the thirteenth and the dinner ended on a rough note. Woods leveled North with a cold eye. "Johnny, you're just a goddam chiseler!" And left. I don't suppose Woods was surprised that North reneged on our agreement. Maybe I shouldn't have been either, but I never expect a friend to disappoint me until he does. Occasionally I wondered how Johnny felt leaving me, his "brother," hanging in midair with a wife, children, no income, and no bank account. At the time I thought it was an act of world class shittiness.

Eventually Johnny sold the Circus and the Florida real estate for several millions of dollars, bought gold against expert advice, watched his investment soar from thirty-five dollars an ounce to over eight hundred, saw his precious metal grow to outweigh an elephant herd and, now richer than his uncle John Ringling had ever been, worried the question of how to take it with him.

But in the fall of 1956 my problem was simpler; I sold our car in order to pay for our rooms at the Wyndham Hotel on West Fifty-eighth Street and aimed at the television business. I liked the kind of people I had met when NBC and CBS televised the Circus spectaculars. That's what I wanted to do next, and quickly; I had no other car to sell.

# Broadcasting

# IO

TO THIS point I had accepted options presented by someone else: to join the OSS, to membership in the CIA, to run the Circus. Certainly they were tasks I was attracted to and knew I would be happy doing. I was pleased to have been sought out because people saw in me something useful to them, and I entered no occupation with reservation or later regret. Nevertheless, I had accepted or rejected opportunities rather than charted a course of my own design. Now the moment had come to find a direction of my own. Whatever that might be, I would bring to it a series of experiences which, in their specifics, might be inapplicable. I would have to learn a new trade and learn it on the job. Broadcasting attracted me. I would apply myself to it intensively, if I could find a way in.

C. D. Jackson, then the publisher of *Fortune* magazine, invited me to lunch. He had followed the swings and roundabouts of my Circus adventures, particularly those with Hoffa, and was intrigued by their mutations.

"What will you do now?" he asked.

"Broadcasting," I said. "I'm trying to get into the television business. It appeals to me. I don't know a damn thing about it. But I've got a gut feeling I'd like it."

"Do you know anyone?"

"Well, I know Pat Weaver at NBC. Superficially. Though when I saw him in his office he was very tentative, almost evasive. And since I met with him I heard he's about to get the chop. And I know a couple of people at CBS. I did some Circus television spectaculars for them. I like them."

"Do you know Frank Stanton?"

"The president-of-CBS Stanton? No."

"Would you like to meet him?"

"Very much." Urgently, I said to myself. I needed a job. The nervous tension of being unemployed was mounting by the day. I forced myself to keep a calm-looking surface, but my gut was churning like a cement mixer.

"I'll give him a call and let you know."

C. D. must have pumped me up to Stanton. He had the look of a man who has been many years inside a suit. I found him gracious, attractive, in middle years, blond, blue-eyed, and neat. His features, his dress, his office were orderly and clean-lined. His mind was as fastidious as his desk. He was open, easy, and friendly and said CBS was always on the alert for "a good piece of manpower." The need was always cropping up for a vice president of this or that facet of the company's operations. He commended CBS to me. I didn't tell him that in 1948, when I was scraping out less than a living writing film subtitles and other oddities, I had a job interview with the infant CBS television department and had been rejected. Stanton arranged for me to meet the president of the television network and Hubbell Robinson, its programming chief. Robinson was the best programming executive in the business. He had created the live, hour-long dramatic programs *Studio One* and *Climax* and made television history with *Playhouse 90*, which spawned writers, directors, and producers who, having learned and honed their trade, moved out to spectacular success on Broadway and in Hollywood. He programmed the CBS network with *Ed Sullivan, Gunsmoke, Perry Mason, Lucy,* and *Bilko,* and left the competition searching for his track. A small trim man of fifty with slick Indian-black hair, Robinson dressed with a Savile Row flair and married girls who sang — Margaret Whiting for a few minutes, Vivienne Segal for a longer, louder time. He was literate, Anglophilic, devoted to Brown University, and rabid about its football team. As for many men, business success and professional sophistication had not diminished his undergraduate admiration for athletes, even ex-athletes. I worried that football talk might take up our entire interview. But he hired me at a very good salary.

"You understand I know nothing at all about television." I wanted to be sure that plain fact didn't get lost, to everyone's later dismay.

Robinson brushed that aside. "Quickest and best way for you to learn is to sit in my office for two or three months. Keep your eyes and ears and mind open."

"You mean you want me in here all day? Every day?"

"Sure. Ten o'clock in the morning until I go home at night. If I have to go to some meeting without you, I'll let you know. Otherwise I want you here with me. Or in one of the studios. Soak up as much about production as you can. Make your own arrangements about that." His generosity on so brief an acquaintance secured my friendship for life.

I thought Hubbell might become bored with my riding his coattail, but he didn't. For the next three months I was at his elbow listening to every phone conversation and sitting in on every discussion of a prospective new television series, of solutions to problems with existing shows, of subjects for live dramatic programs, of deals with actors, writers, directors, and producers, of evaluation of their suitability for one production or another. Gradually strands of programming a network, seen from Robinson's perspective, came together in a pattern and a texture. As inconspicuously as possible I kept copious notes in a black loose-leaf book, recording specifics to be remembered and impressions gained of the CBS attitude, the CBS perception. My self-conscious notetaking was not noticed. Everyone made notes. Lunching with Frank Stanton, I saw that there was always a pad and pencil at the right side of his plate. In most offices a bank of television sets played all day, the sound turned up when someone wanted to hear a particular program or segment — CBS, NBC, or ABC. And at home at night I viewed everything I could see until midnight, studying the medium. I wanted to be acquainted with everything that was on the air and to have an objective impression of it. I didn't ever want to find myself in a discussion of a certain program and not know what everyone was talking about.

The weekly program meetings were instructive and revealing. Robinson chaired them, following an agenda of items. Mr. Paley, the chairman of CBS, dominated them. Paley struck me as keen and vigorous and more handsome in his late fifties than he looked in earlier photographs. His great personal charm set aside, Paley was all business in these planning sessions attended by half a dozen of Robinson's immediate subordinates. He arrived hurriedly, seemingly pressed for time, and left as though hurrying off to an appointment for which he was already late. There was no small talk. Restlessly patient at the outset, Paley was soon cutting through to the heart of any matter, brushing aside nonessentials. Sure and confident of his judgment, his perceptions, his feel for public taste, his sense of what made a program work, Paley voiced opinions, gave directions, and made decisions swiftly and clearly. He seemed to me to possess the skill and experience in his field that made everyone else look a bit clumsy, like Joe DiMaggio gliding under a deeply hit ball that another outfielder would have strained to miss. I admired him.

When my daily apprenticeship in Robinson's office ended, I launched myself into other working parts, spending time with the story department, with Dick Lewine, who produced musical specials, with Spencer Harrison of Business Affairs, who negotiated the deals for the shows Robinson chose to do, and with the production units of *Studio One* and *Climax,* the weekly live dramatic shows. In short, I spent ten months educating myself, excited by a new adventure in a new field, stimulated by the very nature of the business, driven to catch up with what my contemporaries already knew, beckoned by the opportunities of an expanding field. CBS was the place I wanted to be. Now I must make a place for myself within it. The ball was in my court.

CBS was an extremely attractive place to work in those times. Robinson's entertainments, Mickelson's news, and the Ed Murrow–Fred Friendly public affairs programming dominated NBC. ABC was a new entry scrambling for traction in the marketplace. CBS was comparatively small, even intimate. The everyday presence and impact of Paley and Stanton knit us all together, giving us a sense of cohesion, purpose, and direction. I felt I had joined an elite group, was made to feel valued and welcome, and was thankful for the good luck of it all.

Timmy and I found a bright, pleasant duplex apartment for us on the top of 39 East Seventy-second Street and enrolled the girls at Miss Hewitt's Classes. For the first time I experienced the simple joy of walking them to school in the morning on my way to work. After the frenetic Circus existence and the catch-as-catch-can family life it imposed, the routine of going back and forth to one place every day, putting the children to bed at night, playing with each one his own silly little made-up game that sent them off to sleep laughing, sleeping myself in the same bed in the same city was warmly satisfying. The change to a more normal life-style, the anxious post-Circus unemployment behind us, understandably gave Timmy a surer footing, and she set about making the apartment a place we, especially the children, could think of as home. It was a good and sensible thing to do, though at the time I did not fully appreciate why Timmy was so strongly determined, almost compulsive about it. I took for granted, unthinkingly, the security of my own family background, having grown up in a cocoon of parents and grandparents and open, warm-spirited houses where you were always at home, always surrounded by friends. For me home was wherever I happened to be. Without being conscious of it, I suppose I transmitted that attitude to my children. No doubt Timmy drew on her own early experience of rootlessness and felt they needed the reassurance of a physical place where they belonged. I did not fault or contest that. I simply didn't feel as emphatic about it.

In time Hubbell Robinson said, "I want you to go to Europe and develop programs from there." The assignment was logical, for I was as much at home in Europe as in New York. Within the CBS television network structure, immediately under Robinson, was a vice president for network programs, New York, and a vice president for network programs, Hollywood. I was to take a comparable position for Europe and establish a headquarters in London.

Timmy refused to come. She insisted on remaining in New York to complete her home and to give the children a full sense of place before spinning off into the world once again. Her stand baffled me. Simplistically I thought that a wife's place was with her husband, wherever. I only partially appreciated her need to put down a stake. Because she had moved as a young child from one relative to another after her father's death, having been displaced by me during ten married years from Beverly Hills, to New York, to Italy, to Germany, to Washington and Sarasota, to New York again, her attitude was perfectly logical. But to me movement was so natural I failed to consider that she might by now be asking herself whether she had married a tent dweller, an Arab with a horse whose "part was to sow and ride away."

Of course Timmy was right to gather our possessions and turn the duplex on Seventy-second Street into an attractive home, a place tastefully fitted with antiques, mostly things she had bargained for in the back streets of Rome, Munich, Paris, and between. She was right to let the sediment settle. Conversely, I was wrong for ten separated months in Europe and understood this only later, on reflection. I realized, too, that reflection had not been my long suit; my attention was fixed on the present and the future.

In June 1957 I left for London half angry, half sad, but stronger than both emotions was the lure of an opportunity to be seized and the excitement of creating a new function in Europe. And I was driven by the indelible memory of being broke and unemployed in the late forties. I moved into a small suite high at the back of the Savoy Hotel, overlooking the Thames, where a valet, a waiter, and a maid, old retainers out of my earlier era, polished as old silver, looked after me with care and concern. From the Savoy I launched our new CBS business, making my mission known, making new acquaintances among television, film, theatre and publishing people, among writers, directors, producers, and their agents.

Perhaps London at any time, but certainly London in the late 1950s and early sixties, was a desirable place to be. The physical scars of war were healing and a fresh spirit gathered momentum. Independent television challenged the BBC with a competitive service; the Royal Court Theatre in Sloane Square was the showcase for John Osborne and the Angry Young Men. Laurence Olivier created Archie Rice in *The Entertainer*. Ian Fleming invented James Bond. *My Fair Lady* opened in its natural ambience, Covent Garden, starring Rex Harrison, Julie Andrews, Bob Coote, and Stanley Holloway. Silk shirts with frayed cuffs were still worn unself-consciously by the gentry. Carnaby Street was beginning to create the mod styles that would leap to America. The Quarrymen were about to become the Beatles. Inflation was an uncommon word, and one pound sterling, valued at four dollars, went a great distance.

I returned to New York for Christmas and by spring 1958 Timmy had completed decorating the apartment to her satisfaction, rented it furnished to Ricardo Montalban, in from California to do a Broadway play, and she and the three children sailed on the *Queen Mary* to Southampton. We resumed a normal pattern of life, though the unease of long separation did not disappear entirely. Awkwardness stilted the first days after I had met their ship at Southampton. Ours was not the hungry reunion of lovers, rather it was strained by the guarded, tentative behavior of two people feeling unsure but not quite certain what they were unsure of, wary lest some unknown happening in the time apart spring at them. I could not get past Timmy's defense and wondered if I was being walled out. Was she concealing a privacy of her own from me? I was genuinely and demonstrably glad to have them all in London and distressed when the initial strangeness did not dissolve in renewed acquaintance, in the daily run of domestic life. My obvious enthusiasm for our being together again did little to diminish Timmy's reserve. I was puzzled and frustrated and wondered if she had been forced to make a hard decision in New York whether to come at all. Clearly a distance of some dimension — broad or narrow I couldn't tell — had opened between us. Whatever its dimension, the gap fixed itself into our relationship.

I don't know how derivative, but an incident occurred that perhaps had no lasting relevance to anyone but me. I had enrolled Doreen in Lady Eden's School, and shortly after their arrival in England, I took Doreen and Timmy along to meet Lady Eden. She was a gentlewoman and a serious professional, formal and correct. Doreen, at ten, now entering her fifth school in her fourth country, was nervous and responded uncertainly to some of Lady Eden's drawing-out questions. Her mother, for reasons perhaps she herself didn't know — frustration, stress, anxiety in a strange new circumstance, displeasure with me — suddenly unleashed a litany of the child's academic shortcomings. It embarrassed Lady Eden, stunned me, and undid the child before her new headmistress. On the back seat of the cab I held Doreen in my arms as she sobbed all the way home. Her mother sat silently in the opposite corner, cool and aloof, and I wondered what unspoken anger and personal hurt mingled in her soul. Because it hurt Doreen, wiped her out at a moment when she most needed our support, the episode fixed itself in my permanent memory, and I wondered if it was a sin of the father visited upon the child. This was a facet of Timmy's character that remained unfathomed, one that I tried to convince myself was an aberration. Imperceptibly, without design or perhaps awareness, we slipped into a condition of communicating about everything around us, the everyday things, but not at all about what was inside us, each gingerly skirting the other's inner privacy until it became a fixed, if subliminal, pattern.

Private tensions aside, London was lotus-eating time for us. Mr. Paley decided the CBS flag should be planted formally in Europe, hence CBS Europe was established in Zurich as an umbrella for our foreign operations and a subsidiary, CBS Limited, was formed in London. I was made president of both. Business flourished and profited. Timmy found a lovely four-story town house, owned by the Duke of Westminster, in Chester Square in the elegant Belgravia section of London. We made a wide assortment of friends and professional acquaintances in broadcasting, films, journalism, publishing, and theatre, and Timmy lengthened her own list of friends among the titled and the landed gentry. Each morning the two girls walked to Victoria Station and paid threepence fare on a London bus to Lady Eden's in Kensington. Mouse startled her class responding to a teacher's question of what the little girls wanted to do when they grew up. Most aspired to be a Lady-in-Waiting to the Queen, to marry a duke, to be a film star. Mouse said she wanted to work in John of Knightsbridge, a hairdresser's. On days when I wasn't in Paris or Rome or Munich or Stockholm on CBS business, I dropped Peter at Westminster preschool on the way to my office in the Strand, near Charing Cross Station. At the Christmas season we carried on a custom started in Germany, holding open house for close friends: Eric Sevareid, the CBS European correspondent; Charles Collingwood, the London Bureau chief; Drew Middleton, the *New York Times* London Bureau chief; Michael Powell, who directed the classic *Red Shoes,* and a number of BBC and commercial television people. I also rediscovered British wartime friends. Timmy was a superb hostess.

Part of Christmas Day was shared with Deborah Kerr and her two daughters, schoolmates of Doreen and Mousie. Each year the children performed a Christmas pageant in our drawingroom, staged against the backdrop of a ten-foot Christmas tree standing between two long windows that looked out onto the private gardens of Chester Square and across to the symmetry of Georgian facades, mirroring our own. A log fire to

one side warmed the predisposed audience and costumed players alike. In the cast Doreen was Joseph, Melanie played the
Virgin Mother, Peter an aging but obliging infant. The Wise
Men were reduced to two, Francesca and Mousie, and George,
our dog, was a doubtful albeit obedient sheep.

We found, too, an Elizabethan house to rent in the hamlet of
Fawley Green in the Chiltern Hills above the Thames at Mar-
low, where we spent parts of summers and long weekends.
Hidden away at the end of a lane that passed through a tunnel
of privet, the house settled in eight acres of lawn, flower gardens, kitchen gardens, and orchards, adjoining a five-hundred-
acre stud farm where we rode. The scale of the house delighted
the children; from the second-story leaded casement windows
I could reach down and touch Doreen's upstretched hand as
she stood in the garden. A brick-floored main room ran the
width and nearly the length of the house and a man could
stand in the fireplace at one end. Fixed to the low ceiling beams,
a U-shaped trolley bracketed the wide chimney and carried a
heavy brown velvet curtain which on cold nights could be
drawn around to create a cozy family space and contain the
fire's warmth. At bedtime it was a cold dash to unheated rooms
and beds warmed by hot water bottles. Cheers Orchard was an
especially happy place for the young.

Doreen, Mouse, and Peter had been wonderfully well taught
by Captain Sumowski, a tough, demanding former Polish cavalry officer, at his stables near Robin Hood Gate in Richmond
Park. I totally abandoned golf and tennis to ride with them
every weekend and whenever else we could. Horses were a
serious part of life. They drew us tightly, happily, sharingly
together. When the girls went off to boarding school in the
New Forest, Mouse, aged ten, wrote me this letter:

> Fritham House
> Lyndhurst
> New Forest
> Hants.    11/62

Dear Dado

Thanks for your letter. I am always hoping for one to come and
today one did. I knew who it was from the very second I saw
the writing and rushed to the bathroom to read it.

We did miss Halloween but Lady Eden made up for it by making sure we had a super dinner e.g. Coca Cola etc. We were all stuffed. Then we played games and danced. We had great fun.

Daddy, this is very important and the answer has to be quick and it has to be yes or no. Annabel's brother's pony is going to be sold. He goes very fast, he's nearly fourteen hands, he jumps 3ft. 9ins. with a heavy boy. He's iron grey and a blue roan in the winter. In the summer when there are shows and he is meant to jump in the ring he stands up on his hind legs. He needs a very, very good rider to get on him and whack him over the first fence. Then he jumps perfectly. You have to repeat this last three times when he plays up. He is apt to nip but he is very kind and gentle and is good tempered. Hunting he goes like a bomb. His name is Crusada. He is very good natured in the stable and is a bit greedy. He has a terribly good mouth. The bit must be a rubber snaffle. He is positively for sale. Annabel is letting me see a picture of him and if she lets me I will sent it to you. Write soon.

Lots of love<br>Mousie

Give my love to Pete!!!

Annabel's brother's pony was sold while the English post made its way from the New Forest to London and back, but Adam Faith, a blond-maned roan named for a contemporary rock star, made Mouse equally happy. Doreen had a black Connemara named Kinvara, and Peter's pony was called JP. When they weren't actually riding, they pretended to be and set up jumps for themselves in the orchard, and they kept their mother and me up to date with news of the mares and foals on the neighboring stud farm.

In London our domestic life was supported by a butler, a cook, and a nanny, freeing Timmy and me to travel together, particularly during the children's school terms. It was Timmy who first became interested in Africa and urged me to read Alan Moorehead's books *The Blue Nile* and *The White Nile*. Enticed and armed with scant additional knowledge beyond the danger of flash floods in the rainy season, we left London on an East African Airways Comet for Rome, Khartoum, and Nairobi.

For a month we wandered Hemingway's green hills of Africa

in a Land Rover — Kenya, Uganda, Tanganyika, Zanzibar — having rejected the option to join an organized tour; far better, we decided, to make our own way, to leave something to chance. Distant from London and excited by the prospect of a new shared experience, the clutter swept aside from our relationship, we dissolved the tensions between us, and an easy camaraderie slipped into its place. This time away from the demands and alignments of the familiar world renewed our capacity for friendship and loosened an emotional tautness. How much, it was difficult to say, but we were not back at a pure, unbruised beginning. Africa, though, reached out for Timmy and planted in her a lifelong love.

In uncertain English summers we looked for sun — in Saint-Jean-Cap-Ferrat, on the French Riviera, on Corfu, or sailing through the Greek islands. As I said, it was lotus-eating time. Years later, when she was a student at the Sorbonne in Paris, Mouse — I should call her Michele — took a French friend to London and showed her the house she had lived in on Chester Square and Lady Eden's School and the stable at Robin Hood Gate in Richmond Park where she had first learned to ride. Afterwards she wrote me to tell of her visit and ended the letter: "You know, Pop. I had an idyllic childhood."

In the summer of 1962 Frank Stanton came to visit our London office and together we went on to Zurich. He was visibly impressed with what he found and probably surprised when I said it had become all too easy for me now. The foundation had been laid; I was coasting and I couldn't abide it.

"My engine is turning over at half speed. My personal plant is operating at half capacity." I actually used such ghastly metaphors. Instead of advising me to study the English language, he responded very positively, suggesting one job that did not appeal to me, and agreeing that I would wait until he returned to New York and spoke with Mr. Paley.

Timmy thought I had gone out of my senses when I said it was time for me to go back to New York. However seductive the quality of life, however agreeable the creature comforts, however much I loved Europe and my ease within it, I could not imagine topping out there. I was drawn irresistibly to the main event. Perhaps one day in the future I would come back to live happily in Europe, a day I would recognize when it arrived, but now I was compelled to go to work. I was deeply marked by my own footless plight in New York after being dismissed from Warner Brothers. Then I would have worked twenty-four hours a day if anyone would have had me. Now I feared nothing but missed opportunity, missed for lack of reaching, missed by reason of self-satisfaction or complacency. I was wary of the status quo and will be until the world stands still.

None of this was easy to explain convincingly to the popular, gregarious mistress of 25 Chester Square, London SW1. She considered her life-style, if not our relationship, ideal. But whatever unspoken reserve divided us, she was the woman I loved. Also I owed her a considerable debt for the threadbare years in New York between the passionate, carefree beginning in California and the good years in Rome and after. She had endured that meager time without complaint, and I had vowed to myself that I would make it up to her. Now I attempted to explain that we had had the best of CBS in Europe and that nothing stands still. No matter how fervently any of us would like to capture and hold steady an agreeable situation, life is always in flux. If we hung on we would discover our mistake at a future time and it would be too late. There was more that I must do. I did not know precisely what it was, but I had to create a new opportunity and step into it. It would be against my nature to settle for something less than I might achieve. I reasoned that the decision to go back to New York was a responsible one and I asked Timmy to accept my judgment. She was disappointed and unhappy and I understood why. But I held myself accountable for tomorrow and all the tomorrows. Only time and events would confirm or refute the wisdom of returning to New York. In the autumn of 1962 it was not an altogether popular family decision. We left the girls to finish their semester at boarding school in the New Forest and Timmy, Peter, and I flew to New York.

## II

A GOOD OMEN made me smile. Setting out for the office to start my new job, I realized that it was the seventeenth of September, the exact same date I had joined CBS six years earlier. I don't know why this coincidence pleased me so much. I am not normally given to omens or superstitions, except that I always pull on my left riding boot first and never, never put a hat on a bed. But this bright, clean, autumn day everything was pleasing. I was elated by the moment and sprightly about the future, reason enough to smile on any day, and striding down Park Avenue and across Fifty-seventh Street to Madison, I was stopped in my tracks at my reflection in a store window and laughed aloud. I wore a hat from Locke in St. James's, a blue Savile Row suit, a striped shirt with a detached collar made in Jermyn Street, and in the pocket of my jacket a Smythson Bond Street blue Feather-weight diary rested slimly against my chest. London had left its mark. At the office everyone but me got rid of his jacket first thing. In sparsely heated Europe, jackets were worn as much for warmth as correctness. In New York I was too self-conscious of my wide suspenders to doff mine. That night both the hat and the suspenders went out with the trash, and my speech gradually shed the phrasing and colloquialisms that had seeped chameleonlike into my vocabulary. Common coin in English English sounded out of joint, even pretentious, in American. More lasting was my deeper appreciation for civility and manners. I had been brought up to respect both: "Be sure to mind your manners," my grandmother Bridget Fleming reminded me often enough, and at Kingswood School civil conduct was a tenet. But five years in England brought them into more thoughtful application, and lent not only form but substance to behavior. Edmund Burke wrote that manners were more important than laws; Rebecca West said civility is the very stuff of a decent society.

Almost immediately, in a very practical way, I was grateful that the five years in London had also shaped Peter; he had arrived there at age two. I rang up a friend and asked where you put an eight-year-old in school. He named some boys' schools — Trinity, Collegiate, Buckley, St. Bernard's, and so on. Peter in hand, I went from one to the next and received the same response. Impossible; the class is full; most children are enrolled at birth. Buckley turned us into the street with arrogant speed, though other schools were polite enough to give Peter an examination. Having been a pupil at Westminster Junior School, he tested well, but there was no space for him. I despaired. Then out of the blue a call came from Mr. Westgate, the headmaster of St. Bernard's School, a Canadian who had studied in England and was an Anglophile.

"I have made room for your son Peter," he said.

"Wonderful. Did someone drop out?"

"No. We have squeezed him in."

"That's extremely good of you."

"Would you like to know why?" Mr. Westgate's question ended with a chuckle.

"I would indeed."

"Because with his round pink face and piping English accent he looks and speaks as Winston Churchill must have looked and spoken when he was eight."

By the time Peter's sisters had returned from England and entered Spence School, Timmy had found us a smashing penthouse apartment at Ninety-third and Park, and one night, as I sat alone by the fire waiting for friends to arrive, my idle thoughts came to rest on the spacious room itself, almost as though discovering it for the first time. Airy and bright, it ran the length of the building, and french doors at either end opened onto garden terraces. The furniture Timmy had searched out and collected in the back alleys of Europe was beautifully accommodated in its near ballroom size: the gilt mirror out of some Roman *palazzo* could have been made to hang above the fireplace; the noble lineage of green damask drapes, threaded with gold, added a graceful sweep to the long windows; the exquisite craftsmanship of an Aubusson rug subtly coalesced pieces of furniture out of French and Italian antiquity. I wondered why, while she had been searching and collecting, I had not been more appreciative. Perhaps my mind had been concentrated more intensely on the day's occupation than I had realized. Piece by piece I had thought of them only as possessions and, as possessions, they had little meaning or value to me. But collectively, now discerningly placed, they created an ambience that took me almost by surprise, filled me with a sense of pleasure and well-being, and I wondered if the nomad in me had quietly given up his tent, never again to roam.

"Your new title will be Vice President of CBS Inc. for Diversification," Frank Stanton said. "We want to expand beyond broadcasting and records, to get into new lines of business. There is an office for you here on the twentieth floor with the chairman and me. I'll send the Knoll people around and you can redecorate it any way you like." I don't know whether this was a liberty given everyone or whether, having seen the decor of offices I established in London and Zurich, he trusted my taste. A few nights later Stanton and I dined with Mr. Paley in the chairman's private diningroom in the CBS building at 485 Madison Avenue. I don't suppose I actually heaved a huge sigh of gratification as I sat down, but I could have. Finally made it. Not Everest, of course, but a plateau I had been struggling to reach, without knowing its name or its location or its altitude, since I had left Germany in 1954. But in my own terms to have become a vice president of the corporation — there were dozens of vice presidents of various subsidiary divisions of CBS — and to be sitting down to a private business dinner with Paley and Stanton gave me a very real sense of accomplishment, a credential I would always have. It didn't matter to me that to the business community at large my appointment was obscure and unnoteworthy. Mine was a very subjective measure of success. Once again I would have to push beyond myself and reassure Paley and Stanton that their choice had not been a poor one. There was a great deal I didn't know and I set out to know it.

Everyone referred to him as "the Chairman," everyone addressed him as "Mr. Paley," except Stanton, who called him Bill. Over dinner Mr. Paley laid out his criteria for acquisition: The acquired company should be the class of its field, should have the same passion for quality as CBS; should be compatible with what we know and like — for example, publishing as opposed to manufacturing — should be a business we would enjoy and one that would enhance the profit and prestige of CBS. And I was given a subsidiary assignment: investing in Broadway shows. The phenomenal success of *My Fair Lady*, financed entirely by CBS, had whetted the chairman's appetite for more.

The Lerner and Loewe musical was a smashing success in New York and London, of course, and when I became involved it was mainly to deal with the subsidiary rights, negotiating with the Japanese for a Tokyo production — how 'Enry 'Iggins came out in Japanese I'll never know — and with Lars Schmidt for most European countries. Lars was an attractive and profitable partner and had no trouble persuading me to come to Berlin, Stockholm, and Munich openings; all were sparkling occasions and Munich was especially memorable. Lars was married to Ingrid Bergman, and, together with Ingrid's daughter Pia, we attended the Munich premiere, joined a gay posttheatre supper and, when Lars and Ingrid said they had had enough, Pia and I found a late-night bar, drank a bottle of champagne, listened to a piano, and talked. At the time she seemed lonely and adrift, and I felt a warm affection for her. On Ingrid's 1964 birthday, Lars drove me out from Paris to their house in Courcelles. Ingrid had imported from their summer home in Sweden a shipment of *kräfta,* a kind of crayfish, which she cooked expertly, and the three of us sat beside the pool under an April moon drinking cold *akvavit* and gorging ourselves with the succulent meat, building a mountain of shells. If one had to work for a living, this line of trade wasn't too objectionable.

A minor flap developed over the *My Fair Lady* stock and amateur rights. Ralph Colin, a member of the CBS board of directors, asked me to lunch with him and his longtime friend Richard Rodgers at the Four Seasons. Like most everyone else in the civilized world, I had enjoyed Rodgers' music and was delighted at the chance to meet him. Over lunch he told me he owned a music publishing company which published his own music and he wanted CBS to license the stock and amateur rights to his firm. I had expected to license the rights to Tams-Witmark, whom I thought the best in the field, but I met with

Rodgers and his people, and, having looked at the operation, said I did not think their facility was adequate. Rodgers asked for thirty days to gear up for *My Fair Lady* and I agreed. Thirty days and more came and went. Nothing changed, and I told Rodgers I would have to make the best arrangement I could elsewhere. Some days passed and the chairman rang and asked me to step across to his office.

"What the hell have you done to Dick Rodgers?" he asked. "He's just left my office. And he's furious with you." I described chronologically what had taken place.

"Have you made the deal with Tams-Witmark?"

"No. But I'm about to."

"Is it a good deal?"

"Yes."

"All right. That's fine." I heard nothing more from Mr. Paley. But some time later Ralph Colin told me that Paley had rung Rodgers and said, in essence: Michael Burke has related the facts to me and I accept them entirely; he is an officer of the Columbia Broadcasting System and he is a friend of mine. That very generous statement closed the subject, not endearing me to the egocentric Rodgers.

Nor did I endear myself to two other famous theatrical names, Josh Logan and Leland Hayward. Their lawyer, Bill Fitelson, rang me at CBS one day to say that Logan and Hayward were all set to produce a musical version of William Inge's play *Picnic*. Eight hundred thousand dollars was needed to finance the show, and Fitelson asked if I would attend an audition at Hayward's apartment. Both their wives, a pianist, and a boy and a girl singer were already there when I arrived. I was the audience. Pamela Hayward was beguilingly solicitous of the comfort of my chair and the quantity of whiskey and soda in my glass, while Logan sat on a high stool reading excerpts from the book and the boy and girl sang. I had imagined Logan to be a sophisticated man and was surprised, even embarrassed, by his sophomoric performance; or perhaps he thought I was so unworldly that life had to be explained to me in sophomoric terms.

"You see," he enthused, "the hero's the kind of guy who's never paid for a piece of ass in his life." I finished my drink, thanked them, and, smiling a lot to disguise my lack of interest, left. Fitelson rang the next morning. "Well, what do you think?" His question sailed with confidence.

"We're not interested. I wouldn't dare ask Mr. Paley for $800,000 for that show. It's dreary."

"I can't believe my ears. You'll have the cast album for Columbia Records."

"No, Bill. As a musical it's no good. It won't work."

"You must be crazy. This is a Pulitzer Prize play!" His voice grew shrill, his anger mounted.

"Grand play. Terrible musical."

"I'm going to have Leland and Josh call Paley." Threats repel me. I either explode or turn to excessive politeness.

"That is perfectly all right, Bill. I wish you would, Bill. Please do." Eventually they talked NBC out of $800,000, and the network took a complete bath. The show opened and closed in Boston, never to be seen again. Nor did Hayward and Logan ever speak to me again.

On the other side of the coin, I received a call one day from Fred Coe. Fred had been a *Studio One* and *Playhouse 90* producer when I first came to CBS and worked for Hub Robinson. Would I come to an audition? Of course. It was August 7, 1963. We met in the Sardi's building, I think. Coe had also invited Larry Shubert Lawrence, an old chum with whom I had played basketball in college, and his principal aide, Alvin Cooperman. Larry had inherited the Shubert theatres. The audition was for a musical, and the two men who wrote the show played and sang. Their names were Sheldon Harnick and Jerry Bock; their show was called *Fiddler on the Roof.* I loved it, and Fred and I had a drink in Sardi's and worked out the terms of a deal for CBS to put up the full financial backing.

"I'm satisfied if you are, Fred. Now it's up to me to get the money from the chairman." I told Mr. Paley I had just heard a wonderful show with superb ingredients: Zero Mostel would play the lead; Jerry Robbins would do the choreography; the book was based on Sholom Aleichem stories.

"You think we ought to do it?"

"Absolutely."

"Do you have a script I could read tonight?" I gave him my copy and we met again next morning. Paley's expression was doubtful, but I assumed he was playing the devil's advocate.

He always tested your enthusiasm, your information, your judgment.

"You really like this, do you?"

"Very much."

"And you don't think it's too depressing?"

"No. In what sense?"

"Well, the poverty. The pogroms."

"No I don't see it as downbeat. It's funny, poignant. A triumph of spirit."

"Can you get out of the deal?"

"We don't have a deal. I worked out the terms with Fred, but he understands we don't have a deal unless I can get the money."

"Do you think it's too Jewish?"

"That hadn't occurred to me. As a non-Jewish person, I think I saw it as a folk tale. Could be Jewish, Polish, Irish, anything. It's universal." We talked it around a bit more and Mr. Paley asked again if I could get out of the deal. "We don't have a deal unless you agree," I said. And as I spoke it began to seep into my dense Irish head that Paley was uncomfortable with it. My own enthusiasm hadn't taken into account any ethnic considerations on his part.

"Would you rather not do it?" I asked.

"I'd rather not," he said matter-of-factly. The play's Jewishness may not have been the reason he turned it down; it was simply my impression. Back in my office I rang Coe.

"Fred, I'm sorry. I can't get the money. I'm afraid I've failed you." Coe turned to another producer, Hal Prince, who was able to raise the money and produce the show. I missed the party celebrating its tenth anniversary on Broadway.

Over the next couple of years our search for expansion ranged through book publishers, magazines, newspapers, musical instruments, toys, map makers, information systems, cable television, pay television, music publishers, soft drinks, dictionaries. We climbed up and down the New York Stock Exchange list and drifted as far afield as baseball. I knocked on strange doors, met some grand and generous people, sought direction from all quarters, built up a debt of gratitude to many who led me by the hand. Paley and Stanton and I met regularly at ten o'clock every Thursday morning — and some weeks many more times. Paley's vigor and restless imagination led the way. He was an enthusiastic, acute, intellectually tough boss. With him you had to be thorough, precise, and accurate. Or you were lost. For me it was a disciplined, mind-stretching process, a tremendous learning experience. Early on, book publishing seemed to be the place to start our search for CBS acquisitions and I set myself to learning the lie of that land as fast as possible — the firms, the people, the potential prospects — and finally recommended that we buy Scott Foresman, an educational book publisher in Chicago, and Holt, Rinehart and Winston, the general book company in New York, both willing prospects.

"Don't you think you ought to see Scott Foresman before we bid for it?" I asked Mr. Paley, and he agreed that we should visit Chicago. The two of us flew out in his plane, accompanied by his butler, who brought along a hamper of sandwiches and other sustenance for the two-hour flight. The butler first served Mr. Paley a plate of five or six small triangular sandwiches and, while I waited for mine, Mr. Paley offered me one from his plate. My sandwiches were served within a few minutes, but by then Mr. Paley's were all gone. When his plate was empty, I offered him one of my triangles.

"Oh, no, thanks," he said, but his tone was unconvincing and his expression covetous.

"But I owe you one."

"You do?"

"Yes." He swept it away in a flash. I loved his enthusiasm for food.

A car met us at O'Hare Airport, and driving into the city Mr. Paley began to reminisce about his Chicago boyhood. "There was a vacant lot next to our house where we played baseball, and Tinker and Evers and Chance, those great old Chicago players, used to pass by and talk with us. The house seemed big to me then, but it was a very ordinary two-story frame house. Every night at dinner the question was whether my father should buy the vacant lot. Some nights the decision was yes; some nights it was no. He never bought it. It's probably still there." He spoke with great warmth and affection. "Would you like to see it?"

"Certainly." Clearly he himself wanted to and asked the driver if he knew his way to the address.

"Yes, I can find it. But you wouldn't want to go there. It's a kind of rundown Jewish neighborhood."

Paley winked at me and laughed. "I know what kind of neighborhood it is." The chairman could be tough; he could also be very winning. As it turned out we couldn't take the time for a detour without being rudely late for our appointment with the Scott Foresman chairman.

Eventually, at meetings in New York with their chief executives, both the Scott Foresman and Holt, Rinehart and Winston deals were turned down. Mr. Paley would not agree to meet the price. But a year or so later CBS returned to the bargaining table and acquired Holt, Rinehart and Winston, at a price higher than they had originally asked.

We flirted with the *Wall Street Journal*, the *Los Angeles Times Mirror*, *The New Yorker* magazine and, after I had held a number of preliminary discussions with Ed Baker, an opposite number at Time, Inc., Paley, Stanton, and I had lunch in the chairman's diningroom with Andrew Heiskell and Jim Linen, the chairman and president of Time. Everyone agreed it would be a match made in Heaven; equally it was agreed that the United States Justice Department would never allow it to happen. It was a delightful luncheon. The Fender Guitar Company came to me over the transom, was acquired, turned over to Columbia Records. With every other youngster in America seemingly an aspirant Mick Jagger or Paul Simon, the guitar company gave a dashing start to a new CBS musical instruments component. The Steinway Company came later, after I had long gone. As did other acquisitions.

Paley and Stanton were two fascinating personalities, particularly in relationship to one another. Paley had the advantage of a running start in the world. His father had made two fortunes in the cigar business, first in Chicago, then in Philadelphia. But as a very young man Bill Paley had the vision and courage to acquire the fledgling CBS radio network — it then occupied the top four floors of 485 Madison Avenue, studios and all — as well as the talent and acumen to build it into one of America's great institutions. In his field, he stands alone. Stanton came out of Ohio, a researcher. In 1946 Paley made Stanton, then thirty-eight years old, president of CBS. Stanton was a buttoned-down administrator and no detail was too small for his attention. The Paris CBS News correspondent once sent out Christmas cards with periods following the letters C B and S; Stanton reprimanded him: CBS stands alone, unpunctuated. Stanton's idea of a day off was to come to the office on Sunday in a sports jacket. I found him a most sympathetic man, invariably thoughtful and considerate. Yet I don't know a soul who has ever seen the inside of his fine-looking town house on Ninetieth Street off Fifth Avenue. He, too, was a singular figure in broadcasting. No one came up to his status. The two men were an exceptional pair to be associated with. In the course of a day's occupation they afforded me an indelible, unmatched education; carelessness of substance or form was intolerable. Honest error was forgiven, once.

In the early sixties their own relationship was becoming progressively more awkward. One day at the end of a discussion Mr. Paley and I were having in his office he turned the conversation to Stanton.

"What the hell does Frank want?" Paley demanded.

"He wants to be named the chief executive officer of CBS. And he wants that more than anything in the world."

"Why, for God's sake? He is the president. Everybody thinks he runs the place anyhow. He's always running down to Washington to testify before some damn committee. Always running off to meetings of the Business Council or whatever." Paley became more excited as he talked. "Why does he want to be called the chief executive officer?"

"I don't know. You'll have to ask him."

"Hell, I've always been able to find a Stanton." A measure of their mounting testiness with one another.

It wasn't my province, but, positioned where I was in a kind of catbird seat, I gained a perspective on how CBS was functioning, distilled some thoughts about it, and took them to Stanton. I have been staring at the wall for a couple of days, I said in essence, thinking about the CBS that I first joined and the CBS I see around me now. It's lost something. Lost the character and the very definite personality that you and the chairman gave it when you were running a smaller store. Now it's beginning to founder, to give the impression that no one is in charge. We're squandering something of great value. I think the whole company needs to be restructured. The present structure is simply outmoded. The increasing number of disparate CBS divisions, all reporting to Paley and Stanton and

fragmenting their attention, should be realigned into four ho-
mogenous groups, each with its own chief executive, each one
of the four responsible directly to the chairman and the president. This, I suggested, would be a more manageable, less cumbersome alignment for an expanding business.

Stanton listened, stony and silent. He had created the structure and was probably thinking it was none of my goddam
business, not in my brief at all. Gradually his body became less
rigid, his expression more reflective. He seemed to be gathering thoughts of his own, debating whether to voice them. We
talked quietly for two hours or more. A stream of problems
poured out of him, problems he had had with Paley, matters
he had perhaps shared only with his wife. His facial expression,
his tone of voice, his very body language reflected frustration
and hurt, disappointment rather than anger, and toward the
end he said sorrowfully, "Paley may have destroyed me for the
number one spot." I had the feeling I was hearing more than I
wanted to know. I thought to say, why don't you quit? But I
knew he loved his position, his credentials, his surroundings
too much. The thirty-fifth floor of the new Saarinen-designed
CBS building where Paley and Stanton — and three or four of
us — officed was the most elegant, tasteful business accommodation I have ever seen. Its appointments reflected commercial
success with rare dignity and discernment, and expressed the
aesthetic sensitivity of both men. Instead I moved gingerly back
to the subject I had come to discuss. He agreed with my observations and said something should be done. I asked if he would
follow up with the chairman; one of us must. We should sleep
on it for a few days, he said, but in any event I shouldn't raise
it. "It would undermine your relationship with the chairman."
I felt a certain compassion and sympathy for him, for I knew
he had no enthusiasm for a confrontation with Paley, prefer-
ring a placid surface to the turbulence below. To the world at
large Stanton was at the top of his line — wealthy, president of
the most successful and prestigious broadcasting company in
the world, spokesman for the industry in Washington, esteemed throughout the business world. Yet he was troubled
and unhappy, reaching for the brass ring that remained just
beyond his grasp.

A week or so later I had a morning appointment with Mr.
Paley at his apartment. He was suffering a chronic bad back.

The stunning Mrs. Paley opened the door dressed in her robe, and I apologized for taking her by surprise. She laughed gaily. "Come on in, Mike. We now share a secret. Not even Bill has ever seen me without my makeup." With or without makeup, she looked more beautiful than any living creature. "Bill's in the sittingroom. I'll bring in some coffee." The chairman too was dressed in his robe.

At the finish of the business I had come to discuss I said, "There's one other matter. I may be out of order and I may not have a job when I go out the door. But I'd hate myself if I didn't tell you what's on my mind." I was determined not to cast the stone of silence. He laughed lightly at my serious tone. His back was hurting him less and he was in a cheery frame of mind. "It can't be that bad. Say whatever you want to say." He had a wonderful smile and was altogether a man of great personal charm when he turned it on.

"I should tell you first that I laid this all out for Frank a few days ago and he thought it would *not* be a good idea for me to bring it up with you."

"Well, if you think it a good idea, go ahead. Let's have some more coffee. What about some croissants and marmalade?" He was always eager for an excuse to eat. I told him about CBS having lost something, that its luster was diminishing. It needed to be regalvanized, given a fresh sense of direction, restructured. I had even sketched out the new structure to illustrate what I was talking about. He was intrigued and stimulated.

"Damn! I'm delighted you raised this! It's exactly what I've been concerned about. And for some time. We've let our authority slide. We're too fragmented. I can't dredge out of the operating divisions information I want." He became so excited he forgot his ailing back. "You say our luster is diminishing? You're wrong. It's lost." He said we must restore CBS to its former position of prestige and honor. Now that the air was cleared (he had rid CBS of a vexing problem when he fired Jim Aubrey as president of the CBS television network a short time before), he felt free to make the kind of moves required. He was exhilarated, wanted people to have fun working at CBS, and particularly wanted to feel secure about his legacy.

"Did you say you gave Frank your thoughts on this?"

"Yes. Just as I've described them to you."

"Where are you going now?"

"Back to the office."

"Tell Frank we've had this talk and ask him to come over here at four o'clock this afternoon. We'll discuss this thing and get it moving." The chairman was charged. "Stanton can't be so damned antiseptic, though. Always wanting to do things by the book. I'm really bullish about this. About the future."

I had been there most of the morning and he sent me back to CBS in his car. On the way I made notes of his points, his phrasing, so I could relate our conversation to Stanton with flavor as well as accuracy.

"Frank, I had an appointment with the chairman this morning and when we finished our business I blurted out my whole story about what CBS has lost and how it was drifting." Stanton did not look pleased. "What did he say?"

"He's delighted. He said he was delighted I brought up the whole thing. And he'd like you to come over at four o'clock this afternoon so you two can talk about it privately and decide what to do." Referring to my notes, I gave him a full rundown. It was seven o'clock when Stanton returned from Paley's apartment and stopped by my office door. "How did it go?" I asked. He stared at me blankly for several seconds.

"Paley never brought it up," he said and walked away, expressionless. It seemed inconceivable. I wondered what they had sparred about across the gap that separated them and seemed to have been widening since I had returned to New York in 1962. For a moment I was concerned lest Stanton think I was involved in some political ploy, some power play of my own, but on reflection I was sure he knew me well enough not to worry about that sort of thing. I stayed far clear of cliques and cabals, hated political maneuvering. One CBS television network president invited me to join his division, promising wildly, "We'll take the company over from these old farts." Since Paley virtually owned the store, this hardly seemed a sensible ambition. The next network president asked me: "How do you play Paley?" I found such a nonsense question hard to credit.

"Straight," I said. He didn't last long in the post either.

Meanwhile the Paley-Stanton relationship remained civil and my business with them carried on evenly.

Once or twice we had spoken, though never seriously, about buying a football team, but one day over lunch it was Frank Stanton, an improbable source, who first proposed baseball. Frank's deepest venture into sports was driving a fast sports car on occasion.

"What about the New York Yankees?" he asked.

"Terrific idea," I said. It had not occurred to me that either would consider buying a sports franchise.

"How do we know they can be bought?" Paley asked.

"Dan Topping is a friend of yours, isn't he? Why don't you have him to lunch and ask him?" I suggested. Topping and his partner, Del Webb, had owned the Yankees since the late forties. Paley did lunch with Topping and stopped by my office afterwards. His broad smile telegraphed the answer. "He said yes. I told him you would come around to his apartment this afternoon and start working out a deal."

It wasn't quick and easy, but by late summer 1964 we had reached an agreement in principle to buy eighty percent of the club valued at $14 million. Topping and Webb were each to retain a ten percent interest, and CBS would have the option to buy them out within five years. The purchase was to be formally closed after the 1964 World Series — the Yankees lost in seven games to St. Louis — and on November second, majority ownership passed to CBS. Paley, Stanton, and I became members of the new board of directors, representing CBS, together with Topping and Webb from the old partnership. Topping would remain active operationally as the club's president, but before the ink was dry Webb decided to sell his remaining ten percent interest and asked a proportionate $1.4 million. Apparently he needed additional cash for some tax purpose. Paley trotted out his tough-negotiator persona; he wasn't going to let Webb off that easily. The CBS figure-men recommended paying Webb $1,150,000. Paley offered him a flat $1 million, and Webb took it. When he left the room Paley turned to me with an object lesson. "Never be afraid to ask for more than you think you can get." He was very pleased with himself.

I became the working stiff on the board and loved it, visiting the spring training camp in Fort Lauderdale and, during the regular season, going to night games at the Stadium after the CBS work day and on Saturdays and Sundays. There was no need for me to be around that much; I simply enjoyed baseball and the whole scene. I thought of it as a pleasant bonus. But I began to see that CBS had bought a pig in a poke. True, the Yankees were the most famous and most successful team in baseball. They had won more American League pennants, more world championships than any other team, by far, and had finished first in the American League in each of the five years prior to the CBS acquisition. Beyond question, the Yankees were a class act. Over a span of more than forty years they had had but two general managers, both the very best in the business: Ed Barrow and George Weiss. In 1963 Weiss quit in anger, crossed the river, and joined the then hapless New York Mets, leaving behind him an aging championship team. His vaunted farm system dried up, semineglected in the sun. Even on Stadium maintenance Topping had permitted only the most essential expenditures; the profit-and-loss statement was primed for a sale.

In 1964 the team won on momentum, on the sheer will of tiring champions who managed to win virtually all their games in a late September rush for the pennant. Immediately after the CBS purchase the team fell to an embarrassing sixth place in 1965 and was headed lower. Topping spent more and more time on his yacht or at his home in Florida, less and less with the Yankees, and, as a consequence, I spent more and more time at Yankee Stadium. Under manager Johnny Keane, the 1966 season opened disastrously. I think we won only two of the first nineteen games and late into several nights I discussed the situation with Ralph Houk, at first hoping he would volunteer, then urging him to go back to field managing, his natural bent. Houk had managed winning teams in 1961, '62, and '63 before Topping appointed him general manager, succeeding Weiss. Finally he agreed. Johnny Keane had won the 1964 World Series with St. Louis immediately before coming to New York but simply couldn't cut it with the Yankees, so we thought. In truth, he had no team. The Yankees sank into the League cellar for the first time in half a century.

Paley and Topping weren't speaking. At a board meeting which Topping chose not to attend — he went fishing on his yacht in the Florida Keys instead — it was decided that he should be bought out. Paley refused to see him and gave Stanton the disagreeable chore of settling with Topping for the same $1 million figure paid Webb, not the $1.4 million Topping demanded. The question arose: who would replace Topping as the club's president? The Yankees were at once an opportunity and an escape. I had to escape. I had been entangled with the business of acquisitions for almost four years and had long since realized that it was not my line of country. After the initial, riveted attention to educating myself and the stimulating process of discovery and searching out new people, I found it difficult to sustain genuine interest in price-earnings ratios, balance sheets, and annual statements. The signing of a merger deal didn't thrill me at all; I experienced no emotional highs, or even emotional lows, in the business of doing business. I was conscientious but uninspired in the field of acquisitions and mergers, a runner in cement shoes compared with my friend Felix Rohatyn of Lazard Frères, who was Mercury himself. There were dozens of people better qualified technically, better suited temperamentally than I. But at least I had got the process under way, pathfinding for Paley and Stanton. Some of us are better scouts than settlers.

At a board meeting on September 6, 1966, I was elected chairman and president of the New York Yankees. Stanton insisted I should have that dual title, "so there won't be any question about who's in charge." Paley said, "If you're in real trouble, let me know. But I expect you to run this thing in your own way." I thanked him and took him literally. The team I inherited was deep in last place; the only young person on the roster who could play the game was Bobby Murcer; he was twenty years old.

# The New York Yankees

## 12

THE DAY was all wrong for baseball. A thick mist turned into a thin, mean rain. Not drenching, just disagreeable. At Yankee Stadium four hundred and thirteen incorrigible fans and sixty-two thousand empty seats, both equally mute, watched two teams plodding through the mechanical motions of a meaningless game. A shotgun fired in any direction would have wounded no one. For the first time in half a century the Yankees were in last place, in the American League cellar. The date was the twenty-third of September, 1966. It was my first game as chairman and president of the New York American League Baseball Club. Friends thought I had lost my mind, surrendering an enviable CBS position, a luxurious office, and a butler in a starched white jacket who brought orange juice, croissants, and coffee each morning, opting instead for a fallen baseball team and a crumbling stadium in the Bronx. I, on the other hand, was happy as a soaring lark. This was my natural environment, the time and place for me. The route from Franklin Field in Philadelphia to Yankee Stadium in the Bronx had been circuitous, but sitting next to the Yankee dugout, trench-coat collar pulled up against the rain, I knew I had been once again touched by outrageous good fortune. The Yankees lost.

On a Sunday afternoon a week earlier, two days before a scheduled press conference to announce Topping's resignation and my appointment, the phone rang at home. One of the children answered and called from the pantry that it was Mr. Paley.

"You don't have to do this if you don't want to," he said.

"I know. I appreciate your thinking of it. Of the chance for me to opt out. But I really want to do this. Both eyes open."

"The press will be harpooning you from every point on the compass, you know. 'Madison Avenue takes over Yankees.' You know the kind of thing." Almost two years had passed since the sports writers had put the lash to CBS for the Yankee purchase but Paley's press-sensitive skin was still raw.

"That's OK. No mortar fire. No machine guns," I laughed; after all, I wasn't being led off to die, unless it was to be from an excess of pleasure.

"Good luck then."

"Thanks. Thanks for both. For the out and for the good wish."

The Yankee Stadium Club was crammed with press, radio, and television people. Topping spoke first, awkwardly in incomplete sentences, his voice more gravelly than usual. He was never at ease with the press, or with people generally. Milton Gross, a *New York Post* columnist, wrote a scathing good riddance. "My bile has been rising for twenty years," he told me.

For my part I sensed among them a pressing curiosity but no hostility. They would put my feet to the fire, of course. They would be skeptical and cynical, having experienced fakers by the carload. Rather than standing at the microphone as Topping had, shifting his weight about, communicating his discomfort, I decided on the spur of the moment, responding to some instinct, to sit on a tabletop, my legs dangling, at once diminishing the sense of ceremony, conscious that I wanted to separate myself from Topping in style and substance, to establish my stewardship not only as new but different from the past. I was surprised how much at home and at ease I felt and how much I was enjoying myself. I wanted them to feel the same with me. I thanked them for coming and said that from that day onward I was in the baseball business, totally and exclusively. Mine would not be a part-time stewardship. I would move out of CBS, would close the Yankee offices at Fifth Avenue and Fifty-seventh Street — the mid-Manhattan offices Topping had occupied — and would bring together the whole operation in the Stadium, where it belonged. This was something I had thought about and decided upon beforehand, of course. It made sense and I did not want the Yankees to smack of absentee ownership, absent even by the distance of one borough. And I said Ralph Houk would remain as field manager; he was our guy. Howard Cosell, covering for ABC television, asked if I had said *guy* or *goy*.

"Had I taken diction lessons from you, Howard, you would have understood me to say 'guy.' " Everyone laughed too hard, too pleased to have Howard put down, though I liked Howard and intended merely a friendly quip.

I sensed from the lively interest and good-humored give-and-take that the reporters quickly grasped that this was more than a routine management change — one guy in a gray flannel suit for another and, most important, that here was fresh material for them. They were enjoying the exercise as much as I. The press conference stretched out and was followed by individual interviews with columnists each looking for his own angle, and separate interviews with radio and television people. Frank Gifford, the marvelous former Giant football back, was then reporting for CBS Channel 2 in New York; he and I did an interview for the six o'clock news. Mr. Paley, apparently pleased with both his employees, rang and said, "Good questions; good answers."

Topping had always been aloof and withdrawn, as had most of the Yankee front-office staff. I aimed to change that from the very outset. "Gentlemen, going in you have my respect as professionals. Having once been a highly paid stringer for the *Hartford Courant* — ten cents an inch for anything published — I've had a worm's-eye view of your profession. But seriously, I appreciate the job you have to do. Obviously access is essential. I just want all of you to know that all of us are available to you. In case you want it, my direct line at the office is JUdson 2-4303. And my home phone number is ATwater 9-8053. If you need me, call at any time." As the press conference broke up, Maury Allen of the *Post* asked the Yankee publicity director if I meant it. Knowing I did, Bob Fishel encouraged him. "Phone him and see." He did. "Sure, Maury. I'll meet you for breakfast. What time? Where?" His next column was very up-beat: the Yankees are different now! Part of my job, as I saw it, was to personalize, to warm up the Yankees, especially in their deplorable position.

We needed all the friends we could win. The Yankees were more often cast with General Motors than with the common man. CBS also, in the common view, was a faceless, bloodless,

unfeeling corporate giant. How could it relate to the man in
the street or the man in the street to it? How could the blue-
collar fan trust something as personal as his baseball team to an
austere building on Sixth Avenue called "Black Rock"? The
"owner" had to be a person whom they could identify. He had
to be a flesh-and-blood target for their complaints, a person to
be for or against. That came with the territory. The public
relations problems were quite simple to perceive, relatively easy
to attack. The sports press was essential to us. My object was to
make it easy for them to write about the Yankees; and my leg
up was that I gave the writers something slightly different to
write about from the usual sports team owner. Given my Circus
and CBS background, I suppose it was predictable that Leonard Koppet of the Times would ask if I considered baseball
entertainment.

"Not in the pejorative sense," I replied. A Phi Beta Kappa
from Columbia University, Koppet was amused to have a fifty-
cent word crop up in a baseball interview, and the next morning in his Times story he reported wryly that a new standard of
literacy had been set among baseball executives. The Post described the Yankee leadership as young, vigorous, smiling, gregarious, and exciting; Newsday said that the new president had
been about everywhere, done about everything; and Arthur
Daley wrote that the new man was unawed by the monumental
problems confronting him and showed how smart he was by
enthusiastically endorsing Houk as manager. In fact, Daley, the
prestigious "Sports of the Times" columnist for his newspaper,
wrote of "the new Yankee" on two successive days. Only once
before in his career had one person been the subject of a two-
part column. The other, he told me, was the incomparable
Connie Mack. Mr. Mack was a man I had admired from a
distance. When I was a college boy in Philadelphia I used to
watch him in the Athletics' Shibe Park dugout dressed in his
black business suit and high starched collar managing the team
he owned, directing the placement of his players with a waving
scorecard, the only manager ever permitted to manage from
the dugout in street clothes, I believe. I could live a thousand
years and not acquire a fraction of his baseball knowledge, and
I was flattered to be bracketed with him, if only in dual Times
sports columns.

From the outset the press was astonishingly generous to me. They even appeared sympathetic to the formidable rebuilding job to be done with the team on the field. In the farthest reaches of my anticipation I would not have dared to predict so voluminous, widespread, and favorable a reaction.

Needless to say, I was especially pleased by this extravagant press coverage because it gave me an instant identity in a quarter where I was an unknown, the quarter where my new work lay: rebuilding the team, establishing a new Yankee persona with the public and gaining an effective place among my baseball peers, among the Lords of Baseball, as the *Daily News* called them.

Also to my advantage the reporters discovered that I had been an authentic athlete when Penn was a national football power. They interviewed George Munger, my old football coach at Penn, and he said he remembered vividly how well our teams had played and that I had been "a happy-go-lucky guy. Lean and tough, yes. But a gentleman." From Navy Department records they found that I had not spent the war years issuing underwear from the ships' stores. From me they learned that as a child I had seen my first major-league baseball game at Yankee Stadium. One thing I did not reveal was my CIA service in the early fifties. I rang up Dick Helms, then the director of the Central Intelligence Agency and a longtime friend, and asked his advice. Though it was not a point of any great moment, he thought I should finesse it if I could without embarrassment.

Baseball was now my bread and butter and I loved the game and the lads who played it. It's a boy's game, of course, and should be kept in proper perspective to the living of life. Baseball doesn't pretend to be a basic commodity like oil, or grain, or fish from the sea. But it is a vivid, lively part of the American fabric. Withdraw it and the whole scene would be thrown out of balance. Where else would millions of fans unloose their summer passions? Relive their summer fantasies? There must be, particularly in our insistently technological society, some romantic quality, some escape from the hard world of fact. Baseball is a beguiling place to go. Admission to a ball park buys instant respite from the frenetic pace and uncertain values of the real world in which mechanization obscures the point that the most important element in all of life is a human being. But in a few strides — through a turnstile, down a ramp and along an aisle to a seat — baseball quickly reestablishes the individual.

One man with a bat challenges one man with a ball. A young man poised alone on a mound pits his skill and courage against the skill and courage of a young man waiting alone beside a rubber plate. The essence of this contest is fundamental to man's nature and as unending in its appeal as the cowboy and his horse against the elements. The ball park itself remains an oasis in a city desert of steel and concrete. Life slips back to a human scale. Soft grass rests the eye and white-uniformed players, gracefully positioned in defense, stand clearly visible. In contrast to the wound-tight world outside, this linear game unfolds at an ordered pace and drama builds around its split-second timing and precise geometry, clear for all to see and comprehend. There is no uncertainty about individual performance, no waiting for Monday's films to discover who did what, no sharing error with unidentifiables. The shortstop glides in front of a ground ball, scoops it up, and throws, all in one flowing motion. Or he boots it. The center fielder in a minor miracle of timing spears a line drive at sprinter's speed. Or it bounces off the heel of his glove, irrevocably. No assignment of blame elsewhere. One individual makes the play or he does not, for all to see.

This is especially so in the batter's box. Four or five times a day — twice that in a double-header — a batter, alone and exposed, steps to the plate and lays his talent on the line. No equivocation. No quarter asked or given. Only the exhilaration of a hit and the dash down the baseline, or the humiliation of a strikeout and the excruciating journey back to the dugout. Elation and depression. The human condition operates on every pitch, physically and emotionally. A player is wrenched from the heights to the depths and back again every day. His guts must be made of rawhide to endure his highly visible trade. He cannot allow a mistake, or a series of them, or boos from the crowd ("Ya bum, ya!") to upset his finely tuned physical and psychological equilibrium. His sport demands more keenly honed skills than any other.

The owner of a ball club is a custodian; the team belongs to the citizenry, of course, to everyone who buys a ticket to a ball park or a newspaper to read the box score. The man who doesn't understand that has missed the main point. No one roots for or against a button factory in Queens, but the local ball club is everybody's business. Every fan has a proprietary interest. And the wonderful corollary is that running a ball club puts you in touch with the whole city on a first-name basis. Perhaps it is a contradiction in an essentially private person, but I loved that. The luck of the draw had let me function at every level except deep poverty, learning respect for all kinds of people, sustaining one's own self-respect in all kinds of circumstances, holding the marvelous adventure of unfolding experience in common-sense perspective, rooted in my own common beginnings. Varied experience had conditioned me for the New York Yankees, for the open invitation to know thousands of new people. None would be a stranger.

Some people maintained that baseball was out of joint with the times and my response was that we should be grateful if it were true — the times being made up of a number of appalling ingredients — and proposed that people should come out to the ball park twenty minutes before a game when absolutely nothing is happening except a couple of fellows arching a lazy spray of water over the infield. It allows time to shift down into a lower gear. Nor should a person bother to bring his watch; time here is measured by runs and innings and shadows moving out towards the pitcher's mound. There is no race against the clock. Relaxed, the mind is free to notice two elements that make baseball increasingly attractive in these swift days: its essential nonviolence and its individualism.

Every action has a definite outcome, each dependent on the performance of a single individual, alone and exposed for all to see. A throw from the outfield beats the runner to the plate by a stride, but the catcher drops the ball. It lies there on the ground in full view. The runner is elated, the catcher devastated. And we in the stands are ecstatic or desolated, depending on whether the scoring runner belongs to our city.

There is little enough to draw us together, it seemed to me, and the simple verities that keep life in some balance are not always visible to the naked eye, but there is something cohesive about a baseball crowd rooting for the home side, some restorative value in the human rhythms of the game.

A bus stopped at the curb, picked up passengers near where I stood on Fifth Avenue and Ninety-second Street and the driver shouted, "What're ya doin', Mike?"

"Waiting for a taxi to run me downtown."

"C'mon! Get in. I'll get ya down there faster." I dropped my coins in the box, held onto the rail around his seat, and talked about his teenage son's professional baseball ambitions until he dropped me off at Fifty-second Street. A neighborly opening to a new day. And one Saturday night I held Doreen's hand in one of mine, Mousie's in the other, waiting to cross Madison Avenue in midblock on our way to dinner. A taxi driver jammed on his brakes, stopped, leaned over and rolled down his right window. "Hey Mike, we won two today!" He was ecstatic.

"Yeah. And we'll win another one tomorrow!"

"Who's pitching?"

"Fritz."

"Goin' for his sixteenth." Fritz Peterson had won fifteen games thus far that season. The unscheduled stop drew a complaint from the passenger and we heard the driver explain over his shoulder, "I just wanted to talk to Mike." He waved goodbye and drove on and the girls and I crossed to Pia's eight-table restaurant.

A young man in a t-shirt and blue jeans stopped me in the Stadium ramp. "I think you're doin' a good job, Mike, doin' OK. But my old man thinks you stink."

"Do I know him?"

"Naw, he just doesn't like you. I tell him you're OK but . . ."

"Does he say why?"

"Naw. Yer hair's too long, or somethin'."

"Oh well, that seems reason enough. Anyhow, thanks for putting in a good word for me." We shook hands.

Would you come to the Awards dinner at Mount Loretto, a Catholic institution on Staten Island for unmanageable kids? Sure. Would you visit the irreparably wounded in the Veterans Hospital? Of course. Would you speak to the Law Society, the

Meriden Boys' Club, the unwed mothers at the House of Good Shepherd? Yes to all. Will you really join the auxiliary mounted police and patrol Central Park? Yes, really.

Stephen had been a bellhop at the Plaza Hotel for forty years or more. I had known him for half that time at least. He had an Irish name and an Irish way with whiskey. One morning I met him, pale and pained, walking along Fifty-eighth Street towards the Plaza and the day's work.

"Bad night, Stephen?" He shuddered.

"Worse morning. The night itself was grand." We chatted for a few moments and I started to move on.

"Hang on till noontime. It gets better after that," I said sympathetically.

"You know," he said, laying an arresting hand on my arm and looking me in the eye, "before you go. Some of us were talking about this the other day. You know, you're very nice with people." I was touched by what he said and the serious way he said it, and put a hand on each of his shoulders.

"But Stephen, people are very nice to me." It was so. East side, West side, up and down the town. I once said that I would rather be a lamppost in New York than a millionaire in any other city. And that is so. I loved New York from one end to the other and everyone in it. I thrilled to surging current of events that the city paraded day and night, grateful day and night for my own good luck to be alive and moving to the beat of its tempo, to be one of its citizens. I am always encouraged by how much goodwill is gained not by calculation but by common courtesy, simple good manners, and affording any man the dignity that is his natural right. I'm sometimes disappointed that some among us think rude and offensive public behavior a better defense against whatever it is we're defensive about, and I wish more of us had the courage to be polite, to know that toughness lies in good fiber, not in disagreeable behavior, to understand that courtesy is a matter of choice, not submission. I am always surprised that more of us don't appreciate how much favor is won so effortlessly.

On Saturday, my second game as president, four street urchins yapped and leapt around me like hungry puppies as I crossed 157th Street from the fenced parking area to the players' entrance to the Stadium. "Take us in, hey Mike. Hey Mike, take us in, will ya?" They were unwashed and untamed.

"OK. Come on." They could hardly believe their change of luck. The uniformed guard at the door made a grab for them. "It's all right. They're with me." His expression told me what he thought of me: you dummy; you don't know nothin'; these are bad kids. They followed me into the ramp, along a cross-over, and down the aisle to my seat next to the Yankee dugout. It was an hour or more before game time. The teams were limbering and taking batting practice. I tossed my topcoat over the back of a seat. The experiment might cost me a coat and it might not. "You kids stay here. Look after my coat. I'll be back." When I returned, three of them had run off, probably to steal candy from a concession stand. But one had been left to guard my coat. After the game a Chicago baseball writer traveling with the White Sox said, "I saw you bring in a bunch of street kids, didn't I?"

"Well, four."

"The Specials think you're nuts. They tell me those kids are thieves. A menace."

"Yeah, probably. But maybe today they just wanted to see a ball game. Anyhow, who got hurt?"

"Jeez," he said. "This is the Yankees?"

"Got to loosen up the joint a little. We're not at war with kids, you know."

No city police are allowed to work within the Stadium, of course; legislation precludes it. Rather, security is provided by Special Officers dressed in blue policelike uniforms. Some weren't always flexible enough to keep their combat attitude in neutral until it was needed to control the unruly. They would best learn directly from me, I thought, the difference between their legitimate safeguarding role and gratuitous hostility — the us-against-them mindset, particularly with young people. After one game, in those beginning times, I left my seat beside the field and filed up the aisle, behind the departing crowd when five or six boys, perhaps twelve to fourteen years of age, came running after me. "Mike, Mike. The cop took Frankie's bat away from him."

"What bat?"

"Mickey gave him a broken bat and the cop took it away from him."

"Which one?"

"That one. That one standing in front of the dugout." We walked onto the field and along to the officer. "Did you take this boy's bat?" I asked.

"No."

"He did. He did," the kids cried.

"Get the bat," I said, quietly. Grudgingly he retrieved a cracked bat from the runway leading from the dugout to the players' clubhouse.

"Whose bat is it?" I asked the boys. They pointed out a shy, nice-looking lad, dressed in clean, ill-fitting hand-me-down clothes.

"Give it to this boy." The Special stuck it out angrily, hating my guts, no doubt, and scuffed away mumbling and surly. I did not like embarrassing him, demeaning him, but his feelings were less important at that moment than to establish that bullying was out, that a cop taking a bat from a kid was intolerable. The bullies among them would have to learn a new attitude and one direct action was worth a thousand written instructions; the spoken word traveled faster and farther.

The kids scampered off happily shouting a lot of "Thanks, Mike" over their shoulders, happy to have found that the fellow who ran the store was a friend. I liked young people and it showed, I suppose. Anyhow they knew. It helped to be named Mike rather than Cuthbert or Peregrine. "Mike" presented no artificial barrier. I certainly wanted none. In his *Daily News* column, Dick Young once wrote that I dressed like an Edwardian fop but had the soul of a ward heeler, determined to shake hands with every New Yorker if that will make him a Yankee fan. I liked that description.

The best Stadium happenings may have been the young, their wonderment, their sober concentration, their brimming anticipation. It is a joy simply to know that this still existed, undiluted. Papa's loyalties may have been fixed on Ruth or DiMag. Crosetti may have been my folk hero. But who can prove to a lad of ten that his Reggie Jackson isn't equally heroic? Or that a pop foul he caught isn't as precious as Carl Yastrzemski's homerun ball you recovered in the Fenway Park bleachers in some unknown time familiar only to grownups.

Next best may be the next youngest, if there are any grada-
tions at all — the high school and college-aged kids; we wanted
them in our ball park. They came and brought their liveliness.
One spring, though, they erupted in what some newspapers
called a mini-riot. It was an Easter holiday double-header.
There were lots of school kids, and they got restless as the
afternoon stretched out. Paper cups, apple cores, and rubber
balls bombarded the field, just for the hell of it. Then two or
three thousand swarmed over the fences after the last out in
the ninth inning, thinking the game was over. It wasn't. The
score was still tied. The running-wilds had to be coaxed back
into the stands with the warning that the Yanks might have to
forfeit the game. A lot of hand-wringing and finger-pointing
followed. Sports writers wrote: Burke, "too permissive,"
wanted them; he got them; now what's he going to do with
them? Similar unruliness had broken out at the same time in
Chicago and I think Pittsburgh. Concern about safety was genuine. The inclination was to clamp down, taking physical pre-
cautions. Like wiring-in the bleachers. We rejected that. To do
so would be out of joint with the whole purpose of baseball.
Ugly and offensive. Instead, we appealed to their better nature,
to their love of the game, and especially to their identification
with our very young ball team. Ellis, 21; Munson, 22; Kline, 21;
Murcer, 24; Kenney, 24, were all one of them, not one of us
elder types on the other side of the generation gap. I wrote a
message in longhand, had it blown up and hung as signs all
over the Stadium:

> Hey young fans —
> We love you!
> But don't blow it . . .
> Throwing things, interfering with play — man, that's really
>     nowhere.
> If we have to lose a game, let's make the other team beat us —
>     not our fans.
> So cool it, kids.
> Let these young Yankees do their own thing.

Simple. Simpleminded even, but the response was instanta-
neous and complete and for the balance of the season not a

single object, paper airplane, or youngster sailed onto the field. Their ball-park manners were super; I loved them for that and for a host of other good reasons. I was determined to establish my own ethos on the Yankees. At the time, Mike Nichols' *The Graduate* became a watershed film and from the score Paul Simon's "Mrs. Robinson" became a hit song. I borrowed one of the lines — "Where have you gone Joe DiMaggio" — and mounted it on the Stadium signboard so commuters driving along the Deegan Expressway on dismal winter days would, I hoped, smile and know that the New York Yankees might have lost their top standing for the moment but not their sense of humor. Baseball was never meant to be a business run by people who wore iron pants, people unlubricated by life's natural juices, strangers to laughter. The sport is lighthearted; its function is respite and release.

In the late 1960s there was little of either respite or release for thousands of kids in the ragged areas of the city and it seemed obvious that we should try to cheer them up, even if only briefly. We invented the Yankee Kids program. In groups of three or four thousand, youngsters would be invited to a number of games throughout the season. The only requirement was that each ten children would be accompanied by an adult to look after them. Howard Berk, whom I'd borrowed from CBS, organized the idea into a program and when Consolidated Edison became a Yankee broadcast sponsor, Chuck Luce, Con Edison's chairman, undertook to have his company administer the program and be identified with it. During the next decade well over a million ConEd kids enjoyed a free day at the Stadium. In earlier years a limited number of free tickets was allotted to cultivate young fans, but these were targeted for upmarket, well-behaved suburban children. By the late sixties it was high time to give attention to the inner-city kids who had nothing at all going for them and to face up to the different deportment problems they might bring.

On a more selective scale we created a Martin Luther King scholarship. Each June, in collaboration with the New York Board of Education, we selected needy students from high school graduating classes — students who had been accepted at a college — and contributed to their tuition fees. On June 26, 1968, for instance, the auditorium of Benjamin Franklin High

School in East Harlem was packed with relatives and friends of white-capped and -gowned students. From the stage where I sat with the faculty I could make out no white face. It was a rough environment. The worst tales you've heard about ghetto schools were played out there. Yet out of the pack emerged two who qualified for Ivy League colleges. Presenting their checks, I spoke to the students and their families about the Yankees being a neighbor, a member of the community, as well as a ball club, about education giving a man or woman a sense of himself, of self-worth. This kind of participation in the life about us made no news, sold no tickets. But in those years the blacks particularly felt a mounting isolation, desperation. It was of moment to them that someone showed an interest, someone showed up. Not all our players understood that, but most were sympathetic to what had to be done. On a given day they would all pile into a bus and visit areas in Brownsville or Harlem, blocked off for the occasion, and sign autographs and answer questions. Individual players visited schools to encourage youngsters not to drop out. In a crowded gymnasium, youngsters sitting on windowsills when floor space ran out, a grateful principal thanked Roy White: There are a dozen boys here we haven't seen for a month, but they're back now.

Our feel for the mood of the day, hence our motivation, stemmed from the fact that we lived on the edge of Harlem, separated by a narrow span of water and a short bridge over the Harlem River. Riots and fire raged through the black ghettos of Los Angeles and Detroit, Newark and Washington. Rage smoldered and the same anger might have broken loose in New York had not John Lindsay walked the streets of Harlem in his shirtsleeves, his very presence cooling tempers. But Watts and Detroit and Newark aside, you could not, unless you were bloodless as stone, drive through Harlem to and from the Stadium once, twice, three times a day without experiencing some human reaction, without saying to yourself: there, but for the grace of God and an accident of birth, go I. And ask yourself what can I do that I am not doing? What signal of hope can the Yankees give? We could solve no fundamental problem. But I knew there must be something within our particular competence that might be useful, and an idea was sparked by a television documentary about Grambling State University in

Louisiana. *One Hundred Yards to Glory,* it was called. I turned it on because Howard Cosell, who had become a good friend, was the narrator. Grambling is a small black university that has sent an extraordinary number of players to the National Football League, hence Cosell's specific sports interest. At that point Grambling had been undefeated in three years of play against other black colleges. I telephoned the Grambling coach, Eddie Robinson.

"Coach Robinson. My name is Michael Burke. I'm president of the New York Yankees. I saw Howard Cosell's show last night and thought it was wonderful. Inspirational. Congratulations."

"Thank you. Thank you very much. Who did you say this is?"

"Mike Burke. I'm president of the New York Yankees and I called to see if you might be interested in having your football team play a game in Yankee Stadium."

"Come on, man, who is this?"

I laughed. "Seriously, coach. It isn't a gag. I'm sure it sounds a little weird coming out of the blue like this. But it's for real."

"This is straight?"

"It's straight. You can phone me back at Yankee Stadium if you want to make sure."

"No. No. I've just got to get it through my head. You want . . . ?"

"I don't know if it would fit your schedule or not. Or whether you would want to do it at all. But I thought you might bring your team here and play some other black college and we'll raise some money for the New York street academies or something like that."

"Bring Grambling to Yankee Stadium!" From his tone he had grasped the idea and was warming to it.

"Would your kids like to come to New York?"

"Man, we wouldn't need no plane to fly there."

"What team should you play, coach?"

"Morgan State. They're best next to us. Undefeated for two years."

"Who's the coach there?"

"Coach Banks. Ernie Banks."

"Could you play a game in late September?"

"I think so. I'll have to look at the schedule."

"Should you telephone Coach Banks or should I?"

"I'll do that."

"OK. Why don't you two fellows talk it out and then ring me whenever you're ready. Here's my phone number."

We three — Robinson, Banks, and I — met in New York at the Plaza Hotel for breakfast. Robinson was tall, extroverted, looked a bit like a heavyweight Sugar Ray Robinson. Banks dressed as conservatively as an Ivy League athletic director and was built like a fireplug. Both were keen on the idea. We arranged for fees to be paid each school, for the net proceeds to go to the New York Urban League, and for the game to be played in September 1968. Not everyone in the world was enthusiastic about the idea of bringing two black college football teams to Yankee Stadium. Visions of all sorts of disastrous results danced through timid heads. Certain CBS colleagues thought I'd lost my senses: you won't have a stadium left when those blacks get through with it. This unfortunate line of thought gained some momentum, and I rang Mayor Lindsay.

"John, will you please send me a letter, quickly, saying what a great thing it is to have the Grambling–Morgan State game in the Stadium. Great for the city and so on. Perhaps you could congratulate CBS and the Yankees for being so enlightened. You know the line. And would you send a copy to CBS? Some people there are getting antsy. And could it be today, John?" It was done.

Sixty-two thousand people bought tickets. A few whites must have been present, but they were lost in a black sea. Wearing their Sunday clothes and their Sunday manners, the black population poured into the Stadium, filling it to capacity. Their sense of pride was as clear and native as the sound of Louis Armstrong's trumpet. These were their kids, their own black kids, down there making their own history on the field Ruth and Gehrig and DiMaggio hallowed for baseball, where Army and Notre Dame had fought their classic football battles, where Joe Louis had beaten Schmeling, Galento, and Conn, where a Pope had said Mass, where the Baltimore Colts and the New York Giants had met in what many called the greatest football game ever played. The spectacular Grambling marching band sashayed through its intricate patterns, blaring out its jivy rhythms, and its team scored one more touchdown than Morgan State. After the game I stood at one of the exits watching the exhilarated crowd empty into the streets and flow across the 157th Street bridge to celebrate at the Flash Inn, the Red Rooster, Jocks, and other watering places down along Lenox and Seventh avenues. Coming out, three young men in colorful sports jackets taunted one another good-humoredly about a bet won and lost and money changed hands and as they passed me one said to his friends: "Man, it don't matter who scored the most points. We all won today."

*Hate* is such a violent word, sweeping and categorical. Its connotation is so ugly. It is a word whose use I skirt. So I was deeply distressed to find in one morning's Yankee mail a letter from a teacher at Junior High School No. 13 on 106th Street and Madison Avenue in East Harlem. It was a long letter detailing his unhappiness with treatment at a Yankee game the previous weekend. The reason for his distress was understandable, his reaction unfortunate. He had bought eighteen general admission tickets to a Yankee–White Sox game, along with about 60,000 other people, and brought his class of twelve-year-old boys to the game. The general admission section was full, he claimed, so he sat his group in reserve seats. When the legitimate seatholders arrived, the teacher and his boys were told they had to move. It is entirely possible that the usher did not handle the situation with sweet diplomacy. The teacher left the ball park in high dudgeon, dragging the disappointed boys with him. On the following Monday his assignment to the class was to write letters to me. Written in struggling twelve-year-old script, sixteen letters were attached to his own typed complaint. One who lived on 108th Street wrote: "Now I hate the Yankees . . . now I hate Yankee Stadium." Another whose home was on 112th Street wrote: "Now I know the Yankees hate negroes." No letter omitted the word *hate*. It was a time in New York — in Harlem, in Brownsville, in all the nation's deprived areas — when bitterness and despair outstripped hope. Immediately I wrote a longhand letter to each boy who had written to me, and I wrote to the teacher apologizing for his unhappy experience. I invited them all to another game and deplored the use of the word *hate* in the boys' letters. But that didn't put my mind at rest. I was still deeply distressed. I had driven past Junior High

School 13 perhaps hundreds of times on my way to the Stadium, up Madison Avenue to the Madison Avenue Bridge, through the dilapidation, the burned-out boarded-up storefronts, the dim corner *bodegas*, the rubble of collapsed buildings, the clumps of jobless black men passing a bottle held in a brown paper bag, the island of a housing project, and across the Harlem River. The next morning I stopped, found the principal's office, and explained my purpose. I wanted to talk with the boys personally, to invite them to be my guests at another game. I wanted to meet the teacher to ask if there wasn't enough hate in the air without his teaching it to impressionable youngsters. That was putting it nicely. What I really wanted to do was to kick the teacher's ass all over Harlem for being so stupidly irresponsible. When he was brought in, my anger fell apart, changed to dismay. He was a young twenty-four-year-old, slightly built, white upper-middle-class Harvard graduate. He was teaching English to black and Hispanic kids in a ghetto. If his judgment was flawed, his sense of mission was not. If he had not yet learned to handle the minor inconveniences, the petty disillusionments of life, his heart at least was in the right place. He understood, on being told, that irritating misunderstandings can take place in the confusion of a crowd of 60,000 people in a ball park. More to the point, he recognized the disservice he had done his students in assigning them to write letters of hate, permitting his personal pique to induce hate at the moment when many of us were trying to heal the breach, to overcome the growing ethnic mistrust that spread across the country. It ended well. The Harvard boy brought the boys to another game. Singly at first, then the whole lot came to say their polite thanks, piled in with me, a couple on my lap, taking snapshots of one another, happy, no longer believing the Yankees hated negroes or Puerto Ricans or anybody. In his commencement speech in June the Junior High School No. 13 principal, Leonard Loeb, told the Puerto Rican and black students and their parents: "You are not alone." He said he was able to show "that people, no matter their duties and the call on their time, do care. They are interested. I tried to explain that there are times in life when unpleasant things happen. Life is not easy, but that does not mean people are against us."

Life is generally easier for the kind of people who are usually invited to throw out the first ceremonial ball on opening day of the baseball season. Flying to spring training in Florida, I let my mind wander as far afield as whim would carry it, away from presidents and governors and mayors who traditionally opened the Yankee season. Politicians did not fit my sense of opening day. Invariably they were booed when their names were announced over the public address system, and they added not one whit to the fans' expectations of this springtime rite. As soon as the plane landed in Fort Lauderdale I wrote Marianne Moore asking her to honor us with her presence on April 10, 1968. Hearing nothing, I sent a follow-up telegram and received a prompt response, chiding me. "Did you think for a moment," she wrote, "that I would not accept even though I do not have the best arm in baseball." I coveted her for the New York Yankees, her doubtful arm, her frail form, her white wispy hair straying from beneath her tricorne hat, her delicate gentle face that could only be a poet's face. She had been a Dodger fan when they both lived in Brooklyn. Now she had been deserted by the Dodgers, fled to Los Angeles, and she herself had moved to my old Manhattan neighborhood, West Ninth Street. More, she had memorialized the Yankees in her poem "Baseball and Writing," which contained these excerpts citing Mantle, Ford, and Howard:

> It's a pitcher's battle all the way — a duel —
> a catcher's, as, with cruel
> puma paw, Elston Howard lumbers lightly
> back to plate. (His spring
> de-winged a bat swing.)
>
> . . . . .
> "Mickey, leaping like the devil" — why
> gild it, although deer sounds better —
> snares what was speeding towards its treetop nest,
> one-handling the souvenir-to-be
> meant to be caught by you or me.
>
> . . . . .
> like Whitey's three kinds of pitch and pre-
> diagnosis
> with pick-off psychosis.
> Pitching is a large subject.

On a pure Florida day when I swam in the sea in front of my bungalow at the Lagomar Hotel in Sarasota, breakfasted in the morning sun near the pool, played pepper with Frank Crosetti, Elston Howard, and Gene Michael at the Fort Lauderdale ball park and sat behind the batting cage with Houk watching wary veterans taking early spring training batting practice against swift eager rookies with uncertain control, Miss Moore, braving a raw March wind, knocked politely on the side door of Yankee Stadium. She had never actually been on a major league baseball field and wanted to see from ground level where she would perform. Gail, a personable young woman in the public relations department, took her in hand, assured her she would not have to throw the ball from the pitcher's mound to home plate. Whitey Ford would do that on opening day. Gail showed her the first-row box seat where she would sit and explained that she would throw the ball from there to a catcher twenty feet away. Also Gail had the good grace to give Miss Moore a glove and a ball, which she took home and kept under her bed. The poet was keen "to warm up the old soup bone" practicing with her brother, a young man of seventy-odd. On opening day she was in midseason form. Miss Moore threw a perfect strike to the handsome Yankee catcher from Staten Island, Frank Fernandez, a young man with his own sense of occasion. He handed her the ball as a keepsake, kissed her warmly on the cheek, and, in the final inning, hit a home run to win for the Yankees, 1-0. Miss Moore came to the Stadium fairly frequently after that, sitting comfortably in the closed owners' box on the mezzanine, once through a twenty-two-inning game with the Boston Red Sox which went on well past one o'clock in the morning. She brushed aside suggestions that she might like to leave at eleven, at midnight, at half-past twelve. A day or so later she wrote thanking us for such an exciting game, describing some of her impressions: Elston Howard "crouching on legs that a frog would envy."

By her eighty-third birthday she was no longer gadding about. A friend rang to say Miss Moore would celebrate quietly and with a very few friends and would like me to come. "Do you have any idea what kind of gift might please her?" I asked.

"That's so difficult, isn't it?" The lady thought for a moment and added, "I've heard her admire the Yankee warm-up jacket." Pete Sheehy, who has looked after the Yankee clubhouse and the uniforms of every Yankee player from Babe Ruth to Reggie Jackson, had a jacket wrapped for me. Her birthday fell on a Sunday. We had a Giant football game at the Stadium and I was late arriving at her apartment. It was not large — a sittingroom, two bedrooms, a kitchen — but entirely in character. Spare, polished, and Colonial. You would not have been surprised to be told that George Washington had slept there. Dark polished floors were uncarpeted. Books or pictures and photos covered every wall. An old Jefferson desk stood against one wall, a grand piano in the opposite corner. Windows, deepset in thick walls, looked out on West Ninth Street. Miss Moore reclined in a cot-sized hospital bed, its adjustable back tilted forward supporting her in a sitting position. Her legs lay wrapped under a blanket and over her nightclothes she wore a white lace bed jacket. She looked sweet and frail, her skin clear, fresh, almost transparent. I kissed her lightly on the cheek and put the box containing my present on the piano along with six or seven other unopened boxes.

"Would you open it for me?" she asked.

"Now?" I was hesitant because other gifts lay unopened on the piano.

"Yes, please." I held up the blue warm-up jacket with "Yankees" written in white across the chest in cursive Yankee style. She admired it and seemed immensely pleased.

"Would you put it around my shoulders?" she asked, leaning forward so I could fit it around her. She smiled and tugged it together in the front and said she would keep it on.

"It truly is the best arm in baseball," I said. She had taught Jim Thorpe, the great Indian athlete, as a schoolboy in Carlisle, Pennsylvania. James — she always referred to him as James — was assigned to carry the picnic baskets when she took her class on spring outings "because he was so very strong." A young man played the piano and we had cakes and tea and left as she seemed to be tiring.

Not long afterward she died peacefully, and at her funeral service in the lovely old church in Brooklyn, all sorts of charming memories flowed into my mind and I caught myself smiling, remembering one bit of overheard dialogue. A rather aggressively literary man, no doubt well-meaning, challenged her. "Miss Moore, your poetry is very difficult to read."

"It's very difficult to write," she shot back.

In the years that followed, other lovely people helped us open the Yankee season: Simon and Garfunkel one spring; Paul had been an enthusiastic stickball player in the New York streets. Whitney Young, president of the National Urban League, brought his elderly parents up from the Carolinas. "I never thought I'd live to see a black man throw out a first ball at Yankee Stadium, or any other stadium," said Mr. Young, Senior, on the occasion. And in 1973, the fiftieth anniversary of Yankee Stadium, there was Mr. Bluestone. Mr. Bluestone was not as old as Miss Moore, but almost. As long as I could remember he had been the pharmacist in the Plaza Hotel drugstore. Occasionally I stopped there to buy toothpaste or shaving cream or aspirin, not a very exotic customer. A short, polite, fastidious person, Mr. Bluestone, respectful of himself and his profession, always dressed meticulously in a gray suit, white shirt and dark tie.

"You will be going down to spring training soon," he said.

"In a day or two. Big year coming up. Some writers have picked us to win. First time in a long while."

"Oh, wouldn't that be a pleasure." His eyes danced and he rubbed his hands at the possibility of another championship.

"Fiftieth anniversary of the Stadium, too, you know."

"I know. I was there on the opening day in 1923. The first game they played. I sat in the bleachers. I think we paid twenty-five cents. Or was it a dime?"

"Did you live in that neighborhood?"

"Yes. Just off the Concourse."

"Would you like to come to this year's opening game? And bring your family?"

"Would I!" A toothy smile broke through his professional reserve.

"Well, then, would you honor us by throwing out the first ball?" He fell silent for several seconds. A pharmacist in a white coat who had been mixing a prescription a few feet away stepped to the counter.

"He's just dazed, Mr. Burke. Speechless. He can't believe it. Neither can I."

Mr. Bluestone launched the 1973 season for us, completing his fifty-year cycle. The governor was present, and the mayor.

But they sat behind the pharmacist, his wife, his children, and his grandchildren. In his time, from a distance, Mr. Bluestone had seen President Herbert Hoover, Governor Al Smith, Mayor Fiorello LaGuardia pose in the front row holding a ball aloft for the press photographers. Now he took his place with them, proud before his family, his neighbors watching on television, his customers looking in ("Isn't that our pharmacist!"), proud as a king. It was lovely to see, one of those intangible perquisites available for the taking, available in many guises, to anyone who looks after a sports team.

~~~~~~~~~~~~~~~~~~~~~~~~~~~~~~~~~~~~~~~~~~~~~~~~~~~~~~~~~~~~~

# 13

BY 1966 THE Yankee dynasty had collapsed and perhaps could never be rebuilt. Born in 1903, the Yankees were just another American League team until Colonel Jacob Ruppert, the New York brewer, bought them in 1915 for $460,000. He had plenty of money and the will to spend it on a winning team. From the cash-starved Boston Red Sox he bought Babe Ruth, for $100,000, and fourteen other outstanding players: Hoyt, Dugan, Pennock, Bush, Schang among them. Then, in a stroke of genius, he bought Boston's field manager, Ed Barrow, and made him the Yankees' first general manager. Ruppert built and opened Yankee Stadium in 1923 and the Yankee dynasty was launched. Over the next decade Barrow, the astute experienced baseball man with complete business authority, bought players from minor-league teams, most of them independently owned. Then he began to develop his own extensive farm system and hired another immensely effective young baseball executive, George Weiss, to run it. The Yankees had two advantages over the rest of the League: money to spend and good baseball brains to spend it. Ruppert died in 1939 and the club was bought by Topping and Webb in 1945. Three years later the shrewd, experienced Weiss inherited Barrow's job as general manager and the Yankees went off on another spate of success, ten pennants in twelve years. Then Topping silently rang the death knell. In an act of arrogance and misjudgment he fired his most winning combination: Weiss and manager Casey Stengel; both crossed the river to join the Mets, New York's new National League team. The championship team Weiss and Stengel left behind to be managed by Ralph Houk was young enough and healthy enough to win four more pennants before age and injury demolished it, precipitously. In two years, 1965 and 1966, the team fell from first place to last place

264

in the American League standings. The baseball establishment drove the final nail in the Yankee coffin. In 1965 they adopted a free agent draft. Thereafter, each team, in reverse order on the previous year's standing, would acquire the right to negotiate with a young prospect. This new legislation would preclude the Yankees' picking off the best of the new crop as they had done in earlier years. Ball clubs were no longer allowed to scout and sign the best young players coming out of high schools and colleges in free competition with one another. Henceforth the Yankees, like everyone else, had to take their place in line and in their turn select new players from a pool. The rationale was to spread the best new talent evenly among all teams, with particular benefit to the weaker; unofficially the objective was to hobble the Yankees, to pull them back to the rest of the field. Prior to this draft regulation, for example, the Yankees might have signed six or seven of the best twenty prospects in the country. Under the draft system they would be permitted to sign only one of them. For the Yankees, its once-abundant farm system now almost barren of talented youngsters, the new regulation could not have come at a worse time.

To say that CBS had bought a bare cupboard is not wholly accurate without elaboration. The Yankees were indeed appallingly short of promising players and the Stadium itself was in disrepair and deteriorating. Institutionally, however, the Yankees were the most famous team in professional sports. The name was magical. Yankee Stadium was unique, rich in sports lore. And New York was New York was New York. There was, in short, a lot to work with.

We needed all the help we could get from whatever source, to induce fans to come to our ball park while we slogged through the agony of rebuilding a quality team. A generous press gave us a running start, but we had to get up every morning and keep running, hustling every angle we could think of to keep the Yankees in the public's favor.

I had no intention of pretending to know baseball and how to judge baseball ability in a professional sense, and my first priority was to get a professional baseball man to restock the anemic farm system and to rebuild the major league club. Lee MacPhail was the person I wanted to join the Yankees. Lee had been in baseball all his adult life. His father, the flamboyant and brilliant Larry, had operated the Cincinnati, Brooklyn, and, briefly, the Yankee clubs, and Lee himself, after an apprenticeship in the Yankee organization, had built the Baltimore Orioles into a championship team. He agreed to become our executive vice president and general manager and would devote the bulk of his time to the vital area of player talent. Lee was the antithesis of his volatile father, but his solid baseball judgment, his common sense, his uncommon decency were esteemed through the baseball world, and certainly by me. Actually Ralph Houk had wanted both jobs. When he agreed to return to the dugout as field manager he sought to hold on to the general manager's role as well. I told him it wouldn't work. It was not simply that Ralph was an excellent field manager and a mediocre general manager, though that was an accurate evaluation, I believe. More to the point, these are two quite different, full-time functions. One or the other suffers if a single man attempts to perform both. I appreciated the ego factor and, equally important, Houk's concern over who would become the general manager and his immediate boss: would he and an unknown newcomer be professionally compatible? The choice of Lee MacPhail reassured him. Actually the two had once been together with the Yankees' minor league team in Denver, Lee as business manager and Ralph as field manager. They were good personal friends and completely in sync professionally. We found ourselves a close-knit, comfortable tandem: Houk, MacPhail, and me.

The year 1967 we called Year One of the new Yankee era. I wanted to mark a clean beginning, to leave behind past Yankee surliness, to take along the best of the Yankee tradition. When the 1967 season opened the fans were welcomed to a stadium that had been given a million-and-a-half-dollar red, white, and blue face-lifting. During the winter the prison-gray outer surface was painted white; the seats, which had been seventeen different shades of bilious green, were painted uniform blue, the foul poles red. To decide on the shade of blue, I had two sections of a hundred or so seats painted different shades and asked Frank Stanton, whose discriminating aesthetic taste I respected, to give me his opinion. One sunny February morning we studied them from the infield. Stanton asked which I preferred.

"The one on the right," I said.

"So do I," he agreed and left. To my knowledge that was the only time Stanton was ever in Yankee Stadium. Like television programming, Stanton considered the Yankees Paley's private preserve and trod carefully there. The blue seats that we chose is the same blue I selected for the refurbished Yankee Stadium that reopened in 1976. Yankee blue, it is called. For distribution to advertising agencies, to prospective broadcast sponsors, and to New York opinion makers we published an especially handsome thirteen-by-ten-inch brochure. The texture of its beige paper, the dramatic impact of its full-page sepia photographs, the distinctive red lettering reflected the quality tone we set for the new Yankee operation. Its text stated succinctly what we were going to do. And we set to work doing it. Attendance rose twenty-seven percent that first year. We did at once all the things we could do with time, energy, and common sense.

One pace we could not force, had we worked twenty-four hours a day, was the team's development. In Bill Paley's early days in radio he had given CBS a giant leap forward, enticing Bing Crosby and Jack Benny away from NBC. He kept urging us to buy stars. Money was no object. But no one would take our money, no one would sell us players, no one wanted our players in trade. The Yankee roster was either too gray or too grassy green. On the playing field we were still in the throes of decline and fall. One day in Detroit, the magnificent Whitey Ford was driven off the mound after pitching three innings, showered, dressed, and boarded a plane to New York before the game ended. He knew he could no longer pitch. His friend Mantle, moving from center field to first base to conserve his ailing legs, struggled on gallantly and achieved his five-hundredth home run before he too decided he could no longer get his bat around. The New York fans' animus for Roger Maris, mostly for having broken Babe Ruth's home run record, was unrelenting. He would have quit baseball rather than endure another wrath-filled New York season. We virtually gave him to the St. Louis Cardinals, where he had two marvelous years, personally and competitively. Elston Howard went to Boston because Tom Yawkey, whose Boston team was making a run for the 1967 pennant, telephoned me and asked me for him. Boston needed an experienced catcher to handle their young pitchers. I liked Tom Yawkey and said, "OK, with the proviso that when Elston finishes playing for you, we will get him back with the Yankees. We want him here as a coach. This is where he belongs." Yawkey loved baseball and baseball players as much as any man and had spent tons of money to bring a winner to Boston. My son Peter, now age twelve, was the only Yankee fan in his prep school just outside Boston. Loyally he wore his Yankee cap and wrote me: "Dear Pop, How could you do such a terrible thing to Ellie?" I sent Elston Peter's letter. Howard helped Boston win the League championship, and brought tears of joy to Tom Yawkey's eyes before returning to us in New York as a Yankee coach.

On the field the New Yankee Era began with an embarrassing shortage of playing ability but our cellar finish in the 1966 League standings gave us top pick in the player draft. Thurman Munson, a catcher, was our choice. Bobby Murcer, at twenty-three, returned from his Army service and joined the twenty-one-year-old Munson. They became the cornerstone of the new Yankees. It was a beginning. But only a beginning. These two boys, blessed with exceptional ability and the elusive chemistry of stardom, became fellow members of the American League All-Star team for four consecutive years, became the closest of lifetime friends. A decade thence, Bobby would deliver an eloquent, moving eulogy at Thurman's funeral service in Ohio, fly to New York with his Yankee teammates, and that night, having not slept for forty-eight hours, rise to a poetic moment. With the capacity of occasion only the gifted possess, Bobby drove in all five runs — three with a home run — to win a game that the Yankees, wearing black armbands, dedicated to their lost captain, dead of an air crash.

At the beginning of his rookie year Munson couldn't buy a hit, as the saying goes. Sitting in New York listening to the radio broadcasts of Yankee road games, I suffered for him each time he came to bat and sat down hitless and began to worry about his morale. Ralph Houk had been a successful manager of an inherited team of seasoned old pros with whom he had won three pennants: Mantle, Ford, Richardson, Kubek, Howard, Boyer, and their crowd. I wasn't sure how much time he would give a struggling rookie, or whether he would leave the boy to find his own way, make it or not make it. Growing

concern prodded me to take a plane to Baltimore, a taxi to the
Orioles Stadium, and seek out Munson sitting in the dugout
during pregame batting practice. I put my arm across his
chunky catcher's shoulder — his pals called him Beach Ball —
and told him he had nothing to worry about, reminded him of
Mantle's rookie experience — no hits in nineteen consecutive
at bats — tried to be reassuring. He listened expressionless,
studied his thick thighs, reflected for a moment then, in a tone
of matter-of-fact confidence that annihilated my concern, said,
"Hell, I'm going to hit .300 in this league." I watched the game
and went back to New York feeling rather sheepish. Munson
hit .302 for the season and was named the American League's
Rookie of the Year.

Under Lee MacPhail's direction the farm system began to fill
out with new talent, especially with good pitchers: Stan Bahn-
sen came up as the 1968 Rookie of the Year; Ron Guidry and
Scott McGregor were learning their trade in the minor leagues
— both destined for brilliant major league careers, both would
become winning World Series pitchers. At the major league
level a gentleman, a true gentleman, from the Los Angeles
black ghetto of Watts, emerged almost silently, certainly without fanfare, to gain a place among the all-time-great Yankees.
His name was Roy White. Over a fourteen-year career his performance placed his name among the top ten Yankees in games
played, hits made, runs scored. White batted in more runs than
Murcer or Munson. In 1971 he led the American League in
outfielding. As seatmates on a Los Angeles to New York flight
we tackled the *Times* crossword puzzle together and Roy's word
skill left me at the post. We traded the incomparable but aging
Clete Boyer for Atlanta's most promising minor-league player,
Bill Robinson. Robinson was tall, lithe, handsome; his wife,
Mary, lovely as the morning sun. Billy's father was a Pittsburgh
steel mill foreman. The black ghettos of New York and Los
Angeles were foreign to his middle-class experience. In Washington President Johnson threw out the first ball to open the
1967 baseball season, and Billy Robinson, in his first major
league at bat, hit a home run. I don't think his feet touched the
ground until he tagged home plate. He would be a huge success in New York, I thought. I was wrong. New York tensed
him. A Roman Catholic, he crossed himself swiftly each time

he came to bat, but God chose to let him face the opposition pitchers alone. Before one game in Yankee Stadium I ambled out to center field, near where the Ruth-Gehrig-Huggins monuments used to stand, and chatted idly with Billy between lazy fly balls he and some others were fielding. I sought to relax him. Wishing him good luck, I held my hand for a moment at the small of his back. His muscles were tightly coiled springs. He couldn't find the release.

I took him and Mary to the theater to see *The Great White Hope* and to supper after at Sardi's, trying to help them feel more at home, to think of New York not as ominous but open to opportunity. It didn't work. Billy struggled for three seasons and in the end had to make the disheartening descent to the minor leagues. Adversity, Hemingway wrote, is a tough town to play. But we kept in touch by mail. Often Billy was discouraged to the point of quitting, didn't, finally made his way back up to the Philadelphia Phillies, was traded to the Pittsburgh Pirates and won his world championship ring. Late in the final World Series game Billy got a key hit, and was on base when Willie Stargel came to bat, and scored ahead of him when Willie hit the game winning home run. Next morning the front page of the *New York Times* carried a four-column picture of Bill Robinson standing at the plate waiting to be the first to congratulate Stargel, captain of the newest world champions. It filled my heart. Billy Robinson, promise fulfilled, championship ball player, on the front page of the *New York Times* in the city that had beaten him but not defeated him. I had the page reproduced on a metal plaque, mounted on a wooden backing, and sent it to Mary and Bill for Christmas with my love. (Years later, just before I left for Ireland, some valued sports-writer friends organized a small dinner at Joe's in the Village. As a wonderfully thoughtful surprise, they invited Mary and Bill Robinson to drive in from Pennsylvania. He wore his championship ring; she was more beautiful than ever.)

In the winter of 1972 Boston needed and obtained from the Yankees a journeyman first baseman. In return we took from them a relief pitcher called Sparky Lyle, who apparently had been troublesome to the Boston management. As a Yankee he was troublesome only to other American League clubs. In his first year with us he saved thirty-five games, set a major league record, won the Cy Young Award as baseball's best pitcher, and became a cult figure. Late in the game, the opposition threatening a Yankee lead, play would halt and a pin-striped Datsun would emerge from the bull pen. "Pomp and Circumstance" thundered from the organ and the fans came to their feet with a roar of expectation as Sparky Lyle stepped from the car, tossed his jacket to a batboy, bit off a huge chunk of Red Man chewing tobacco, and strode to the pitcher's mound, his body language spewing disdain at the waiting batsman. A fast slider was his best pitch. Sparky was a natural showman, and he would have been an equally natural long-haul trucker pushing a cross-country rig. Unbeknownst to most of his enthusiastic fans and masked by his unfettered behavior, Lyle was a surprisingly sensitive photographer, mostly of flowers, and a keen amateur astrologer. You had to know him for a long time to discover either.

The same year, Bobby Murcer hit thirty-three home runs and, five years into the New Era, the Yankees were once again in the thick of a pennant race and were not eliminated until the first day of October, 1972. Some baseball writers predicted we would win the League pennant in 1973.

In purely personal terms those were the best of all possible years. They dealt me a full share of human happiness.

Unquestionably the most lovable single day of the lot was Sunday August 10, 1968. The Yankees were struggling toward a fifth-place finish while the Detroit Tigers were gliding toward a World Championship. Exasperatingly for the Tiger manager, Mayo Smith, our ragtag team beat the Tigers on Friday night and again on Saturday afternoon. By Sunday, the Yankees had simply run out of pitchers. Ralph Houk assigned a tired Fred Talbot to start and to go as long as he could. Then he tapped Rocky Calivito to pitch. We had picked up the famous Cleveland outfielder, as he neared the end of his career, to add hitting strength to our lamentable bench. After four innings Detroit was ahead 5-0 and Talbot was spent. Houk signaled the bull pen. The crowd thought the public address announcer had gone bonkers. But incredulous eyes confirmed that it was indeed the Rock striding purposefully towards the mound, the mound famed by the incomparable Whitey Ford, Lefty Gomez, Red Ruffing. A mounting roar moved from stunned disbelief through astonished delight to wild enthusiasm for the sheer bravado of it. His first pitch was a plate-splitting strike to a bemused batter and an ear-splitting cheer for Calivito. A weak fly ball retired the first batter. One out for Rocky. He could have been elected borough president of the Bronx on the spot. Two more easy outs, and Whitey never walked off the mound with greater aplomb. Serious, gentlemanly Calivito turned a simple baseball afternoon into a Roman holiday.

The fans cheered every pitch, roared on every out, and gave Calivito a standing ovation at the end of every inning he survived, as he set down batter after batter, and his teammates somehow conjured up six poetic runs off Detroit's best man, Mickey Lolich. Winning pitcher, Calivito. Lifetime record: Won — 1, Lost — 0. But it was a day for the cup to run over. Rocky played the second game in right field, his undefeated arm hanging limp by his side. And of course Calivito the hitter hit a game-winning home run to sweep the four-game series from the incipient World Champions.

When I first arrived in the Bronx, Mickey Mantle and Whitey Ford were Yankee heroes in their deepening twilight. We became good friends. Our off-the-field relationship began when a man who owned El Morocco rescued us from one of those countless sports dinners that pile up in winter. He invited Ford, Mantle, Hank Bauer, and me to his nightclub. Bauer, their former teammate, then managed the Baltimore Orioles. We drank champagne at the bar and were possibly a decibel or two more boisterous than the regular clientele. Someone next to me made what I thought to be an unkind remark about unmannered ball players and I took hold of his shirtfront. Laughing, Mickey pulled me away, and in mock anxiety told Whitey they had better get me out of the place before I got them all in trouble with the ball club. It was a silly, laughable nonincident and the owner quickly herded us to an upstairs lounge and called the house photographer to take our picture, all of us sitting on a piano, arms across shoulders, grinning foolishly, Bauer's face looking less like a clenched fist than it did under a ball cap. Only Whitey appeared more or less sober. Bauer wanted to hear some jazz and insisted on a dingy bar that only he liked and was dislodged from only because he decided he was hungry and wanted to go to the Stage Delicatessen. At five in the morning the Stage was closed. Bauer was ready to put his fist through the glass door to get at the corned beef but was persuaded that there was an easier way to find breakfast. In a taxi en route to Reuben's, Mantle turned to Ford with a mischievous grin and in his Oklahoma drawl said, as though he had just remembered some fundamental truth, "You know, Whitey, this is the first owner we haven't drunk under the table."

Mickey was lost when Whitey decided he could no longer pitch and abruptly left the club. Except for Simon and Claude, the two young men I had been with in France, I have not known two men who shared such a deep affection, such love and admiration for one another. Like Simon and Claude, in a different crucible, Ford and Mantle lived through every experience together from hard-won World Championships to private shenanigans. At first glance it was an improbable pairing, on second a most obvious one. The street-wise New Yorker — Mantle called him "Slick" — and the native country boy from Oklahoma. However rough-cut or unsophisticated they may have appeared from the gentler slopes of society, they possessed world-class talents and, in human terms, they possessed a world-class friendship. Not much tops that.

When my friendship with Mantle was secure enough, when I judged that he felt comfortable enough with me, I asked him to stop by my quarters at the Stadium one day, no hurry. I had designed my office to be unofficelike. So that people would not have to face me across the barrier of a desk, I had no desk. Instead I used a round marble-topped table surrounded by four or five soft leather chairs. At the other end of the rectangular room two coffee-brown sofas faced one another. Set at right angles to them were two matching armchairs. In front of each pairing stood a glass coffee table. Bookshelves stretched along the end wall. Southern light from big windows along the 157th Street side brightened white walls and red carpeting, giving the room a cheerful, upbeat look. And it could be transformed from an office to a livingroom simply by clearing papers from the round table. I wanted people to feel at ease there.

Mickey sat on a sofa and I in an armchair, and we drank beer I had fetched from a small kitchen down the hall. I said, in essence, I had heard all sorts of opinions about his financial situation: that he had invested his money well and was in solid shape financially; that he had been profligate and had no income but the $100,000 a year the Yankees paid him. My only concern in raising the question was his financial well-being. If his affairs were in good order, fine. If there was anything helpful we could do while he was still in Yankee uniform, we were prepared to do it. Mantle was embarrassed and asked if we could put off any talk until an Oklahoma friend, Harold Youngman, could come to New York. Youngman was a kind of surrogate father to Mickey, a successful building contractor and a first-rate person. He was, I discovered, perhaps the only person who had ever been gratuitously and constructively helpful to Mantle in business. Youngman had put him into an Oklahoma motel venture that was sound and profitable; otherwise Mickey had not made the best commercial use of his baseball fame. It was agreed to make a late commercial start. I asked Mark McCormack to represent Mantle. Mark had made a phenomenal success handling the business interests of golfers Arnold Palmer, Gary Player, and Jack Nicklaus. But it was too late in Mantle's career, McCormack said; he coveted Murcer and Munson. Finally, a good young lawyer in Texas, Roy True, took hold.

The 1968 season had been a painful struggle for Mantle and he was not sure that he could play another. "Come to spring training, Mick," I suggested. "If it doesn't feel right, pack it in." When he arrived in Fort Lauderdale we met for dinner in the restaurant on top of the Yankee Clipper Hotel. The color scheme was dark blue, the lights dim, an ambience that matched Mickey's mood.

"I can't do it," he said sadly. Clearly he didn't want to embarrass himself, to play to a standard less than his best. In two All-Star games during the two previous seasons, he had come to bat as a pinch hitter. Both times he struck out. In the stands you felt the burning humiliation of a man proud of his top form, devastated by its loss, and understood his decision.

No one has ever done it better. And as long as there are bats and balls people are going to say: "That Mantle! What he would have done if he had two good legs!" He had been careless about his body, his unconcern rooted, it seemed, in the assumption that like his father he would die young. The postoperative exercise routine prescribed to rebuild his damaged knees was virtually ignored, so for most of his career he carried bandaged legs and pain into every game.

We held a career-ending press conference the following morning. It surprised no one. And on June 8, 1969, we retired his uniform in a ceremony at Yankee Stadium. Sixty-two thousand people came to say Hail and Farewell. Standing on the infield grass, Joe DiMaggio presented him the plaque that would be mounted on the Stadium's center field wall. Whitey Ford handed him his uniform shirt, number 7, symbolic of retiring that number from Yankee use along with Ruth's number 3, Gehrig's number 4, and DiMaggio's number 5. The pennants of all the pennant-winning teams he had played on were laid out symmetrically across the outfield grass. Beside each stood a fellow member of that year's team. Over the public address system Frank Messer, the broadcaster, recited Mickey's accomplishments of that year, and one by one the teammates trotted in to take a place on a line along the infield base paths until they formed a semicircle behind Mickey, standing near the pitcher's mound. When he came to the microphone sixty-two thousand people were on their feet. A sea surf of cheers rolled down, swelling to a new crescendo again each time he raised his hand asking for quiet to speak. For eight solid minutes they cheered.

The finale I borrowed from the Spanish bullring — an open golf cart picked him up at the mound and drove him slowly around the warning track so the fans in the box seats, in the outfield stands, in the bleachers could share him equally. From photographs I had seen, the famous good-byes of Gehrig and of Ruth had been made from home plate. I wanted Mantle's to be an upbeat, a happier, a more directly shared event. Mickey was uncertain when Houk told him of the golf-cart ride and sought me out.

"Do you think I ought to do that?" He was concerned it would be too showboaty, too hotdog.

"Yes, it's something you should do," I reassured him. And as he took his seat in the cart next to Kenny, the grounds keeper–driver, I put my hand on his shoulder. "Mick, this is something that's never happened before. May never happen again. It's yours alone. Drink it in. All the way round." It was a curtain call of heroic proportions. Appropriately.

## 14

ODDLY, IT WAS the National League people who made me, a stranger, most welcome at my first major league meeting in Pittsburgh, in December 1966. The buffet table in the Hilton Hotel's Terrace Room was heavy with mass-produced food, none of it appetizing, but I filled my plate, reminded myself that men in a Siberian gulag would kill to get at such a table, and wondered where to sit. Warren Giles, the president of the National League, walked quickly across the room, his hand extended in greeting, a smile on his jolly pink face, a friendly sparkle in his eye. He had the carry-on of a man a political machine could keep reelecting to the House of Representatives as long as he was willing to run for office, and I learned in time that behind an almost professionally gregarious, courteous manner was an authentically warm human being and a gentleman. Of all baseball's administrators, I was to become most fond of him. His sparse hair was white and mine dark then, and I addressed him as Mr. Giles. He led me to his table and sat me next to someone I did know, Horace Stoneham, the San Francisco Giants owner. Horace invited me to his room for a nightcap, but I slipped away; I had picked up enough baseball lore to know that Horace sometimes locked people in his room and threw the keys out the window in order to secure a drinking companion. Mr. Giles said he wished I had joined the National League and, at that moment, I wished I had. My new American League colleagues' approach was gingerly, uncertain what kind of partner I, a CBS person, would make. They didn't have long to wait.

A fellow newcomer to baseball at that same moment was Marvin Miller. Miller had been retained by the players to represent them, to organize them into an effective negotiating body. He arrived with outstanding credentials as an economist for the Steelworkers, recommended to the players by a distinguished professor at the University of Pennsylvania's Wharton School. The Lords of Baseball received him with minimum courtesy and zero enthusiasm. The president of the American League, Joe Cronin, presided over the meeting at which Miller first spoke to the owners, sitting at tables formed in a hollow square. He had, if I recall, a singularly modest demand: that the minimum salary of a major league player be raised to $10,000 and $12,000 in the two succeeding years. It was then $7,500. When he finished, Cronin thanked and dismissed him. Miller was plainly puzzled. He expected there might be some discussion of his proposal. No, there would not be, he was told. "These gentlemen will consider it and we'll get back to you," Cronin said.

Three months later I had a phone call from Miller. Could he see me? Of course he could. He asked if I remembered hearing Cronin say in Pittsburgh that Miller would be given some response to his minimum salary proposal. I did. Was I, as one club owner, aware that he had heard nothing? No, I was not. I confirmed that we owed him an answer and rang Cronin to find out what we were going to do to fulfill our commitment to Miller. Oh, that was a matter for the commissioner. I rang General Eckert. There would be a meeting baseball's executive council on April 27 in his office at 680 Fifth Avenue, where the matter would be discussed. Would I like to attend, ex officio? Yes I would, I said, unaware that I would be as welcome as the mumps. The commissioner, the two league presidents and two owners from each league were the executive council members. The ubiquitous league lawyers were there too. Walter O'Malley of the Dodgers, a shrewd, clever, bullying man, ran the meeting. The process was feudalistic. The guileless Eckert turned O'Malley purple with suppressed anger as he explained that he had invited me inasmuch as I had expressed a special interest in the subject. Little of substance was discussed. But there was a lot of moaning and hand-wringing about the threatening emergence of Miller, much hankering for the dear simpler days. I sat silent on the sidelines as long as I could, listening impatiently to the circumlocution.

"Gentlemen, as your invited guest, permit me to make a simple point. Marvin Miller is here, like it or not. If he were the devil himself you'd have to deal with him. The Alka-Seltzer tablet is in the water. It's fizzing. You can't reach in and take it out. We have to move on." Someone wanted to know what I would suggest. "Marvin Miller is an experienced professional. He knows his business. He's good. We're going to have to get someone equally skilled to deal with him. Someone who knows that world of union negotiations. Someone who understands that baseball players are contemporary people, living in a contemporary society."

Bowie Kuhn was present as the National League's lawyer. Whether as O'Malley's cat's-paw or on his own I don't know, but he inferred that I was somehow in league with Miller, demanded to know what was my true relationship and what authority I had to meet with him at all.

"As president of the New York Yankees I'll see Miller any time he asks me to."

"What more went on between you and Miller that we don't know about?" he asked insolently. I paused to hold my irritation in check and to let the question hang in midair for a moment, isolating itself. Then I looked Kuhn in the eye and quietly laid down the gauntlet. "Are you questioning my veracity?" He backed off; my question needed no verbal response, and the discussion moved along.

Mr. Giles asked if I could suggest an appropriate person to represent baseball. I did, having done some homework and got a recommendation from labor relations friends at CBS. Kuhn pooh-poohed the idea of an outsider, someone who knew nothing of baseball's special problems. He averred he would handle Miller; thus the lines of a Kuhn-Miller battle that was to last over the next sixteen years — most of them during Kuhn's commissionership — were drawn. Aided by an impenetrable absence of foresight on the part of the major league clubs and an untimely arrogance on the part of the commissioner, Miller out-generaled the lot, won the battles one at a time, and won the war. Baseball players have the best arrangements of all professional athletes.

The unfortunate Eckert was not long for the baseball world. It was foregone. At his induction the New York press immediately had tagged him "The Unknown Soldier." Stiff and lackluster, Eckert was an honorable citizen from the provinces of life, unequipped by experience or personality to cope with the hard light of public position, the litmus-quick judgments of a hard-nosed press or the basket of eels who had voted unanimously to hire him as their commissioner. Walter O'Malley, the Los Angeles Dodgers owner, had plucked him out of Air Force blue and made him commissioner. There were voting formalities, of course, but O'Malley, who wasn't even on the selection committee, arranged for the appointment of a man responsive to him. It had been self-serving and unkind on O'Malley's part, but in character. Unlike the Wrigleys, the Busches and most other club owners, O'Malley had baseball as his main business and he worked at it shrewdly and very successfully. But arrogance warped his judgment in Eckert's case.

Football was riding a flood tide of popularity. Its commissioner, Pete Rozelle, was a skillful administrator and a particularly astute public relations person. Baseball, on the other hand, was becalmed. The American League appeared to be sinking. In 1967 Carl Yastrzemski of the Red Sox was the only American League player whose batting average was over .300. No other player in the League reached that level. In desperation the Americans lobbied for interleague play to bolster fan interest. The Nationals, led by O'Malley, reacted as though their American League peers were a leper colony. Baseball needed Rozellian leadership.

The Edwardian Room at the Plaza Hotel was my breakfast place three or four mornings a week; a meeting there over orange juice and eggs saved people a trip to the Bronx. The lofty oak-paneled room, its giant windows taking the morning light from Central Park on the one side, Fifth Avenue on the other, its solid masculine furniture designed to comfort men of Edwardian proportions, its texture of permanence made it an agreeable place to start a day. One sunny morning at a table between the two corner windows that look out on the Park and the Avenue, Dick Meyers and I met secretly and agreed that Eckert had to be replaced. Meyers was executive vice president of the Anheuser-Busch Brewing Company and a highly respected person in the brewing business; he also looked after the St. Louis Cardinals baseball team for Gussie Busch. We agreed that a swift silent coup should be mounted. Wisely, but surprising to me because Busch appeared always to be guided by O'Malley, Meyers made an overriding condition: O'Malley must be kept totally in the dark. Given one whiff of our plan, O'Malley would sabotage it, because it was not his. He must be taken totally by surprise. Before our second coffee we had composed a short list of sensible and sympathetic peers. Discreetly, Meyers would approach four National League owners; I would do the same in the American League. Signing the breakfast bill, I was already feeling badly for the unfortunate Eckert.

Bob Reynolds, who ran Golden West Broadcasting and the California Angels for Gene Autry, and Gerry Hoffberger, owner of the Baltimore club, were at the head of my list and joined at once. We would make our move at the annual baseball meeting in San Francisco in December 1968. On the final day of meetings a few of us met for breakfast in my suite at the Palace Hotel — Hoffberger, Reynolds, Meyers, and Frank Dale, the publisher of the *Cincinnati Enquirer*, who was also president of the Reds baseball club. We rehearsed our tactics. Immediately after the final agenda item and before the meeting was formally adjourned, Hoffberger would respectfully request the commissioner to leave the room so the owners could meet in executive session. This request and its timing would surprise and irritate those who were not in on the plan. They would grumble but, we calculated, they would charge this off to Hoffberger's reputation as a maverick. That crazy Hoffberger again!

When the time came, the commissioner left the oak-paneled Comstock Room as he was asked. Reynolds rose, made a prefatory comment, and read a resolution to remove Eckert from office. Dick Meyers and Frank Dale and others voiced strong support and, very speedily, the resolution passed. O'Malley was flabbergasted. Not only had his man Eckert been unseated, but he had played no role whatsoever, probably for the first time in his long baseball career. The press hailed the Young Turks who had taken over from the Old Guard. Eckert looked relieved, a man rescued from quicksand, and readily volunteered to serve as a lame-duck commissioner until a new man could be found. A two-man restructuring committee was formed — Meyers and Hoffberger — to find a new commissioner. Speculation started at once. A United Press columnist wrote: The baseball people have already found their new commissioner; he's Mike Burke of the New York Yankees. When Joe Durso of the *New York Times* asked me about it, I said I was not a candidate but that I had some ideas about what should be done. The velocity of life has changed, I told him, and baseball's state of mind must change with it. We had to admit that baseball was in trouble and we could not lay that fact at Eckert's door. I said I didn't think we should ever change the nature of the game. Its geometry was spectacularly successful: the distance between the bases, the split-second skills, all those things were sound. Neither did I think we had to panic. That always ended badly. I thought that the more life became mechanized and computerized, the more popular baseball would become. A nonviolent sport in a violent time, it would remain a kind of oasis where a person could sit peacefully, participate vicariously, and restore some balance to his life, a life surrounded by mounting levels of civilian violence.

Like Mark Twain's, the announcement of the Old Guard's death was premature. O'Malley was stung, humiliated, angry as a wounded bear. I decided to visit him on his home turf, to get the feel of him privately, and flew to Los Angeles. We met in Chasen's restaurant, where the portrait of W. C. Fields as Queen Victoria in the entry hall always made me smile. It was the last smile of the night. O'Malley had enthroned himself on the leather banquette of the booth just inside the door on the left, lording it over the rest of the room. He was a man who wanted even strangers to realize that he was someone important, and his ostentatious manner ensured that the point was not lost on the most obtuse passerby. Subtlety was foreign to his heavy hand. O'Malley was a beefy man, girth and jowl; an abundance of good food and good drink filled out an expansive vest and overlapped his collar; a fleshy Irish face was thin-lipped and stubborn-chinned. Behind glasses, his eyes were alert, intelligent, and suspicious. Almost convincingly he affected openness and affability.

Throughout dinner he saluted people coming and going. My lateral vision saw that some he greeted looked surprised and wondered why they had been singled out for a hearty hello and a jolly wave, unaware that I was the intended audience. It was a rather pathetic exercise, so unnecessary. Mrs. Chasen's cooks gave us delicious steaks and O'Malley, between gestures to his public, made some gruffly humorous, ice-breaking comments about warring Irish tribes — the chieftains of the Young Lions and of the Old Guard breaking bread. His approach was oblique, his message clear: he would remain in control of baseball. His native suspicion harbored an inordinate concern about the powerful CBS somehow wielding its power within baseball, at his expense, and his only straight-ahead line was to urge me to buy the Yankees from Paley. He avoided entirely any discussion of the new commissioner. That was a subject reserved to himself and his friends, not to be shared with an adversary. Over a cheerless brandy he left me in no doubt where I stood. O'Malley dropped me at the entrance to the Beverly Hills Hotel and we said good-bye with a handshake and a forced heartiness.

Two weeks after Eckert had been deposed, the two leagues met in a Chicago hotel. Going in, there was strong National League support for Chub Feeney of the San Francisco Giants; he was related to Horace Stoneham. And, according to the newspapers, all but one American League club wanted me to become the new commissioner. In a ground-level room looking out on a wintry patio, twenty-four club owners sat elbow-to-elbow at tables set out in a hollow rectangle. Selected to chair the meeting jointly, representing their respective leagues, O'Malley and Gabe Paul of Cleveland took places at the center of one long side. I sat at one end between Bob Reynolds of California and John Fetzer of Detroit. In the early feeling-out talk one hostile question from Atlanta — "How much CBS stock do you own?" And one loud aside from Houston — "His wartime friend Henry North got him his Circus job" — showed the lie of the National League land. O'Malley had his side well coached. Feeney and I were asked to leave the room so there could be uninhibited discussion of our qualifications. Before leaving the table I whispered privately to Bob Reynolds, "If this thing gets serious, you can tell them I couldn't possibly take the job for less than two hundred fifty thousand a year." I knew that would stop cold any ground swell for my candidacy. Eckert's annual salary was sixty-five thousand dollars.

Feeney and I were friends. For a while we stood at the bottom of a dim stairwell and then, sensibly, moved to the bar, and

I tried to persuade him to take the commissionership. Look, my argument went, I don't want to be anything but a New York Yankee; I think you would make an excellent commissioner; we appear to be the only two candidates; I'll withdraw my name, and that will be that. He argued that he should withdraw in my favor. And we played Alfonse and Gaston until, at length, I convinced Chub that I really and truly did not want the post, that I had given Bob Reynolds a price tag that would surely preclude my being considered. We shook hands, finished our drinks, and walked back downstairs. The meeting had taken a coffee break, but O'Malley and Paul remained at the table sifting bits and pieces of paper, ballots I assumed. We asked what was happening and were told that after several straw votes the two leagues were evenly divided in support of Feeney and me. When the meeting was reconvened, I requested the floor, withdrew my name from consideration, and moved that we elect Feeney the new commissioner by acclaim. Frank Dale jumped up and seconded the motion enthusiastically. Everyone was thrown off balance by the quick move, and the ensuing discussion was disjointed and confused. A vote for Feeney as the sole candidate failed to produce a sufficient number of ayes. The meeting broke up with an acceptable candidate still to be found. My American League friends were disappointed at my unwillingness to run for the office. It would have suited their purpose. Possibly, if I had forced myself, I might have become a creditable commissioner, but I doubt it. The role didn't suit me; I couldn't imagine working as a hired hand for twenty-five O'Malleys. Or even one. The mere thought of it turned me cold.

In the weeks that followed, the search went on and I actually went along to see Bowie Kuhn to ask him if he would consider the post. It seemed to me that he could be recommended on two counts at least: he was familiar with its administration and favorably known within baseball, and he was well regarded as a lawyer at a time when legislative attention to professional sports was increasing. Having worked together with him on a number of baseball-wide assignments, I had a high personal assessment of him, our early irritating encounter notwithstanding. I would be willing to canvass for American League support. No, he said, he was too private a person, and preferred to spend his summer weekends quietly at his summer home in Quogue, tending his roses, playing a bit of golf. Perhaps he was waiting, prudently, for O'Malley's invitation rather than mine. O'Malley was his more natural sponsor and, in the end, a successful one.

Kuhn became the compromise commissioner and I remained encamped happily in the Bronx tending my own store, happy to be alive and well, happy to be in this world at this time and in this place, connected to this game. Tending store meant a number of extracurricular activities remote from box scores and league standings, activities that were nonetheless part of the persona of a ball club, if the principal fellow has a sliver of social awareness, an extra ounce or two of energy, and doesn't take himself too seriously.

For me, tending the Yankees was not work. Rather, it was a long lilting holiday. The days and nights were full, of course, but filled with an exhilarating variety of things to do under very agreeable circumstances. No day was like the one before or the next, except for the set schedule of games during the season. And even those were never quite the same; the outcome of a game was never foretold. The unpredictability, the emotional excitement of winning and losing, my empathy with the players — good days and bad — the awareness that over days and seasons, my own success or failure was riding on the outcome — all these came together in an addictive potion. All the ingredients were human, strength and frailty cycling through the mix.

An ordinary day often started with breakfast at the Plaza with a magazine writer assigned to a Yankee story, or with the director of the Repertory Theatre at Lincoln Center to lend a hand to his problems, or with Marvin Miller to work out an accommodation with the Players Association, or with a valued broadcast sponsor. A morning could be taken up with a concoction of appointments: a Yankee board meeting with Paley; a contract negotiation with the local television station, a visit to a player recuperating in Lenox Hill Hospital, a press conference announcing Whitey Ford's retirement, a session with Yankee scouts and minor league managers to review our young talent, a meeting with the Yankee staff to schedule promotion days — Bat Day, Cap Day — for the following season, a hell-raising session with the Stadium concessionaire. I might lunch with Lewis Rudin at "21" to enlist his political help with the city, or with Jack Kent Cooke and Lamar Hunt in a Waldorf Towers suite to talk about the Yankees' buying a soccer franchise, or alone at the Flash Inn at the top of Harlem, just across the 161st Street bridge from the Stadium, drinking a beer and eating the chef's delicious special salad. An afternoon could include seeing Wellington Mara about the football Giants' tenancy at the Stadium, talking with Bill White about joining our broadcast team, visiting a deputy mayor at City Hall, taping a David Frost show with Pearl Bailey, attending a National Book Committee meeting, contesting with the commissioner of baseball, defending a boy vendor fired by the concessionaire because his hair was too long.

Almost always before each game I visited the Yankee clubhouse, loafed about the field at the beginning of batting practice to chat with our players, the visitors, whomever; drank a beer and gossiped with the writers in the press room, where we fed them a very good meal. Never was I so dopey as to tell Houk how to manage a game. The phone in my box next to the Yankee dugout kept me in touch with every part of the Stadium during a game, but I never once rang Houk. Nor did Lee MacPhail, except to give Houk a weather report so he could hurry or stall if rain was in the offing, depending on whether we were ahead or behind and what the inning was. After a game, too, I briefly visited the clubhouse to say a word to the boys who had played especially well and, more importantly, to touch the shoulder of a player who had blown a game and sat dejectedly on a stool before his cubicle. A touch on the shoulder told him all he had to know. It was a good idea, I thought, for the players to feel my involvement on a personal level. But I was careful to stay well short of impinging on Houk's turf; it would have been bone stupid of me to diminish his managerial authority in any way. When I had opinions about our players I gave them to Houk or MacPhail privately.

On nights when no games were scheduled, Mouse and I would see a ballet or go to the Philharmonic. There were dinners on end to speak at: the Cartoonists, the Investment Association, the Lighthouse for the Blind. Saturday and Sunday mornings I rode my horse, and on Sunday nights Timmy made spaghetti and a green salad, a good way to end the week.

When the children were home from boarding school or college they often joined me at the Stadium, though the girls found baseball a funny game and were not as keen on it as Peter was. Away from the public venues my private life was closed off, not furtively but rather as a nonpublic time out, spent with family and friends. I gave up sporadic games of golf and tennis to ride with the children on weekends and holidays. Sharing the sport equally — equally because each of us had one mount to ride, one saddle to sit in, one bridle to guide his horse; equally because we walked, trotted, or cantered together as a group, sharing the same enjoyable experience, unweighted one way or the other by age or youth, parenthood or childhood — an already loving relationship bonded us even more commonly, enduringly. During their early years in New York, after we had returned from England, we made time to be together — riding of course, ice skating at Rockefeller Center, rounding Manhattan on a Circle Line boat, or simply walking down through Central Park to the zoo or the carousel. Some of our liveliest laughing times happened when their mother was in Africa, not because of her absence but because the absence of a mother's level, practiced hand, with only their father for the moment, allowed us to invent every day, to make it a kind of game, an adventure. I taught Mouse to whistle through her fingers, and the shrill blast from a petite angelic-looking schoolgirl stopped the most indifferent cabbie at a hundred paces. As Mouse grew into becoming Michele, she took me to poetry readings at the New School. She will herself be a good poet; is now, I believe.

When Peter was a freshman at the University of Pennsylvania, I visited him and, for auld lang syne, we went to a football game in Franklin Field. I found it rather sad. Penn hadn't had a good football team for years — not since they had joined the Ivy League and curtailed recruiting — and three-quarters of the great stadium seats were pathetically empty. I asked Peter why he didn't join in the traditional songs, and he said he didn't know the words; he'd not been to a Penn football game before. I smiled, thinking of my brother quitting freshman football to join the Mask and Wig Club, and it pleased me to observe how much Peter was like him — in looks, in temperament, in turn of mind. Now and again for a split second, or sometimes in a half-dream, my mind fused the two, then sorted and reidentified them. The Penn team fell behind badly and we left to stroll around the campus where a mailman in a blue-gray uniform, lugging his shoulder bag, waving his cap, hailed us. He was a man of sixty, I gauged, handsome, with wiry iron-gray hair and dancing eyes. A broad smile rolled back from magnificent teeth, illuminating a happy man.

"President of the New York Yankees," he announced, pleased as though he had found a ten-dollar bill in the street.

"I am." We shook hands.

"Mike Burke! My Mike Burke!"

"Yes." His easy possessiveness made me laugh and his enthusiasm was so disingenuous, so infectious that it pleased me that his discovery so pleased him.

"I used to deliver your mail. 3908 Spruce Street, right?"

"Right. You've got some memory."

"I'm Horace."

"My God, Horace. I'm glad to see you. You're not supposed to have gray hair. Not my Horace."

"What about my Mike?" And we laughed together at what time had done to our black hair.

"You look handsomer than ever," I said. "This is my son Peter. He's a freshman." They shook hands.

"I used to deliver mail to your daddy. All those football players that lived at 3908. Shinn, Fielden, Tony Micho. I knew them all. Your daddy was a scat back. He could scat!" Peter stood back a pace from this unexpected reunion, slightly shy on the rim of an acquaintanceship almost twice as old as he was. "I told them I knew the president of the Yankees. I told 'em it was true."

"And for a long time, Horace." He asked me to write a little note on the back of the football program I carried, confirming our friendship.

"Don't you worry about Peter," he assured me. "I'll look after him. Same as I looked after you and Frank Reagan and all you boys." To have been remembered by Horace was surprising and gratifying, and it made me doubly glad to have come to Philadelphia. Perhaps the chance encounter would say to Peter that a vast university need not be an entirely impersonal place and that healthy acquaintanceships neither dim nor lose their flavor over long broken time. I asked him what was the most exciting experience of his first semester.

"A lecture by Louis Kahn," he said. Kahn, the famous architect, was a member of the university faculty. "I taped it," he added with a sly smile. Since the age of twelve Peter had been on a straight line towards architecture. Well-meaning friends warned that it wasn't a lucrative profession, as though that mattered, and his mother and I encouraged him on his course at every juncture.

We had bought a penthouse apartment at 17 East Eighty-ninth Street and yet again Timmy made an exceedingly attractive place to live. Probably I became a more neglectful husband than I realized, too taken up with the number of things to be done, especially in the early Yankee years, and the endless invitations to do more. I rarely said no. It was in large part my inattention that veered us apart.

Two significant things happened that rightfully enhanced Timmy's sense of herself. First she uncovered her own distinguished ancestry. In the seventeenth century her forebears had moved across from Scotland to Ireland and established themselves in Drumaboden Castle and from there a younger son emigrated to Virginia. A later-generation Campbell pushed through the Cumberland Gap to Tennessee to found a distinguished banking family. The family home outside Nashville, built by Timmy's grandfather and the birthplace of her father, is a classic antebellum plantation house. Tall white pillars and a red brick facade look out across lawns and paddocks that slope away to a private lake flanked by great old trees. The Civil War battle of Franklin was fought in the surrounding fields, and today Magnolia Hall is listed in the national directory as a Historic Site. This discovery plucked Timmy from limbo, placed her in a distinguished lineage, qualified her for membership in the Daughters of the American Revolution.

Then, too, she took up her extensive travels in Africa, exploring and writing about places few Americans had been, and, in the process, establishing a healthy identity of her own. *Holiday* magazine commissioned her to write about one four-month journey, and titled the piece: "Ladies Day South of the Sahara; a New York Yankee Wife Skips Spring Training for a 10,000 Mile Trek of the Sahara." In subsequent years Timmy visited all parts of Africa — sailed the Bend of the Niger to Timbuktu and Mopti, trekked by Land Rover across 1,300 miles of the

Sahara from Algiers into the remote Ahaggar Mountains, found her way into Chad, where a French Foreign Legion convoy found her in Abéché and lifted her clear of revolution, was arrested in the Sudan for unwittingly taking photographs of a desert military camp, and was looked after by Catholic missionaries in the Zaïre jungle. Most of those journeys she undertook alone; all were daring. Each time a combination of blithe innocence and good Scots fiber, firm purpose and the magic of femaleness, carried her to and from her remote destinations and back to New York unharmed.

At home she tended towards the grand houses along Newport's Belvue Avenue where her best friends lived, deep in old American money, while my compass pointed to the sweatier poles of Yankee Stadium and Madison Square Garden. In time our marriage foundered and failed, though lawyers haggled over a divorce settlement for five separated years. The countless nights I had not been home for dinner — or at all — had a price. Timmy kept the apartment and, except for my books, everything in it, which was fair and just. It was she who had assembled everything that was there; I nothing. Our divorced relationship was civil, as it should have been, and our three children were old enough to understand that their parents could be unmarried and not unfriendly, not uncaring of the past. They, together with Patricia, clung together, looked after one another with exceptional care, swept to and fro collectively like a flock of birds.

I was in my office at Yankee Stadium when my mother telephoned from Old Saybrook, where she and my father had lived since he retired, there where the Connecticut River flows into Long Island Sound. He loved to be near the water, to walk the shore in winter, and to swim every day as soon as the weather was fine, diving off a rickety board at the end of an old wooden pier when the tide was in and the water deep enough. On his walks he carried a blackthorn stick I had brought him from Ireland, not because he needed it but because I had brought it to him, I think; and when he swam an old-fashioned, tireless sidestroke, or floated on his back gazing at the sky, or, eyes closed, drifted in his own memories, reliving his own secrets, the waves lifted and lowered him gently as a caring friend.

"Your father had to be committed to Norwich." Her voice was clinically flat. She did not attempt to be oblique or to cushion a harsh fact. That was her way. I repeated the sentence to myself to comprehend it, like repeating to yourself a sentence in a half understood language, striving to get the translation correct.

"You mean the insane asylum?" I held my breath, praying that I had misread her tone and that Norwich had some less sinister meaning.

"Yes. He . . ." I don't think I heard much of what she said about his having become increasingly unreasonable, unmanageable, fleeing the house at any hour of the day or night, and more.

"How long has he been there?"

"Two days."

"Are there visiting rules?"

"There's no point in your seeing him. He won't know you."

"That doesn't matter." I sat still for a long time trying to fit this rough jagged piece of news into my mind, but a sluicegate had opened and a torrent of recollected images, sounds, phrases, places, plunged through a raceway of my mind, a current too swift and turbulent to admit a new unhappy fact. When I was away at war, I had written him, recalling, among other things, a father-and-son golf tournament we had played in and won when I was about sixteen. He wrote back:

> . . . It once again proves the power of good example, more often than not given unwittingly with no thought of the impression being created. I was deeply touched and am grateful to you.
>
> My memory of that game takes another tangent. I can recall hitting a few other tee shots that day that for me were *good*, about 225 down the middle, but they were still about 25 yards short of yours, so the old man just picked up. Under ordinary conditions that would have been a minor tragedy, but on that occasion I was bursting with pride and joy at your accomplishments, such as I have been fortunate enough to experience on numerous occasions since and in many different and more important affairs.
>
> I like to think that the first step in making you a man was the occasion in Springfield when you came home weeping because

three kids had been picking on you and I told you the story of the bully and what a cad he is, really a coward at heart, admonishing you to lay into them which you did to your entire satisfaction and mine on the very next day. You will recall that they did not bother you again. I am sure that was one lesson in life which made a lasting impression, because no one has pushed you around from that day to this. That often came to mind when you gave it and took it with relish in Franklin Field and it never mattered how big they came. That physical courage is a great asset to you now and I know you will meet any situation that may arise, solely on your own, if need be. . . .

I am going back to New York this afternoon and am planning to see your darling Patricia tomorrow. Somehow or other seeing Patricia is like visiting with her dad. Yes I'm a funny guy. I'm slow on the uptake, as far as my heart is concerned. Just as I stood in awe of you as a baby for the first six months or so, not being able to get used to being a father, so it has been with Patricia — admiring her of course and thinking of her as a sweet and unusual child. But now she has made her way deep into my heart, just as you did, and there she shall remain. Mine is a slow-burning fire, but when it flares up it is all consuming. I love her deeply, Mike, and I am very happy about it. I hated to see you kids grow up, but Tricia is filling that void that perhaps only little innocent children can really fill. I think when they are young, children are loved by their parents in the same sort of way, making no distinction, just plain loving, as they grow up they develop their own individual characters and love branches out into deep respect, or sympathy, or concern or whatever feeling the particular child may engender. So while the old love is basic, it expresses itself in devious ways. Anyway it's all intensely interesting, as you will find as you go along. . . .

And at the time he retired we were living in Germany. I wrote him then and still have his response:

My dear Mike,

Many thanks, Mike, for your touching letter about my retirement. What you think of me is of the greatest consequence. Having observed me under all sorts of conditions or circumstances, and knowing my faults and foibles, I feel that I have passed the acid test in the crucible of fatherhood in winning your affection and respect and retaining both, and am a father not without honor in his own family. Consciously or unconsciously, one presents only his best side to the world and in a sense practises a mild form of deception, but his family cannot be deceived. They know the old man all too well. So my cup of happiness is over-flowing and out of it pours my heartfelt gratitude and thanks to you for your words of commendation.

I fear that the parade will remain a figment of your imagination unless perchance you can, one day, acquire possession of a Ringling Brothers bandwagon. Perhaps a calliope would be more appropriate, placed as I soon will be at the tailend of the procession. One is gone and promptly forgotten.

The only big news I have for you is that we have purchased a house in Old Saybrook, within a hundred yards of Long Island Sound. . . .

Hurricane Hazel came too close for comfort but we are not even inconvenienced. Trees fell around and about us and many of our neighbors were without electricity for days, which of course meant nothing functioned. Another Martini or two were recommended for Mother to quiet her fears. As a result I passed out about 5 p.m., about two hours before the full force of the storm hit this area. In consequence, I just added to her anxiety the worry as to how she was going to drag out this bulk in case we had to quit the house. Some help! Some fun! Love as ever, Dad.

Last time I had seen him was at his Old Saybrook home watching a horse race on television with half an eye. When I asked he couldn't remember the winner, but as we spoke he described to me with total recall his student days and an encounter with a Jesuit priest on the first day of a new school year. It was in a hallway beneath the shoulder-high sill of a fanlight window. The priest-professor thrust a Greek book at him. "Read that." My father had been failed in Greek the previous term. Morning light slanted down through the window and across the book, opened at random halfway through. He read a page or two, translating as he read, read along easily until the priest snatched the book out of his hand and snapped it closed. "Who says you don't know Greek?" he said and strode on, pleased to reverse the earlier year's failing mark.

Of my three college backfield mates my father was particularly fond of Jimmy Coulter, our blocking back. Two, Frank Reagan and Jim Connell, had died young, and for years I could not trace Coulter and feared he had been killed during the war. Then late in life I found him: Colonel Coulter, a retired professional soldier, still blond and firm-featured. Like most of us, immediately after college Jimmy had enlisted in the Army and had married a girl to whom Faith introduced him, a lovely black-haired girl with whom she had modeled.

When we met he carried a dogeared canceled check dated 1942, made out to my father in the amount of two hundred dollars. He had saved it for thirty years to show me and told me its story. "When I graduated from Officer Training School at Fort Belvoir and got my second lieutenant's commission, I was posted to Oregon. I wanted to take Helen with me but we didn't have the train fare. We had no collateral. Couldn't get a loan, anywhere. Finally Helen and I went to see your father. Did you know this?" he asked.

"No. I didn't."

"You know, he asked us only one question. 'Jimmy, how much do you need?' And when I told him, he just wrote out a check for the two hundred dollars. Didn't ask when we would repay him. Nothing. Just wished us luck, kissed Helen and told her to watch over me." Coulter hesitated for a moment to overcome a catch of grief in his throat. "Did he ever tell you about it?"

"No, Jimmy. That was between you and him."

"We'll never forget him. We paid him back as soon as we could. Before I shipped overseas in '42. We've talked about him a thousand times. And about you. I wish Helen had lived until your letter came." She had died two days before my letter reached him. I handed him back his canceled check and he folded it carefully into his wallet. My mind's eye could see Jimmy vividly as a running play started, rolling out, number 11 in blue on the broad back of his white jersey, blocking a defensive end, leaving me a hole to run through.

"You know I love you, James," I said, my arm across his shoulder.

"I know," he mumbled, hanging his head, his nature even now too shy not to be made slightly self-conscious by such an open expression.

The State Mental Hospital at Norwich is an old institution. Set well back from the road in a walled, parklike setting, at first glance it might have been a small New England college. I drove through the gate and along a curving gravel drive and parked the Ford Mustang on a lawn near a line of old elm trees. Only when the eye moved away from the administration building did it pick up restraining bars at the windows. At a reception desk I asked a polite young woman in civilian clothes if I could see patient Patrick Burke. Yes certainly, she said and an orderly led me along a broad, high-ceilinged corridor.

A slight draft of fear chilled me, a fleeting fear from the past. At sixteen I had a summer job driving a dry cleaners' delivery van. One of the weekly stops was a private mental home, where I made pickups and deliveries as swiftly as possible, half afraid of the silent, ominous man who gave and received the cleaning. He looked like Boris Karloff's Frankenstein monster, and I imagined fearsome things in the dim silence behind him. The same boyhood sensation of half-fear stirred from its forgotten place and I shivered.

We turned off the corridor into an open deck perhaps fifty feet square, open except for heavy steel netting that made it a cage. A dozen or so patients, mostly men, had been let out in the midday sun. Four or five sat a few feet apart in an uneven circle, tossing a red, white, and blue beach ball to one another with varying degrees of lack of interest. My father watched them from his chair; he would have been terribly embarrassed if the ball had come to him. Politely he would have tossed it back, disguising his annoyance at their invasion of his privacy. His expression was serious, thoughtful, distant. He wore clothes he often wore walking along the Sound — a beige cloth cap, a long-sleeved maroon flannel golf shirt, a beige cashmere sweater, gray slacks, and brown shoes, the same style shoes, brown or black, he had worn ever since I could remember, shoes made by Church or someone in New York. He always dressed conservatively and well. Since his law school days at Yale, J. Press had made his suits, and when Louis Praeger and Sid Winston split away and started Chipp in New York, he went along with them, always complaining a little about their tailors' not being what they used to be but never abandoning them. I couldn't approach him for a moment or two. At first sight my heart split in two. Like a melon cut by a meat cleaver, it lay open and hurting, and I didn't know how you approached a man committed to an asylum. I walked across the deck and, at half the distance, he looked up and saw me coming towards him.

"Hello, Michael," he said quietly, as though he was expecting me. I kissed him. He always kissed his father; I always kissed mine; my son always kisses me and I him. I drew up a chair and we talked for an hour or more as a father and son who have been lifelong friends. His brain worked perfectly. He was totally articulate. Sentences and paragraphs were perfectly structured. His vocabulary had unlimited range and his language flowed beautifully from its source in Jesuit scholarship and law. But his mind had jumped to an adjacent track. He spoke as though I had found him at a convention of the American Bar Association. He was dreadfully sorry he had come and would leave tomorrow. He had found no old friends. The quality of membership had deteriorated badly. All through the night there were the most awful commotions; people screaming and yelling. Not having a good time, just behaving crazily. As soon as he got back to his office he would write the president of the association resigning and expressing his regret that the affairs of the association had fallen into disarray. He would not mention the other members' coarse behavior. He simply wanted out, to have done with it. I fell in with his delusions and we discussed this and other things at length. I wanted nothing more than to take him by the arm, escort him to the car, and drive him back to the city with me. I was repelled by the thought of his spending another lonely night, confined, listening to the terrifying night sounds. When I kissed him good-bye he promised to be home the moment the convention adjourned and never to attend another.

I was born at home in my parents' bed. My father held my mother's hand and in her pain she dug her nails into his hand until it bled and, bleeding, he held her hand and she his fiercely with the pain of me until I arrived. She told me this. And holding my hand, figuratively, he had given me a sense of the fundamental decencies.

He was moved to a nursing home in Windham, not far from where my sister lives. When I visited him there, he didn't know me and asked my help, whoever I might be, to unfasten the hasp that locked him into a special chair. A traylike contraption across his lap, not unlike a baby's high chair, held him prisoner.

Without understanding either his crime or the punishment, he was a man confined to the stocks. A nurse came into his spartan hospitallike room with capsules for him to swallow.

"Can't we let him out?" I asked.

"No, I'm sorry. He becomes quite violent once he's released. He wants to run away."

"Jesus!"

"What did you say?"

"He's my father. What are those things you're giving him?"

"Sedation and other things."

"Christ, you're not trying to keep him alive, are you?" She looked at me as though it were none of my affair. He was passing through the land of the professionals now, a land to which neither kith nor kin could gain entry or have a voice. Fortunately he escaped them soon.

After the funeral I drove alone back to New York, and going to an empty apartment and an empty bed was not an attractive option. The Yankees were playing a night game. I sat alone in the small closed owners' box that used to hang on the face of the mezzanine along the first baseline, half watching the game in process, half remembering my first game here, with him. A gust of rising wind blew rain in my face and brought me back to 1969. In moments, a tempest raged into the Stadium. Players fled from the field under a deluge, and the ground crew, rain suits glistening in the floodlights, fought gale-force winds that whipped the tarpaulin out of their hands, blowing it like a loose sail in a wild sea, lashing it twenty feet into the air and a man with it if he didn't let go. You are not going "gentle into that good night," I thought, as my father's spirit passed through the Stadium en route to join my brother.

On a wintry Sunday morning, riding my horse in Central Park, charged with more zest than wisdom, I cantered across the frozen ground, over a rise and onto a sheet of ice, seen too late. Horse and I went down together and together slid fifty feet or more, our slide stopped roughly by gravel where the ice ended. Only a damn fool would have ridden into such a hazard, and I was too embarrassed by my stupidity — and perhaps a little stunned — to feel any hurt. The horse had slid across the ice on top of my right leg, which was skinned and bleeding slightly. Like me, the horse was wet all along one side, more frightened than hurt, and no doubt wondering why he had trusted himself to the hand of such a bloody idiot. We put ourselves back together and moved off quickly to avoid explanations to early-morning joggers running to view the outcome of the spectacular fall.

It was several weeks before tiny black spots began to appear in my right eye. I blinked each morning expecting they would go away — I always thought any malfunction or illness will soon go away — but they didn't and one day I realized that through my right eye I could see my hand only if I held it at shoulder level. It disappeared if I lowered the hand to my waist. So I asked the Yankee team doctor, an orthopedic specialist, if he knew an eye man. He suggested Lenox Hill Hospital, where our players went when they were injured. Dr. Sweet — that is not his true name — made his examination, seemingly with increasing care. Finally, a very solemn expression on his face, he laid a hand on my shoulder and I saw the bad news coming.

"I'm very sorry to tell you this, young fella, but the eye is going to have to come out." For some reason I was not altogether taken aback. That possibility had occurred to me. Yet I took a deep breath and let the air out slowly. It gave me a moment to accept a new fact, to say to myself, OK, that's it; no point in pissing and moaning. "Let me show you," the doctor said gravely, and described accurately reactions I did or didn't have to various lights and instruments. He diagnosed a malignant tumor. "I'm terribly sorry to have to tell you this." He continued to be apologetic.

"It's all right, Doc. I'm rather lucky, as a matter of fact. That eye has never worked perfectly anyhow. I'd be pretty damned pissed off if it was my good eye." I was surprised at how swiftly I was accommodating to having one eye.

"I'll make the arrangements. You should check into Lenox Hill about noon on Thursday, and I'll remove the eye on Friday morning. Would you like to get a second opinion?"

"I don't know another eye doctor."

"Well if you do find someone, you could stop by his office on your way to the hospital on Thursday." I went into a bar across the street for a drink. Glass eye or patch? Which do you think? Probably should have another opinion. Normally I tend to accept professional judgments. If the dentist tells me I should have my wisdom tooth out, I agree; if a surgeon said I had a hernia, I'd say sew it up. I stopped in to see Mr. Paley and told him that Yankee affairs were in order and that I would be away for a couple of weeks.

"Where are you going?" he asked, assuming a winter holiday.

"To Lenox Hill Hospital."

"Oh really?" He looked anxious. "What for?"

"I have to have an eye removed."

"My God, you can't go to Lenox for that. You've got to go to the Eye Institute at Columbia Presbyterian Hospital. It's the best in the world. I'm on the board there."

"Thanks. That's very kind, but I don't think taking an eye out can be all that complicated and the arrangements have already been made." But for a second opinion he suggested Ira Snow Jones of Columbia's Eye Institute, and en route to Lenox Hill Hospital I stopped by to see Dr. Jones. I was attracted to him at once, personally and professionally, and even more so after he examined me and, in my presence, telephoned Dr. Sweet. Much of what Ira Snow Jones spoke into the phone was incomprehensible to a layman's ear but I understood when he said that it was not a foregone conclusion that I must lose the eye. I asked Dr. Jones if I could switch my business to him but he declined regretfully, saying I was Dr. Sweet's patient. So I called Dr. Sweet and said I felt more comfortable with Dr. Jones. He was a bit miffed but agreed to cancel the hospital arrangements and, free of that commitment, Dr. Jones accepted me as his patient. "Have a good weekend and come to the Columbia Presbyterian on Monday. I'll operate on Tuesday." Ira Snow Jones is an absolutely top-flight surgeon and a beautiful man, speaks softly with a slight Southern accent, is a profoundly serious professional but witty and, as the Irish say, has a bit of fun with him. On Tuesday he performed a two-hour operation. I hadn't a tumor, but a retina tear. Apparently these come small, medium, large, and economy sizes, and I had the economy size, so severe that the first doctor had misdiagnosed it. I had to lie still for some days and when I left the hospital, wearing black glasses with pinprick holes so that the eyes looked straight ahead and didn't move from side to side, I took a room at the Plaza Hotel because I would need the better service. Mr. Paley had delivered to me three huge jars of especially prepared soup. Dr. Jones liked the progress.

"What happened to that red spot that used to be on the side of that eyeball?" I wanted to know.

"Oh, we moved the furniture around a bit while we were in there," he said with a sly smile. "Merry Christmas."

Timmy had all four children and me for Christmas dinner. Patricia's own mother lived in Florida, and over the years Patricia and Timmy were together so much that people thought them natural mother and daughter. This pleased them both, and they disabused no one who made the assumption.

## 15

A SUNDAY morning in November was dull, damp, and unpromising for the New York Giants football game scheduled to start at one o'clock. I walked through the Stadium to make certain that concessionaires had not left unsightly empty cartons lying about, that the Special Officers had been issued overcoats, that the members were being properly looked after in the Stadium Club. Jimmy Esposito's ground crew had finished freshening the white yard-line stripes on the green turf, tortured by football cleats, and now probed the undersides of the overhanging decks with long poles, poking loose chunks of dank cement that needed little urging to fall. In football season it was our urgent Sunday prayer that decay be spotted and knocked harmlessly onto the empty seats before it was jarred loose by 62,000 Giant fans stomping for warmth or for a Fran Tarkenton touchdown pass. In the winter of 1968 tons of paint, white outside, blue within, had been lavished on the Stadium's face and in the April sun she had looked a spring chicken to the hasty eye. But her body knew the deeper truth. In the cold cruel light of Sunday morning each crack and crevice of her forty-eight years haggarded her and saddened me to realize the end of her glorious career, her one-of-a-kind career, was closing in.

Often at midnight, after a summer ball game — the crowds gone, the players showered, dressed, and away, the press box empty of the last sports writer polishing his story, only an occasional worklight burning in the soft still darkness — I sat alone in the company of great ghosts: Ruth and Gehrig, Gene Tunney and Red Grange, not that I had ever seen Tunney or Grange perform, but I could see them through the scrim of time and story. And more contemporarily, Joe Louis defeating Max Schmeling and Billy Conn, Sugar Ray against Joey Maxim; Johnny Unitas and the Baltimore Colts against the most magnificent of all the Giants — Gifford, Connerly, Webster, Summerall, Robustelli. All recalled themselves to careful memory in the night. At the onset of 1970 the Stadium was literally beginning to crumble. But however decrepit she had become, however declassé her neighborhood, Yankee Stadium still exuded more allure, remained more awe-inspiring than any of the new symmetrical ball parks. I loved her and it seemed slothful, almost sinful, not to make a flat-out effort to renew her.

I started with a visit to New York City's planning commissioner, Don Elliot. He was sensible and sympathetic, but repeated trips to City Hall, knocking at administrative doors, made it plain that only the mayor could say yea or nay to my plea.

Every summer the Yankees and the Mets played a Mayor's Trophy game to raise funds for sandlot baseball. John Lindsay accepted our invitation to attend. After the game a number of people — the mayor's friends, my friends — gathered for drinks in my rooms behind the mezzanine deck on the first-base side of the diamond. Needless to say, by indirection we had let Lindsay know that he might be waylaid by me on this subject. Linsday carved out a corner of the room for us, near a window looking out on pedestrians and a line of clogged motor traffic homeward bound along 157th Street and River Avenue.

"What can we do?" The mayor's tone, expression, body language all signaled that this was a sincere question, not a sidestep maneuver to finish his glass of wine and whizz off.

"Whatever the city did for the Mets," I said. The city had built Shea Stadium and leased it to the New York Mets baseball team, owned by the very deep-pocketed Mrs. Joan Whitney Payson.

"Why don't you come to my office on Tuesday at, say, ten o'clock?" At ten o'clock on Tuesday morning I was at the mayor's office in City Hall. Dick Aurilio, the deputy mayor, was there; so was Norman Redlich, the estimable corporation counsel, and others. The mayor let me start.

"The Stadium is starting to fall apart. We have had the architects who built Shea Stadium and Dodger Stadium in Los Angeles make a preliminary study to see whether it's feasible to renovate the Stadium, removing the pillars that support the mezzanine and upper decks. The pillars that block some views. And, if that's feasible, to estimate the cost. Their study — I'll leave it with you — finds it can be done and would cost about eighteen million dollars. And, as you probably know, the ground on which the Stadium stands, eleven acres, is owned by the Knights of Columbus. The Stadium itself is owned by Rice University. Both are willing to sell. Or be compensated equitably if the city condemns the property. I think their combined price would be, maybe, four million dollars. What I'm asking you to consider is taking over the Stadium, renovating it, and leasing it back to the Yankees on some kind of lease comparable to the Mets'. Simply put, we are asking the city to equate us to the Mets." A great deal of discussion followed. Would we consider sharing Shea Stadium with the Mets? Yes, as a second choice. Our first choice would be to maintain our own identity in our own ball park. Why doesn't CBS put up the money? Can't; it would be an irresponsible private investment. The stockholders would sue the management. All the new stadiums in the country were financed by municipalities — Houston, Atlanta, Cincinnati, Kansas City, Minneapolis. Not to mention New York. What if the city can do nothing? Then the Yankees would have to consider moving. "Frankly, this would be an anathema to me. The Yankees belong in one place, the Bronx, New York. They are New York. The New Orleans Yankees is beyond my ken," I said.

John Lindsay had heard enough. "The city will do for the Yankees what was done for the Mets. My financial people tell me the city spent twenty-four million dollars on Shea Stadium. We'll do the same for the Yankees." That was Lindsay's marching order to his staff.

When I met with them two days later in Aurilio's office, the air was heavy with negative vibes. Aurilio said they couldn't justify committing twenty-four million dollars to Yankee Stadium. No one actually said I should go away quietly, but it was clear they wished I would. They estimated that at the very outside the city might commit ten or eleven million dollars, but certainly no more. The twenty-four million dollars Lindsay had cited was out of the question.

"Is that the final word?" I looked from face to face, from one locked expression to another, and needed no further answer. "This must be one of the shortest meetings you guys ever had." I drove up the FDR Drive, along the East River, back to the

Stadium, and telephoned Lindsay. He returned my call the next day. "Mr. Mayor, thanks for ringing back. I just wanted to say how sorry I was that we're not going ahead with the Stadium project."

"We're what?"

"Not going ahead. Your guys said they had some second thoughts. The city might go ten or eleven million, but you can't do for the Yankee Stadium what was done for the Mets."

"Who said that?" His tone was sharp.

"The fellows you asked me to meet with."

"Mike, I said twenty-four million and that's what I meant."

"That's what I thought. Perhaps you could let them know and we'll start over."

"Don't worry! I'll get back to you." He did and we resumed discussions. The city picked up negotiations with the Knights of Columbus and Rice University and made its own contract with the architects, Praeger, Cavanaugh and Waterbury, to develop the preliminary work they had done for the Yankees into a full-blown engineering study. When the Yankee Stadium matter was scheduled for a public hearing before the city council, the mayor's office asked me to attend. The council chamber, designed like a huge Federal drawingroom, would have looked more natural if it had been filled with Jeffersonians. Contemporary dress seemed out of place. I took a seat in the rear row, expecting the corporation counsel, Norman Redlich, and the economic development commissioner, Ken Patton, to testify in support of the main proposal, anticipating that I might be called to answer a technical question or two. So I was totally unprepared to be called as the first witness. Chatting with a friend, he interrupted me in midsentence. "They're calling you."

"For what?"

"To be the first witness." Redlich and Patton sat in the front row, laps piled with reference papers. I didn't even know where the witness was meant to stand.

"Why didn't you guys let me know?" I said passing them. They appeared as nonplussed as I. But by now, March 1971, I had lived with the subject long enough. Most of what I would need was in my head. The rest I could speak from my gut. Responding to questions, I made our case as best I could. Ironically, Bill Paley's son-in-law, Carter Burden, fresh out of Harvard Law School and new to membership on the council, was the most hostile. I assumed Burden was trying to put an official distance between himself and his father-in-law and avoid any trace of apparent favor, but his insinuation that I was up to some kind of chicanery was personal and irritating.

"If you are misreading me, Mr. Burden, I would like to remind you that, while I am chairman and president of the New York Yankees and speak for them, I am also an officer of the Columbia Broadcasting System, which owns the Yankees. Therefore I speak in the name of CBS and wonder whether you're calling *their* straightforwardness into question as well." That was a low blow, but it depersonalized his attack. Nevertheless, councilman Burden had posed a perfectly legitimate question: could spending twenty-four million dollars on Yankee Stadium be justified in the face of the need for schools, hospitals, and libraries? That was not for me to answer. I strove to spin intangibles in among the arithmetic and spoke of the psychological advantages of a team's presence, the disadvantages of its absence, trying to speak for the people whose voices are not heard.

New York is millions of anonymous people. Not all of them read books, go to the opera, belong to a club, own a white collar. At no cost — no initiation fee, no dues, not even the price of a ticket — an anonymous person can acquire instant identity: I am a Yankee fan; that is who I am. He can wear the team insignia on his cap, or on his sleeve. He belongs, he is a member, and when his team triumphs, he triumphs. We're number one, he will cry. This man, or this woman, who will never be number one at anything, becomes number one vicariously and his self-worth is lifted. And in a sometimes lonely city no one need be totally alone. A lone person is free to make a friend of an athlete, to take free possession of him, to devour everything written and broadcast about him, to invent a relationship more real than the imaginary playmate of a lonely child, to have a companion he will never meet. But meeting doesn't matter. In a saloon, a ball park, a subway, you will hear him say: "Mantle's my man" or "Jackson's my man." He may even have the player's autograph to authenticate his friendship. Subtract the bread and circuses — the sports team to possess, the athlete to identify with — and the city would go tilt.

Next morning I was pleased to read in the *Times* that they had used as their quotation of the day something I had said to the council: "A baseball club is part of the chemistry of the city. A game isn't merely an athletic contest. It's a picnic, a kind of town meeting."

The *News* was not so generous and ran up a red flag: WORST FOOT FORWARD. They warned of the mayor's committing the city piecemeal and that the estimate board members would have to be fifty-seven varieties of chump to hold still for such tactics, even though sentiment argued that New York should make every effort to keep the Yankees in the home they had graced so long with their presence. One major consideration could strengthen or weaken our position: would the New York Giants football team remain in a refurbished Yankee Stadium?

Wellington Mara and his family owned the team and had been our tenants in the Stadium during many football seasons. He and I talked and I outlined my plan, which included a design to accommodate his football team. Mara was a good friend and good tenant, but he was cool to the idea. He did not believe Lindsay could deliver on what he had promised. Mara also had an alternative, a sure and attractive one. Sonny Werblin, then head of the New Jersey Sports Authority, invited Mara and me to his United Nations apartment and described his and Governor Cahill's plan to build football and baseball stadiums in East Rutherford, New Jersey. Four miles from Lincoln Tunnel, he repeated emphatically, "part of the megalopolis." The new home of the Giants and the Yankees. Attractive leases could be drawn. Sonny was a superb salesman. He led us to the top of the mountain and showed us the green valley. More precisely, he took us up in a helicopter and showed us a gray swamp. Impressive architects' sketches demonstrated how the two adjoining ultramodern sports facilities could be co-beneficiaries of spacious parking lots and linking highways.

I knew in my bones that the Giants were gone. Equally I knew that I would stay in the Bronx, where the Yankees belonged, if I could possibly manage it. I understood Wellington's susceptibility. In the Bronx he was our tenant; in New Jersey he would have his own home. In the Bronx he would have 60,000 seats, in the Meadowlands 74,000. In the Bronx he would have Lindsay, in whom he lacked confidence; in New Jersey he would have Werblin and Cahill, in whom he had implicit faith. Mara opted for New Jersey. I put my money on Lindsay and New York, knowing it was a gamble, knowing that I was rolling for a hard four, not an easy eight. No one could spot the political mines that could blow us out of the water. But it was a gamble we had to take. At least all my instincts told me so. Instincts, if they are any good, usually tell you what to do long before your head has figured it out.

At the time the city of New York was being maligned and deserted. The Johnny Carson show guaranteed itself easy laughs with any anti–New York joke, however lame. Major firms were abandoning the city for the suburbs: Pepsi-Cola decamped to Westchester, Chesebrough Ponds to Stamford. The football Giants, as New York as Times Square, were by comparison minuscule in size, of course, but more visible. The Yankees were equally indivisible from New York. Over the long championship years they had become as fixed and as unique as the soaring skyline. If we, too, were to abandon the city, the negative psychological impact would be severe. Disproportionate, perhaps, but damaging nonetheless. How many impressionable people would jump to the conclusion that the city must be going down the tube? First the Giants, now the Yankees. Do they know something we don't know? In this climate of uncertainty would it not be an act of faith in the city for the Yankees to stay, to say to an audience of proud, tough, emotional, resilient New Yorkers: We're with you; we're going to hack it out here with you; this is where we were born; this is the turf we fought for; this is where we will remain. Every fiber of me dictated that this is what we should do. In my own mind there was no debate. Maybe we could halt, even reverse, the downslide of the Bronx, create a beachhead against decay, building out from there. A dreamer's dream? It was worth the candle. At least we could demonstrate that, in the popular slogan of the day, we gave a damn. Besides, there were sound economic reasons for the city to keep the team in New York. Its presence created revenues otherwise lost. For example, the mayor of Kansas City, arguing on behalf of an American League franchise for his city, estimated that a team would generate fifty million dollars in additional revenues for the city's businesses —

hotels, restaurants, transport, bars. And that was Kansas City.

Werblin telephoned Paley for an appointment, which Paley, bless him, said would be pointless. "I think Mike has already made a commitment to Lindsay."

Later in the day Paley asked, "Have you?"

"Yes. I have." That was it. Paley never wavered.

I had a vividly clear vision of how I wanted the renovated Stadium to look. Uncountable hours were spent with the architects, planning the renovations in infinite detail. Fundamentally I wanted the Stadium to retain its unique shape and its essential character. Also, although it may seem relatively unimportant, I was dead set against a rainbow of color-coded seats. This was more than an aesthetic preference. A single color would be more unifying, more democratic. Everyone in the ball park is there to share the same experience, eat the same hot dogs, drink the same beer. The physical fact that everyone doesn't sit in the same seat was no reason to separate people into reds and oranges and greens. I felt there was, as there should be, a subliminal cohesion, with everyone being a blue. It was also more pleasing to my eye. Another high priority was to retain the copper facade around the top of the grandstand. If in a photograph you saw nothing but the facade, you knew it was Yankee Stadium, no other. I lost that one. Time and again the architects told me my facade demand was impossible, were sent back to the drawing board, and, finally, convinced me that if we were to be rid of the girders, to give everyone an open view of the field, the new structure would not support the facade.

"Then take it down and mount it around the perimeter wall behind the bleachers. We've got to preserve that characteristic somehow. Come back and tell me you can do that." They found a way. Years later, long after I left the Yankees, I happened across a television interview with George Steinbrenner. The reporter asked him about preserving the facade, applauding the fact that it had been done. In response George related how it came about. "You see, I was watching a game at the Stadium one night in 1972, the last year in the old park. My good friend Cary Grant was my guest. 'George,' he said, 'you've just got to keep that facade. It's so characteristic of the Yankees.' 'OK, Cary,' I said; 'we'll do it for you.' And we did." Oh, well.

In a letter to John Lindsay I had set out our Yankee requirements, or at least how I thought the understanding should be considered and accepted or rejected by the city. As the architects progressed with their detailed study, estimated costs mounted and before the mayor took the project to the board of estimate for a vote, I wrote him a summary letter to make certain everyone was focused on the facts.

> We are now faced with a new and difficult arithmetic. The cost of acquiring the building and land would probably be at least $5 million, the assessed value. Modernization of the Stadium would be $27 million, possibly more. A total cost for the Stadium alone of $32 million, or more.
>
> To this sum must be added the costs of creating 10,000 parking spaces contiguous to the Stadium, a new road system including widening and ramping the Deegan Highway and an overall upgrading of the environment. . . .
>
> The cost of these supporting facilities will add several millions to the $32 million estimate for remodeling the Stadium. Everyone involved should face the financial magnitude of the total project realistically and decide whether attempting to modernize Yankee Stadium and dramatically upgrade its supporting facilities is a practical course, particularly with the New York Football Giants having committed to move to a new stadium in the Meadowlands in 1975.

Lindsay held to his course.

The hearing played to a full house. The Yankee Stadium item headed the day's agenda and there was no vacant seat in the board of estimate's beautiful Federal-period room on the second floor of City Hall on the twenty-third of March 1972. Outside, through the high, deep-silled windows, the stone and steel canyons of lower Manhattan contrasted with the quiet dignity of the board's chamber. Spectators sat in rows of white churchlike pews, cushioned in red. New York's prominent ancestors looked down sternly from portraits hung high on white walls, or perhaps they chose to look out the window if the subject did not interest them. Corinthian columns supported an ornamental dome, and across one end of the room the members presided from a high semicircular dais, their view angling down on spectators in their seats and on the witness in the well. A lady sitting in the pew behind me tapped my shoulder and said she would be a hostile witness. I thanked her for letting me know, and when my name was called out, rose and walked forward to stand and be questioned. Respectfully I asked permission to make an opening statement. The board's president, Sandy Garelik, agreed, although I knew his thumb was already turned down, no matter what I said. It was an open secret that the Praeger, Cavanaugh and Waterbury in-depth study now estimated the Stadium renovation at thirty-six million dollars, in contrast to the mayor's original twenty-four-million-dollar figure, which matched Shea Stadium's cost. The climate for our plea was an uneasy one. Among other things I said:

> Our decision to stay was, in a sense, a declaration of faith in the City and its future. It was made at a time when there appeared to be a mounting inclination on the part of both business and private citizens to flee the City. We felt differently. We have deep roots in the City and a long tradition. Our history is a dramatic part of the City's history. The Stadium and the Yankees are an integral part of the character and chemistry of New York. We may both be a bit bruised at the moment, but not to the point of diminishing our pride, our belief in ourselves and our sense of occasion. We have staked our future on the City.

The board voted 12–6 in favor of renovating the Stadium. Garelik and Abe Beame were among the six negatives. Beame was to become the mayor who officiated at the Stadium's reopening in 1975. Editorials in the New York press were antagonistic. The *Daily News* comment was headed: STADIUM STINKEROO. And the *New York Times*': STEALING HOME PLATE.

Approval by the board of estimate was more a beginning than an end. I must have made a hundred trips to City Hall to thrash out things with engineers and financiers and, most important, to negotiate a lease with the corporation counsel, Norman Redlich. It was a long and intricate business. Redlich had written the Warren Report on the Kennedy assassination and would later return to New York University as its dean of the Law School. Negotiating with him was a rewarding experience professionally and personally. He is a gentleman of rare quality. Subsequently he told John Lindsay that the negotiation with the Yankees was one of the most intellectually stimulating exercises he had known. It was for me as well, though some days, as the process slogged on, I was glad of an extra inducement to yet another early morning at City Hall.

At the corner of Broadway and Centre Street a turn-of-the-century bakery served superb coffee and fresh orange juice at a counter near the front, and at the back, in clear view, huge black ovens turned out trays of fresh bread and rolls, muffins and pastries, cookies and cakes. Cheerful ladies picked your choice off a tray straight from the oven and set it warmly before you. I'm in their debt for refreshing my body and my spirit and lifting both across City Hall Park to the negotiating table.

When the Stadium reopened in 1975, Irwin Shaw, friend of thirty years, now more, and I went together, as had become our opening-day custom. After the game we joined the line of cars filing out of the new four-deck garage alongside the ball park. A lad of about eighteen ran up to the open window, thrust in his hand and shook mine.

"Thank you, Mike. Thanks for the new stadium." Irwin thought it a charming gesture. So did I. Common man always seems to understand the main point.

"Would you like to put together a syndicate and buy the Yankees?" That was Mr. Paley's question to me in the summer of 1972, a very generous question. He and I sat in the subdued elegance of his office on the thirty-fifth floor of the CBS building, its austere black granite shafts soaring sheer and straight out of Manhattan's rock base. We sat at the antique drum table he preferred to a conventional desk, its forest-green Florentine leather top blending with forest-green paneled walls. A rich textured carpet, fine as an English lawn, muffled sound. A stark white life-sized figure of a man seated on a straight chair, leaning forward examining his foot, startled the eye, created the oddly uncomfortable sensation of another human presence. The Picassos, hung against the dark walls, were more agreeable, and I sat with my back to George Segal's mummylike sculpture.

Mr. Paley's question was not unexpected. For some time I had wondered how he would approach selling the team, once he had made up his mind to do so, as surely he would. Anticipating it, I had reflected on the options of returning to the main body of CBS or hiving myself off with the Yankees. The time invested in CBS, sixteen years, the generous benefits that accrued to a CBS executive, the agreeable atmosphere among old friends argued for returning to the structured discipline of an affluent corporation. But that would mean giving up the freebooting quasi-independence I so thoroughly enjoyed in the Bronx, departing from a business I liked, one in which I had made some kind of mark. And abandoning a ball club, a group of people, I loved. It would have been spineless not to cut the CBS cord and cast my lot with the Yankees.

"Yes, I would. Thank you." Paley had positioned me just where I wanted to be, and I knew it suited his purpose as well as mine. Apart from his personal enthusiasm, the Yankees had not fit comfortably into the CBS composition. An overall homogeneity existed among the other CBS operations. Its four main groupings fell into a neat structural balance, while the Yankees dangled in a small, lonely box at the end of the schematic plan, relating and reporting only to the chairman. Anti-Yankee agitators, some rather petty, cropped out of the executive ranks. One television network president — the turnover in that post was frequent — complained, "I haven't seen Paley in a year. You see him every week!"

The main and urgent reason for selling the team was clear and sensible. It would be extremely embarrassing to have the city of New York renovate Yankee Stadium at great cost to the commercial advantage of the dramatically profitable Columbia Broadcasting System. Paley did not need the public outcry this would provoke. The press had been hostile when CBS bought the Yankees. It would be immeasurably worse in the case of a new stadium built for them at public expense. Thus far, the newspapers had singled me out by name: "Michael Burke Steals Home Plate," and so on. In my reading, it was a matter not of whether Paley would decide to sell the Yankees, but when.

I took the proposition to a succession of obvious and prominent New Yorkers and to some less obvious, less prominent persons in New York and beyond. With no success. No one would touch the Yankees. They either did not want to distract themselves or divert any part of their wealth to the baseball business. Or they were dubious of my forecast of what success lay ahead for a rebuilt team and a new stadium. Or they had subjective reasons undisclosed to me. However unencouraging, all their negative reasoning was legitimate. If you are looking for the best return on an investment of capital, a baseball club is not the place to invest. In addition to money, a person must have a very compelling reason to buy a team. Mrs. Payson, Gene Autry, Tom Yawkey were avid fans. Apart from those whose aim was to sell more beer or chewing gum — Busch and Wrigley — most other owners had become wealthy in some unglamorous business only to find the purses full, themselves unfulfilled, their egos unsatisfied. Team ownership offered ego gratification and instant escape from anonymity.

Gabe Paul telephoned and asked me if I would be willing to talk with George Steinbrenner, a Cleveland shipbuilder. Gabe ran the Cleveland Indians for Vernon Stauffer and was a shrewd old baseball hand. Steinbrenner, he said, had recently failed in an attempt to buy the Indians, his hometown team.

Steinbrenner and I met for the first time for lunch at the Brussels Restaurant on East Fifty-fourth Street, where the veal was especially good, the tables far enough apart for private conversation and the maître d'hôtel a rare breed, a French Yankee fan. George was a bustling fellow, as tall as I but thicker. His dress was businesslike, neat and square. A military prep school had left its mark on his hairstyle and bearing. He admired General Patton, I learned, and one could see the reflection of this esteem. *Fortune* magazine had described him as young, forty-two, a "mover and shaker," and that appeared accurate. He was confident but not at ease. One sensed that congeniality was not a natural asset, but he put his best foot forward. The porcupine quills of his personality lay folded back. His business mind was keen; he was savvy about numbers. Altogether, he was an intelligent man in a hurry and bursting at the seams of Cleveland.

George said he had virtually a ready-made syndicate, some left over from the failed Cleveland negotiation, some with whom he had participated in other ventures. It was a feeling-out ground-laying tack and ended on both sides with a sense of promise, a sense that, on balance, the fit was probably right. George could raise the money. He would buy a fifteen percent interest himself. I would deliver the club. He and I would be the general partners; the other investors would be limited part-

Mousie enjoying a cruise
down the Florida coast on
Dan Topping's yacht,
1965 (*Michael Burke*)

Announcing to the press
that I had become
chairman and president of
the New York Yankees,
replacing Dan Topping.
Yankee Stadium Press
Room, September, 1966
(*Louis Requena*)

Lee MacPhail, Yankee general manager, William S. Paley, chairman of CBS (on his first visit to Yankee spring training in Fort Lauderdale), manager Ralph Houk, and I, 1967

Our host, standing between Whitey Ford and Mickey Mantle, shepherded us upstairs at El Morocco and out of harm's way. Burke, Hank Bauer, Ford, and Mantle, left to right, celebrating a season's end, 1967

Central Park, 1967. Batting in the Broadway Show League, I was the second baseman and pull hitter for the play *Scuba Duba*, against Mayor Lindsay's City Hall All-Stars. (© *Bert Andrews*)

Anxious days in Yankee Stadium. The caption under the *Daily News* back page photo pleaded: "Don't Jump, Mike." (*New York Daily News photo*)

Ernie Sisto/NYT Pictures

"I do not have the best arm in baseball," the poet Marianne Moore protested. But on opening day of this 1968 season at Yankee Stadium, she made a perfect pitch to the catcher, "crouching on legs that a frog would envy."

Yankee Stadium, June 8, 1969. Mickey Mantle's retirement ceremony. The crowd of 60,000 gave him an eight-minute standing ovation. Here as he is about to circle the stadium's warming track in a golf cart I'm reminding him to savor every second of a once-in-a-lifetime experience. *(Michael Grossbardt, N.Y. Yankee photographer)*

Reading the names of war dead from the pulpit of Trinity Church at Broadway and Wall Street. A protest against the Vietnam War

Yankee spring training, Fort Lauderdale, 1970

Whitney Young, president of the National Urban League, and Mrs. Young, throwing out the first ball on opening day at Yankee Stadium *(Michael Grossbardt)*

With Frank Stanton, president of CBS, Inc., at a Plaza Hotel dinner given by the National Association of Christians and Jews, which invited me to be the guest speaker

1972, New York City Hall. Mayor John Lindsay and I admiring the model showing how the refurbished Yankee Stadium would look

With Manager Ralph Houk sitting in the Yankee dugout watching infield practice before an early 1972 game. Ralph is working on his first-of-the-day chaw of Red Man tobacco. *(Michael Grossbardt)*

The two Yankee
general partners,
George Steinbrenner
and I, at 1973 spring
training in Fort
Lauderdale

With Sharon Alvarez
de Lobo making
way through the street
crowd in front of
Carnegie Hall
en route to a Frank
Sinatra concert

June 1976, Yankee Stadium. Signing Muhammad Ali and Ken Norton for their September fight in the ball park.

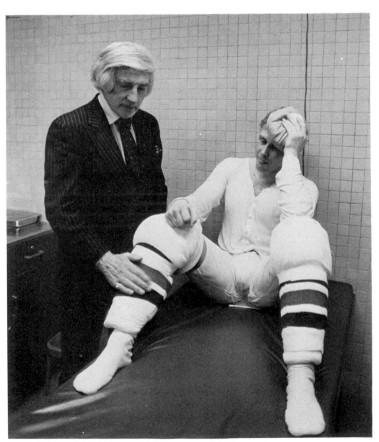

Visiting New York Ranger Anders Hedberg in the training room after a particularly rough game. The marvelous Swede was given a rugged indoctrination when he came into the National Hockey League. *(George Kalinsky)*

With rock star Billy Joel, and Yankee pitcher Ron Guidry at Madison Square Garden after a Billy Joel concert. Yankee players were especially welcome at Garden events and, happily, came often. *(George Kalinsky)*

Bill Cartwright, the Knickerbockers' young center, is happy about the outcome of a game. So am I. *(George Kalinsky)*

Hou Het, capital of Inner Mongolia, China, 1981 *(Bob Shipstad)*

Peter and Michele posed by their sister Patricia, Wainscott, 1976
(*Patricia Burke*)

The farmhouse in
Wainscott where,
Michele said, "Nothing
ever goes wrong"

At the rostrum as chairman and toastmaster of a General William J. Donovan Award dinner in New York. Left to right: Jeff Jones, president of the OSS Veterans Association; John Shaheen; William J. Casey, director of the Central Intelligence Agency; and William Colby, former director of the CIA

CB after schooling over fences at Toppings' stables in Sagaponack (*Photograph ©1984 by Jill Krementz*)

Molly at Michele's wedding to Leslie Majer in Peter Burke's SoHo loft (*Patricia Burke*)

CB taking the fence in front of James Jones's house in Sagaponack. We were invited for Sunday brunch.

My grandson, William Sorrell, in Wainscott on his first trip to America, 1979 (*Doreen Sorrell*)

Patricia in the garden of her house in Water Mill, Long Island, 1981

Doreen (holding William), I, Michele, and Peter in front of Wainscott, 1979
(*Patricia Burke*)

Doreen and William, from a portrait painted by
Doreen's husband, Richard Sorrell, at their home near
King's Lynn, Norfolk, England (*Mike Grenham*)

Old Northbrook House, Aughrim, County Galway, stands on a piece of land which Henry North acquired years ago. My original plan to restore and live in it proved impractical. The dog belongs to Henry's son John. (*Michael Kelly*)

CB settling in at Aughrim after his flight from America — and looked up to by his new friend Dunnie (*Michael Kelly*)

ners. George had a shipping business to occupy him; I would continue to run the baseball operation. I would put up no money but would acquire a ten percent equity in the club and a long-term personal-services contract.

Before we met again I checked out George further in several appropriate places. He was financially solid, his family distinguished and honorable. The family shipping business enjoyed a first-rate reputation. Other investors carried even stronger financial credentials — Bunker Hunt of Dallas, Marvin Warner, the future American ambassador to Switzerland, Lester Crown, who seemed to own something of everything. At face value and taken at his word, George Steinbrenner appeared to have the ingredients of a good buyer and a good partner. I expected a less stiff, more supple personal relationship would come along with time.

George and I met again for breakfast at his hotel, the Carlyle, and Teddy Kennedy, who was staying there as well, joined us for a cup of coffee. I gathered George had hired a plane and put it at Teddy's disposal for some journey he had to make, and Teddy was very grateful. When Kennedy left George said Bunker Hunt and some of the other investors wouldn't stand still for my getting ten percent equity but would agree to something less. I wasn't sure whether George was invoking the absent Hunt as the bad guy to help achieve his end, but it didn't matter. I flipped it quickly through my mind and agreed without haggling on my equity and a five-year personal-services contract with a five-year option. I was happy with the financial arrangement. Important too, I had an obligation to Mr. Paley to get the club sold. I could not possibly let the deal founder because I failed to squeeze the last drop of personal advantage.

We pushed aside the coffee cups and I laid on the table a piece of foolscap on which I had jotted in longhand the points of agreement between us — my equity, salary, and so on, ten points in all. In my business life I had done a thousand handshake deals. Contracts trailed along later when the lawyers got around to drawing them. In this instance, instinct prompted me to get something in writing. We both initialed each point and signed at the bottom of the page. It was a vital slip of paper.

"We can buy the ball club for ten million dollars," I told George. "We cannot get it for nine. We do not have to pay eleven. In my judgment, we will get it for ten million dollars, but it must be in cash. I have signed a deal with the city and redesigned the Stadium. They will renote it and we'll have a thirty-year lease on good terms. The terms protect us on the down side and give the city a break on the up side. We have a team now that could win the pennant in the next year or two and be off running for some years to come."

I scheduled the two of us to meet Mr. Paley in his office at three o'clock in the afternoon of December 19, 1972. George and I lunched on calves' liver at the Brussels, shook hands on our personal arrangement, and agreed to offer CBS ten million dollars in cash. George was wide-eyed at the luxurious appointments and private art gallery look of CBS's thirty-fifth floor. Mr. Paley was in his most charming and engaging form when I introduced them. I said we had come to make a firm offer of ten million dollars for the Yankees and Paley said it was a very respectable offer, one he would discuss with the CBS finance committee and have an answer for us within a few days. He turned his attention to George. "I assume that you and Mike have worked out an arrangement that is satisfactory to him."

"Absolutely. We wouldn't go into this deal without Mike as a partner. If he wasn't going to stay on, I'm not sure we'd be interested." I related my financial arrangement to Mr. Paley.

"That's important to us," Paley said, still addressing George. "According to Red Smith he's now Mr. Baseball to the New York fans." A faint pleased smile shadowed across his face when he mentioned the *Times'* Pulitzer Prize columnist, as though Smith's comment endorsed his own judgment for having let me take charge of the club in its doldrums six years earlier. "Mike's identified with the Yankees more than CBS is. We think that continuity is important. You know, there was some severe criticism when CBS bought the team. No tears will be shed when we sell it. But it makes good sense from our point of view — and I would think for new ownership as well — for Mike to look after the Yankees. Though we'd certainly be happy to have him back at CBS if he wanted to come."

"Mr. Paley, I can assure you we wouldn't want it any other way. I've got a ship company to run. I won't have much time for baseball, so Mike'll have to carry the load. And follow up with the city on the new stadium. All you have to do is walk around the city with him. He's Mr. Yankee and that's a helluva asset." George spoke convincingly. A day or two later Mr. Paley rang to ask $11 million. I telephoned George, said we should hold firm at $10 million and he agreed. Paley accepted our original offer. He had taught me well. A memorandum of understanding was drawn and executed before the year's end, completing the sale. George pooled $4 million in cash from the investors, including $600,000 of his own, and borrowed $6 million from a bank to pay CBS $10 million. Mr. Paley made one personal caveat: he asked me, in response to an anticipated press question, to make clear the fact that the $10 million cash sale had made CBS whole on its original $13.2 million investment in the Yankees. Tax writeoffs of player contracts plus the cash received made the Yankees a break-even venture for CBS. It was important to Paley to be able to say this publicly. In order to avoid any misunderstanding, I suggested that the CBS public affairs vice president, Kidder Meade, compose wording that would suit Mr. Paley's quite legitimate purpose. This would be the basis of any comment I might have to make.

Bob Fishel, the Yankee public relations head, set up a noon press conference at Yankee Stadium for January 3, 1973, my father's birthday. The deal had moved along so quickly that none of the ten limited partners was available and we told the press we would assemble them all in a week's time and buy the writers another lunch. Our purchase of the Yankees created headlines as far away as Bombay. In New York the *Times* ran a photo of George and me and a story in the middle of their front page. The headlines across the back page of the *Daily News* read:

TEN MILLION BUYS YANKEES
CBS SELLS OUT TO BURKE, ELEVEN OTHERS

Almost everyone liked the idea. Faithful to Paley's caveat I was quoted as saying, "CBS substantially recouped its investment." But Steinbrenner, in his exuberance and in the tone of a man who has pulled off a business coup and wanted all the world to know it, said, "It's the best buy in sports today. I think it's a bargain." In a stroke this statement destroyed my relationship with Mr. Paley. The damage was irreparable. Explanation was pointless. Everyone knows you never erase from the public mind the first impression of a newspaper story. Subsequently I learned that Paley held me responsible for Steinbrenner's boast and felt I had not been faithful to his request. I regretted this very deeply, still do. I felt a sharp sense of loss of a valued friendship and the respect of a man I regarded highly. In actual fact, the value of the Yankees had been written down substantially on the CBS books, and the $10 million cash sale resulted in a book profit of more than $5 million. Thus the moment of elation was tempered by a distressing discordant note.

A second discord sounded within the week. We scheduled a press conference in one of the private rooms upstairs at "21" on January tenth to introduce our ten limited partners. During the week following the announcement of our purchase, George added three partners, including Gabe Paul, who arrived on the run with his coattails flying behind him. Only that morning, the tenth, had Paul completed a transaction to divest his interest in the Cleveland team and resign as its general manager. During the week Steinbrenner had telephoned me from Cleveland to say that Gabe would purchase a five percent interest in the Yankees if he could sell his Cleveland shares. "Gabe is sixty-three, you know. He has a home in Florida, and he and Mary will retire there in a couple of years. An association with the Yankees will be a nice way for Gabe to end his baseball career." Again at face value, taking the man at his word, it was an acceptable gesture, though Gabe would bring with him a history of discord in various baseball jobs. At a partners' breakfast in the Carlyle Hotel I learned to my astonishment that Gabe expected to announce his presidency of the Yankees. George had promised him that post. Steinbrenner withdrew to his bedroom to comb his hair, leaving Paul and me in the sitting room "to sort it out." We did quickly, if temporarily.

"Gabe, there is no fucking way we're going to make such a stupid fucking announcement at the press conference!" My Irish was up. "I'll explain your presence exactly as George explained it to me on the telephone from Cleveland: this is a nice swan song before your retirement to Florida." That is the way we handled it at the press conference, but the New York sports writers, shrewd and perceptive, smelled the rat. Duplicity added itself to my perception of Steinbrenner's emerging character. It was apparent that he and Gabe had reached an understanding about Gabe's role different from that described to me. It was a clear warning.

Then there followed great difficulty in translating my personal arrangement into legal documents. Lawyers tugged back and forth without success. Finally George and I, together with our lawyers, arranged to meet in Florida, where the team was in spring training, and work out a formal agreement. We did. For hours. Outside, the Yankees and Detroit played an exhibition game. Each lawyer took notes and then, all points agreed, the two attorneys — Bruce Haims of Debevoise and Plimpton for me and George Martin of Mudge Ross, Richard Nixon's law firm, for Steinbrenner — flew to New York together and en route put to paper the finally agreed-upon contract. The following morning, Monday, Haims received a call from Tom Evans. Evans was George Martin's senior in the law firm, was a limited Yankee partner, a college friend of Steinbrenner's, an associate of John Mitchell, with whom he worked closely as a Nixon fundraiser. Haims telephoned me.

"Steinbrenner has repudiated the deal."

"How can that be? George and I shook hands on it."

"He says the paper George Martin and I drafted coming back from Fort Lauderdale on the plane does not reflect what was agreed at the meeting."

"It does accurately reflect our agreement, doesn't it?"

"Of course it does. Martin is as chagrined as I am. As long as I've been practicing law I've never experienced anything quite like it."

"OK. That wraps it for me. The man's word is worthless." My anger was cold and contained. The latest twist was not a surprise; I could feel it coming.

"What do you mean when you say 'that wraps it'?" Haims asked.

"It means I've made a decision. I'm going to disengage."

"Pull out?"

"Yes."

"You mean just walk away?"

"Hell, no. Withdraw on my own terms in my own way. I'll get the season opened. That's only a month from now. Meanwhile George will get more and more agitated, more and more paranoid about my presence. By the time I tell him I've decided to withdraw, he'll kiss me."

"Not likely."

"More to the point, I'll be able to make a good and quick settlement."

"You think so?"

"Of course. That piece of foolscap George and I signed in the Carlyle Hotel tells me all I have to know."

"When are you going to do this?"

"Not sure. Sometime after the season gets under way. I couldn't in good conscience pull out before that. I read people pretty well; I'll know the moment."

"What do you want me to do?"

"Just carry on with Steinbrenner's lawyers. As though you didn't know what I just told you. I don't want anyone in the world to know that except you and me."

Usually spring training was a loose, happy time, especially with the Yankees. We liked one another, spent pleasant times together away from as well as at Fort Lauderdale's gem of a minor league ball park. My winter home was one of the beach bungalows at the Lagomar Hotel. Peter and Mouse came to spend their Easter holidays from school with me. Peter once arrived in a van with three girls. Doreen was abroad, studying design in Italy and in England. During exhibition games a Dixieland band wandered through the stands making lively music. Tourists lounged in the sun getting acquainted with the names and numbers of the youngsters we had poured into the Yankee system, and DiMaggio pulled on his old uniform and, looking trim as ever, was mobbed for autographs, obligingly given.

One day in that first partnership spring photographs of players and staff were taken for the official yearbook and Steinbrenner and I were scheduled to have our picture taken together as fellow general partners. Normally I dressed pretty casually around the Stadium and especially so in Florida — a ball park is hardly the Royal Enclosure at Ascot — and I turned up wearing a faded blue denim workshirt from the Army & Navy store, a pair of white flannels gone a bit yellow with age, and loafers that probably should have been thrown out. In contrast, George was neatly tonsured and dressed in a neat sports shirt, neat blue flannel jacket, neat gray flannel slacks, looking altogether well scrubbed and fit to pass a spit-and-polish inspection. His unspoken displeasure at my impromptu attire screwed his face into a sour glare. I still have the picture, framed and hanging on a wall, and it makes me smile every time my eye catches it. It tells the story of the time and the difference between us. George is tight, angry, and uncertain. I am relaxed and content, a man with a secret, certain of where I'm going and how it will come out in the end. He is still plotting my undoing, and I know that he can't win; I have already left.

A few days later George telephoned from Cleveland. It was a conference call. His lawyer, Tom Evans, was hooked in from New York. Whatever the subject, George obviously wanted a witness. He was angry as a storm at sea.

"Did you give Murcer a new contract for $100,000?" he demanded.

"Sure. What about it?" I asked.

"What did he get last year?"

"Eighty-five."

"Eighty-five! And you gave him a hundred! What do you think this is, a money tree?" He was screaming now. So I yelled back, and Evans tried to restore some calm. So did I.

"Listen, George, if we keep at each other's throats like this, the partnership won't last out the week. So cool it." He apologized for screaming, and I went on, "Bobby had a good year. He hit thirty-three home runs, for Christ's sake. Led the team in batting. Lee offered him ninety-five thousand. Then Carl Rosen came to me privately . . ."

"Who's Rosen? Some agent?"

"No. He's a very successful businessman here who advises Bobby. Rosen said Bobby wanted desperately to get a hundred thousand. To come up to the Mantle level. I knew the extra five thousand would give Bobby a terrific psychological boost. He's the only guy we've got who sells tickets. I told Lee to give him the hundred thousand." Steinbrenner was mollified, for the moment, but still peevish.

"Well, just remember this partnership is no money tree."

Opening day Steinbrenner arrived from Cleveland with an entourage of sycophants, pushing through the office door, blustering into the lobby, posturing for the benefit of his little clique, throwing down the gauntlet to anyone within earshot.

"Now we'll see what this hundred-thousand-a-year ball player can do!" Of course it took only about ninety seconds for the story to reach Murcer, dressing for the game in the Yankee clubhouse. Bobby came to bat in the bottom of the ninth inning. A hit would have tied the game, a double would have won it. He struck out. Trailed by his hangers-on, Steinbrenner swept down the narrow hallway towards my office. We met head-on halfway.

"There's your goddam hundred-thousand-a-year ball player. He's not worth a —"

"Knock off that shit, George!" I yelled. The yes-men sucked in their breath and pressed against the wall, wishing that they were somewhere else. "Bobby Murcer will strike out again, knock in runs again, hit home runs again. So unless you want to destroy the boy let's not have any more of that chickenshit." Such dialogues don't tend to be elegant. I walked on, down to the clubhouse to see the players. At the season's end Bobby Murcer had batted over .300, hit 22 home runs, and knocked in close to 100. Baseball people will tell you that's very good indeed.

On April twenty-fifth, three weeks into the 1973 season, I wrote George a formal proposal that I become a limited partner and cease to be the club's chief operating partner. I wanted my message to be precise and to be in writing. Some days later George came in to New York and joined me at the round marble-topped table in my office. It was, I said, time for us to admit that we were incompatible. It made no sense for us to try to work together. We came at the world from two different poles, and Yankee Stadium was too confined a space to contain us. I proposed to retain my equity in the club and make a settlement on my personal-services contract. George, as I anticipated he would be, was immeasurably relieved. We talked sensibly, settled my contract, shook hands, equally glad it was over, and left it to the lawyers to draw up the necessary papers. Some days later George brought them in and laid them on my table for our signatures.

"Will you change your mind and stay?" he asked.

"No. That would be the wrong thing to do. Too much blood on the carpet. We'll be better going our separate ways. No regrets. I've loved it. Had a great ride. And I'll always be a Yankee." I held out my hand. "Good luck."

"You too." The fever had broken. The personal conflict was over. It was the only sensible course to take. Once it was taken, I was more disappointed than angry. Even a bit sad. The years from 1966 had been idyllic; nothing would be quite like them again.

Afterwards we stood together on the edge of the field, tying off bits and pieces of Yankee business, watching the crowd depart an afternoon game. It was a foregone conclusion that Ralph Houk would leave at the season's end. He couldn't abide George's intrusions. Most likely he would go to Detroit or Boston. George asked me whom we should get to manage the team.

"Billy Martin. Get him at the first chance. He and I used to have dinner whenever his club came to New York. When he was managing the Tigers we talked about his coming to New York, and the Detroit owner all but had me up before the commissioner on tampering charges. Billy's driving ambition is to become the Yankee skipper and baseball's first hundred-thousand-dollar manager. He'll be difficult but worth it. As soon as he's free I'd get Billy." That was my first, last, and only act as a Yankee consultant. A couple of years later, when Billy was fired in midseason as the Texas Ranger manager, George rang me at my summer home to say that he had sent Gabe Paul to search out Billy somewhere in Colorado. And he rang again a few days later saying, "We've got him and he's your problem." We laughed easily and agreed that it was a great move. I was especially happy for Billy; a Yankee is all he ever wanted to be.

I never went to Yankee games at Shea Stadium when the team played its home games there during the two-year renovation period. It was more discreet to be not only a limited partner but a silent and distant one. Hanging around the perimeter would demean me and disquiet everyone else, especially George. A buffer of absence would avoid tensions. From the very first George had been bugged by my New York visibility and the amiable relationship I enjoyed with a variety of people. In his mind I represented, if not a threat, at least a distraction. He was discomfited by my easy camaraderie with Yankee organization people contrasted to his own rough exercise of authority. He shouted and blustered for lack of fundamental self-assurance, terrible-tempered for reasons perhaps as unclear to himself as to others. And when the Yankees returned to their beautifully renovated Stadium, I went to and from my box behind the Yankee dugout, not stopping at the offices, certainly not intruding into the Yankee clubhouse to visit the players, not even when they had won the World Championship. I would have felt out of place and uncomfortable. Whatever it is that gnaws at George would have bitten him sharply, and I did not want to draw his wrathful reaction down upon the players, especially those with whom I had a long friendship. They knew how I felt about them and tacitly accepted the situation. Some didn't give a damn, of course. They would come over and shake hands across the top of the dugout — Murcer, Munson, Nettles. And of course Billy Martin. Occasionally Billy would give his lineup card to the home-plate umpire in the usual pregame formality, then trot a direct, defiant line to the dugout step opposite my seat and extend his arm for a handshake, his eyes alight with mischief. "George has got his glasses on us, you know. This'll really burn his ass." Billy made taunting mischief wherever he could, but this was his natural home and everyone knew it.

Beyond a leavetaking press conference a few days thence, I hadn't a clue in the world what I would do next. I knew only that it would be something I liked and wanted to do. I was deeply pleased with what I had done last. How it had started, how it went in the middle, and how, after some awkwardness, it ended. I knew, too, that there was nothing I couldn't do if I liked doing it. For the moment I would simply drift in the afterglow of a marvelous experience.

Taking honest account, I concluded that if clairvoyance had permitted me to see how my personal Yankee saga would unfold, I would have done nothing differently. Knowing what I now know, I asked myself, would I do it all again? Would I do it the same way? Would I have agreed to the same outcome? I came down with an unequivocal yes. I had taken a gamble of sorts leaving the luxurious climate of CBS and had come out far ahead. I had thrown a big seven on the first roll. I owned a piece of the club whose value would rise. I had a few dollars in my pocket and the world was full of infinite possibilities. It was, in truth, the proper time to move along. However arrived at, the moment invariably reveals itself.

The Yankees had been a great joy, a perennial holiday. I had indulged myself extravagantly. Running a ball club was not the world's most demanding occupation. This was as true of the Yankees as any other; the unhurried pace of the game itself seduces its administrators into a leisurely business tempo, often mistaken for work. It would have been only a matter of time before I became sated and restive, not with the game itself, but with the business of baseball. Even during the busy restructuring years my energy had overflowed into all kinds of extra-Yankee activity: the National Urban League, the National Book Committee, the Board of the Faculty of Arts and Sciences at the University of Pennsylvania, Multiple Sclerosis, the Auxiliary Mounted Police, even a series of lectures across the country.

And, above all, a very private life of great intensity. For those were the main years of the Big Love Affair, the perfect joining that would last for ever and forever after that, the match made in Heaven, Héloise and Abélard.

Suddenly, there she was and life changed for all time. A gentle September breeze brushed her bright summer dress lightly against her slender limber body; long lovely legs moved her fluidly across Sixth Avenue, other pedestrians blurred and irrelevant. Some elemental passion slipped into a vacant, waiting place inside me. A year, perhaps two, had passed since I had last seen her and then glancingly, perhaps at a crowded cocktail party, perhaps in a theatre lobby. Now she smiled gaily and we kissed cheeks, as casual friends, openly delighted by the chance meeting on the corner of Fifty-second Street across from the CBS building, a two-person island in the stream of lunchtime traffic.

Yes, she would love to have dinner one night; please phone. I forced myself to wait through the interminable afternoon. I thought you'd never call, she said, laughing. The Lafayette was a fashionable French restaurant then; even jaded heads turned, for she was that kind of breathtaking girl, not showy, not flashy, but truly beautiful and dressed in exquisite taste. She was that elusive unknown creature who lived deep in the psyche just out of sight, just beyond reach. I felt myself slip-sliding away and I knew I would be forever lonely without her. In truth, her thrall had been upon me from that time a decade ago when we had first met and she was twenty-three.

We agreed to meet again the following night at Joe and

Rose's on Third Avenue. I sat at the bar drinking a Jack Daniel's sour, talking sporadically to the busy barman, when she came up behind me, crooked an arm around my neck and, squeezing tightly, kissed the side of my face, hard. We dined in the back room on black and blue steaks. I told her quite simply that I loved her, and she took from a leather bag a candid photograph of me, one I had never seen. Since we had first met she had kept it secreted in a book of Chekhov's stories.

There followed the best of all possible years. But the gods who fashioned the ingredients that fit us together lived in a simpler place, far from the ordinary ways of earth, and earthbound realities proved too complex even for an *ange* such as she to resolve in our favor. The desolation to come, no less than the love that went before, would echo and reecho in the canyons of the heart. The story did not end as a love story should, happily ever after, but we knew the years together had dealt us an unreasonable share of human happiness. I have thought of you only twice, she said when she learned I was leaving to live in Ireland and telephoned: night and day. And I her.

My active life in the New York Yankees partnership had lasted little more than a hundred days. On April thirtieth the sports writers were invited to an informal press conference in my office. Throughout, they had been exceedingly kind to me. Some had become very good friends, and I owed them a word of farewell. When I had taken over the club from Dan Topping six years earlier I had sat on a table top, feet dangling, comfortable and at ease and wanting the reporters to be at ease as well. Now on this last day in my office I sat on the credenza, my books aligned behind me, a baseball lithograph made by H. Samhein of Boston in 1894 on the wall behind my head. Next day a Red Smith column in the *Times* said, "Burke talked first, his manner as relaxed as his attire — navy blue turtle neck, dark handkerchief peeping from corduroy jacket. Steinbrenner, a collar and tie man, listened with arms folded and chin jutting."

I made no bones about having enjoyed my position and, though there was a certain lingering sadness in giving it up, one had to be pragmatic. "If I may borrow a line from Yeats: 'I

balanced all, brought all to mind,' and three weeks ago proposed to George the arrangement now agreed on." To one of
the writers who inquired I answered, "It's a line from Yeats.
'An Irish Airman Foresees His Death,' ironically enough." And
to another question: "I suppose at the root is the fact that we
are two rather independent individuals with different points of
view. It was something neither of us anticipated, but as we
talked through the situation, we were confronted with — perhaps we created them ourselves — areas of disagreement. We
would have preferred a different outcome but, after some
rocky times that George and I had together I am pleased that
we've resolved our differences sensibly."

George said, "A myriad of things came between us. It may
be hard to understand this, but I think Mike and I are on a
closer personal basis now than before." The journalists, professionally skeptical, were doubtful. My chemistry and George's
could not mix without exploding. Professionally separated, we
could be personally civil.

Red Smith threw up his hands. Now they're the Cleveland
Yankees, he wrote. I said I would be seeking gainful employment outside baseball. Bill Lee, the venerable sports columnist
of the *Hartford Courant,* whom I had known since I was a
schoolboy at Kingswood, writing as though I were his favorite
nephew, wrote that I had often said, "The Yankees are part of
my chemistry and perhaps I of theirs." And he thought it "a
pity that baseball had lost the chemistry of which Mike Burke
is made."

I left baseball with a sense that my visit had been worthwhile.
The years had been pleasurable beyond my most extravagant
expectations. I took a final remembering look at the intensely
personal office that would soon disappear. On Sundays during
the football season the credenza across the end of the room
offered a buffet for a dozen or two invited friends — Irwin
Shaw, Felix Rohatyn, Brud Holland, John Lindsay, a mixture
of chums and their ladies. A neighbor brought around barley
soup and cheesecake from his wonderful delicatessen on 161st
Street. There were black bread and biscuits for the Brie, fruit,
a tall silver coffee urn. Now, as on ordinary days, the credenza
held a long line of my books, which would be sent along to me
later. Prints of baseball in earlier times hung cool and refresh-

ing against the white walls — Abner Crossman's *The American Baseball Player in England: Match between the Red Stockings and the Athletics, Princes Grounds, Brompton* and *The Match on Lords Cricket Grounds between the Red Stockings and the Athletics*. A bouquet of fresh cut yellow 'mums stood in vases on each of the glass coffee tables and the leaves of the tree standing in a corner were shiny green in the afternoon sunlight. Through the big windows the sun's slanting rays warmed the red carpet and the rich brown sofas, brightened the room, and cheered me with lighthearted memories of agreeable friends gathered there.

I liked having been there and having them with me. I would miss the daily friendship of MacPhail, of Houk, of Fishel, miss the easy camaraderie with George Schmeltzer the electrician, with Jimmy Esposito and his ground crew, with Pete Sheehy in the clubhouse, with Mike Rendine in his box office, miss the special breed of sports writer that covers baseball, the young new breed who had made me an honorary Chipmunk and given me one of their Chipmunk sweatshirts. I would miss the annual Yankee picnic in right field and the softball game between the ground crew and the office staff, enlivened by quantities of beer, miss the Yankee Christmas party where Johnny Johnson lampooned all of us with film and commentary and Joe Pepitone sang ballads and Jim Bouton read his poetry, miss Anne and Rita who ran the switchboard so amiably, miss the players, knowing I would never again visit the Yankee clubhouse to congratulate or console them. The Yankees were a very close-knit family in those years, drawn closer in adversity perhaps. Anyway, it had been a lovely ride. But now it was over and I would have to find something new to engage me.

The cumbersome freight elevator — we had no other then — lowered me to the ground floor and I crossed 157th Street to the players' parking lot, slid in behind the wheel of my Datsun 240Z, and drove across the Harlem River for a farewell beer with the lads at the Flash Inn. It was a quiet, satisfied ending.

~~~~~~~~~~~~~~~~~~~~~~~~~~~~~~~~~~~~~~~~

# Madison Square Garden

## 16

YANKEE STADIUM was no longer my stadium, no longer indivisible from me, no longer my center of gravity. Once again I was in limbo. Again the bridge was burnt behind me without my having any notion of how or where I would next make my way. Oddly, I had no misgivings, but rather a sense of elation at cutting loose from what had developed into a disagreeable situation. I was comfortable with myself for having valued self-possession more than a lucrative contract, and was amused at myself for taking this financial measure, knowing that in the not so distant past I might have sold my soul for less. Admittedly, a touch of sadness mingled with weightless freedom, the kind of residual sadness that lingers at the end of a long love affair, not morose or anguished or bitter, but a muted, accepted sadness, knowing that a period of your life had been better than all others, that it was over, and that life might never be quite so good again. But that very good slice of life, I knew, was a private possession, a part of me. No one could ever subtract it, not for one day, not for one hour.

True friends always know when to reach out for you. In June 1973, Bill Horrigan, my old OSS colleague and the godfather of my daughter Doreen, telephoned from his home in Bermuda inviting me to use his guest cottage. The food was good and the rates right for an unemployed person, he said. He and his wife, Mary Kay, met me at the airport with a warm Brooklyn Irish welcome and a loose schedule of golf and swimming, cocktails and dinners, that promised several days of no deeper concern than how to hit a ball straight after a twenty-year abstinence from golf.

When I returned to New York to search out a new place, Felix Rohatyn, another longtime friend, rang to say that Charles Bluhdorn, chairman of Gulf & Western, was looking for someone to become president of Madison Square Garden and wanted to see me. Felix, a partner in the investment banking firm of Lazard Frères, had, as chairman of the Municipal Assistance Corporation, almost single-handedly saved the city of New York from bankruptcy. He and I lunched in Bluhdorn's private diningroom in the Gulf & Western building at Columbus Circle on Monday June 18, 1973. Gulf & Western owned the controlling interest in Madison Square Garden and called the major shots. Characteristically blunt, Bluhdorn made it clear that he was fed up with the incumbent, Irving Felt. A Bluhdorn monologue took up the first half hour. Later Felix and I laughed when he told me Charlie had not been impressed by me at first; it was only over coffee that he began to see my possibilities. We laughed because talking against a Bluhdorn monologue is like spitting into a gale. When I did have a chance to say something I told him I could be interested in running the Garden's sports and entertainments — the Garden itself, the racetracks in Chicago and on Long Island, International Holiday on Ice — but I was neither knowledgeable of nor attracted by the corporation's other interests: office buildings, hotels, real estate. I suggested he consider a different person to look after that part of the business, and we agreed to think about it and talk again.

Other people came along with a variety of proposals. None appealed to me. I thought seriously of transplanting myself to Ireland but, on reflection, it seemed too soon for that. A month after our luncheon meeting, I went back to see Bluhdorn in his large, characterless office. Expensively furnished, it reflected the impersonal taste of a decorator; I doubt Bluhdorn could remember what it looked like once he walked out the door. His opening remarks took me by surprise. He let loose a barrage of criticism. Is this guy some kind of nut, I wondered. If he thinks this ill of me, why did he ask me back? To be abused?

"Look, Charlie, I'm not here hat in hand. You invited me. I wasn't sure I wanted this job at all. Now I know I don't. You sound as though you have been talking to my worst enemy, whoever he is. If you wanted to know something about me, why didn't you talk with Paley or Stanton? I worked for them for fifteen years." Bluhdorn changed direction in mid-stride; his tone switched from hostile to solicitous, and he called in the president and the financial vice president of Gulf & Western to join our conversation. Both were very pleasant. The president, Jim Judelson, being supportive, said he presumed the reason the Yankees had such a long difficult climb from the bottom of the league was because CBS had held me on a short financial rein. I could buy no outstanding players.

"No. Not at all. Paley did not hold a tight pursestring." Judelson looked astonished.

"Don't you know you're indicting yourself when you say that?"

"You may read it that way, but you're wrong. It would be a real copout on my part if I told you anything different. What I said was a simple truth. Money was available, if we could have used it. The slow Yankee rebuilding can't be charged off to a shortage of money. The problems were much deeper, much more complex. I'd be glad to analyze them for you someday, if you like." Judelson couldn't figure out whether I was being too honest or too dumb. He simply couldn't fathom why I hadn't seized on his first assumption and in effect protected my own ass with a simple "Yes." I rather enjoyed his bafflement. Don Gaston, the financial man, asked another Yankee question. Bluhdorn didn't know one sport from another and followed the dialogue like a spectator at a tennis match. Suddenly he jumped back into the discussion. "Yes! What do you say to that?" he challenged.

"That Don doesn't know what the hell he's talking about." Bluhdorn slapped his thigh and laughed uproariously, perversely tickled that I would have been so blunt with Gaston. I hadn't meant to be a smart-ass but rather to be clear that he was off the track. Gaston understood that and was not offended, having asked a fan's question, pretending no expertise. Bluhdorn suggested that the three of us go along to Judelson's office and get better acquainted. Before we left he said, "I don't want you to leave here until you agree to take over the Garden. I don't care about anybody else's opinion. I've got my own good nose, a good smell, a good finger feel. I can feel, I can smell when something's right. And when something's wrong. I've been trying for two years to find you. I want you to promise me to take it. I don't want you to leave the office before you promise me." He spoke rapidly, almost wildly in a salivated

Austrian accent, his arms waving and jabbing as though words alone were inadequate to carry the force of his message.

In Judelson's office the talk was very friendly, as though I were already a colleague. Quite abruptly Judelson's tone changed from light to serious and lowered confidentially. "Did Charlie tell you he spoke to Paley?"

"No, he didn't. As a matter of fact, when I told him that he should, he changed the subject."

"You ought to know this." His eyes were level and intent. "Paley cut your balls off." That took me aback. Shocked me.

"How do you know?" It was such an astonishing statement and I wanted to make sure it wasn't hyperbole.

"Charlie told me. Did Charlie rough you up at the beginning?"

"Yes. I told him I hadn't come to be abused. I didn't give a damn about the job. But for the record he ought to call Paley or Frank Stanton."

"Paley cut your balls off."

"Thanks for letting me know." The pit of my stomach went hollow. It was difficult for me to believe that Paley would have done that, but Judelson was very positive. I let word get back to CBS that I knew the thrust of Paley's remarks to Bluhdorn. A few days later Paley's personal lawyer, a man I didn't know, telephoned and suggested that we meet, but I declined. His lawyer, for Christ's sake! It seemed to confirm Judelson's story, though I had hoped it wasn't so. Apparently Paley was still seething at Steinbrenner's comment to the press seven months earlier that the Yankees were "the best buy in sports," implying that we had got a bargain, that Paley had been bested in the deal. Paley still held me responsible. Perhaps he had adopted Jack Kennedy's motto: Don't get angry; get even. Or perhaps he had given Bluhdorn his honest opinion. At first I was angered; later it seemed regrettable and very disappointing.

I was immensely pleased to be at the Garden and felt immediately at home. All the threads of my earlier life came together in a single strand — Yankees, television, circus. Even the CIA experience, where I had devised a pattern for directing a large, complex operation and had developed a style of supervision that encouraged people to perform happily and well. Though the modern Garden was a corporation owned by 85,000 stockholders, its shares traded on the New York Stock Exchange, I was possessive of it, proud of it, loved it, perhaps not with the same passion as the Yankees but loved it well. A circus tent, a stadium, an arena — all shared grounds that united different elements of society; places where I always seemed to feel at home; places where people came to be entertained and went from having been entertained, where performers performed and where, when it was empty and still after a night's performance, I could walk around and savor the day past, anticipate the day ahead, consciously happy that this was where life had set me down. I approached it every morning and left it late each night as though the Garden were mine alone, alone to share enthusiastically with as many millions of people as I could possibly entice to its ambitious schedule of events. The place would be mine to run and I liked that, preferred that it be a problem to be worked at rather than a perfect machine to be maintained. I liked the loneness of decision, the responsibility, the commitment to a seven-day week, to working all hours. I would have felt only half-employed in a business that closed down at five o'clock in the afternoon. I liked the fact that the Garden was an institution, that it was a kind of Piazza del Popolo, a place of the people, where millions came each year to see a variety of events and that I could expand the range of entertainments and reach still farther out into the citizenry. I liked the sense of continuity and continuing change, of history and history to be made. I liked the feel at the center of the city's great throbbing night-and-day engine, the feel of the Garden pulsating to the same raw rhythms as the city itself.

The Garden was almost one hundred years old, lodged in its fourth home, when I arrived. William Vanderbilt, son of the famous commodore, had converted the old New York and Harlem Railroad freight shed and stable to a new purpose and opened the first Garden on Madison Square on May 31, 1879 — the very same Madison Square where Alexander Cartwright, the architect, laid out the first baseball diamond, the bases ninety feet apart, and established the concept of three outs to a side and a nine-inning game. Not a flimsy idea. Vanderbilt's announced plan was to create a new athletic center, though the new arena's opening event was a concert and the *New York Times* wrote: "It is the purpose of the management to give concerts nightly. The programs will be of a popular character and suited to the demands of most pleasure-seekers, who do not wish to be called on for any serious mental effort while taking their amusements."

Concerts alone would hardly suffice. In 1882, shortly after he had won the heavyweight boxing championship of the world, John L. Sullivan, the Boston Strong Boy, became the Garden's star attraction. Sullivan filled the building to its 10,000 capacity in a fight with the British champion Tug Wilson. A year later Sullivan was stopped, not by his opponent, but by the police. During the second round the champion was arrested for "outraging decency and tending to disrupt public morals" — the law of the day took a dim view of boxing.

Horse shows, dog shows, circuses, and track meets came and went regularly each season and the star of the 1880s was Jumbo, a twenty-two-year-old elephant imported from England by the incomparable Phineas T. Barnum. But in the end there were fewer attractions than days in the year. Always the spectacular event filled the house, suffused it with enchantment or charged it with excitement. It was the other days, the dark days, that tested the ingenuity, patience, and financial resilience of successive entrepreneurs. In his charming book *Madison Square Garden: 100 Years of History,* Joe Durso wrote: "Sellouts were few and far between" and "the Arena was swamped with silence more often than noise. There were many nights society went through the marble doorway, not enough when the masses went through." Thus the Garden became "a patched up, grimy, draughty, combustible old shell," according to *Harper's Weekly.* Losing money was no more fun for a Vanderbilt than for the rest of us. He decided to call it quits.

But the National Horse Show people rallied around J. Pierpont Morgan to buy the site and commissioned Stanford White to design a new Garden. By 1890 a Moorish castle emerged alongside the tree-lined square, a yellow brick and Pompeiian terracotta structure with a soaring 320-foot tower: "A sort of pleasure exchange and central palace of pleasure," *Harper's* called it. And the *New York Times* wrote, "We don't understand how we lived so long half content without it." Augustus Saint-Gaudens' thirteen-foot bronze statue of a naked Diana the Huntress sent shock waves all the way to Philadelphia, causing the *Philadelphia Times* to deplore "the depraved artistic taste of New York." Not to be outdone by a statue, White himself died notoriously in the luxurious rooftop supper club he had designed, shot down by a jealous husband, the millionaire Harry K. Thaw, who pumped bitter lead into White's body for having trifled with Evelyn Nesbitt, one of the theatrical beauties of her time and famous as "The Girl on the Red Velvet Swing." As White sank to the floor, mortally wounded, the band was playing, "I Could Love a Thousand Girls."

Stanford White's magnificent Garden II went bankrupt in 1913, and the New York Life Insurance Company, which held the mortgage, suffered it until Tex Rickard and boxing bailed them out, leasing the Garden for ten years at an annual rent of $200,000. (In the 1970s that sum would rent the Garden's four walls for four days, maybe.) Then in 1925 Rickard and John Ringling teamed up to build Garden Number Three on Eighth Avenue and Fiftieth Street, and when it wore out, Irving Felt, then chairman of the Madison Square Garden Corporation, erected Garden IV atop the Pennsylvania railroad station at Seventh Avenue and Thirty-third Street. When its doors opened in 1968, Red Smith wrote in his column: "It is quite simply, the most famous and most glamorous arena in creation."

Madison Square Garden approached its one-hundredth anniversary, its spirit contemporary, its fundamental character unchanged, the pattern of its life surprisingly consistent: dazzling events and dark nights, enduring staples, fortune and misfortune, stars at the top of their form appearing in the Main Event. The Circus, the National Horse Show, the Westminster Dog Show remained constants. Jenny Lind gave way to Frank Sinatra, heavyweight champion John L. Sullivan to Muhammad Ali, miler Paavo Nurmi to miler Eamon Coghlan, wrestlers Yussif the Turk versus the Russian Lion to Bruno Sanmartino versus Ivan Koloff. Proprietors with the gilt-edged names of Vanderbilt and Morgan, Rickard and Ringling, stood aside for the corporate arrival of Charles Bluhdorn and Gulf & Western Industries, but the more it changed the more it remained the same. Throughout its century the Garden reflected the tone, the texture, and the taste of its day. The *New York Times* had rated the first Garden "one of the greatest institutions of the town to be mentioned along with Central Park and the Bridge of Brooklyn," and in the early 1970s a *Times* opinion poll selected twelve New York institutions, including Central Park, and asked their readers to choose the places they most preferred to visit. Madison Square Garden and the Metropolitan Museum of Art, nine years its senior, ranked one and two at the top of the poll. To the public the Garden remained an exhilarating state of mind, its business vicissitudes unnoted and of little concern to them. They were *my* problem.

Before the key went into the lock of a morning in 1973, the Garden owed the city of New York $15,000 a day in real estate taxes alone and the daily building costs were another $25,000. Survival meant booking as many as seven hundred events, performances, a year if we possibly could; dark days were as endearing as the black plague. When I arrived, the Garden was no less a challenge than it ever had been. I leapt in, stimulated by the tumbling variety of it all, clear that it was the masses we must draw through the turnstiles. We needed to tend carefully to our meat-and-potatoes presentations and at the same time widen our search for new events, new publics. We could not let our ambition fall short of making the Garden, if not all things to all people, then at least *some* things to all people.

The 1973 Garden management was disheveled. Chairman Irving Felt's long suit was real estate. Only a real estate person would have changed the century-old, world-famous-name Madison Square Garden to Madison Square Garden Center, as though the Garden were a suburban shopping mall on Seventh Avenue. When I first saw it I wondered if Felt had ever heard Broadway's seasoned wisdom: Never rewrite a hit. Felt was an unnatural in the world of sports and entertainment. His capacity to deal effectively with the press and the public was virtually nil. In a business where the human factor is overriding, he was once described in a magazine piece as "a man with all the warmth of an unlit gas chamber at San Quentin." That's too vicious a condemnation of anyone, but it pointed up a shortcoming for a person in a highly visible, people-intensive business.

Crossing the threshold as the new president, I was cut off at the knees by a press relations fiasco. *New York* magazine featured an exposé of newspaper and broadcast people who received free seats to Knickerbocker basketball and Ranger hockey games, in addition to their entirely legitimate working press credentials. These seats had a certain dollar value. A chart of the arena illustrated exactly where each person's seats were located, how many he received, and identified him by name and company, causing acute embarrassment to the individuals and their organizations and prompting the *Times* and the *News* to issue explicit instructions to their staffs not to accept free tickets from Madison Square Garden. In early years, when the Knicks were struggling to attract fans and press coverage, a number of important writers and broadcasters were courted with season tickets. Later, when Knick and Ranger tickets became a hot item, the Garden wanted them back but was fearful of alienating the journalists whom it had courted in needier times. Hence the less than brilliant scheme to plant a story and expose them publicly.

I hurried around to the managing editors of the *Times* and the *News* to apologize. "Why didn't you just let us know what you wanted, and we would have taken care of it?" they protested. I attempted to disassociate myself from Felt's misguided maneuver, pointing out that it predated my arrival at the Garden, but the nicety of timing was too slender a reed to stand against their fury. I was tarred with the same brush and off to something less than a glorious start.

Internally my impression was that Felt dabbled in Garden operations. The daily business of the corporation was run by a handful of opinionated young accountants grouped physically around Felt's office on the eighteenth floor of the 2 Pennsylvania Plaza office building. They lacked guidance, judgment, and experience. The Garden itself — the Round Building — stood physically and spiritually apart, connected to the office building by a broad public mall. The key operating people in the Round Building were the best in the business. Richard Donapria, the building superintendent, had been making this Garden and its predecessor go for almost half a century, adapting it with uncanny skill to hundreds of differing events each year. A smallish, well-made man with small balanced features and gray hair, Donapria wore three-piece tweed suits and button-down Oxford shirts and smoked a pipe. Set down on a college campus, he could easily be taken for a benevolent Humanities professor.

Alvin Grant booked all Garden events except the Knickerbocker and Ranger games and was the dean of his breed in America. Gentle-mannered, soft-spoken, he had learned his trade managing ice shows, was acquainted with everyone in the arena business around the world and knew from experience when to book an event, for how long and how to sell it to the public. These two quiet professionals, Donapria and Grant, were immediately recognizable as mainstays. Jim Norton, the head stagehand, and Norm Leonard, the chief electrician, stood close behind them. They could rig and light anything from a circus to a rock concert, a fight to a horse show.

It was a measure of arrogant immaturity that the eighteenth-floor financial chiefs were both ignorant of what made the Garden tick and disdainful of the Indians who did know. Understandably, the Indians had a low opinion of the know-nothing young chiefs. Communication between the two was akin to shouting across the Grand Canyon in a gale. Things were so obviously out of joint that it was clear how to begin to put them right. Felt's corporate staff people were wary of me, sensing their free-wheeling ungoverned status threatened. Apart from apprenticeships in accounting firms, their real-life experience was limited to the spasms of pygmy warfare that distorted Felt's administration. Though it took a while, the immature accountants were supplanted by their own subordinates, who proved to be entirely worthy.

The Garden was an extremely complex operation physically compared, say, with Yankee Stadium. At the Stadium we put on eighty-one baseball games each year, not a burdensome task for the stadium manager and the ground crew. At the Garden during a 350-day span we had to present at least 650 events, preferably more, in our three venues — the Main Arena, the 5,000-seat Forum, and the Rotunda. And the Rotunda was unavailable during the Horse Show, the Dog Show, and the Circus, when it was given over to stabling 250 horses, to benching 3,000 dogs, or to housing a menagerie of circus animals whose aroma lingered on into the summer. Needless to say, it was essential to book and to schedule events with great care, working around the staples: 41 Knickerbocker basketball games and 41 Ranger hockey games — usually Wednesday and Sunday nights for hockey; Tuesday and Saturday nights for basketball. Tons of dirt covered the floor during the National

Horse Show and locked the arena into that single event for a week each November. In the spring the Circus took over for eight weeks. But when the teams made their league playoffs, Circus performances were interrupted. Shows might be given earlier in the day. Then the rigging was tucked up and ice or a basketball floor laid down for the night's game. There was always a debate whether ice could be left under the Circus performance or not. The building superintendent preferred not to make new ice; the quality of old ice is better. The Circus disliked playing over ice.

For all the hundreds of events it was vital that the booking people and the building people mesh, making certain that events could be got in and out without the chaos of an overlap. The stream of events required to sustain the Garden as a viable business left no time to spare, no room for error. All departments had to be synchronized: production, box office, publicity, advertising, security, all the facets of the building operations — electricians, stagehands, carpenters, painters, ushers, ticket takers, Specials, sweepers, and so on. It was possible for the Garden to present more events by far than any other arena in the nation because Garden hands, men and women, were just so damn good at what they did.

Presiding over the operation, I roamed the whole place, though organizationally I had only seven department heads report directly to me, leaving aside lawyers and financial people: the Rangers, the Knickerbockers, boxing, Holiday on Ice International, broadcast, bookings, and administration. Our broadcast department bought time on local television and radio stations, produced our own game and other event programs, and sold our own sponsorship time. And not long after I came to the Garden, we created our own Madison Square Garden cable television package, which we sold to cable systems in the metropolitan area and, later, nationally.

Bookings, under Al Grant, and administration, headed by Jack Fitzpatrick, were the cornerstones. Grant and his people sorted out the entertainments we wanted, negotiated the deals, dealt with their production and promotion. Fitzpatrick supervised the building's operation and everything to do with tickets — box office, group sales, season sales. The two men and their colleagues meshed all the gears.

As with the Yankees, the granules of any two days at the Garden were unalike. The two jobs had shot me into a visible place on the New York scene, into a role I fitted naturally enough, but one that left little private time available. When the day was closing down for most people and their hour had come to catch the express to Stamford, a taxi uptown, or the F train to Queens, my day was stepping up to a game, a concert, a track meet, an ice show. Nine-thirty in the morning and midnight bracketed my normal working day. Friends were faithful about coming to various events — Felix Rohatyn to hockey, Kurt Vonnegut to basketball, Benny Goodman to tennis, Irwin Shaw to baseball — and a good deal of social life melded with goings-on at the Stadium and at the Garden, followed by late supper with those patient enough to sup with me as one day passed into the next.

Except for those mornings on which I had a breakfast date at the Algonquin, Rosanne Miskow, looking scrubbed and bright and attractive, started my day with freshly squeezed orange juice and coffee and cheerful pleasantries. Rosanne, pretty, dark-haired, divorced, was more a member of the family than secretary. The natural warmth and easy friendliness of her personality was undiminished by the telephone system; she came through as a lively flesh-and-blood person to hundreds of people whom she had never met. More often than not her desk was decorated with flowers or other gifts from appreciative people who had gained something from her special thoughtfulness. She was a personage in that magical telephone network of young New York women who, among them, seemed to know how to dredge up a pair of tickets to a sold-out Broadway show, to get you on a fully booked flight to Paris, or to organize the menu for a dinner party in a private room at "21" without ever leaving their offices.

In the month of May I might see Eddie Donovan, the Knick general manager, several times a day to discuss player trades or our selections for the upcoming NBA draft of college athletes. I pretended no professional eye for player talent; people who had spent their lives in the game were well paid to provide that specialized knowledge. But I probed Donovan, the scouts, the coach for opinions, pressed them to think hard and shepherded them towards commitment until we were agreed on a course of action taken for the right reasons. Were we of one mind about our most urgent need? Did we all agree that player A was the one we coveted most? Were we agreed to trade our player Z? Was it agreed that I should fly to Los Angeles to meet with Bill Russell and the Seattle team's owner to try to buy Spencer Haywood? Draft selections made, trades done, I might not see Donovan for a month.

Then, too, a week might pass without my seeing Al Grant, and he would ring to say he had a half-dozen matters that needed decision and we would spend an hour or two discussing and deciding: to create a new Garden event, the Americas Cup, an international gymnastics competition; to promote a wrestling event in Shea Stadium during the Circus run (our monthly Monday night Garden wrestling program was suspended while the Circus was in the Garden); to try to move Ice Capades a week up in the schedule to make room for a tennis tournament; to finance a live production of *Sesame Street* for the Forum and a national tour. Any given day could include a meeting with Dave deBusschere to arrange a date to retire his number at a Knicks game; a meeting with Skee Goodhart, president of Holiday on Ice International to determine whether we should add a fifth unit to our four shows touring Europe and South America and to schedule another trip to Moscow in connection with a Russian tour for one of our units; a visit with a friend's son looking for a job; a talk with a man running for governor and wanting help in his campaign; a labor negotiation with Jimmy O'Hara, a longtime friend and head of Local 3, the electricians; a meeting with a designer to look at his sketches and choose a new Knick uniform; a meeting with Jack Fitzpatrick to set ticket prices for the upcoming season or to scale the house for a fight; a budget review with the financial staff. And some days were just up for grabs.

Basically I ran an open-door office, literally and figuratively, told people to bring me the problems they couldn't deal with on their own: if you feel comfortable with it, go ahead; if you get stuck and need help, come to me. Gradually I grew to know to whom I could give a lot of rope, whom to keep on a tighter line. My colleagues, in turn, learned the kinds of decisions I wanted to be involved with and those I didn't. From the beginning I moved around. I wanted to know my own people, wanted to know that "Tiger Bait" Land, the Garden's most expert rigger, had once fallen into a tiger cage when a rigging cable snapped, wanted *The New Yorker* to do a piece on him and raised hell when *The New Yorker* writer told me that he was being frustrated by my own public relations people. I wanted to know everyone we trafficked with. We put on a lot of rock concerts with two New York promoters, Ron Delsner and Howard Stein. I wanted to get the feel of them as people rather than names, wanted to get the feel of a Ray Benton who promoted tennis tournaments, of Howard Schmertz who put on the Millrose Games, of the men who organized the antique shows and the stamp shows in the Rotunda.

Most importantly I searched for new ideas, for additional events appropriate to the Garden, some as far away as Mongolia. A rock manager whose acts played the Garden found himself holding rights granted by the Chinese government to bring the Mongolian Horsemen on a tour of the United States. The prospect was beyond his capacity and he came to me. "I thought with your Circus background and the Garden's know-how about arenas . . ."

It was arranged that we meet in Tokyo: together we flew to Beijing and from there over the February-frozen Sparrow Mountains, formidable as the Rockies, into Inner Mongolia. Hou Het, the capital, is a city locked in the Middle Ages. The Mongolian Horse School, operated by the government much as the Russians run the Bolshoi Ballet, selects young men and women from the nomadic tribes of the Grasslands, which lie beyond the Great Green Mountain and border Soviet-controlled Outer Mongolia. They are descendants of Genghis Khan's Golden Horde, who dominated the known world of the thirteenth century, and their twentieth-century horsemanship is spectacular. There was a great deal of patient, painstaking work that remained to be done to build their raw material into a spectacle attractive to Western audiences. As individuals they were hospitable to a fault, warm and altogether winning. I liked them immensely and found it difficult to tell them that their act wasn't ready.

As 1974 began I had been at the Garden half a year and the Garden and I were synchronous, going full tilt, going well. One particular week had its own spectacular dimension. Arithmetically, it was a week in which 140,000 people paid $2 million to be entertained by a heavyweight fight, three rock concerts, two Ranger games, and two Knickerbocker basketball games. During that week the Garden demonstrated its universality as it has perhaps never done before in its history. In the space of three days, we hosted three events, any one of which could have sent a spark of drama coursing through the city. The heavyweight fight rematched Muhammad Ali and Joe Frazier; the basketball game featured the traditional rivalry between the Knicks and the Celtics; and the concert was Bob Dylan and The Band, Dylan's first concert tour in eight years. For those days the center of New York's social life was firmly anchored at Thirty-third Street and Seventh Avenue. The whole city seemed to be caught up in the intense Garden excitement. Restaurants and nightclubs were berserk with business. People from all over the country suddenly remembered urgent business commitments in New York. Five non–David Merricks called for my friend Merrick's fight tickets. He already had them in hand. Woody Allen, Dustin Hoffman, Elliott Gould, and 19,000 other New York fans cheered the Knicks to a win over the Celtics. Mouse and Peter went to all three Dylan concerts, and the aroma inside was neither tobacco nor legal. No one ever got busted for rolling a joint at a Garden concert, and the older ushers stuffed their ears with cotton to defend against the quadraphonic sound.

ALMOST FROM the first day I was plunged into the murky world of boxing where the incidence of rogues and rascals, chancers and conmen must be the highest in the world. The fierce competitiveness of Broadway (not only should I succeed but my best friend should fail) is sweetness itself compared to the vendettas of boxing, whose alliances shift as unpredictably as the sands of the Sahara. A second Ali-Frazier fight was in the offing.

The first Ali-Frazier fight had been held in Madison Square Garden in 1971, the most glamorous sporting event in living memory. Joe Frazier won a fifteen-round decision to become undisputed champion of the world. The unique chemistry of a heavyweight championship, the magnetism of these two boxers fighting for what was then the largest purse in history, $5 million, drew a dazzling Hollywood-to-Harlem audience in plumage to shatter a peacock's ego. Ali-Frazier II was headed for Houston's Astrodome and somehow had to be rerouted to Madison Square Garden. Ali-Frazier I had been promoted by Jack Kent Cooke and Gerry Perenchio of Los Angeles, Cooke putting up $4.5 million of the fighters' guarantees. Madison Square Garden added $500,000 to buy the live gate and bring the fight to New York. But there the long fingers of the New York State's tax department fixed themselves around $350,000 of each fighter's purse. Neither Ali nor Frazier thought this a hospitable gesture, and their pained cries for an equitable tax settlement failed to penetrate the state's vault. For this rude reason New York was not their first choice for a rematch. But it was my first choice and, at that early stage of my Garden life, my first priority. I hustled after it.

Perenchio telephoned about selling his interest in the rematch to Madison Square Garden. I was ready to talk, but as it turned out he had nothing to sell. The rematch provision in the original Ali-Frazier I contract obtained only to a championship fight. Ali-Frazier II would be a nontitle fight, for a year earlier in a stunning surprise George Foreman had beaten Frazier for the title. Thus neither Ali nor Frazier felt an obligation to Cooke or to Perenchio. But Cooke was a business friend; as owner of the Los Angeles Kings and the Lakers, he was a fellow governor of the National Hockey League and the National Basketball Association, and he had indeed anted up the lion's share of the purse for the original bout. If he wanted to invest in Ali-Frazier II, we should make room for him. He said he did want to participate and confirmed that Perenchio had no position whatsoever.

Bob Arum was Ali's lawyer. Bruce Wright, a Philadelphia lawyer, represented Frazier. Arum was not everybody's favorite fellow but was emerging as a potent boxing figure, primarily because of his association with Ali. The old boxing maxim held for Arum: Whoever controls the big name among the heavyweights controls the sport. Arum didn't control Ali, but his placement within the Ali camp gave him considerable influence. Arum's own first look into the backrooms of boxing was from a post in the United States Attorney's office. He was asked by the IRS to prevent money from a Patterson-Liston bout from escaping to Switzerland. Arum was a quick study. He learned the business. Jimmy Brown, the former Cleveland football star, introduced Arum to Elijah Muhammad, who had converted Cassius Clay to the Muslim faith. A new company was formed to promote the renamed Muhammad Ali. It was called Main Bout and it was run by Arum. A Harvard Law School graduate, the astute Arum began to practice more boxing than law from his Park Avenue office. Why with such remarkable success? "Because there are so many dummies in this game," Arum told a *Sports Illustrated* writer.

Bruce Wright practiced law, dressed in unpressed tweeds, smoked a pipe, lived in a Philadelphia suburb, and was dedicated to Joe Frazier's getting a square deal and conserving his earnings. The three of us — Arum, Wright, and myself — negotiated and struck a deal. Each fighter would be guaranteed $750,000 against thirty-two percent of the gate receipts and ancillary rights, ancillary rights meaning closed-circuit television and delayed network broadcasts. There was one threatening proviso. Madison Square Garden must arrange a satisfactory settlement of the $750,000 in taxes withheld by the State of New York from the Ali-Frazier I fight. And that the same settlement formula must obtain for Ali-Frazier II. I had twenty-eight days, until October 30, 1973, to do it. If not, the fight would move to Houston. It said so in the contract we had signed.

I called on a friend, Alton Marshall. Marshall is a big, vital, handsome man; an abundance of prematurely gray hair accentuates his ruddy complexion. He was then Governor Rockefeller's executive secretary and virtually ran the State of New York during the long months Rocky was campaigning for the vice presidency. Marshall was savvy, responsible, and exuberant; he worked twenty hours a day and was as keen at the twentieth as at the first hour; he was, and is, straight as a taut wire. His only question was: How can I be helpful in getting the fight to New York?

After the 1971 fight the state levied its tax against the boxers' total income — that is, their share of gate receipts and *worldwide* closed-circuit television. The formula Madison Square Garden now proposed was that New York State tax the boxers' share of gate receipts and revenue from closed-circuit venues *within* the State of New York. This seemed rational and equitable. A blizzard of notes, telephone messages, memoranda, and other documents swirled through the next several days, intertwined with the normal skein of the day's occupation — preparing for a new basketball, hockey, and entertainment season. We missed the contractual deadline but persuaded the principals to give us a week's extension. Finally, on November second, Arum, Wright, and I met in the offices of tax commissioner Mario Procacino and arrived at an understanding acceptable to everyone.

As the fight's promoters, Cooke, Arum, and I structured a three-way deal over dinner at "21" on September 25. We would be equal partners. The Garden would handle the fight itself and the live gate. Arum would organize the closed-circuit telecast and guarantee a certain revenue from it. Cooke, an unusual state for him, would be a silent investor.

As a boxing neophyte, I leaned heavily on the knowledge of

Harry Markson, president of Madison Square Garden Boxing, and Teddy Brenner, the Garden's matchmaker. As a young man, Markson had switched from journalism to boxing as the public relations man for Mike Jacobs. Having survived the journey through the netherworld of Jacobs Beach to the newest Madison Square Garden without stain or sorrow — a kind of reverse crossing of the River Styx — he had to be a sainted man.

Teddy Brenner was a different stripe. A tough, cynical, sardonic old pro, he had clawed his way up through the outer precincts of fight clubs to the pinnacle of Madison Square Garden, his arrogance mounting stride-for-stride. Brenner hated Arum. In Teddy's more generous moments Arum was The Snake. Brenner's bias aside, Arum appeared to me, on brief but concentrated exposure, to be the ablest fellow around by far. He knew the closed-circuit television business and was laced into the Ali camp, into the big name. If he was slippery as a peeled peach, so be it. You simply had to know you were not dealing with a turnip and be prepared to work as smartly as Arum. Arum and I got on together, in part because he knew that I understood the impact and importance of the television aspect of boxing. On the other hand, he didn't endear himself to Brenner by calling him "a boxing traditionalist and extremely unimaginative."

The Fight of the Century, we labeled it, and called a press conference in Madison Square Garden's Hall of Fame to let the world know. By prearrangement Frazier was taken to rooms some distance from my own in the Pennsylvania Plaza office building. Ali, his wife, Belinda, and infant child came quietly to mine. Ali lowered himself carefully into a leather sofa. The baby, gently held, slept on his shoulder. Belinda wore plain pearl-gray Muslim garb, her head wrapped in a nunlike wimple. She sat straight and self-contained, looking a perfectly beautiful Arab woman. She spoke no word, and no change of expression disturbed her composed dignity, nor hinted at her secret thoughts. Ali and I exchanged small talk softly until someone came to the door and said it was time to go across to the Garden. Tenderly Ali transferred the sleeping child to Belinda's shoulder and silently, the mood traveling with us, we rode the elevator to the ground floor, crossed the Garden Mall, and rode up an escalator to the Garden's Hall of Fame Club. The moment the door opened, admitting us, Ali shifted from low to overdrive in one swift stroke, leaping like a sprung jack-in-the-box into his wild, unbridled runaway public role, baiting and insulting Frazier from the first word. We jostled our way through reporters and cameramen to a long table, me in the middle and Ali and Frazier on either side. Contracts to be signed lay on the table before us and, across it, more than a hundred writers and photographers, television and radio reporters, elbowed for position. Frazier at first shrugged off Ali's barbs, then the poisoned arrows began to pierce his defenses. "White man's nigger," Ali taunted him. Infuriated, Frazier sprang to his feet, knocking over his chair, and lunged at Ali. People behind grabbed at him and restrained him. I spun towards Ali as he leapt up to counter Frazier, instinctively wrapping my arms around his chest, leaning the weight of my body against his, holding him back. His arms flailed at Frazier over my shoulder. Suddenly, sandwiched between insults hurled at Frazier, Ali's whispered message in my ear to make certain I understood the charade: "This is a lot o' shit, man. This is a lot o' shit." Shortly everyone calmed down and the contracts were signed, pictures taken. I was launched into boxing.

The fight was a great success. The $100 ringside seats were the first to go, populated by the Kennedy clan up from Washington, high-livers from Hollywood and Harlem, bankers and bookmakers from Manhattan. Ali won. At a postfight party in the Garden's Penn Plaza Club I threw my arm across Arum's shoulder, a gesture of congratulation. Brenner, persistently the dog in the manger, couldn't resist another thrust at Arum. "I see you'd even put your arm around a snake." I refused to take the bait, to let him spoil the moment of elation. "Why not? We just made three and a half million for the fighters and netted seven hundred fifty thousand for Madison Square Garden. Not a bad night's work to start 1974. Come on, Teddy. Let's you and I have a private drink and think up another night like this." He laughed a short hollow laugh and followed me to the bar. A hard man. I needed his expertise. He was the best matchmaker in the business.

Next time I ventured onto boxing's treacherous slopes with a major heavyweight fight, my colleagues Markson and Brenner thought I had gone round the bend. They tried to save me. I, on the other hand, was certain we could fill Yankee Stadium. And gambled eight million dollars that it would not rain on Tuesday the twenty-eighth of September 1976. The match between Muhammad Ali and Ken Norton for the heavyweight championship of the world was an idea of no one in particular; rather it was the obvious next move for both fighters.

Two years earlier we had offered Ali and George Foreman $7.5 million to fight for the Garden. But a little brotherly persuasion from promoter Don King and a ten-million-dollar contribution from President Mobutu won them to Zaïre for their Rumble in the Jungle. At the Garden we contented ourselves with showing the fight on closed-circuit, sold $413,000 worth of tickets, and, ironically, were one of the few involved, other than the fighters, to make a profit. Not long after I was amused to read in the *Times:* "The State Department officials are expected to decide in a few days whether to go ahead despite objections from key Congressional leaders with an emergency loan of $10 million to Zaire. Officials of the African Bureau of the State Department argue that the $10 million is urgently needed to meet the deteriorating economic situation in Zaire." I wasted no time considering whether State would bail out the Garden if we blew our bet.

The Garden needed to promote a major fight. Twenty years earlier, when Jim Norris owned the Garden and Mike Jacobs owned boxing, the government charged them with monopoly and a Judge Ryan decreed that henceforth the Garden could sign a fighter for no more than a single bout. Now Bob Arum and Don King, two of the swifter elements in this society and archenemies, cottoned onto the Garden's limitation and began signing fighters to multiple-fights contracts, eroding Madison Square Garden's long first-rank position. The game grew increasingly incestuous, not for maiden ladies. Arum's position in the Ali camp slipped. He had promised Ali $6 million for a freak match in Tokyo against a Japanese wrestler, Inoki, came up $4.2 million short, and lost favor.

Don King took over the rail position. Herbert Muhammad, Elijah Muhammad's business-minded son, dealt on behalf of Ali — and on behalf of the Muslims. Herbert gave King until April 10 to come up with the purse for Ali-Norton. We lay back in the weeds watching and awaiting our opportunity, letting Herbert Muhammad know where we were. A few days after King's deadline had passed, Herbert's lawyer, Charles Lomax, rang me to say what was wanted.

"Herbert's asking eight and a half million," Lomax said. "We have some automobile people in Detroit ready to put up that amount, but Herbert wants to deal with the Garden." Invariably, some ephemeral individual, syndicate, Arab sheikhdom or Third World nation hovered just offstage ready to put up the asking price, a threat meant to hasten a decision to match the phantom competition. "Detroit" and "Boston" were as narrowly as our competitors ever came to being identified. We made our own calculations of how much the fight was worth — the live gate at Yankee Stadium, the closed-circuit television revenues, a delayed network broadcast, the foreign-broadcast rights. On the twenty-fifth I rang Herbert Muhammad at his home in Chicago and told him $8.5 million wouldn't wash but maybe $6 million would.

"We've got an area to talk," he said. "Make me an offer." First there were some things to be done: secure the Stadium, reconfirm the state's agreed formula on the fighters' personal tax liability, strike a deal with Arum to organize the closed-circuit telecast, review with Richard Donapria the field seating conformation at the Stadium, a hundred other things, and, not least, negotiating a deal with Ken Norton's manager, Bob Biron. Biron appeared to be a nun in a carnal house; he was a retired vice president of General Dynamics and vice chancellor of the University of California at San Diego. Bob Arum claimed he had the rights to Norton's next fight. Biron swore to me that Arum did not. No love lost there. We sorted out that contretemps and in a couple of phone conversations with Biron agreed tentatively to a $1.5 million guarantee for Norton against fifteen percent of the gross revenue, whichever was greater, plus $100,000 for training expenses.

On May tenth Herbert Muhammad flew from Chicago and we met in my Garden office. Herbert, a short, stocky, almost roly-poly man, dressed conservatively in gray business suits and wore a gray caracul fez, indoors and out. He was a shrewd, serious, unsmiling man though not a lugubrious one. He knew what his act was worth and was coolly clever about getting it.

Accepted wisdom in the trade had it that Herbert — or the Muslims — received one third of Ali's purses, maybe twenty million dollars, over his career. Herbert dealt straight and we got on well. I offered him a $6 million guarantee for Ali plus $250,000 for training expenses and fifty percent of the gross receipts over nine million dollars. He accepted. Two days later Arum and I caught the 8 A.M. American Airlines flight from LaGuardia to Chicago, took a taxi directly to Herbert's office, and, page by page, went through the contract we had brought with us. Herbert found it was in order for Ali to sign.

"Let Lomax take you to lunch," Herbert suggested. "I've got to find Ali. As soon as I heard Don King was tailing you out here, I had Ali leave his house. Get lost. Otherwise King would crash in on him moaning and groaning and falling on his knees, crying, begging, getting the fighter all upset. Now I've got to find Ali and have him sign the contract. I'll see you back here about three o'clock." We found Lomax in the prestigious Sidley and Austin law offices — Adlai Stevenson's old firm — and had a delightful visit with another member, Newton Minow, the former Federal Communications Commissioner. They treated us to an excellent client's lunch. The signed Ali contract in hand, Arum and I boarded the 6:20 P.M. American Airlines flight to San Diego, dined with Bob Biron at the hotel he owned in La Jolla, and met with him again in the morning at our airport hotel rooms. For some forgotten reason, Teddy Brenner had joined us but was obliged to remain in his own rooms. Biron felt he had been jobbed by Teddy in some previous encounter and refused to do any business with the Garden if Teddy were present. Except for Norton, I doubt Biron liked many people in the fight racket. A courteous, soft-spoken, rather frail gray-haired man with a subsurface prickliness, he would be typecast as a university vice chancellor. A fight manager was the last thing you would expect him to be. His man Norton had beaten Ali and broken his jaw in their first fight and Ali had squeezed by him in their rematch. In the event that Norton won the rubber match and the championship, we did not want to be shut out by the two-decade-old Ryan decree, which limited the Garden to signing Norton to this one fight. So Biron and the unrestricted Arum signed a deal for Norton's first three title defenses with the tacit understanding — one hesitates to say gentlemen's agreement — that the Garden would promote these fights. Arum and I were back in New York before midnight.

An enraged Don King, stung by the Garden's getting the fight, railed foolishly against Herbert Muhammad's selling out to the white man. Dick Young opened his *Daily News* sports column with a note that made me laugh and gave my children new material for ragging their father. Young wrote that it was "a personal triumph" for me and that I hadn't done much in recent years.

"What ya been doin' in recent years, Beeg Mon? Goofing off?" That was Michele.

"Where you been hangin' out, Pres? On the street corners watching all the girls go by?" That was Peter.

"Not much action lately, hey Papalovich?" Michele again. How I loved them, their perception, their perspective, their capacity for laughter, our priceless gift for laughing together. They knew I took work seriously, never myself. Life is too serious not to be taken lightly, as Lawrence Durrell wrote. No doubt I should have genuflected to Young for raising me Lazarus-like from the dead; he had officially buried me when I left the Bronx and the lead sentence in one of his columns intoned: "By next week nobody will remember there was a Mike Burke connected with the Yankees."

A few days later, as I returned from some uptown luncheon meeting, an agitated colleague intercepted me in the reception area. "You can't go into your office," he said nervously.

"Why not?"

"It's been taken over by a gang of black toughs. They pushed right past the receptionist, stormed through the halls, and took over your office."

"Who are they?"

"I don't know."

"How long have they been here?"

"Half an hour. About. Should I call the police?"

"Hell no."

"Are you going in there?" He was genuinely frightened.

"Of course." Invasion of privacy angers me, and this was an infuriating sight: seven self-styled tough guys littered my office. A black man, about thirty-five years of age, going to fat, in a rumpled dark suit and black hat, sat in my chair, talked into my phone, his feet up on the oval-shaped green marble-topped table I used for a desk. I yelled from the threshold, "Get your fat ass out of that chair!"

Startled, he slammed down the phone and jumped half out of the chair in one knee-jerk reaction but recovered quickly enough to be affronted and retort in caricature pulpit tones, "No one has ever spoke to Reverend Sharpton like that!"

"Well, Reverend, this will be a new experience. Get your ass up out of my chair." As I crossed the room, rounded the table, and bore down on him, he moved swiftly out of the chair. I ranted in genuine rage at their muscled entry, at their terrifying the receptionist, at their frightening the staff, at their hoodlum behavior. I did not know who they were or what they were after, but I did not have to be clairvoyant to know that I was being set up for something, apparently racial and potentially newsworthy. An alerted NBC television crew and a still photographer from the *Amsterdam News* shoved themselves through the doorway. I chased them away and turned back to the intruders. It was abundantly clear that I should not call the cops and have them dragged away, which was precisely what they would have liked. That was an easy one to read.

"Okay, Reverend, what's the plot? What the hell are you doing here?" It turned out to be two things, neither clearly stated: a harassment by Don King and a shakedown. King would never admit to it, of course, and later when I threw it up to him he laughed as though it were a private joke we shared. Sharpton was more explicit. I was antiblack; I had done in Don King; Ali had sold out to the honkies. Ergo, the Reverend and his gorillas were going to picket Madison Square Garden and Yankee Stadium, discourage the black community from buying tickets, and disrupt the fight. I told Sharpton he had better check out my race relations with about a hundred different black leaders in New York before trying to cast me as antiblack. He wanted to know if I'd meet with Shirley Chisholm, the black congresswoman from Brooklyn. Of course I would. Any time. He made a couple of phone calls, ostensibly to set meetings — first at 2:30 and then at 3:30 — across Seventh Avenue at the Sheraton Hotel. The calls were fake. The antiblack accusation collapsed. It was groundless and Sharpton knew that. Then we got to the shakedown: financial support for Sharpton's less than modestly named National Youth Movement Inc. They would be giving a fund-raising dinner at "21." (At "21"! I pictured these slugs lounging along the bar at "21.") Madison Square Garden would be expected to take several tables at $1,000 each. They would be sending me a letter confirming this requirement. I shook hands with each one as the gang filed out sullenly. Except for a front-page *Amsterdam News* picture of Sharpton sitting at my desk, the episode died as quickly as it had arisen. It had not been one of Don King's more adroit maneuvers.

Nothing went smoothly with Ali-Norton. I made a deal with the city to rent Yankee Stadium for $125,000 and sought George Steinbrenner's agreement that the fight could be held there. The lease I had negotiated with the city back in 1971 required the city to obtain Yankee approval before renting the Stadium. George was not happy, but it appeared untenable for him to refuse. Some months earlier he had been criticized severely for having blocked a Frazier-Foreman fight at the Stadium. It was lost to the Nassau Colosseum. Even so, George never did things the easy way. Yankee and Garden people worked out an agreed procedure, but Steinbrenner failed to sign it, and our lawyers came back empty-handed.

"Not to worry," I told my colleagues. "I'm going to the game at the Stadium on Saturday. I'll see George and get him to sign it." At the Stadium I did interviews with Bill White on radio and Phil Rizzuto on television to promote the fight and, as George wasn't around, told the team lawyer, Ed Broderick, that I would expect George to sign the agreement the following day, Sunday. I would have it picked up the first thing Monday morning. On Monday Broderick telephoned to say that George hadn't signed the paper and couldn't be reached. He was thought to be in the air, flying to Buffalo. Or somewhere.

"Listen carefully," I said into the phone, "It's now eleven-seven. Mayor Beame is doing a publicity thing on the steps of City Hall at twelve noon with Ali and Norton. So you'd better get through to George wherever he's hiding and tell him he has fifty-three minutes to sign the agreement that everyone at the Yankees and everyone at the Garden has already agreed to. If not, the mayor will announce from the steps of City Hall that

there will not be an Ali-Norton fight in Yankee Stadium because George Steinbrenner blocked it." And hung up. Before I
left for City Hall at 11:40, Broderick rang back confirming
George's approval. "Thanks. I have someone waiting at the
Stadium to pick up the signed contract."

Early on I was puzzled as to why George chose to make
patently simple things so difficult, seeming to choose the painful way because it was painful. Then I realized that the energy,
the trust, the good mind that made him a mover and shaker,
the sum total of him, was hooked on power, power in whatever
sphere he operated, wherever it could be applied, power to
reduce a secretary to tears, power to hold up the Garden and
the city to the very last anxious moment, power to hire and fire
managers of the baseball team, to hire and fire public relations
men. The point of application really didn't matter. However
exercised, it was the power switch that turned on his juice,
nothing else. Once that basic fact was understood, everything
else fell into place. He is not the first nor the last man to suffer
that torment, a habit as insidious as the roughest narcotic.
However perverse, it is also one kind of motivation that has
moved the world along, like it or not.

On Monday it rained. On Wednesday it rained. But Tuesday,
the day of the fight, was fair. God was with us, but New York's
Finest were not. In addition to the advance ticket sale, we expected to sell twenty thousand seats at the Stadium on the night
of the fight. All the ticket windows opened and manned. We
sold two. Not two thousand, two tickets. The previous night,
Monday, striking off-duty police had besieged Gracie Mansion,
the mayor's official residence. Only a police van barricading the
gateway prevented a wild, angry mob of cops in mufti from
storming it, like the Bastille. Dissatisfied with pay and work
schedules and determined to attract maximum attention, they
felt that the Ali-Norton fight presented a perfect vehicle for
them to create havoc. People, including Governor Carey and
his party, literally had to fight their way into the Stadium. John
Lindsay got out of his car and walked in front of it clearing a
path to the VIP parking area. Uniformed police stood about
doing nothing to curb their off-duty comrades. No attempt was
made to maintain order. The strikers, mob-crazed, incited vandals and spurred street gangs to terror. One group organized

a band of teenage hoodlums into a human battering ram that
thrust itself against one of the gates, trying to break through.
Ticket takers were terrorized with impunity, and no one could
guess how many non-ticket-holders bulled their way into the
Stadium. An old gentleman's kidneys forced him to use one of
the portable toilets set up around the outfield wall, and two big
dudes demanded one hundred dollars for his safe passage.

In the street I jostled, shouldered, elbowed my way through
the crowd looking in vain for a ranking police officer and at
one moment had to jump aside quickly to avoid being trampled
by a herd of a hundred kids rampaging through the street
alongside the Stadium, running over people, running God
knows where or why except for the sheer unbridled, unchal-
lenged hell of it. Uniformed cops to whom I appealed
shrugged their shoulders and turned away, indifferent to my
problem, sympathetic to their off-duty comrades. In a parking
area enclosed by high wire fencing, entered through a single
control gate, vandals jumped up and down on the roof of the
governor's car, bashing it in. Cops assigned to guard the area
watched cynically. Hundreds of people with tickets took one
look at this melee, turned and went home. People expecting to
buy tickets at the Stadium retreated. Instead of a stream of
pedestrians advancing across the 161st Street Bridge from
Manhattan, a horde of people fled to the safety of Harlem.
Inside the Stadium ushers and our Special Officers were em-
broiled in an all-night wrestling match, wrestling floppers out
of seats and making room for ticket holders. Swifty Lazar, the
incomparable literary agent, sitting in the second or third row
at ringside, shouted my attention to a bewildered, frightened
French girl hovering nearby. She had no English, no ticket,
and had become separated from her friends. I sat her in my
seat, comforted her, told her to sit still — we would get her
back to her hotel after the fight. Somehow her friends found
her. During the fight I sat in the first row separated from Charlie Bluhdorn by a lady between us. After the third round he
wanted to know who was winning.

"I don't know. It's too early to tell."

"Who's winning? Who's winning?" he demanded. "You're
supposed to know these things! You're the sportsman!" He was
irritated by my ignorance. I was not sufficiently prescient to tell

him that the fight would not end well for Norton. At the end of the final round, the fifteenth, the challenger threw his arms into the air and his handlers lifted him off his feet in jubilant bear hugs. He and they thought he had won. So did half the audience. And much of the press. But the judges determined that Ali's final round attack and Norton's caution, preserving what he thought was victory, tipped the decision in favor of the champion's retaining his title.

When the financial results were tallied up, Madison Square Garden had barely broken even. I had expected we would make a million-dollar profit. In hindsight, had we held the fight in Madison Square Garden instead of Yankee Stadium, we would have fared much better. So, at the end of the day, Markson and Brenner had been right. Right for the wrong reasons.

Editorials the following morning were too late to help. The *News* cried OUTRAGE IN THE BRONX and the *Times* warned A THREAT OF ANARCHY. Both decried the fact that lawless bands had rampaged inside and outside the Stadium, egged on by off-duty police while on-duty officers left the public to the mercy of muggers and thieves. An Associated Press reporter asked me the obvious question. "No," I replied, "I don't think we'll have another fight in Yankee Stadium for a long time."

Time passes. Wounds heal. The following spring Herbert Muhammad telephoned me to talk of another Ali fight. At the time we were promoting a match in the Garden, this time between Norton and Duane Bobick, a "white hope." Herbert thought Bobick would be an ideal opponent for Ali, once Bobick had disposed of Norton. We agreed in principle.

"But, Herbert," I said, "it would look pretty bad if we made a deal now based on Bobick's winning. Word would get out, surely, and the story would be that the fix was in. Why don't you come into New York for the Bobick fight and we'll meet the following morning for breakfast and make a deal?" That was agreeable to him, but the script went awry. Norton knocked out Bobick in the fifty-eighth second of the first round. I felt badly for NBC, for I had sold them the live television rights for $1.5 million.

I had invited Bill Paley to the fight, having heard that he had been devastated by his wife's recent cancer death and thinking that the distraction of a boxing match would not be out of place. Whether he still harbored any ill feeling about me I didn't know, but the disappointment I had experienced when he had apparently denigrated me to Charlie Bluhdorn had evaporated. Whatever he might have said at the time had done me no harm, and there was no anger hidden in my mind. On the contrary, Mr. Paley had put me in the way of the Yankees and I would be eternally grateful for it. Less subjectively, I held his accomplishments in high regard. Paley and CBS, it seemed to me, fit Thoreau's observation that "an institution is but the lengthened shadow of one man." I was pleased when he accepted, sat in the same row at ringside as the NBC people, and teased them goodhumoredly about their fifty-eight-second million-and-a-half-dollar program.

Herbert Muhammad, Charles Lomax, and I had arranged to meet for breakfast next morning at the Plaza Hotel. Waiting for them to arrive, I sat at the same corner table where Dick Meyer and I held our first conversation about unseating Spike Eckert as the baseball commissioner. And looked out on the fresh spring green of Central Park, at pretty girls in their spring dresses hurrying to work, at the polished brass of carriage horses reflecting the bright spring sun. I floated high on a tide of well-being. The Garden's profit from the night's bout had been $750,000. Better than a sharp stick in the eye.

I stood and we shook hands when they arrived. "I don't suppose we have much to talk about after last night's outcome," I said, "so we might as well enjoy a good breakfast." But they had come for more than eggs and bacon. Ali, they explained, must have a fight in order to pay the previous year's income tax. It was that simple.

"What kind of purse do you need?"

"Three million dollars."

"Well, let's talk about a suitable opponent." Over an extra cup of coffee or two we agreed on Ernie Shavers. I went back to the Garden and stopped by the boxing department to see Teddy Brenner. "How much would we have to pay Shavers to fight Ali?" Teddy made a quick mental calculation.

"One hundred fifty thousand dollars."

"Then sign him for a September twenty-ninth fight. I'll sell the live television rights to NBC. They deserve this one. They may have winced at Bobick-Norton. But they sure didn't whine." Days passed. Teddy said Shavers' people wanted two hundred thousand dollars. "Fine. Tell them we agree. Get his name on a contract and get it filed with the commission." More days passed, and I bugged Teddy about the contract. My nervous system signaled something untoward was in the wind.

Teddy gave me a verbal pat on the head. "Relax. Relax. Stop worrying. Everything is agreed. I told Frank Luca to send me a telegram confirming the deal." Teddy was a great matchmaker; he knew what two fighters would make a good fight. His genius stopped there, though few of us escaped the sting of his sardonic humor and slashing tongue. He made the common mistake of overestimating himself and underestimating everyone outside his immediate clique.

"Telegram my ass, Teddy. Get the goddam contract signed."

"They're coming into New York next week to sign."

"Teddy, get up to Akron or wherever it is that Shavers comes from. We can't wait around till they come to us. You've been screwing around with this thing now for weeks." Dialogue in the boxing business is rarely poetic. Later in the day Teddy walked triumphantly into my office and handed me a telegram addressed to him.

Madison Square Garden Boxing, 6 Penn Plaza, New York, New York. Ernie Shavers will box Muhammad Ali for the heavyweight championship of the world in Madison Square Garden on or before October 10 1977. Shavers is to receive a minimum guarantee of $200,000. If bout is not signed for by June 15 1977 $10,000 will be forfeited to Shavers. Shavers will grant Madison Square Garden Boxing option of first refusal on first and second title defenses at terms mutually agreeable. Thank you. Frank Luca.

"Fine, Teddy. Now put the contract in your pocket. Get on a plane to Akron and have Shavers sign it." Brenner couldn't get through to Shavers or Luca or anybody by phone. No one knew where they were. More worried than ever, I went out to my summer house on Long Island for the weekend, and Teddy telephoned me there. Arum had signed Shavers for $300,000. I rang Arum and yelled at him, more angry at Teddy, at myself, than at Arum, who had seen an opening and moved swiftly with an effective blocking maneuver. Deplorable ethics but legitimate boxing.

I had already sold the fight to NBC for $4 million. They had even been appreciative. Al Rush, with whom I had made the deal both for Norton-Bobick and for Ali-Shavers, had told Herb Schlosser, president of NBC, "Mike could have run an auction. But he didn't. He came straight to us."

Now what? This was the situation. Shavers' business manager, Frank Luca, had sent the Garden a telegram agreeing to terms. A few days later Luca went around and signed a contract with Arum's company, Top Rank. Arum had promised Shavers $300,000 and Ali or, if the champion was unavailable, some other prominent opponent. We went to the state athletic commission waving our telegram from Luca. Arum flashed his contract. The commission ruled in favor of the Garden, and Top Rank went to the state court, which temporarily vacated the commission's decision. We responded in federal court and obtained a preliminary injunction enjoining Shavers from fighting except for Madison Square Garden. Luca testified that he had moved the fighter from the Garden to Top Rank because the Garden was too slow with a $30,000 advance. He received the money from Top Rank. Granting his injunction, Judge Owen had this to say:

> Both Luca and Shavers testified before me that they did not consider that they had a deal until they had the $30,000 advance. I do not credit their testimony. The advance was not mentioned in the telegram.
> Luca also testified that he specifically told Brenner that not only was there no deal until he received his advance, but also that until that time they would continue to negotiate with Top Rank. Brenner denies being told this and I credit him. I observed both men on the witness stand. It is inconceivable that Brenner, knowledgeable, energetic and vocal — having an option agreement with Ali which would expire on July 1st and a multi million dollar contract in hand for television rights to the fight with NBC, would not have pinned down this alleged last item of the deal if Luca had told him what he says he told him. I reject Luca's version of this conversation.

I am glad the judge didn't put me on the stand and ask me to substantiate his assessment of Teddy's energy and efficiency in this fiasco. Lawyers drew up their battle plans, but we settled out of court. Arum was bought off for $300,000 and we added

$100,000 to Shavers' purse. Slothful attention to our business had cost us $400,000 and lawyers' fees. We had no one but ourselves to blame. I credited my instincts and kicked myself for not having been more insistent goading Brenner to action. Teddy hadn't yet grasped that the time had passed when he could sit arrogantly in his Garden office and let the boxing world flock to his door. Having been king of the hill, perhaps he was shackled by pride. If so, it was a false pride, one we could not afford.

The fight itself was a compelling spectacle: the man some had called a "dog" against the most charismatic champion of all time. Ali survived on guile and guts, "covering his diminished skills with a magic show," according to Pat Putnam in *Sports Illustrated*. His foil was a shaven-headed thirty-three-year-old puncher, a crude workman who was expected to last six rounds or so. Ali labeled him The Acorn because of his bald pate. In Las Vegas the bookies considered Shavers too far out of his class. Everyone liked him but no one bet on him, or even against him. He had won fifty-two fights by knockouts, lost three the same way. He had never fought over ten rounds and the few times he had gone that far he had finished so exhausted he could hardly stand. This night, the thirteenth round was Shavers' best to that point. The fourteenth even better. At the opening of the final round an exhausted Ali sucked in a deep breath, called on his tremendous willpower and launched a furious offensive. Shavers' body sagged but not his spirit. Ali won, of course. But never again would anyone call Shavers a dog. His courage, his will matched the champion's. Only his skill fell narrowly short. For all his forbidding bulk and skinned head, the brave challenger was a warm and sweet man with a little-boy smile. An entirely sympathetic man. Of boxing he said: "It's a coldhearted business where out of twenty-three people, twenty-two are thieves. I was too nice."

At NBC, Al Rush and his friends were ecstatic. Al telephoned to tell me the New York overnight Nielsen ratings achieved a sixty-one-percent share of audience in the opening rounds, growing to eighty percent in the final half hour. "These are the highest ratings I've ever seen." I was happy for him, grateful to him. The fight had netted an $800,000 profit on the night. I would have been happier had it been all ours. But $300,000 went to Arum, a neat payoff for his swift move into an opening our lead-assed action had left him.

Things were not going well for the New York Knickerbockers. In the spring of 1973 they had won the NBA championship, beating Los Angeles. But, then, Willis Reed, their heroic captain, Dave deBusschere, Jerry Lucas, and Dick Barnett were suddenly gone and age was nudging Bradley, Frazier, and Monroe past their physical best. The delicate balance of the championship team was lost, vanished except for its permanent place in the record books and in the memories of millions of New Yorkers who had been levitated by its play. Not an encouraging start for my stewardship. I had fallen into another Yankees 1966 situation. A championship team had disintegrated; its holdovers were in decline, and I knew even less about basketball than baseball.

I had been at the Garden one month when the giant form of Willis Reed limped into my office and overflowed a chair, a long stiff leg stretched out before him. It was our first meeting. He had no idea what kind of reception he would get from me, a stranger, nor did his agent, Larry Fleischer, who was with him. Willis was at first defensive, even sullen, and prepared to argue strongly; Fleischer, a bright able lawyer, was assertive. Clearly they had mapped their strategy before coming in. The problem they brought was simple. Willis had two years to run on a contract to play for the Knickerbockers at $250,000 a year. He was committed to play for the Knicks and we were committed to pay him. But Willis would be physically unable to play without another, a third, operation on his knee, the knee on which I had seen him hobble off the bench the previous spring into the early moments of the championship game with Los Angeles, and score two quick inspirational baskets against Abdul-Jabbar that set the packed Garden into a frenzy and his team to an ultimate victory. Willis explained that he had consulted his surgeon, Doctor O'Donoghue, in Oklahoma City. Dr. O'Donoghue doubted that another operation would improve Willis' condition. His knees were simply worn out from years of pounding up and down the hard basketball surface; strong thighs sprang him into the air and his 240-pound body hammered his legs back against the unyielding boards. Willis did not want to go through the agony of a third operation, a third painful therapy, and another punishing basketball season. But he wanted to be paid his contracted salary. His and Fleischer's fear was that I would insist on an operation, gambling that it might be successful, successful enough to get another year's play out of him, pain notwithstanding. It was not I who would have to pay the price in pain. Their tone and argument indicated that this was the response they expected from me. I listened attentively, asked a few questions, glanced through Dr. O'Donoghue's report of his latest examination, observed Willis' mindset as he talked, mentally sifted the contractual niceties that Fleischer had marshaled and said quietly, "Willis, I wouldn't think of asking you to have another operation. And of course we'll honor your contract." It was a logical decision that also happened to be a decent one. You read a situation, you make a decision; the case would be no different in a day or a week, nothing to add or subtract, nothing to be gained by procrastinating. Probably something to be lost. Willis had paid his dues, in full. Neither he nor Fleischer was prepared for so quick and painless a resolution. That is how the Knicks lost their captain.

My start with Coach Red Holzman, fresh off his championship years, was prickly, first over a trivial matter, then one more substantive. Early on I had looked into the pattern of ticket allocations among various Garden people and found it was, by my measure, profligate. Of course there are legitimate business requirements, but allocated tickets are the bane of a ticket-selling business. It is a necessary practice, but I wanted to make certain that none were going to some fellow's butcher so his wife could get a better cut of meat. It was our business to sell tickets, not to give them away, and the public's right to know that, except for a limited number required to meet legitimate official requirements, all tickets were available to them. Holzman was petulant about having the Knicks' allocation cut back. They had grown accustomed to a certain level of patronage. I refused to be dissuaded. Words were hot and the atmosphere cool.

"You're not going to tell me how to coach the basketball team too, are you?" Red asked the question derisively and left in a surly mood. Like most resisted change, this one took but a short time for everyone to adjust to and accept.

The second Holzman issue was more basic. For some years

— ever since the former Knick general manager Eddie Donovan had been lost to Buffalo for want of a $5,000 annual raise — Holzman had held the dual job of coach and general manager. He had bypassed Ned Irish, then president of the Knicks, and sold his bill of goods directly to Irving Felt. I believed the concept to be fundamentally wrong. I told Red candidly that I thought him unsurpassed as a bench coach — no one would refute this — but, as I saw it, the Knicks' general managing function had been virtually unattended. The Knickerbockers' draft picks over the past few years had been hopelessly bad, their names as easily forgotten as an umbrella. He wanted to know who I had in mind and I said Eddie Donovan. Actually I did not know Donovan, but Ned Irish had advised me to get him back at the first opportunity. Donovan was credited with having brought Dave deBusschere to New York, the move that tipped the Knickerbocker team into perfect balance and produced the two Holzman championships. Subsequently Donovan had done exceptionally well as general manager in Buffalo. Holzman was cagey, and I guessed he was privately confident that Donovan wouldn't challenge him and that his influence would remain overriding. Before he joined us, I had no idea how tough or how timid Donovan would be; I knew him favorably by reputation, and I had Irish's recommendation.

As time passed I grew to like Red very much. Among other things he was a great trencherman, and, as we became more comfortable with each other, he invited me to go along with him one night to a dinner with his informal eating club. A group of a dozen men, all Italian except Red, dined together every month or two at Alfredo's restaurant on Fifty-ninth Street. Each member in turn arranged the meal in advance, vying to outdo his fellows. The quality of the food was superb and the quantity ample. Red gave me high marks for eating everything and was fascinated by my habit of eating one thing at a time. Even though there might be two or three foods on one plate, I ate all the zucchini, say, before touching the veal. "You didn't embarrass me," he said. For Red this was glowing praise.

The magic had fled the court at Madison Square Garden, Holzman's genius notwithstanding. Absent Reed, deBusschere, and Lucas, the team finished the season seven games behind

Boston and lost four out of five playoff games to Washington. The Knicks needed help, and a prospect presented itself. A player agent, Irwin Weiner, came to tell me that one George McGinnis wanted to play basketball in New York. Freely translated, that meant Weiner thought he could get more money from the Knickerbockers than elsewhere. McGinnis, a young man of quality and a gifted player, would give the Knicks a great boost. He was the kind of player who could, as they say, turn a team around. For the previous year's play in the American Basketball Association he had shared the Most Valuable Player award with the incomparable Julius Erving. But there was a major catch. McGinnis had played out his ABA contract, but if he were to come into the National Basketball Association he would belong to Philadelphia. They held his draft rights. The Knicks couldn't even talk with McGinnis without Philadelphia's permission. Holzman and I telephoned Pat Williams, the Philadelphia 76ers' general manager, and opened negotiations to acquire their rights. It was tortuous. As the summer weeks dragged on Red became impatient and irritable, postponing and rescheduling, postponing and again rescheduling his vacation in Puerto Rico, where he fled each year to escape hay fever. "When can I leave?" he pleaded.

"If you were the coach you'd be long gone. But as the general manager you've got to stay here and help me. I don't know enough to do this alone. You've got to tell me what he's worth to you." In time we struck a deal, agreeing to Philadelphia's tough demand: the Knicks would have thirty days during which to negotiate with McGinnis; if we signed him, Philadelphia would receive from the Knicks Earl "The Pearl" Monroe and two of our draft picks; if we were unsuccessful within the thirty-day limit, all bets were off and we would revert to the status quo ante. We battled out a rich but fair contract with the player's agent, Irwin Weiner, and Weiner and I flew to Indianapolis with a contract in hand for George McGinnis to sign. A splendid-looking, personable giant, McGinnis met us in a hotel room at the airport, but we had come too late; too many weeks of summer had been used up dickering, first with Philadelphia then with Weiner. The Indianapolis team's preseason training and exhibition games were already under way. He would have signed the contract and come with the Knicks,

McGinnis said, had we arrived before he had rejoined his team. Now he felt morally obligated to go through with one more season in Indiana. He was apologetic. I told him I was sorry and very much regretted he would not be with us in New York, but respected the decision. It was refreshing to meet a young man who honored moral obligations. I tore up the contract and flew back to New York.

The next spring Weiner was back in my office to reopen negotiations. I rang Philadelphia. The general manager said no. They would sign McGinnis themselves. I rang Irv Koslov, the owner, an exceptionally nice man who ran a paper company. He said no. So I told Weiner we could do no business. Three, four times he returned, urging me to defy the League. "Sign him. They're not going to touch New York. We'll sue the League for dictating where George has to play, for stripping him of his freedom of choice. It's against the law." That was Weiner's line of attack. Each time I sent him packing, then flatly refused to talk to him about McGinnis.

Time passed. It became May 21, 1975. I had flown across from London the night before and was sorting through the mail that accumulated during my week's absence. Rosanne came in with a message. "Alan Cohen wants to know if you could join him in the Conference Room."

Alan Cohen had come from a prestigious law firm, where he had been an expert in tax law, via Warner Communications, where apparently he did not fit comfortably, to the presidency of Madison Square Garden Corporation. His presence could be laid at my door for recommending to Charlie Bluhdorn that he find someone more qualified than I to deal with the Garden's real estate business. Bluhdorn was under the illusion he had spirited Cohen away from his archrival, Steve Ross of Warner Communications. Ross' view, I was told by one of his associates, was that he had fobbed off a problem. Cohen had a good legal-financial mind, an unprepossessing personality, frail judgment in human relations, little feel for life inside the constantly exposed skin of the Garden. He suffered a compulsion to become a sports personage with little chemistry for it.

From the first, my very presence made him uncomfortable. In the limited world of sports I was a known entity. He was not. When the governors of the NBA appealed to me to become their commissioner and proposed a long-term $250,000-a-year contract, Cohen urged me to take it and was crestfallen when I rejected it out of hand. Shortly after he joined the corporation, there was a press conference at the Garden about boxing. I was out of town and Cohen decided to attend. Unfortunately, so did a *New York Times* reporter, who asked Cohen a sidebar question about the Knicks and Rangers. Cohen was naive enough to say that, given a choice, he would rather the Garden make a profit than have the Rangers win a Stanley Cup or the Knicks win an NBA championship. Next day, Dave Anderson headed his *New York Times* column: NOBODY ROOTS FOR THE BOTTOM LINE. The columnist reminded him in print that the fans root for a team to win, not for a team to make money; root for athletes, not executives. Obviously Cohen's answer to the sly question should have been that championships and profits are synonymous: you build a team to win; profits follow. But having been trapped by the question he was to be known henceforth as "Bottom Line" Cohen.

Now sitting at the conference room table, smiling and jolly, were Cohen, Weiner, and a fellow I didn't know, who turned out to be Weiner's lawyer. Surprise and a sudden whiff of rat undoubtedly showed on my face as I sat down apprehensively. Cohen was bursting with good news.

"We've just signed McGinnis!" I was only half sure it was a joke, that they were sending me up. The other half told me these fellows didn't have the humor for it.

"Say that again."

"We've signed McGinnis."

"We can't."

"We have."

"We don't have the right."

"Don't worry. We've got that figured out."

To get out of the rut I asked, "On the same terms as last year?"

"Oh, no," said Cohen; "we had to sweeten the deal." No wonder Weiner and his lawyer were so jolly. Obviously all these arrangements had not been made around the conference table that morning.

"You guys obviously know something I don't. Explain it to me."

Cohen outlined the McGinnis scenario. Because I had negotiated a contract with McGinnis a year earlier, the one I had torn up, and because I subsequently refused to deal with his agent, McGinnis would sue the Knicks for violation of the antitrust laws, for conspiring with Philadelphia and the rest of the NBA to boycott him. Faced with this threat, the Knicks would sign McGinnis, stipulating that he withdraw his suit against the NBA, thus taking the Knicks and the NBA off the antitrust hook. Because the suit threatened the player draft and the reserve system concept, the bedrock of the League structure, the Knicks would be forgiven their transgression, having saved the League from a devastating lawsuit. I was vexed and disbelieving.

"Don't worry. I've talked this out with Jay Topkis. He's one of the top antitrust lawyers in the country. It's OK." Cohen was immensely pleased with his scheme. Topkis was a member of Cohen's former law firm.

Apparently this convoluted plan had taken shape during the previous week, while I had been in Moscow, attending the opening of our Holiday on Ice show in Lenin Stadium and negotiating with the Ministry of Culture for future Russian tours. Naturally, as the operating head of the Garden and the New York member of the NBA board of governors, I was to be the point man, and would have to carry the can. I was unhappy and unsure of my ground in this legal labyrinth. Both the Garden house counsel and the outside experts, as well as lawyer Cohen, were confident. My mistake was to give them the benefit of the doubt. The case might have some legal merit, but in the practical world the ploy wasn't worth a damn, and I was stuck with it. That night at dinner I even told myself it would be all right, but I knew deep down it would end badly.

At the press conference to announce the McGinnis signing, I knew we were dead. McGinnis himself — he had actually filed an antitrust suit but dropped it when the Knicks signed him — was impressive. But in response to reporters' questions, Jay Topkis, the antitrust specialist and presumably the key to the success of our legal gambit, was astonishingly inept attempting to explain the Knicks' position. Larry O'Brien, the new NBA commissioner, had taken office on June first. His first major act was to convene a special meeting in San Francisco for June fifth, calling the Knicks to account. The commissioner and his staff sat along one side of a hollow square of tables, the Philadelphia people and their lawyer, the famous Louis Nizer, sat opposite, and other owners filled in vacant places along the sides. By chance Topkis and I sat next to Bob Schmertz, the Boston Celtics' owner and a good friend of mine. Schmertz shook my hand without enthusiasm.

"You know, you don't have many friends here. Including me." I nodded. The anti-Knicks sentiment was poisonous. As the governors entered the meeting room, Philadelphia's general manager had stood at the door passing out copies of a memorandum describing what absolute shits we were. A wounded Irv Koslov, the Philadelphia owner, made a brief comment and turned to Louis Nizer to make Philadelphia's case. Nizer wiped us out. My subsequent plea was pissing into a gale, and Topkis made no impact whatsoever. The five-day-old commissioner withdrew to consider his ruling and returned to give it: the Knicks-McGinnis contract was disapproved; his draft rights were restored to Philadelphia; as penalty the Knicks would forfeit their 1976 first-draft choice and reimburse Philadelphia for expenses incurred, including legal fees, as a result of New York's action. Also we would be fined $250,000.

The commissioner was called from the room for press and television interviews. Then I was sought. In a long empty corridor leading to the television room we passed one another, O'Brien returning, Burke going. Abreast, we hesitated for an instant. O'Brien shook his head. "The ball takes some strange bounces, doesn't it?"

"Yes. Even a round ball." The irony in both our minds was that it was I who had asked O'Brien to become commissioner. After his predecessor's retirement a search committee had come up empty and the committee's chairman appealed to me to find a suitable nationally known figure. I had remembered seeing O'Brien at Knicks games in the Garden during the previous season and telephoned him. "If you had called me a year ago — or perhaps a year from now — I'd say no. But at this moment I'd be willing to consider it." It went from there to a long-term contract. The McGinnis case was his first ruling.

As a pillar of the League — of the original NBA members

only New York and Boston survived the formative years — the Knicks lost standing among their peers for having flouted the constitution so unbecomingly. And I, as the most visible target, took a flood tide of criticism, within and without the League, in the halls and in the streets. Cohen was nowhere within sight or sound.

At times I was tempted to cop a plea: it wasn't me, fellows! But that would have been equally unbecoming. And an unconvincing whine. I despised whining. Better to take the abuse and keep quiet. *Qui s'explique s'accuse.* Though I made one exception. Months later at an NBA All-Star game in Phoenix, I took a seat next to Irv Koslov on a bus carting a group of owners from the hotel to the basketball arena. Because he is a serious, moral man, Koslov's sense of honor had been bruised by the Knicks' action; he was deeply disappointed that his faith in me had been misplaced. In pledged confidence, I told him the weird story, not exculpating myself. He was visibly relieved, and the stiffness melted from our relationship, which pre-McGinnis had been especially congenial.

Red Holzman had grown mentally worn and physically tired, suffering, it seemed to me, a psychological downdraft after the heady championship years and the wearing toll of travel from city to city night after night, season after season. Neither his soul nor his body had the same zest for the game. His interest waned, and he agreed it was time to withdraw to the front office, his permanent place in the Knickerbocker organization won, his legend made. General manager Eddie Donovan recommended Willis Reed above all others to replace Holzman. Reed had spent the years since his retirement as a player preparing himself as a coach, singlemindedly and thoroughly. One of Reed's first acts was to exclude Holzman from the basketball department. He wanted Holzman out of the office we had set up for him there. I was taken by surprise and wondered why no one had ever mentioned any ill feeling between the two. Neither man had ever hinted at it. Assumptions are always risky. I had tucked my head beneath my arm and gone along on the assumption that the captain and the coach of two world-championship basketball teams were compatible. Whatever it was Reed held against his former coach, he kept it to himself, but his mind was set on barring Holzman from his new turf. I sought out Red and apologized for Reed's attitude. A pragmatist, Holzman shrugged it off and spent more time shopping with his wife, Selma, at the supermarket and playing tennis at his Atlantic Beach club.

The first Reed-coached team made the playoffs, but Sonny Werblin arrived as Madison Square Garden Corporation's new president before the second season started. Sonny knew nothing about basketball, but someone told him Reed was not a good coach, and Sonny, master manipulator of the press, began to shaft Reed in public print. Reed lost his composure. All his life he had been an unblemished hero — school, college, professional — extravagantly praised, written about in golden terms, idolized. And indeed he was an athlete of heroic proportions, a courageous leader, the captain of champions. Harsh press criticism, often carping and unfair, and public embarrassment were new experiences which he was unequipped to handle. Reacting in anger and dismay, he undid himself and had to be replaced.

Holzman and I had lunch at Alfredo's. The eighteen-month sabbatical had renewed and refreshed him. Tennis and the beach had left him fit and tanned. I asked him to consider coming back to coaching for the balance of this one season and one to follow. No more, just a season and a half. It would have been unwise from both our points of view to go beyond that limited period. Thereafter he could become the Knicks' vice president. Or president, as far as I was concerned. He agreed, and I sent Selma Holzman a dozen roses. (At Yankee Stadium, when a Yankee or a Knick or a Ranger — or indeed one of the staff people — had performed particularly well, I sent flowers to his wife, or his girlfriend, or his mother, drawing her into the play, appreciating her role.)

Through all the comings and goings, the Knicks remained the Garden's most profitable department and one of the most profitable franchises in professional sports.

The New York Rangers hockey team was a private fiefdom, I discovered. They were not in fact, of course, but the Madison Square Garden hockey department thought of itself as something above and apart from the society around it, a state of mind derived in large part from Bill Jennings' personality. Jennings, president of the Rangers, was a semiabsentee lord of the manor. He commanded the drawbridge from his law offices at Simpson Thatcher and Bartlett. Unlike the Yankees, who operated as a self-supporting business, the Rangers — and the Knicks — were freed of the onerous nuts-and-bolts of business, were left free to concentrate solely on playing hockey or basketball. The Garden administration was structured to provide a cocoon for each team, relieving them of any responsibility for operating the building, running the box office, producing broadcasts, selling advertising, supervising concessionaires, and so on. This was a sound practice, but it tended to encourage the prima-donna strain, which particularly suited Jennings, an aloof, withdrawn, painfully unsociable man. Independently wealthy and highly intelligent, he practiced law and was well regarded by his law partners, but the centerpiece of his life was hockey and specifically the New York Rangers. He guarded them jealously, always watched the games on television from a private room just off the loge seating area and, if he ventured into the arena, could walk unrecognized through a game crowd of 17,500 Ranger fans. Except with a handful of friends, he was shy to the point of rudeness. In short, Jennings was not the kind of person one would expect to find, by whatever accident or debt of gratitude, at the head of a professional sports team. When Irving Felt's efforts to complete financing to build the present Garden fell short, Jennings had stepped in to close the financial gap. So there he was, and he lived and died with the Rangers.

Emile Francis was the steward. As its general manager, Francis ran the team expertly. I had known him quite well earlier as the Rangers' coach. He was a baseball fan and had an open invitation to our games at Yankee Stadium, and I had been his guest at Ranger games. I had always held him in high esteem, personally and professionally.

At the outset, as chairman of the Rangers, I attended a few league meetings with Bill and Emile, tested the water, and determined that with the exception of one or two specific matters on which I had particular knowledge, I could add nothing substantive to their capacity to deal with whatever came along. Besides, I disliked the league president, Clarence Campbell. A Canadian in a sport populated by Canadians and claimed as their own, Campbell affected gruff forcefulness that rang hollow and presumed that his title conferred arrogance. He was a poseur, miming a personage he thought he ought to be and I was happy to leave him to Jennings.

Among baseball and basketball owners there were relatively few of inherited wealth. In hockey, Jennings, Billy Wirtz of the Chicago Black Hawks, Bruce Norris of the Detroit Red Wings formed a cabal of family-rich at the controlling center of the National Hockey League. But around the table at League meetings, the most impressive men to me were our own Emile Francis and Sam Pollack, the general manager of the Montreal Canadiens. They stood in a class by themselves, as men and hockey men.

However superficially I was involved in the day-to-day operation of the Rangers, the fans made no fine distinction. Among them, recognizable and held accountable, I was fair game in the corridors after a losing game. "Burke, you stink" was one of their gentler good-nights. They were the most complex of all New York sports fans, "the most vocal, demonstrative, impatient, fickle and frustrated," according to the *New York Times*. Their team had been in the playoffs again and again but had not won the Stanley Cup, the League championship, since 1940. By 1975 their fury reached a new decibel level. Eddie Giacomin, the veteran goalie, was abruptly traded to Detroit and the sometimes spectacular, always kookie, crowd-pleasing Derek Sanderson was sent to St. Louis. Our television broadcasters chose that moment to ask me to do an interview between the first and second periods of a game. The broadcast booth is on one long side of the arena's upper rim among the private boxes and is bracketed at either end by the Blues, the blue seats. At a Ranger game there's never an empty blue seat. They are filled with hockey's wildest fanatics. "Hook sucks!" (substitute any name unfavored at the moment) is one of their chants of derision.

Between the elevator that lets you out on the top deck at one end of the arena and the broadcast booth opposite center ice, there are fifteen hundred blue seats. A four-foot-wide aisle immediately behind them circles the arena. It would have made no difference if the aisle were forty feet wide. I never made it to the broadcast booth, not for the first intermission, not for the second. The first young man to spot me was not quite sure. Could that really be him? Up here? Now? Among us maniacs?

"Mike Burke?" the fellow said, half-question, half-accusation.

"Yeah. How ya doing?" That did it. Fifteen hundred lions couldn't believe their good luck. A Christian with no sword, no shield. Spleen vents opened. At times I had three or four arguments going at once. Women, asking and receiving no quarter from the men, fought their way into the action. Occasionally I could move forward a few feet at a time, then stop again, blocked, penned in, the game on the ice below forgotten. When would they get another chance to tell off this sonofabitch who traded away Giacomin and Sanderson, this guy who hadn't given them a Cup since 1940, this guy who "ruined the Yankees." With some I tried to reason, some cajole, some ridicule to their mates for being bone stupid, some to offer to fight later outside on the street or right now. By the middle of the third period I had progressed — jostled, pushed, pulled, pressed — to section 408, about half the distance. Two fellows elbowed and shouldered their way through the mob and grabbed me by the arm.

"C'mon with us, Mike. We're in this section." Leading me, they shoved a path towards the steps down into section 408.

"C'mon, guys, let 'im through. We're goin' to buy him a drink. At least he's got the guts to come up here. When didja ever see any of them other creeps up here?" Section 408, like most sections in the Blues, was a family affair. All have had their seats for years. Everyone knew everyone else. Mary and Sue, Alex and Tony, Mabel and Mac.

"What's the score?" I asked.

"We're losin'. Five to four. What'll ya have?" They had an assortment: gin, vodka, beer, Scotch, ice, paper cups.

"Vodka."

"We want ya t' know, Mike, we only do this once a year. The game before Christmas," one of my hosts explained, head gesturing towards the bottles. It is forbidden to bring bottles and cans into the arena. No doubt some of our uniformed guardians were a few dollars richer in tips. "Only once a year." I watched the balance of the game, chatted and drank with the section 408 regulars.

It had been an exhilarating night, absorbing a lot of fan

frustration. They had been able to tell the boss, some boss, any boss, a boss figure, to fuck off and it made them feel better, did me no harm. I think they intuitively knew that I understood this phenomenon, a phenomenon they themselves didn't articulate or even identify but only felt, felt in the form of satisfaction and relief, experienced in the unchallengeable fact that each personally and directly, not anonymously or as part of a mob, had enjoyed his say, frankly and without fear, a personal triumph.

"You gotta come next year, Mike. We'll send ya an invitation." Each year thereafter I received an invitation to share section 408's Christmas cheer.

Not all fan encounters ended so pleasantly. Walking through the corridors of the Garden after a game lost, a certain amount of abuse was inevitable: "Buy a new team, ya jerk," "No wonder Steinbrenner fired you," "Those guys stink out the joint." Mostly I ignored it, moved along, let the barbs glance off. Sometimes, on a whim, I stopped and invited a fellow to get off his chest whatever was burdening him. Sometimes it was a boy showing off for his girl. Nothing lost by making him look good in her eyes. But one night a snarling fellow was particularly insulting and trailed me spewing unpleasantness, assuming the right came with the price of his ticket, that he was immune to rebuttal. My annoyance mounted, simmered, and without breaking stride I told him to bug off, to take his sour stomach home and put it to bed. But he stuck like a limpet and his language turned so foul that suddenly I boiled over, whirled on him, gripped a fistful of his shirtfront with my left hand, and shot my open right hand to his throat, catching his Adam's apple in the V of my thumb and index finger, and rammed him back against the wall. It happened so quickly that he went limp with astonishment. Long-buried close-combat reflexes had exploded from some forgotten place within me. The crowd shuffling towards the exits must have been flabbergasted. Fortunately, two of our Special Officers were a few feet away and reacted instantly, pulled me away from the heckler and hustled me across the corridor through a door into the press lounge. "Jesus, Mr. Burke, you can't do that!" I thanked them and apologized and couldn't have been more ashamed of myself. It was an inexcusable act, shameful, embarrassing, and unprofessional, and never happened again. I made a private pledge never again to defend myself, if that was the term for it. But my promise did not include the players.

Another night a ratty-looking man in his thirties, I would guess, sitting eight or ten rows ahead of me on the aisle kept up a steady barrage of insults aimed at Phil Esposito. He had one of those voices that cut through all other sound. Across the rink on the Rangers' bench, when he wasn't skating, I could see Esposito, distracted, glaring in the direction of the heckler, eyes searching out the source. More often than not these types shut up after a while, or people sitting around them will tell them to knock it off. But this fellow was perhaps a little drunk, a little too rough-looking for his neighbors to challenge. I left my seat and sat on the aisle step at his elbow.

"You're laying it on Phil pretty hard tonight."

"Yeah, Mike, what's it to you?" He was defiant and at the same time surprised to find me sitting next to him.

"Quite a lot. We'd like to win this game and I don't like your distracting Esposito."

"He can take it. He's getting paid enough."

"Tell me, would you say those things to Esposito's face, if he were within hitting distance?"

"Sure." Beer had made him cocky.

"Bullshit. You're a tough guy with two hockey dashers and eighty-five feet of ice between you and him."

"Yeah?" He was better at billingsgate than dialogue.

"Would you be yelling those things if Mrs. Esposito were sitting next to you?" No reply. "She's sitting just over there, you know." I pointed her out. "Now if you want your money back I'd be happy to give it to you and you can leave." I reached into my pocket and took out some bills. "Or if you want to stay and enjoy the game, that's fine too. But behave yourself." I went back to my seat and he behaved. After the game I was leaning against the rubbing table in the trainer's room and Esposito came out of the shower.

"Thanks for taking care of that guy."

I kidded him. "I thought you were playing hockey, not watching the crowd."

He grinned. "You'd be surprised what you can see from the bench. Especially before you're married."

For me, of all major league professional athletes, hockey players as a group, seen at closer range than from the stands, are the most attractive, the most likable. I am conditioned by the Rangers, of course. Every sport has its share of especially appealing individuals. There are certain Yankee ball players whose friendship I treasure above all others. But across the board, hockey produces an exceptionally high percentage of engaging young men. Ranger teams, it seemed to me, ranked at the top, and the 1979 Stanley Cup finalists in particular were a wonderful collection of kids; their captain was age twenty-four. And I don't exclude from this definition the veterans who did not think of themselves as kids: Esposito, Tkaczuk, and Vickers. Nor the two Swedes, Hedberg and Nilsson. They were superb players, engaging companions, and gentlemen. In the dressingroom before the first championship game in Montreal, as his teammates legged into their pants and pulled their stockings over their pads, Ulf Nilsson sat before an empty locker, empty of his gear, in civilian clothes, head down, elbows resting on his knees, weeping silently. An injury had sidelined him. Not everyone thinks of a professional athlete so deeply caring about his trade. From time to time a teammate would pass by and touch him gently on the head or shoulder. No word was necessary. The message of friendship and compassion was clear.

I don't remember if it was the same year or another that some of the players — it might have been Pat Hickey, Ron Duguay, and the Maloney brothers — organized a New Year's Eve party following a game at the Garden. They rented a bistro on Broadway in the nineties and converted it into a private disco. Making the rounds before the game, wishing them luck, I was asked by a couple of the boys if I would join them and I did. Fresh from a nicely timed victory, they all came with their wives or girlfriends. When I arrived the smallish restaurant-bar rocked with laughter and happy talk, song and the solid beat of music. Loose and light-hearted, they danced, drank beer, bantered, spoke softly in a lady's ear, living at the top of the world. Oh, to be young and to be a Yankee, someone once wrote; oh, to be young and to be a New York Ranger would not be off the mark. Sure and keen, unself-conscious of their physical gifts and natural courage that lifted them above tens of thousands of aspirants into an elite handful who played their game at world-class level. On the rim of the crowd, drinking their wine, drawing pleasure from their pleasure, I was happy for them and laughed with them at their irreverent discovery, when I was pulled into the dancing, that the only gray-haired person in the room could move to the contemporary tempo, I having learned from my own children of their age. I liked having been invited.

## 18

FAMILIARITY DID NOT improve Alan Cohen's disposition towards me. Up to a point you make allowances, engage in a
measure of hypocrisy, remain tolerant of imperfect situations,
expecting that your colleagues are making reciprocal allowances for your own flaws, for your basic chemistry which can't
be traded in for a new mixture. But beyond a certain point,
when tolerance is overtaken by exceptional unpleasantness, you
have to say to yourself: what the hell, life's too short, or something equally simplistic, and move to the heart of the matter. I
asked Alan if my very presence discomfited him. The direct-
ness of the question undid him momentarily. But after backing
and filling he said, in effect, well, yes, it did. The subject was
neither new nor remote. Cohen had a solution at hand and
proposed that I put together a syndicate to buy the Rangers
and the Knickerbockers. It seemed a rather drastic solution to
a personality conflict, but I went along, curious as to where it
would come out. On September 12, 1975, I wrote Alan this
recapitulation:

> To make sure we are both clear as to where we are and where
> we are going, let me set down my understanding of our recent
> discussion. Needless to say, this surprise turn is of major mo-
> ment to me and is not one I view casually. I feel we both would
> be more at ease and function better with a clear understanding
> of where we want to come out in the end.
>
> A month ago I asked you if you would be more comfortable
> if I were not here; in essence your response was yes.
>
> In that context, you brought up the matter of selling the
> Knicks and the Rangers, describing this as a necessary move for
> Madison Square Garden Corporation. You proposed that I put
> together a group to buy the teams. This would permit a finder's
> fee to be paid me.

When we talked again on September 2nd, you proposed a specific finder's fee and I agreed that that seemed appropriate. You added that this fee could be paid out in any number of different ways.

But it remains to develop a comprehensive sale proposal. The proposal should include sufficient financial information to permit potential buyers an intelligent analysis and a basis for a sound business judgement. Definitive negotiations for the sale of the teams will be conducted by you on behalf of Madison Square Garden Corporation.

In short, we would outline an arrangement for the termination of my contract and develop a comprehensive profile for my purchase of the teams. The two are inseparable.

Throughout a series of discussions, I left unasked, perhaps mischievously, the obvious question of whether Bluhdorn knew of and approved this sale of the two teams. That was Cohen's problem, and I felt no obligation to caution him about going too far down the road without Bluhdorn's endorsement. Of course when Bluhdorn did get wind of Cohen's plan he demolished it in his own crushing style. Alan and I were having lunch at "21" with Victor Potamkin, a flamboyant and successful New York car dealer toying with the prospect of owning a New York sports franchise. Just as Alan's poached sole was served, a waiter plugged in a phone and set it on our table. The call was for Alan, so Victor and I heard only our end of the conversation, a tremulous "yes." Whatever was said to him turned Alan the color of his untouched fish. He leapt up and fled, mumbling that Bluhdorn wanted to see him immediately. Potamkin, puzzled by Alan's abrupt retreat, gazed at the abandoned sole as though it held some explanation. "Victor," I said, "I suspect the Knicks and the Rangers are no longer for sale."

Cohen and I rocked along awkwardly attending to different parts of the Garden business. In a way, quite privately, I felt rather sorry for him. His was a classic case of a man mistakenly chosen and thrust into a post for which he was unsuited by experience, personality, or temperament. Once in position, instead of rechanneling his best talents, he aspired to things he was least capable of achieving, seduced by some romantic notion of himself, by some creature of his mind, foreign to all his natural equipment. His selection was unfair to him and was bound to end unhappily. His behavior became more erratic, and it was a time for me to remain detached and cool. At one board meeting, astonishing everyone, Cohen pulled out a sheaf of yellow foolscap and read his resignation from longhand notes. The board was told he would, having resigned the presidency of the corporation, consider assuming the chairmanship but only with the understanding that he would be available but one day a week. The corporation's affairs warranted no more of his time. The men around the table were embarrassed for him and I wondered if this was some bizarre ploy to have his friend Joe Joyce, who, like me, was a senior vice president of the corporation, installed as its president. Their heads were always together. The embarrassed silence was broken by George Morton Levy, the founder of Roosevelt Raceway and "the father" of harness racing. Gently, the octogenarian Levy suggested to Cohen that this was a poor idea, badly handled, and one he ought to rethink. Like Cohen's peculiar inspiration to sell the two sports teams, this one too evaporated. But I doubt that the incident, when word of it reached Bluhdorn, advanced his cause.

Once again Cohen became near-frantic when he heard that the *New York Times Sunday Magazine* was preparing a cover story about me. Insinuating inside information, he warned me that it was to be a hatchet job on me personally and on the Garden and that we must do everything in our power to stop it. The *Times,* he said, had installed a new editor with instructions to make the *Sunday Magazine* controversial, to get it read, get it talked about. The free-lance writer hired to do the piece won the assignment claiming he could destroy Burke. All this may or may not have been true, but I suspected Alan's motivation was not necessarily to avoid a negative story but to avoid my photograph's appearing on the magazine cover. He contacted Jim Judelson at Gulf & Western and poured vinegar into an unhealed wound. The *Times* in the recent past had flayed Bluhdorn mercilessly in a three-part front-page series. Another destructive story about Gulf & Western's most visible subsidiary was the last thing that was wanted. Judelson rang me in despair to say he had used up his most valuable chip to have the story killed, without success. I asked Alan whether he had seen the story; he had not but had spoken with a *Times* reporter who had. The reporter, a friend, told me that he had not in fact seen the story, although he guessed it would not be very likable. The writer's stock-in-trade was muckraking. I couldn't really get exercised about it. Even if the piece was not something one's mother would write, memories are short. No one remembers except that they saw your photograph on the cover of something. Was it *Newsweek?* Or *New York* magazine? Anyhow, there was nothing to be done and I went off to Paris. We had undertaken to tour the Leningrad Ice Ballet in Western Europe and I wanted to attend the Paris opening at the Palais des Sports and keep our developing relations with the Russians moving along. The author of the *Sunday Times* piece got wind of the maneuvering to kill his story. He telephoned me at the Hôtel Meurice in Paris and wanted to know what the hell was going on. Flippantly I said that by the time the issue with the story appeared I might no longer be with the Garden. That dumb remark only further antagonized him and made me look a bit foolish when it was printed. Until I returned to New York I didn't know how close to being true my flippant remark was. The cover story appeared and wasn't all that bad. The writer, not an admirable fellow, resorted to the usual tricks — implying that a derogatory quote from some bartender I had never seen, much less known, represented a body of disparaging public opinion. But his bias was offset by some facts he couldn't avoid. On balance, it was certainly not a destructive story. But it caused Cohen to lose his head entirely.

He asked me to his office and said, not unkindly, "Charlie Bluhdorn told me to fire you. But don't worry, we'll make a very generous settlement on your contract." He was very solicitous and I listened. As he talked on, my mind raced over this startling bit of news and decided intuitively how to deal with it.

"Alan, don't fret. It's perfectly all right." My tactic was to disarm him, to make it look easy. "I'm sure we can make an agreeable settlement. I know everyone will be very generous. And of course there are a thousand things I can do elsewhere." He was much relieved by my relaxed attitude. "There is only one thing, though," I added. "Just for the symmetry of it. Charlie Bluhdorn hired me. Charlie Bluhdorn is going to have to fire me. Face-to-face."

"Oh, that won't be necessary."

"Oh, yes, it will." Quietly and firmly I closed off the discussion on that point. Together we went to a very agreeable lunch at Giordano's on Thirty-ninth Street at Ninth Avenue. Alan's settlement terms grew more generous with each martini. I didn't discourage him. Lunch over, I telephoned Bluhdorn's office and left a message for him to ring me back. He hadn't by the following morning, so I wrote him a letter and had it hand-delivered. When I returned to the office from a tedious business luncheon about two-thirty, Bluhdorn was on the phone, snarling. "I've got this letter. What is this? I'm goddam busy. My desk is buried with . . . I'm . . ."

His annoyance, his waspish tone of voice made me angrier than I had been for some time. I cut him off, yelled into the telephone. "Listen, Charlie! I don't give a shit about those pieces of paper on your desk! This is my life you're fucking around with!" That was more melodramatic than I intended, but I was pissed off. He did an about-face. Like many of his ilk who shouted at people, Bluhdorn understood only being shouted at. His next words were spoken calmly, even sensitively. "Could you come over at three-thirty?"

"Of course." Bluhdorn had Larry Levinson, his general-purpose assistant, with him. The mood was relaxed and pleasant. "Thanks for making the time. And, up front, I want you to know I'm not here to ask to be un-fired. Alan made a very generous settlement proposal."

"What's this firing business?" Bluhdorn never remained calm very long.

"Alan told me yesterday that you told him to fire me."

"I what!"

"Told him to fire me." Bluhdorn spewed a string of Austrian-accented expletives, his arms flailing the air, and, when he calmed down, he looked at Levinson with a what-next expression. "I told Cohen no such thing!"

"My only purpose in being here, Charlie, is that I want to leave for the right reasons. Not for the wrong ones. I want to leave with the facts clear and the record straight."

"Forget this leaving business! I don't want to hear any more of that crap. But now that you're here, let's talk about some Madison Square Garden things. I've got some things on my mind." They must have been eating at him from the way he attacked the subject.

"OK."

He had a number of pertinent questions reflecting a familiarity I wouldn't have guessed he had. I would have thought him so occupied with the Dominican Republic's sugar, the United States Justice Department's aggressive probing, and any number of heavier matters that the Garden would have been lost to all but his superficial interest.

"What about the fiasco with the basketball player? What's his name?"

"McGinnis. I'll give you a capsule if you like. Apart from Irv Koslov . . ."

"Who's he?"

"He owns the Philadelphia basketball team. Apart from Koslov, you and Larry will be the only people to have heard this from me." I related the salient facts.

"You refused to deal with the agent? You came back from Russia and found the whole cockamamie scheme was done?" Again he and Levinson exchanged some message in a glance.

"Yes."

"You took all the blame, you know. I mean here. From us."

"I assumed that."

"Why didn't you let someone know before now?"

"That's not my style." A line from one of Marianne Moore's poems slipped silently through my mind: "expanded explanation tends to spoil the lion's leap." I had been there four hours. Bluhdorn wanted to know where I was going.

"Back to the Garden. We've got a basketball game starting in about five minutes."

"Take my car." He shouted for his secretary to have his driver take me to the Garden. "Look. I'm glad we had this talk. I never told Cohen to fire you. Never. I want you to stay at the Garden as long as you want. I'm sorry this happened, and I don't want you to leave."

"Understood." We shook hands and I went to watch the Knicks. Cohen was gone before the year's end, eventually to join a company that runs parking lots and such things. The Garden had been a misadventure for him, not without its lessons, not without profit.

Dazzling as their great moments were, each of the three ancestral Gardens suffered a common ailment that plagued successive managements from Vanderbilt and J. P. Morgan to Ringling and Rickard: an insufficient number of events. In its fourth home, as the Garden neared its hundredth anniversary, this fundamental problem was no different. The circus, hockey, basketball, ice shows provided a contemporary base, but plainly the schedule required fleshing out with every appropriate attraction one could think of that people would pay to see. Days with no events were the perennial bane of the Garden's existence; hovering like buzzards, they challenged every management's ingenuity. Looking with fresh eyes, it appeared that to stay alive we must widen our perspective, to reach out to the entire community, a community where each Sunday Mass is said in twenty-two different languages.

Olga Korbut became the darling of the 1972 Olympics, winning a gold medal. She inspired my colleague Alvin Grant to conceive the Americas Cup; eighteen nations sent teams to compete in a new international gymnastics competition. New Yorkers filled the Garden, as they have every year since.

Wrestling was a secret shared only by those who cared about it. If you asked a hundred people on Fifth Avenue and Fiftieth Street if there was wrestling at Madison Square Garden, yes or no, one hundred would say no. Yet on Monday nights once a month 20,000 boisterous fans, none in white tie and tails, filled the arena with wild cheers for the good guys and jeers for the bad. At first glance they may have looked to some a raunchy crowd. Casually dressed and high-spirited, they caused not one jot of trouble. Mostly Puerto Rican and Italian, they were different from the horse-show crowd, noisier and more exuberant, and came from different parts of town. But they were wonderfully well behaved and came in family lots; we had to have a state law amended to permit parents to bring children under twelve years of age. Everyone went home happy. The good guys always won.

Garden wrestling was based on a solid partnership with a beautiful New York Irish gentleman named Vince McMahon. Though his father had been a boxing promoter, Vince veered into wrestling. A theatrical-looking man, he stood apart from the crowd by his manner and business style. Over six feet tall, straight in posture, florid of complexion, with flowing white hair, often dressed in a white belted camel's hair topcoat, he was a refreshing throwback to an earlier, more colorful New York. You could shake his hand on a deal and know it was as secure as any contract you ever signed. I would trust him with my life.

Starting with the Mexicans, we reached out to New York's multiple ethnic populations, ambitious that everyone should know we were thinking about them, wanted them at the Garden. On a Saturday in September we presented a matinee and evening music program produced especially for Mexican audiences. By Saturday morning the venture looked like a dead loss. The advance sale wouldn't pay the ticket takers' salaries. Dejected, I left the building just after midday to get a sandwich and a beer and, scuffing along Thirty-third Street towards Eighth Avenue, hands sunk in my pockets, head hanging, wondered how I could have gone so far off the mark. So deeply was I wrapped in my own gloom that it was some minutes before I became aware of crowds of people emerging from the subway, streaming off the buses, chattering in Spanish, heading for the Garden. My spirits zoomed and were in full flight by the day's end. Both performances virtually sold out the 18,000 arena seats. The Mexicans were late buyers and late arrivers, we learned.

We spread our wings from there, more in the Forum than the arena because its size better accommodated the talent, and presented shows for the special interests of Italians, French, blacks, Dominicans, Puerto Ricans, Jewish, Irish, Chinese, and other specific audiences. At Christmastime the Forum belonged to the children. Parents brought them by the thousands to see Bugs Bunny or *Sesame Street Live*. And throughout the balance of the year audiences could find judo, team tennis, the Moscow Circus, martial arts, est lectures, Special Olympics, graduation exercises, Jacques d'Amboise Schoolboy Ballet, a Muslim convocation, magic shows, ice ballet, club boxing, fashion shows, revival meetings, male beauty contests, union elections, and more. In the Rotunda, when it wasn't used to house circus animals, stable 250 horses, or kennel thousands of dogs, one found antique exhibitions, stamp shows, racing-car exhibitions, furniture shows, the first Ephemera and Collectable fair, a private supper party for five hundred people. During the passage of a year something for everyone turned up somewhere within the Garden's circular walls. Watching the six million people who flowed in and out each year, mingling with them — sometimes anonymously, sometimes not — observing their captured interest, their holiday air, invariably filled me with a rewarding sense that the Garden was playing its role, giving respite from the city's crucible, contributing in its way to the city's balance. There is about the Garden, as there is about the New York Yankees, an absence of pretension. The Garden is what it is, as the Yankees are what they are. Pure and simple. Pretending to be nothing more, nothing less. The Garden sweats the clean sweat of a circus flyer, a basketball player, a jumping horse, a beer vendor, a spotlighted singer, a stage-hand. Pretension is some foreign thing. It lives elsewhere. I was in harmony with this environment.

Team sports — Knicks and Rangers games — I found the most emotional, a great tennis match the most thrilling, a heavyweight championship fight the most colorful. But concerts were the most moving. Paul McCartney, Elton John, The Grateful Dead, Neil Diamond, Bob Dylan, Billy Joel, the incomparable Mick Jagger and the Rolling Stones, others. Each drew his own kind of audience, some more free-spirited than others. Rock music became an increasingly important part of our repertoire. Perhaps it would have knocked us down if we had not made room for it. But to make certain we missed no bets, one of our young people was designated to concentrate on that assignment exclusively, to induce as many rock groups as possible to come to the Garden. Soon we had built to fifty-seven the number of concerts in a single year, every one a sellout. More often than not, before a deal was set or the tickets ordered from the printer, word of a potential concert spread like tinder fire among the young. The music of these marvelous entertainers drew them into a shared human experience, unlike any other. Garden air hung heavy with the scent of marijuana. It was also heavy with a feeling of unity, the rounded edges of contentment and kinship. Absent were the sharp corners of meanness, hostility, constraint. Perhaps these same young people — most were young — might behave differently in the competitive day streets or roaming the night. But in the Garden, suffused in music, moving to its beat, hand-held torches acclaiming the end of a performance, one saw their community, felt their lilt and their lust for life.

All the Garden's events — giving pleasure, giving pause, giving a sense of fulfillment to many people whose jobs do not fulfill their aspirations and who search for self-expression in their free time — filled my own need as a person bent towards giving. Always, giving has been more satisfying to me than receiving. I would rather give a present than receive one. It is a built-in condition, not something acquired, not something learned, but something that was there when I was born, I suppose. Willingly I gave up my body, as they say in football, to a block, a tackle, or a run; voluntarily I gave my body to a war. I am the happier for giving pleasure to a crowd of 20,000 or to a solitary lady. It is my lot; I am content with it, fortunate really.

Every morning when I arrived at the Garden — and before that at Yankee Stadium — Rosanne was there to greet me with a cheerful word on even the dreariest days.

"Well, we've done it again," she announced happily and pointed out a headline in the *New York Post* over a story written by Henry Hecht: THE GARDEN GROWS A WINNER. Hecht wrote that "Mike Burke had an idea as big as the joint he runs." I had told him that I wanted to make a place for the Garden in world tennis. Given a year or two, I thought, the Masters' tennis tournament would take root. "He caught an early bloomer," Hecht wrote. In one stroke, the Masters' had established the Garden as a major world tennis site.

It had taken two years of maneuvering through the administrative labyrinth of professional tennis before we found our way. Tennis at the Garden was hardly an original idea. Exhibition matches had been played there by the great Bill Tilden in the 1930s. And in 1947 Jack Kramer and Bobby Riggs played their famous blizzard match. The day after Christmas a storm worse than the infamous blizzard of 1888 delivered twenty-five inches of snow, the heaviest snowfall in history, and paralyzed the city. A train from Grand Central Station required twenty-four hours to make a scheduled one-hour run. Somehow, 15,000 people appeared at the Garden to see two fellows named Kramer and Riggs play tennis. Rummaging in my head for events that would fill the building with paying customers, I reached for history. And for Jack Kramer. The hour, I sensed, was right for the Garden to get into tennis, not an occasional exhibition but on a solid, ongoing basis. My young colleague Rob Franklin — he had come over from the Yankees with me and had done a superb job handling a variety of events — and I laid out possible approaches and started exploring them. The ladies were our first gambit. In the spring of 1977 we put our money on the women's professional tour finals and brought the top eight point winners from the Virginia Slims women's circuit to the Garden, offering $150,000 in prizes. We got away to a good start, and in succeeding years the prize money quickly jumped to $300,000. By 1980 Tracy Austin played Martina Navratilova for the $100,000 first-place money before the largest single crowd in the history of women's tennis, 13,878. But it wasn't until the winter of 1978 that we landed the men, and not without a little help from our friends.

With the eight top women established as a March Garden feature, Rob and I set out to romance the people at Colgate. Colgate sponsored the men's Grand Prix circuit and we wanted the finals — the Masters' — to be held in the Garden. The Masters' matched the top eight players in the world. We blocked out four days in the Garden's heavy winter schedule to accommodate tennis and, at what we thought was a propitious moment, went along to see David Foster, the Colgate chairman, and Jack Grim, who looked after Colgate's sports operations. It was a brief meeting. Foster said no, more or less politely. He preferred that the Masters' tournament be held each year in a different country to promote Colgate's international sales. He was unmoved by arguments that the great tennis tournaments — Wimbledon, for instance — were not peripatetic but fixed in a single place. Rob and I were disappointed but not discouraged. We had shot for the moon but, if necessary, we would settle for the North Star. We applied for and were given an ordinary Grand Prix circuit date. At least we would have an attractive tournament, if not the Masters' itself, in the Garden. But when you are out moving around, knowing that nothing ever stands still, having an objective, keeping alert and flexible, things happen.

What happened was that David Foster discovered that an itinerant Masters' was impractical for a number of reasons and sought permission of the Men's International Professional Council in Paris to anchor the championship tournament in

Mission Hills, California, a resort owned by Colgate. No dice, said the committee. And our friends at court moved deftly on our behalf. In a quiet aside, Jack Kramer, a member of the nine-man council, recommended to Foster that, as an alternative, he ask to place the Masters' in Madison Square Garden. Bob Briner, the executive director of the Association of Tennis Professionals, used up some of his political capital in our favor. Both were our friends, both genuinely believed that a long-range commitment of the Masters' to the Garden made sense for professional tennis. The International Council agreed, and, within a few minutes of their decision, a telephone call from Jack Kramer let us know that when Foster returned to New York he had but one place to call.

I said we would come to him, and Rob and I met Foster and Grim in the Colgate offices. Yes, we could accommodate the Masters'. From the fifth to the eighth of January 1978. And in the years to come. Needless to say, we struck a better deal for the Garden than we were prepared to make on our first hat-in-hand visit. But everyone was pleased. Foster had the Masters' and no place to put it. We had the building and no Masters'. A very happy solution all around.

From that moment Rob and I set out to give the Masters' a memorable debut. The eight best tennis players in the world playing for $400,000 prize money gave us a running start. We transformed the Garden. I knew how I wanted it to look, just as surely as I knew how I wanted Yankee Stadium to look when it was renovated. We achieved a tennis atmosphere. Tennis fans familiar with the building set up for hockey or boxing or the Ice Capades were astonished and delighted. An azure blue artificial surface, Supreme Court, lay on top of our basketball floor. The perimeter, as at Forest Hills, was lined with hundreds of geraniums and mini-forests of rented trees, and palms grew from the four corners of the arena. In the Forum we put down another artificial surface where the players could practice. And the Forum lounge was laid out like a country club terrace, with trees and flowers and a bar. Once again the ingenuity and skill of Richard Donapria and his people triumphed. The place looked tennis. On the first night, Thursday, Jimmy Connors and Guillermo Vilas were the main match of the round-robin tournament.

I had an early dinner date with Sonny Werblin, his wife, Leah Ray, and Bili Kohm, their brilliant young public relations friend.

"What have you got on at the Garden tonight?" Sonny asked.

"A tennis match." Bothered by a flu bug, Sonny and Leah Ray went home and I took Kohm along with me to the Garden. Shaking his head in amazement, he couldn't believe the look of the building, the electric excitement. Guillermo Vilas outlasted Jimmy Connors 6-4, 3-6, 7-5, before a capacity crowd, the biggest ever, anywhere for a tournament match. An audience of nearly 19,000 roared continuously at the sustained intensity and incredible shotmaking. When the match ended at forty-two minutes past midnight, I had no inclination to go home. I was too high. I watched the fans drift out through the vomitories and made my way to the players' area — the Ranger and Knickerbocker dressingrooms and the lounge between the two had been turned over to the tennis players — congratulated Connors and Vilas on their thrilling match, listened in at the press conference set up in the Rotunda, wandered around the empty arena savoring the aftertaste of a glorious night, hearing again the roar of the crowd, hearing the referee, Frank Hammond, asking for "Quiet please" over the public address system, listening to 18,590 exhilarated spectators hush suddenly to pin-drop silence. Replaying the scenes in my mind, I simmered with satisfaction at a good beginning and the anticipation of more to come.

When a sports promoter wakes in the night, no sheep jump his fence but, in search of the public's intangible preference, notions tumble through his head, notions of what might entice people into his available seats. And his stomach is knotted by the hard arithmetic that today's unsold seat is gone forever, that his stock is perishable day by day, can't be stored on a shelf for a more favorable time. He deals with no solid substance, but sells a small piece of cardboard of no intrinsic value, bearing a date, a seat number, and a price. His goods are intangible, as elusive as the wind. Each event — a game, a gymnastics exhibition, a wrestling match, a rock concert — is caught for a moment, then the moment disappears into history like the day itself. His reward for dealing in smoke is to hear the lovely sound of happy, stimulated people lifted out of themselves, their real-life baggage left aside, enjoying an event that may have taken shape in his head on a sleepless night, to see a crowd figuratively turning thumbs up to an occasion as they drift back to the real world rewarded, refreshed, or merely pleased that they had come. This was how I felt about that good night as I took a last goodnight look around the deserted silent arena. The cheering left no record of itself but echoed in the memory, the mini-forests in the four corners of the arena still in the worklight dusk. A night watchman was on duty at the single unlocked door to the mall leading onto Seventh Avenue. He was one of the older men, and our conversations almost invariably included some reference to a young Met baseball player whose career the guard and his wife followed religiously, as closely as though he were a family member, as though he were someone they actually knew. Always we spoke of the player only as "he" because we both knew whom we were talking about. This night, in the wake of a history-making event, was an exception; he said simply, "Great night, Mike."

"Wonderful. And more to come."

"Great for the Garden."

"It is." He pushed back the door to let me out.

"No coat?"

"Don't need one tonight."

"You don't want to catch cold now."

"I'll walk fast."

"Well, goodnight, Mike." He closed and locked the door behind me and I walked to Gramercy Park, unaware of the January cold, unable to turn off my own emotional high like a light switch.

The final on Sunday matched Bjorn Borg and Jimmy Connors in a showdown of world-class tennis. Eighteen thousand one hundred fifty screaming fans got what they had been waiting for: a player to call Number One. Sometimes a promoter's midnight notion survives a harder look in the cold light of day, flourishes, takes on a life of its own. By 1981 it was Borg and John McEnroe in the final, before 19,000 jubilant tennis buffs. They made the sport of tennis into a fine sort of theatre, Mike Lupica wrote: one of those gripping Garden nights when the

sparks begin on the street, race through the lobby, and fly up
the stairs where the evening explodes.

Abe Beame had become the mayor of the city of New York.
He telephoned to ask if we would be willing to hold the 1976
Democratic National Convention in Madison Square Garden.
Of course, I said. We would be delighted. And would I go to
Washington with the New York City delegation and made a
presentation to the party's site selection committee? I would.
Both were gut responses. Except in the vaguest way, I had no
idea what was involved. I had never been to a National Convention. But in 1976 the city balanced precariously on the brink of
bankruptcy. Governor Hugh Carey was impelled to create the
Municipal Assistance Corporation to take control of the city's
fiscal direction. My friend Felix Rohatyn became the linchpin
of the rescue operation. For our sins, real and imagined, the
Congress and the rest of the nation wished us ill. A *Daily News*
headline conveyed to us a message from the President of the
United States: Drop Dead. Like many New Yorkers in the face
of these unfavoring winds, I thought the convention would be
a boon to the city. The last National Convention held in New
York was in Stanford White's Garden in Madison Square in
1924. After two tumultuous weeks and 103 ballots, Al Smith
and William McAdoo were deadlocked. On the fifth day, William Jennings Bryan had his pocket watch lifted by a pick-
pocket and one of his golden-voiced speeches, according to the
*Times,* produced "more pugnacity, ill feeling, bad blood and
un-Christian ferocity than is seen in the Garden in a whole
boxing season." Finally John W. Davis won the nomination
from wilted delegates. I expected there would be a thousand
and one people who would say that the present Garden
couldn't accommodate a convention, and that it shouldn't be
tried. But all my instincts told me that it was something we
should make a commitment to do and then hustle to make
good on our commitment.

In Washington, the city of Los Angeles was represented by
Mayor Bradley and made a slick Hollywood pitch. Mayor Lan-
drieu of New Orleans was there with an enticing presentation.
Miami and its mayor were old hands at political conventions
and how to persuade a site selection committee. Detroit's ener-

getic mayor headed his city's delegation. I found the New York group in a small, bare office off the Committee Room and enquired about Mayor Beame. He hadn't come down. The mayor was represented by Neil Walsh, the city's dollar-a-year deputy commissioner of welcomes, or some such title. Charlie Gillette, president of New York City's Visitors and Convention Bureau, Xavier Lividini, representing the Hotel Association, and I made up the rest of the New York delegation. I looked around for the charts, photographs, and other physical props that would help make New York's case. There were none. Instead, Walsh pulled a piece of yellow foolscap from a drawer and tossed it on the bare battered wood desk. "What do you think I ought to say?" he asked of no one in particular. Our turn to appear was coming up in about ten minutes. We were going up against the well-developed strategies and sophisticated presentations of four other cities. All we had was a blank sheet of foolscap and three guys looking at one another in dismay. The convention was a prize New York desperately needed, especially for psychological reasons. The rest of the country was taking perverse pleasure in the city's dire situation. And here we were winging it. I turned to Gillette. "Charlie, do you have with you the film you showed the Executive Committee a couple of weeks ago?" The New York bureau's purpose is to attract conventions and tourists to New York. As a member of its executive committee, I had seen a film Gillette had made that put New York's best foot forward. It was excellent.

"Yes. Certainly."

"Look, Neil. Everyone knows New York has hotels and restaurants and theatres and a police force. I would think what these site selection people will want most to know is whether Madison Square Garden can house a convention. Why don't you let Charlie show his film? Then I'll take on their questions about the Garden."

It worked out well enough. Walsh said the New York police were the finest. Charlie Gillette's film was very attractive, Lividini gave them reassuring statistics about hotel space, and I explained how the Garden, admittedly not built as a convention hall, could be converted effectively. The fact that Pat Cunningham, the Democratic Party's leader in New York, was also chairman of the site selection committee did us no harm. It was left that Cunningham and Robert Strauss, the party's national chairman, and a group from the committee would visit New York the following week and tour the Garden with a critical eye before the vote was taken. It was close. Eleven to nine in favor of New York.

Charlie Bluhdorn was in a swivet when the Madison Square Garden board next met in suite 200, a tastefully decorated private apartment just off the main arena where we entertained guests before various events. A rectangular mahogany table seated twenty for dinner and doubled as a board table once a month. Bluhdorn was in full form, shouting and waving his arms. "Tell them to take the damn convention to Poland." That didn't sound sensible even to Charlie. "Or Central Park!"

"What if it rains?" someone asked wryly.

"We'll supply the umbrellas!" Charlie shouted, banging the table with the flat of his hand. When he mounted one of these hobby horses, he often rode it a wild distance from reality. His concern was legitimate but exaggerated. The election laws proscribed our giving the Garden free of charge as the convention site, because this would have been considered an indirect political contribution. It would have been illegal and we would have been prosecuted. To be on the right side of the law we were required to rent the Garden to the city of New York, charging a "normal rent." I estimated that a normal rent figure might be as high as $2 million. The Garden, hence Gulf & Western, could be accused of sticking it to the city at a most inauspicious time. The city was broke. So Bluhdorn fumed, seeing no solution to the dilemma: be altruistic and go to jail; be lawful and invite charges of gouging the impoverished city. Bluhdorn was a constant target for a generally hostile press and, like St. Sebastian, did not need another arrow through his body. He was not happy with me for having encouraged the convention to New York and the Garden.

"Charlie." It was difficult to get his attention when he was off on one of his monologues and I tried a second time. "Charlie. There is a simple solution. At least I think what I had in mind to do will take care of your concern." He snorted disbelief. "I'll talk with Abe Rosenthal at the *Times* and Mike O'Neill at the *News* and someone at the *Post* and ask them to send around a political reporter, someone who may be covering the convention for them, and explain the situation clearly. If we do that, they won't turn on us. They'll put the screws to us only if we try to be clever, try to fog one past them." He ranted a bit more, but that is the way it worked out. The reporters came along to the same boardroom, and over coffee and Danish pastries I told them what we were going to do and why. We got no flak.

The convention would last for four days, but the whole operation would take two summer months out of the Garden's normal life. We made careful, sensible financial calculations and met with the deputy mayor, Stanley Friedman, at City Hall to reach a final rental agreement. There must have been thirty people at the table. I suppose it's the same in every bureaucracy the world over. Friedman sat at one end and I at the other. Some preliminary nuts-and-bolts items were discussed and Friedman said, "We'll pay you one million, seven hundred and fifty thousand."

"OK, Stan. That's a deal." It was too swift for one of Friedman's accountants, who had some other things to haggle about, but Friedman cut him off.

"What's to talk about? I made him an offer, and Mike says it's a deal. That's it!"

Converting the Garden was a monstrous job, but Richard Donapria, Norm Leonard, and other Garden people were superb. So were the outside contractors. There were squabbles and squalls, misunderstandings, conflicts, tests of will, dogs in the manger, opportunists, and people who gave way too soon or not soon enough. But always at critical moments someone with his head screwed on dealt with a problem in a constructive way, and in the end the convention was a huge success — for Jimmy Carter, for New York, and for Madison Square Garden. The total achievement was important for the Garden, but on a far wider and more significant scale for the city of New York. Twenty thousand delegates and alternate delegates to the convention went home to the rest of the country bearing testimony to New York's hospitality and good cheer. Swept up in the sense of occasion, New Yorkers put their best foot forward. In contrast to Chicago in 1968, New York was as peaceful as a Trappist monastery. The police were required to make but a single arrest outside the Garden. Even the prostitutes, the locals and the brigades from out of town, were circumspect. "We are going to move the girls away a little. Talk nice to them. They'll understand it's important," assistant chief of police Dan Courtney told the 1,500 men assigned to the convention.

For its Quotation of the Day on July 10, 1976, the *New York Times* quoted Robert Strauss, chairman of the Democratic National Committee: "Madison Square Garden was not built for a National Convention and just wouldn't work, so they said. Well, the Garden looks magnificent — warm, functional and efficient." As a memento to their achievement and their pride of workmanship I had Strauss' comment etched in metal and mounted on wooden plaques for each of a dozen key Garden people who had made it happen. They had risen to the occasion with magnificence.

The convention in July was followed by Operation Sail in August. Tall ships from all over the globe sailed into New York Harbor and turned the whole city into a spectacular festival. The psychological impact of these two events changed the mood of the city, buoying its confidence, and the nation seemed less inclined to wish New York the worst for its sins.

Again in 1980 New York reached for the Democratic National Convention. This time Mayor Koch, in his inimitable kookie-crafty style, led the delegation to Washington and addressed the site selection committee. Harry Van Arsdale promised them that there would be no labor strife, no strikes; Bob Tisch, the indefatigable chairman of the host committee in 1976, brought a Radio City Music Hall group to sing and pledged that New York would be as hospitable in 1980 as it had been four years earlier; and, in my turn, speaking for the Garden, I simply quoted Mr. Robert Strauss. The 1980 convention was no less complex, no less demanding. But it went off more smoothly the second time around. The trail had been cut four years earlier.

From its beginning in 1879 the Garden's entertainment mirrored the life and times of the city, the changing and the unchanged. Gone a century later were the six-day bicycle races, Stanford White's supper club and girls in pink tights, gone into history like the Wake of John Barleycorn, a bacchanal held on the eve of Prohibition.

## 19

THE RHYTHM of the Garden, in contrast to the Yankees, allowed summer weekends, even summer holidays, and I found a century-old brown-shingle farmhouse on Long Island, a hundred miles from Manhattan. Lying half-hidden behind a high privet hedge, higher than a basketball player can jump, it had front windows that looked out across a mile of potato fields. A garden behind the house produced an abundance of vegetables, and each season vines and bushes along the side borders gave us grapes and blackberries, and two rows of trees bent under the weight of apples and peaches. From the back windows we looked out on a thousand yards of open fields to a lone house against the dunes and the sea beyond. The stillness, especially at sunrise and sundown, was measurable against frail bird sounds and the ocean's deep undertones — a shift-down from the swift and noisy pace of playing host to six million guests during a Madison Square Garden season.

Patricia, my daughter by Faith, had a house of her own nearby. The summer that she had turned sixteen her mother finally consented to her joining us in England, and Patricia became reacquainted with her brother and sisters. Later on she married an attractive Princeton undergraduate, went to live in Chicago, came to see all the Yankee–White Sox games at Comiskey Park and, when the marriage failed, returned to New York to rejoin us. Quick, bright as a button, extroverted, she enjoys an exceptional facility with people and has made her own way very successfully in the motion picture business. She and Timmy had grown close, took holidays together in the Caribbean and, as I mentioned, were sometimes taken for mother and daughter, though Patricia looked strikingly like her natural mother.

Alternate summers Doreen and her husband, Richard Sorrell, a young painter, came from England and brought William, my first grandchild. Doreen had finished her secondary schooling at Spence on Ninety-second Street and wanted to complete her studies in England, where all her chums were. I protested that she was too young. "But, Pop, you left home when you were fifteen," she argued and won and went off to learn fabric design in London and at a studio on Lake Como in Italy. She designed fabrics for Moygashel in Northern Ireland and, given the unrest there, I worried each time she journeyed from London to visit the mill in Belfast to work out colors with the men in the dyehouse. She had met Richard Sorrell while he was studying at the Royal Academy in London; his portrait of Doreen won the silver medal and was hung for a time in the Academy. The whole family flew across for their wedding and, in time, Richard's portrait of their first son was chosen by the National Portrait Gallery for its 1983 competition. William, then five, was quite unassuming about the honor of having his picture hanging in the National.

Michele was the mistress of the Wainscott house. In the spring and fall, heat from a Franklin stove warmed the living-room that ran the length of the house, though its warmth barely touched the third floor, where some of the young slept dormitory-style under a peaked roof. Peter and his friends came and went. On a Sunday morning I never knew whether I would find two or twelve in the kitchen, but we all swam together at the end of the narrow road that ran to the beach. Except on weekends, we rarely saw anyone there but fishermen hauling in their nets in the early morning.

We kept our horses at Toppings' stables in Sagaponack, a mile away, and on Sunday afternoons behind the Bridgehampton High School I played third base for the novelist Willie Morris' Golden Nematodes softball team. James Jones, at first base, found my erratic throws more dangerous than literary critics and he retired to take command of the beer cooling in a tin tub of ice on the sideline. Our pitcher, Billy de Petris, who owned the Triple Crown bar on Main Street and had played high school baseball with the Red Sox' marvelous Carl Yastrzemski, was so good that our team mostly won. Irwin Shaw's son Adam was the fittest, handsomest player, and the prettiest team member was a girl painter who played center field. Some looseness of rule permitted me to play also in the annual Artists versus Writers game in East Hampton, a game to raise money for the local hospital. Bobby Van's bar in Bridgehampton was our common eating and drinking place and message center for friends coming and going.

The pattern of life was simple and private. Mornings Michele and I rode out from the stable along potato fields, deep green in the early light, towards Sagg Pond. In the distance, across the water, tow-colored wheat fields rose gently from the pond's edge to a tree line standing against the horizon as it had for centuries. Waterfowl, taking sudden flight out of the brake, kept the horses alert, and wild roses grew where they chose. Each morning the heavy question was whether the swans, impervious to the world at large, would be above or below the bridge. Across it, alongside the road, a small granite block, a touchstone of time and perspective, bears the legend: "Here stood the first church in Bridgehampton 1686–1737." We passed, thinking of the epitaph on Yeats' gravestone: "Horseman, pass by." And on days when the soft morning fog was in from the sea and the visibility calculated in yards, it was not difficult to imagine that Yeats' tower was a short gallop away.

Sunday, the day Willie Morris' team took on equally nondescript challengers from Cold Spring Harbor, presented another weighty problem: were my reflexes still good enough to play third base, or should I abandon pride and ask to be moved to second? I leaned towards second in the interest of keeping my front teeth.

In Wainscott unread books got read, sun-bleached kindling for the fireplace was gathered from along the beach. Mary and John Lindsay were close by, and Roone Arledge, whom no one could ever reach at his ABC offices, often rang and said, "Come over for a cookout." Happily too, Irwin Shaw spent his summers here, nearer than Switzerland, hence seen more frequently than at World Series time. His lion's laughter rumpled the night as we retold the tales old warriors tell one another of their generation's war. The hype, hustle, and decibel count of the Garden was a hundred miles away — and an immeasurable distance. One of my children put a fine point on it. "Papa," Michele said, "nothing ever goes wrong here."

I nearly made things go dreadfully wrong. Peter and I rode

our bicycles to the beach one day in late September, just before his classes resumed at Pratt Institute in Brooklyn, where he studied architecture. As far as we could see in either direction the beach was deserted and the sea was rough.

"These waves look pretty big, Pop."

"It'll be all right once we get past the breakers." They did look high and broke over and down from the top with a crash, but Peter is a strong swimmer — he swims two miles every day — and I've swum in oceans all my life. I ran and dove under and through a breaking wave and swam quickly out past the following wave. Peter was just beside me. Suddenly I was terror-struck by what I had done. The waves were far higher than I thought. Surging towards the beach, they built to heights of eight and ten feet, curled over, slammed down against the sand and stones with a tremendous crash, and were sucked back by a fierce undertow. Caught at the wrong moment, they could kill, snap a man's back like a dry twig. A local man who had swum in these waters all his life had his back broken in lesser seas a week before. Beyond the breakers mountainous swells lifted us up and slid us down into troughs, and, gathering momentum, one after another, hurtled past, hurling themselves and everything with them against the land. I had committed the most foolhardy act of my life. Above the roar of the surf I yelled to Peter, "Too ugly, Pete. We'll get out the first chance we get. Stick close. When I say go, go like hell!" In that kind of sea ten or fifteen or twenty waves follow one on the other in rhythmic succession. Then, in different places at different times in no predictable sequence, the sea flattens for a few seconds, takes a breath, then picks up its pounding tempo again. I watched for that instant, that brief flat opening through which Peter and I could escape. It came, and we swam for life and, touching sand, raced up the sloping beach before the next monstrous wave broke down on us.

"I'm sorry, Pete. Forgive me. Your father is a bloody damned fool. You had a lot of guts to come with me. I might have got us both killed."

"Couldn't let you go alone, Pop." Until we heard it on the six o'clock radio news, we didn't know that the beaches for the length of Long Island had been closed to swimmers because of storms and the wild seas.

It was in Wainscott, without realizing it, that I first saw Molly. Absent a professional reason to be alert and open to all comers, I tended to withdraw within my own privacy, to abandon my public self in favor of my private self. Perhaps I withdrew to a deeper internal distance than I was aware of. The penalty was that I didn't register seeing Molly the first time or two. Luckily she gave me another chance. One winter's morning, riding in Central Park, we passed. She spoke and I turned. Like a camera coming into focus, there appeared a girl's face that God made to wear a riding hat — a short straight nose, beautifully symmetrical features, wide-set bright eyes, a full mouth, white even teeth, an open smile. Astride a large horse she looked a petite, clean-limbed figure in riding boots and stretch breeches. A tweed jacket fitted trimly around her small waist and gave way to full, fortunate breasts.

"You know, I've spoken to you twice before and you didn't even look at me." She said it with a taunting smile.

"That's hard to believe."

"It's true. Once here, when you came into the stable from riding in the rain and the rest of us were riding indoors. You were soaked and I asked you if the rain didn't bother you and you were unsaddling your horse and said, 'Maybe it will make me grow.' You didn't even look up."

"That was my first mistake."

"Then at the Toppings' stables. We were all curious about you; why you always rode out by yourself. And one day you were leaning on the rail of the hunt field watching Anne give some of us jumping lessons and when I rode out you opened the gate for me and closed it behind me. I thanked you and you said, 'You're very welcome' and didn't look at me at all. I didn't exist. You don't remember, do you?" She was not protesting but rather laughing at her failure to penetrate my shell.

"No I don't. Was I wearing blinkers?" We rode on together.

Her little boy, Johnny, was waiting at the stables, playing with his soldiers and cars, and I gave them a lift home to East Eighty-eighth Street. She forgot her riding crop on the floor of the car. A day or two later I returned it to the doorman of her building, learned her surname, and not long after was invited to dinner. Sitting before her fireplace sipping a glass of wine, thinking well of her paintings, her books, the comfortable furniture — certain handsome old pieces inherited from her family in Virginia — eyes following her coming and going with plates and food, talking, listening to the music, I became aware of a house lived in by a woman, and grew acutely conscious of the want of an ongoing female presence in my life. Until this unfolding moment I hadn't noticed how much the time in emotional hiatus had dimmed my perceptions, how deeply I had dropped into a narrow single existence. I had been in women's houses, surely, but casually and in transit. There were women with whom I enjoyed friendships, but my emotional quotient was tamped down, silently buried. With Molly, as we sat on the floor before the fire, drinking her wine, eating her pasta and salad, I began to realize that my normal emotional responses were not dead. They had been idling and now slowly picked up speed. I had grown so accustomed to the sensation of drift that I assumed it to be my lot, that I had had my season in the sun. Cool gave way to new warmth. Some nameless place in the pit of me that had been sleeping, stirred, stretched, and reasserted itself. Not in a minute, but in time. Molly was a godsend, witty and alive, intelligent and outgoing, good at her profession, and divorced. She brought life back into balance. My children loved her. Patricia wrote her sister Doreen: "Molly is the best of Papa's friends but, drat it, she may be younger than I am."

And another relationship found its proper balance as well. A single sentence sliced through a habit of respectful but sporadic contact with my mother and opened my half-closed mind. A magazine writer asked a number of mothers how they had contributed to their son's lives and I read my mother's quote in the published article, "I encouraged his endeavors and I prayed for their success." It brought me up short; I was unaware that her thoughts turned in that way and that she would articulate them in those terms. I don't really know this woman, I told myself, and, struck by my long obtuseness, I hastened to recover lost time. On her eighty-eighth birthday I gave her my New York Yankees 1977 World Championship ring. It was, she said, the most wonderful gift she had ever received and immediately hung the heavy athlete's trophy on a gold necklace where it dangled on proud display to her banker, hairdresser, doctor, priest, dressmaker, fellow Irish Club members, and the barman at Clarks, who knew her usual order was a Charlie's

Challenge — a triple Tanqueray gin martini served in a chilled carafe. For some reason she had always been fond of baseball, knew how to keep a scorecard before I did, kept up a friendly running feud with an octogenarian lady friend who rooted for the Boston Red Sox. A Reggie Jackson doll, in Yankee uniform, of course, rests on her bed.

One day in a quiet, private moment, she laid her hand on my arm and said softly how contrite she felt about so many things — her harshness to many people, her unintended hurtfulness — and regretted that her chance to ask their forgiveness had been lost to eternity. She spoke as though I shared the image of transgressions that coursed through her mind. I had only a vague notion but nodded understanding because she needed someone to know what she had done or had not done, needed someone close to her, someone who knew her frailties as well as her strengths, to hear her act of contrition as surrogate for those who were on her mind and were long gone from this earth. I told her she must have been forgiven because contrition lay in the depth of her heart; God asked no more; she must put her mind to rest. We had become true friends, and she continued to encourage my ventures and pray for their success. On her ninety-third birthday she danced with gallant young men, her spirit indomitable, her mind keen, her interest in the world alert and current, her handwriting that of a schoolgirl who had just retired the penmanship trophy, her loyalty to Reggie Jackson undiminished when he left the New York Yankees for the California Angels.

I had not met Reggie Jackson before he came to the Yankees in 1977. He introduced himself, in effect, across the top of the Yankee dugout. Henry Ringling North and I were in my box, eating hotdogs, beer containers sitting on the roof of the dugout, watching the teams loosening their legs and arms. Reggie stood on the top dugout step, caught my eye, smiled, and said, "Hi, how are you?"

"Fine. And you?"

"OK."

"Good luck," I said and gave him a thumbs-up sign. He grinned and gave it back. This started the practice of exchanging a small connecting gesture, and it lasted throughout his

Yankee career. Before the start of each game I attended, we would have a word or two across the dugout roof or at least exchange a thumbs-up sign. That is, except on the eighteenth of October, the final game of the 1978 World Series against the Los Angeles Dodgers. That day there was too much commotion. All kinds of extra people trafficked up and down between the dugouts and around home plate — extra photographers, extra broadcast crews, functionaries from the commissioner's office, people who attached themselves to the pregame ceremony. So we missed our little pregame routine. Reggie struck out his first time at bat. The next time up he hit a home run. He crossed the plate grinning, and, trotting to the dugout, he caught my eye and I his. I gave him a thumbs-up — atta baby! — and, as he returned the salute, his arm shot up in a short irrepressible jab: right on, it said. The next time up he hit another home run. I held up both thumbs. Trotting on a line towards me, he gave a double thumbs-up in return, a torrent of adrenaline running. Just before he ducked into the dugout he hesitated for an instant and yelled to me, "I'm going to hit another!"

Timmy was with me. So was Winston Guest, who was a bit hard of hearing. "What did he say?" Winston hollered above the roar of the crowd.

"He said he was going to hit another."

"That's impossible," Timmy said, still applauding. "Isn't it?" She had only to wait until his next time at bat. Reggie hit the first pitch deep into the right-field bleachers, and the defeated Dodgers turned towards Los Angeles. It was a monumental triumph and thrilling to the bone to have witnessed. No one, not even Babe Ruth, had ever hit three successive home runs in a World Series game. "I could hardly believe my ears when he told you he was going to hit another home run. Or believe my eyes when he did," Timmy said, still dazed. But 55,000 witnesses in the park could attest to it as an undeniable fact. It's in the record books.

On summer weeknights during the following season Molly and I went often to the Stadium and after one game drove downtown to McMullen's on Third Avenue for supper. We sat at a table for two against the back wall and halfway through the first glass of wine looked up. Reggie stood there looking solemn. I rose to shake hands and introduced him to Molly, whom he knew by sight.

"Could I join you?" he asked uncertainly. He was alone and looked troubled. As soon as he ordered his food, he prefaced what he wanted to talk about by saying that we did not know one another intimately, but that he knew enough about me to feel he could talk freely. He included Molly, of course; one look at her and he concluded rightly that she was a first-class girl, sympathetic and discreet. Reggie's problem was Steinbrenner. George had laid on a red-carpet campaign to persuade Jackson to become a Yankee, lunch at "21" and the lot. Later George ignored him socially and Reggie felt jilted. More significantly, he couldn't understand why Steinbrenner sniped at him, embarrassed him in the press in a number of minor and not so minor ways. Basically, Reggie wanted to have a heart-to-heart talk with someone who had the feel for the situation, knew the cast of characters, hence might have a helpful point of view, might even help him gain some perspective.

Jackson, an uncommon man as well as an uncommonly good baseball player, is an exceptionally sensitive person and has an exceptionally high IQ. His ego is worthy of a man who has hit two home runs in a World Series game, tells you he will hit a third and does, worthy of a man who had been at the top of his profession from the first moment, worthy of a man who is the most charismatic player of his era. He and his intelligence and his ego present a large target to the slings and arrows of lesser men, most of whom couldn't lift his bat, much less swing it, literally or figuratively. We talked for three hours, talked until Molly began to look at her watch. She would be due in her offices at *The New Yorker* at nine in the morning. Nothing was concluded nor was it meant to be. Reggie wanted simply to establish a firm contact so, in future, he could reach out for private conversation when he felt the need. From time to time he would ask across the dugout roof, "Will you be there after the game?"

"Sure."

"See ya." I'd wish him luck and we'd do a thumbs-up. Usually he met us at McMullen's merely for companionship and once for a unique reason.

One summer the New York Knickerbockers drafted a basketball player named Mike Woodson, a fine-looking youngster just graduated from the University of Indiana. He and Bobbi, a lovely live-in classmate, had come to New York for his contract signing and a press conference, and I asked Mike if he and his lady would like to see a Yankee baseball game and take supper afterwards. Emphatically they would, and Molly came with us. We drove up Madison Avenue and the young lady's eyes danced from one boutique to the next. She was keen to trade in her Midwest chic for New York chic and ambitious for a career on television. Higher up Madison Avenue, passing through East Harlem, both were appalled by the boarded and fallen buildings, and by the derelicts drinking from bottles half-hidden in brown paper bags. A middle-class background and a distinguished Midwestern university campus had not prepared them for the sight of Harlem.

Woodson asked me about Reggie Jackson. "He has his detractors. But he has more intelligence in his head and more character in his little finger than all of them put together." The two kids were almost disbelieving that their first night in New York found them sitting in front-row seats at Yankee Stadium. Their unspoiled reaction was charming to watch. Reggie Jackson finished his pregame sprints and stopped to say hello.

"Who's that you've got with you?"

"Mike Woodson. Mike, Reggie Jackson." They reached across the top of the dugout and touched palms. Reggie disappeared for a moment, popped out of the dugout again, and flipped a baseball to Mike, who caught it deftly.

"Just testing your reflexes," Reggie called, winked and disappeared again. Woodson rubbed the ball, turning it gently in his hands.

"This is the most wonderful thing that has ever happened to me," he said, serious and clearly pleased.

"My God, Mike. What about the four-hundred-thousand-dollar contract we signed this afternoon?" I teased him. "Hell, I could have given you a baseball, a whole box of baseballs." We laughed together because everyone felt good about this good piece of time. Indeed it was a most wonderful day in the life of young Mike Woodson: a new diploma, a new professional basketball contract, a new baseball from Reggie Jackson, and a pretty girl to make a new wife. It was very good to be with them at a threshold time, to see life's possibilities reflected in their expectant eyes.

We took them to McMullen's for supper and, though he hadn't spoken of it at the ball park, Reggie joined us. I had a hunch he would. Generously he had come to offer young Woodson his counsel to a young athlete starting a professional career in New York. Conversation through supper was almost exclusively a dialogue between Reggie and Woodson, perhaps nearer a monologue by the old pro to a still-awed newcomer. It was brother talk, and Reggie started challengingly. "Are you a religious man?" Mike, slightly taken aback, answered softly that he went to church and his sisters sang in the choir. This is what Jackson told him: "It is easy to be a journeyman or even a good professional athlete in New York. But a very tough place to be a star. And stardom is the only status worth striving for. Once attained, you must have the inner resources to cope not only with the pressure of playing competition. That you take in stride. More punishing are the outside forces that try to diminish you, to bring you down, to embarrass you, to lie about you, to create a public image that you yourself wouldn't recognize. You want to cry out: 'Hey, that's not me.' But no one listens. People have read it in the papers, therefore it must be true. Or so-and-so said it and he must know. So you have to be secure enough within yourself to know who you are, to know that your friends know who you are, and to be true to yourself. You will lie awake at night fighting off the demons, wondering where have all the decent people gone, why envy is such a common sickness, why there is more ill-will than good, why distortions are more salable than truths. All those things will drive you bats. You have to have someone to talk to. You have to talk to her," Jackson said, inclining his head and turning his eye to Bobbi. "You can talk to him," he said, indicating me. "I know; I talk to him. You can talk to me." Thus Jackson offered the hand of friendship to a green lad.

Jackson needed to call up all his own advice, to reach deep into his own inner resources during his final year with the Yankees. George Steinbrenner's psychological harassment nearly undid him. Again we met at McMullen's; Reggie's nervous system was strung out on the rack. "Why is he humiliating me?" he asked.

"You know George. He careens through life. No brakes, loose steering apparatus. I'm sure there must be days when he regrets having run down so many people. But of course it's always too late."

"Yeah, but why me, man? I've earned my pay."

"Shores him up. That's his power kick," I said.

"But it's destructive."

"That's the object. To beat Reggie Jackson."

"It isn't being beaten, like somebody wins and somebody loses. He wants to pound me into the dirt. What does that prove?"

"Himself to himself."

"What's that mean?"

"George has to keep flexing his muscle publicly to prove he's not a paper bull."

"What do I do?" Jackson's shoulders slumped, dejected and despairing.

"Well, a couple of things. The way you defeat anyone who rules by fear is not to be afraid. That takes away his best shot. George has frightened you, made you doubt yourself. The physical you were made to take, and the eye examination. Forget that shit. That's a psychological ploy."

"Man, it's sick."

"Another person could simply say: I no longer want Reggie Jackson with my team. Period. George can't. He's got to convince people that you're washed up so he looks smart letting you go. It's not very profound." I grinned at Reggie to lighten the conversation.

"And you have to remember that his ego is even more fragile than yours." He grunted.

"It hurts."

"Sure it hurts. But you have to understand that another man's words do not diminish you. Hurt, disappoint, embarrass. Yes. But diminish? Never. You hold all the cards, for Christ's sake — Reggie Jackson's talent, his charisma, his chemistry. You can take those assets anywhere you like."

"I like being in New York. I like being a Yankee."

"Of course. And I wish you would be forever. But George has written it on the wall in large letters. He's not going to sign you to a new contract. Right or wrong. So go where you're wanted. Go where you'll be happy. As a friend, that's how I see it. I could be wrong, but I doubt it like hell."

Contractually Reggie was a free agent, and the California Angels signed him, made him "the straw that stirred the Angels' drink." He had a superb year, led the team to the Western division championship. The Angels drew two and a half million fans to the Anaheim Stadium, an American League attendance record, and made Gene Autry, the owner, a very happy man.

The year 1981 drew in on its final weeks and it was for me a time to move on. I had been president of Madison Square Garden for almost eight years, longer than I had ever been in one place. The Garden had been a thoroughly enjoyable and successful experience. I loved it. The many faces of it, the built-in demand to continue to learn, the need to cope within the course of an hour, any hour, with a convention, a concert, a fan's complaint, a network contract, a player's ego, a Russian tour, a conflict of colleagues. And to decide. Over the years there had evolved a certain acumen, an intuitive ability to read a situation and to make a judgment. I liked running things. Now, once again, I decided it was time for me to go. Being president of the Garden in 1981 was not the same as it had been in, say, 1973. Changing circumstances and passing time had, like the restless sea, reshaped the ground.

An old friend, Sonny Werblin, came to the Garden. The similarity of our titles — president of Madison Square Garden Corporation and president of Madison Square Garden Center — tended to confuse outside people, but internally the titles as such were of no particular consequence. Nevertheless, once Sonny had been in place for a year or so and had become more involved in its operations, we began to overlap. Our interests were too much akin for a natural division of labor. Was it his Garden or mine? Our friendship was too long and the hour too late to quarrel or even to quibble. The presidency of Madison Square Garden Corporation was very important to Sonny. Not for financial reasons, of course; his personal means were deep and sound. What he needed was a prominent institutional platform. He had once retired from MCA and found that no combination of diversions could absorb his energy, his near-frenetic need to be in the action. A New Jersey partisan, he had seized the almost Sisyphean task of transforming the East Rutherford swamps into the handsome Meadowlands Sports Complex, pro bono publico. Time and again the project faltered and fell back; each time Sonny's guile and guts pushed it forward. Almost anyone else would have failed. And like most successes, this one, once assured, gained a hundred fathers, mostly politicians. Consequently, the ground shifted for Sonny too, and for his own good reasons he had to take his leave. At the age of sixty-eight he came to Madison Square Garden, his body older and more fragile-looking than its years, his spirit demanding that he move to a highly visible place, one that would afford a floodlight of public attention. And Charlie Bluhdorn proffered it.

Personal publicity was as essential to Sonny as breathing. Obscurity irritated and depressed him; not to be in the news was tantamount to being dead, without an obituary. Reading about himself in the newspapers, sitting as a dais guest at an endless chain of black-tie, fund-raising dinners, none distinguishable from the last or from the next, reaffirmed his identity, reassured him, and by his own measuring of things, confirmed his place in the action. More power to him. I would claim for myself no passion for anonymity. But I regarded a good press a business requirement, not a personal one. Along with others who liked him and knew his merit, I observed this facet of his character objectively and with sympathy, appreciating that it was an addiction like any other — danger, alcohol, or solitude. One accepted it as an element of a friend's temperament. His many talent-agent years, when personal publicity for his clients represented very real commercial value, had conditioned his personal values. For Sonny's addiction, the Garden was a perfect fix.

In time, as he found his footing and propelled himself into the Knickerbockers or television or political matters, I withdrew an equal, balancing distance, at first almost imperceptibly. Except for boxing.

I pulled out of boxing altogether when Sonny became infatuated with Don King and made him the de facto Garden boxing promoter. We didn't argue about it; we simply had differing views about the wisdom of an association with King. Long before Sonny arrived I had rebuffed King's ambition to join the Garden. I saw only disadvantage in a close business relationship with a man who made no secret of having been a numbers operator and having served a four-year prison sentence for killing another numbers man. This was not for prissy or personal reasons. Rather, King's natural style would have been suffocated under a corporate blanket, or, ignoring its constrictions, his free-wheeling would have embarrassed Charlie Bluhdorn, already hypersensitive to public criticism. The Garden-King association was a flop and short-lived. Neither did I share Sonny's enthusiasm for a Madison Square Garden venture into professional soccer, having followed the sport's misfortunes and apparent fortunes since the late sixties, when two teams had been our tenants at Yankee Stadium. I had resisted inducements for the Yankees to buy a franchise in the North American Soccer League. Though I didn't see it as a viable business, I did not anticipate the cost to the Garden before we could shake loose of the loss-making Washington franchise.

All this is to say that there were certain business matters on which Sonny and I held differing views. But we neither argued nor bickered; our personal friendship remained close and constant; our social and business lives intertwined without distinction. As always, the key for me was knowing where I wanted to come out in the end. I decided to leave the Garden at an appropriate time. I could not foresee precisely when that would be, but, I having determined the outcome, intuition and a sense of responsibility would dictate the pace. When the time would come for me to declare myself, I wanted it to appear to be a natural, undisruptive evolution, and I moved silently in that direction.

Beyond the Knicks and the Rangers neither Sonny nor Jack Krumpe, who had come over from the Meadowlands with him, were closely clued in to the prosaic bits and pieces that made the Garden tick. Sonny, without appreciating how they did or why they did it, was often prickly or disdainful of some of the people who put the pieces together painstakingly day in and day out. He was a fussy housekeeper, forever picking up a stray gum wrapper or a paper cup from the floor, but hundreds of events and the complexities of mounting them lay on the periphery of his interest. But Jack Krumpe, I knew, would take charge there, and learn quickly. He was a brainy, sleeves-rolled-up Phi Beta Kappa and Dartmouth College football star, an accountant by training, well organized, diverted by no outside interests, and devoted to Sonny with a filial loyalty: "If that's what Sonny wants, that's what it will be." He was a rock-solid associate; Mr. Inside to Sonny's Mr. Outside.

I was in that mindset when Howard Cosell and I found ourselves chance seatmates on a flight from Los Angeles to New York. Howard had just come from broadcasting a fight in Las Vegas and was tired, exasperated, and frazzled.

"You just don't know what it's like to be a supercelebrity," he declaimed. "Did you see what those animals did to me in Baltimore during the Pittsburgh series? Emmy and I might have been killed by that mob. It's too much. Too much. I can't take it anymore!" Baltimore fans had taken exception to comments Howard had made on the air during the Pittsburgh-Baltimore World Series telecast and apparently a mob had threatened him and his wife as they left the Baltimore ball park.

"Why don't you quit, Howard?" As a friend, you had to understand that his outrageous ego was outdistanced only by his total vulnerability. "Pack it in. Take a professorship at some university. You enjoyed lecturing at Yale, you told me. You've got more money than you'll ever need." Howard took my half-jest seriously and became reflective.

"Quit? For Academia?"

"Yes."

"Could you?"

"In a minute."

"Really?"

"Yes, really. And I will one day."

"I doubt I could." His voice was low and his expression deeply thoughtful.

"I know you couldn't. And you shouldn't, really."

"Why do you say that?" he asked.

"A couple of reasons, at least. What you are is who you are. You invented yourself, created your own myth. So the what and the who of Howard Cosell are one and the same. And then, for you there is no such thing as enough money. That's built into your equation. And I understand the why of that."

"Do you know what my family sacrificed to send me to law school? You know where we came from."

"Of course. So I understand the money thing. I'm not faulting you."

"It's true."

"I know. You told me. But most of all you'd go berserk from boredom if you weren't racing from pillar to post for ABC; if you ever stop being the public Howard Cosell. The worst punishment you could deal yourself would be to quit. Not now, anyway."

"And you think you can? Drop out of the limelight? Just like that?"

"I do. The public role is a comfortable fit for me. I like it immensely. But it isn't all of life. At least it isn't all of life for me. Who I am has a private identity all its own."

"What would make you quit all this?"

"Well, most of my life I've worked for someone — Wild Bill Donovan, Johnny North's Circus, Bill Paley, Charlie Bluhdorn. At some point I want to be on my own."

"When?"

"I don't know. But I'll know when the time comes." The stewardess brought us drinks. I was fond of Howard, enjoyed his friendship, told him of my disposition to move to Ireland.

Planning to leave New York forced me to think very carefully about Molly. Selfishly I would have chosen to have her come with me. She had become an integral part of my life, completing it compatibly, convivially, adding the verve and flavor of her bright female presence. A line from Synge's *Deirdre of the Sorrows* pursued me: "It's lonely you'll be the night and the long nights after." And I shied at the prospect of being without a mate, a woman friend. A man alone is such an incomplete thing, always slightly off-center, slightly awkward, like a man with an ill-made limb. Certainly an ordinary man is not equipped to do life alone. I debated with myself, the emotional against the sensible, striving to sort out the right and fair thing to do. Until now, I had not noticed the years passing. My limbs remained limber, my weight and shape unchanged, my appetites the same, my skin had not gone to crepe. In the Garden years, coming across a newspaper photograph of myself, I was invariably startled by the whiteness of my hair seen through the camera's eye. Could that be me? It was and there was no denying chronology. So the decision must be mine. If it should prove a mistake, either way — to ask her to come with me, to leave without her — it must be my mistake. I could not let it be Molly's to regret.

At the end of the day, I could not fairly ask her to uproot herself and her young son and put themselves down in an unknown place, a place and a way of life foreign to everything in their experience. The matter of age was of no consequence at the moment, but years in advance of her I would become "a tattered coat upon a stick."

Alone then, I would take a new bearing among the rain-worn castles, broken forts, fallen naves, and battered sanctuaries in a land where time stands and waits for your next move, a land where a widow is said to weep the fire out and there is a man who can make a cat laugh. A land of consuming loneliness, its weather is always between two minds, its people congenial to many imperfections. A member of Parliament has proclaimed that "a lie is one thing; perjury is another"; and a critic has written that a dramatic performance was so fine that "there's no prize worthy of it." The romantic Ireland of Yeats' invention, and the Ireland of O'Casey as well: "her courage broken like an old tree in a black wind."

The time recommended itself. In the late summer I suggested to Sonny Werblin that he and I lunch together at the Garden's Penn Plaza Club. He drank a vodka martini and I drank a bottle of Kronenberg beer and we shared a tuna-fish salad. I said I would prefer not to serve out the remaining two years of my contract and would like to leave the Garden by the year's end. The conditioning process — the gradual withdrawal, the body language of recent months — had, I think, made this an unsurprising development. Sonny was neither startled nor dismayed, only regretful. He volunteered to alert the Gulf & Western people.

True, it would be a getaway not without material cost. Leaving the Garden two years before the expiration of my contract had a price. Common sense made me take that into account, and I calculated it would mean giving up roughly a million dollars in salary and pension. That seemed a lot to abandon. At Gulf & Western it was taken for granted that I would complete the final two years of my contract, and even look beyond. No one would ever question, even know, if I were vamping. Except me. I knew that if I waffled about for another two years, faking full-fledged engagement, I would be terribly dissatisfied with myself. My self-regard, however well or misplaced, couldn't abide such an empty maneuver. All the visceral signals carried the message that this was not the moment to vacillate over arithmetic, and I felt comfortable with myself for heeding them.

I aspired to no other post in New York; no different line of work attracted me. Having feasted on the best of times, I had no inclination to reheat yesterday's dinner. I had no cause to cling to an institution, no need to be held together by an institutional identity. What I was, what I had become publicly through the Yankees and the Garden, was a role I enjoyed completely, as some actors must enjoy certain roles and could play them again and again, pleasurably. But who I was privately was another matter. My private self — nurtured in family kitchens, tempered on football fields and battlefields, in setbacks and advances, in measured trials and modest triumphs — was capable of existing on its own, drawing water from its own well. And of course I couldn't be idle. New York is too alive to the moment to suffer idlers kindly. I had always vaguely pitied the inactive men seen lunching idly among the business lunchers, their mornings occupied with the wait until noon, their afternoons empty while the rest of us were fully engaged. I vowed never to become one of them, just as I had determined, as a college football player, never to become an old grad who hung around the locker room or the training house on Saturday afternoon clinging to a faded collegiate glory. I would loathe to be a nonparticipant, getting in the way of people with constructive things to do. Thus, I would make a drastic change, strike out for a fresh life-style, open myself to the world's infinite possibilities.

Making a clean break would include selling my partnership in the New York Yankees at some point, when I could find a buyer acceptable to the other partners. I also wanted to leave the Yankee affair in perspective. At my final partners' meeting, because it was true and should not have been left unsaid, I said that George Steinbrenner's performance as the general partner had been unique; that I knew no one who could have matched his formula for success. In response, George told the partners that they should not forget that it was I who laid the foundation for them — the rebuilt team, the new Stadium. "If it weren't for Mike none of us would be here." It was a good and proper ending.

Later George said, "I'm not surprised. You often talked about living in Ireland someday."

Ireland. American friends were astonished, told one another I'd be back in no time at all. Irish friends thought I was insane, coming there of my own free will when I could have chosen Miami. American born and bred, I had not worn Ireland on my sleeve, but from the earliest days of my boyhood in an immigrant Irish community, Irishness had insinuated itself into my bloodstream, fed by improbable tales and sad, going-away songs, by my grandfather's dancing a wild reel to a fiddler's tune or throwing me up on the back of a horse. In manhood I was drawn to the remoteness of Connacht, wind-bent and rain-lashed, and thrilled by the action of a Galway horse clearing a stone wall, galloping across a bog. From the beginning I was conscious of a natural affinity, an absence of strangeness, as though I had known the land for centuries, and repeated visits over a span of years had deepened my affection.

I had no taste for farewells, least of all a farewell party. My preference was to slip away quietly, so when Sonny Werblin proposed one, I waved him off and suggested instead that the Werblins, the Krumpes, and I have a quiet family dinner. Gently he insisted that it wouldn't do, and that I owed a proper farewell to a few good friends, permitting them an au revoir. Halfheartedly I agreed, and he invited a small group. Sonny was right; I would have denied myself a pleasant leavetaking from enduring friends, friends who had added texture to my life. At the end of dinner the men spoke in turn. Sonny said I marched to a different drum; Howard Cosell recalled the black college football teams playing at Yankee Stadium ("We all won today"); Chub Feeney recounted my deferring to him for the commissionership of baseball in the stairwell of a Chicago hotel. Roone Arledge, Felix Rohatyn, and Kurt Vonnegut, all Long Island neighbors as well as city friends, recalled small personal things. Martin Davis, who had dealt so considerately with my resignation and who was to succeed Charlie Bluhdorn as head of Gulf & Western, came to say Godspeed. Elizabeth Rohatyn spoke vivaciously for the ladies; Jill Krementz took marvelous pictures, and Emmy Cosell gave me a mezuzah to fix to my Irish door. I said: For everything there is a season and a time.

I would miss their companionship. I would miss New York. All of it. Uptown and down, east side and west. I had loved every moment, even the early, bone-chilling wintry days on the North River with the wind slicing through my raincoat, and the dead-broke times in a railroad flat on West Ninth Street. I loved the city and all that was in it, threw my arms around its one-of-a-kind, heart-stopping, tough-tender body, the littered gutters and the vermilion sunsets beyond the Hudson Palisades, the derelicts who hustled me for a dollar on the front steps of Madison Square Garden ("Hey, Mike, can you help us out?") and the nuns of the House of Good Shepherd who sent me lovely crocheted bedthrows at Christmas. The roaring crowds at Yankee Stadium and the Garden, the shirtless in the bleachers and the well-turned-out enclosed in the corporate boxes. The city's heart pumped my blood. I would miss the intense humanness of it all, a city and a breed of people untied and undefeated.

Ireland

MARTIN, who looks after me in Galway, had tea on and a blaze going in the library fireplace against the wine-cellar temperature of the house. No one can remember how old Martin is and in Ballinasloe, where we bank and shop, he is said to have a name for good sense and an ear forever cocked for what goes on in the world.

Seeming to jump, as though startled by its own ring, the phone on the desk before the window rang, surprising me as well; normally it was out of order. Tony O'Reilly was calling with an invitation to lunch at Castlemartin on Sunday. "We'll invite some people you would enjoy meeting. And we'll have a Mass for you in the chapel." The ruins of a seventeenth-century private chapel on the demesne had been faithfully restored by the O'Reillys when they renovated Castlemartin.

"Lunch sounds grand," I said. "But why would you give me a Mass?"

"Because you're the first man to immigrate to Ireland since St. Patrick." The notion made me laugh and I accepted gladly.

Martin stirred the fire and asked "Will you be taking anything with your tea, sur?" His brogue was as thick as a summer hedgerow.

"Nothing at all, thanks. You know, Martin, I've agreed to be the starter for the point-to-point." The East Galway point-to-point races are held on St. Patrick's Day over a natural three-mile course of brush and banks and boreens.

" 'Twill be no bother to you."

"Do you know where the starter's flag is?"

"Wouldn't it be in the Land Rover, surely?" It was the kind of flexible response that encouraged you to think that the flag was probably there without actually guaranteeing it and saved him from looking for it, at least for the moment, or maybe ever.

"I'm not sure I remember exactly where the course is."

"They've moved the fookin' thing."

"How far is it? From here, I mean."

"Not far."

"How long do you think it will take us to get there?"

"Not long."

"If we leave here at, say, half eleven, when will we get there?"

"In good time." That is about as close as you can pin down a vintage West of Ireland man. I changed the subject.

"Whom did Paddy's daughter marry yesterday?" I asked.

"Someone from beyond."

"Where from beyond do you think he might be, Martin?"

"I think he be French. But anyway, he be a stranger." He let it stand at that for a moment while he reflected on the law of probability, then added, "But I don't suppose he be a stranger to her." He put more logs on the fire and went to fetch the mail. "Here's the morning post for ye." He handed me a packet of letters, including one from my mother.

"My mother sends her regards, Martin."

"Ah, God save her. She's the hand of a mere girl by the look of it."

"Sometimes she types her letters. Good exercise for her fingers, she claims; says she wouldn't want arthritis."

"Right. Why should she want it?"

"No reason. But she's ninety-three."

"She'll make a hundred, surely."

"Bought a new dress for the St. Patrick's Day breakfast at the Irish Club."

" 'Twill be a grand time. With her dancin' and all." Martin had no trouble conjuring up distant and unknown events.

"She has remarkable energy."

"I'd say that. Like yourself, sur. You'll never die."

"What makes you think that, Martin?"

"You've not the time for it."